T0354166

A Field Guide to
Tropical
Reef Fishes
of the Indo-Pacific

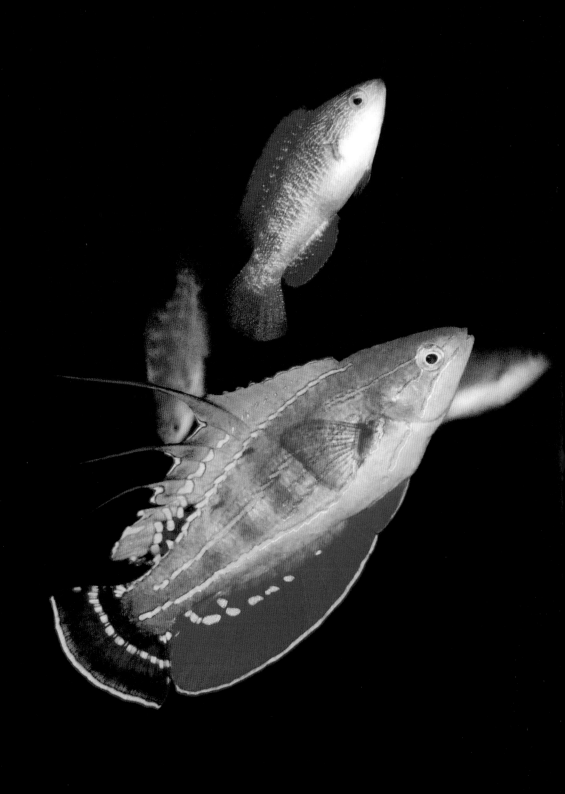

A Field Guide to
Tropical
Reef Fishes
of the Indo-Pacific

GERALD R. ALLEN

ILLUSTRATED BY ROGER SWAINSTON & JILL RUSE

TUTTLE Publishing

Tokyo | Rutland, Vermont | Singapore

DEDICATED TO THE MEMORY OF MY FATHER,
REX ROBERT ALLEN

THE AUTHORS

DR GERALD R. ALLEN is the author of more than 400 scientific articles and 35 books. He served as senior curator of fishes at the Western Australian Museum between 1974 and 1997 and is an international authority on the classification of coral reef fishes as well as freshwater fishes of Australia and New Guinea. Since leaving the museum he has served as a private consultant, primarily involved with coral reef fish surveys in south-eastern Asia for Conservation International. He is also the recipient of several prestigious international awards for lifelong contributions to science including the Kay Radway Allen Award (Australia), Bleeker Award (Japan), Robert K. Johnson Award (USA), and NOGI Award (USA).

ROGER SWAINSTON is acclaimed as one of the world's finest fish artists. His illustrations are more than accurate scientific records. Meticulous attention to detail, coupled with years of experience with marine life, infuse his paintings with a special vitality. His illustrations have appeared in numerous publications around the world.

JILL RUSE was born in Western Australia and is a graphic designer and illustrator with over 40 years of experience. She has done a variety of freelance jobs for the Western Australian Museum and other prominent institutions and companies. Jill does not dive, but has an excellent eye for colours and natural shapes. Most of her paintings in this volume were based on Dr Allen's underwater photographs.

FOREWORD

The present volume is the fifth revised edition of the book that was originally published as *The Marine Fishes of North-Western Australia* in 1988. It was substantially expanded in 1997 and re-issued in 2000 under the title *Marine Fishes of Southeast Asia* with the inclusion of 36 additional plates by Jill Ruse. The 1997 and 2000 editions included additional coverage of northern Australia (including the Great Barrier Reef and offshore reefs of Western Australia such as Rowley Shoals), as well as the Indo-Malayan Archipelago, stretching from Malaysia and western Indonesia to the Solomon Islands and north to the Philippines.

Aside from the correction of several minor errors, the present volume is essentially similar to the third and fourth revised editions with one exception. It contains numerous nomenclatural changes, affecting both scientific Latin names and common names of the region's fishes. Only a few of these involve scientific names, but in all cases these have been made to reflect the current universally accepted nomenclature. Those familiar with previous editions will likely be shocked to see a wholesale change of common names. I offer sincere apologies for what might at first appear to be gross inconsistency. However, the common names used in this book are the result of a recent, major initiative taken by the Australian Government and Seafood Services Australia. For decades a situation existed where there were often several common names used for the same fish depending on geography or even growth stage. In an attempt to stabilise common nomenclature an initial workshop was convened in Adelaide in 2004 that was attended by representatives from the scientific community, seafood trade and the aquarium industry. After a circuitous two-year process an approved list of names was formulated and finally published in October 2006 (*Standard Names of Australian Fishes*, edited by G.K. Yearsley, P.R. Last and D.F. Hoese; CSIRO Marine and Atmospheric Research Paper 009). Hopefully, the new names will be gradually accepted by the public, thereby eliminating the considerable instability and confusion that has existed in the past.

Previous editions of this book have enjoyed remarkable success as an indispensable guide for anglers, divers and aquarists. I sincerely hope that a new generation of nature enthusiasts will embrace the current updated edition with the same enthusiasm.

Gerald R. Allen
Perth, Western Australia.

CONTENTS

The Beaked Coralfish (*Chelmon rostratus*) can be found on reefs throughout the Indo-West Pacific (G. Allen).

TABLE OF PLATES

INTRODUCTION

There are approximately 31,000 types of fishes inhabiting our planet, including at least 16,500 marine species. Tropical seas encompassing northern Australia and neighbouring countries immediately northward are inhabited by the richest fish fauna on the globe. Although official counts are lacking, an estimated 4,000 species occur in the region, including 2,775 coral reef fishes. For most families of tropical marine organisms there are more species present in this area than any place on earth. Intensive studies by the author over several decades have identified Indonesia as the richest country for reef fishes with 2,200 species. The Bird's Head Peninsula region at the extreme western end of New Guinea (West Papua, a province of eastern Indonesia) is the epicentre of reef fish diversity, with nearly 1,500 species currently reported.

Why is this region populated by so many species? No doubt combinations of several factors are responsible. Certainly among the most important are a lengthy history of favourable climatic conditions (e.g. warm water), a diversity of habitat types and a tumultuous geological and hydrological past. In the latter category events such as sea level changes, ocean current shifts, volcanism and continental drift have created isolating barriers that greatly enhanced the speciation process.

One of the most significant factors responsible for the region's great plethora of fishes and other marine organisms is the vast tropical shoreline with an array of diverse habitats. Coral reefs are the most complex habitat system. They provide abundant living space and seemingly endless 'survival opportunities' for a wealth of creatures. Spires of tabular and branching corals are the reefs' equivalent of multi-storey tenements. Not only do they house thousands of living polyps, they also serve as a retreat for legions of brightly coloured fishes that swarm above. Ledges, caves and crevices form the inner sanctum of the reef city, which is populated by shy, seldom-seen fishes that may only emerge for night-time feeding patrols. The sand and rubble fringe surrounding individual reef complexes appears devoid of fish life. But first impressions are deceptive. Close inspection reveals an entire community of specially adapted species. Although this habitat contains far fewer fishes than nearby reefs, its inhabitants are equally interesting. Common adaptations include camouflage colouration and burrowing behaviour. Other major habitats in the region include inshore

The Raja Ampats of West Papua, Indonesia is home to more fish species than any other similar sized area on earth (M. Erdmann).

coastal environments — vast stretches of sandy or rocky shores, interspersed with estuaries and coastal mangroves — and open offshore oceanic habitats. Distinct fish communities populate all of these zones.

This book contains more than 2,000 hand-painted illustrations featuring over 1,670 individual species. The paintings were completed over several years and are primarily based on photographs or colour transparencies of either live fishes taken underwater or freshly caught specimens. In many cases, preserved specimens at the Western Australian Museum have been consulted to ensure accuracy of detail and proportions. The end result is a colourful and highly comprehensive guide to the sea fishes of northern Australia and the adjacent South-East Asian region.

AREA OF COVERAGE

This book provides coverage of tropical Western Australia, Northern Territory, Queensland and the region immediately north of Australia encompassing Malaysia, Indonesia, Philippines, New Guinea and the Solomon Islands. The main emphasis is placed on reef and shore fishes — relatively good coverage is provided except for gobies (Gobiidae) and threefins (Tripterygiidae). Both of these families contain small, cryptic, seldom-seen species whose classification has not been satisfactorily studied — many of the species are difficult to identify, even by trained specialists.

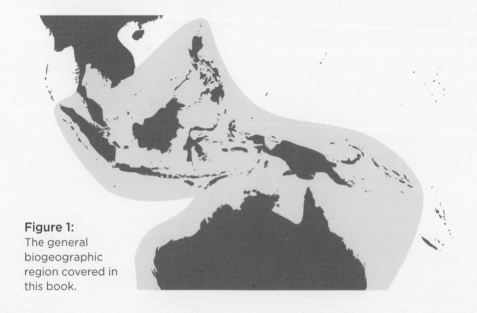

Figure 1:
The general biogeographic region covered in this book.

Relatively good coverage is also extended to families containing species of interest to anglers. Foremost in this respect are the trevallies and their relatives (Carangidae), tunas and mackerels (Scombridae) and billfishes (Xiphiidae and Istiophoridae). Less than full coverage is given to families containing cryptic, hence seldom encountered species (for example Antennariidae), or species living in deeper sections of continental shelves. Excluded from coverage are the true deep sea fishes which, for the most part, live well offshore, below 200 m depth (although some make daily migrations to the surface).

FAUNAL COMPOSITION

Most of the region's reef and shore fishes can be broadly described as being of Indo-Pacific origin. In other words, they belong to the overall reef fish community that ranges across the vast reaches of the tropical Indian and Pacific Oceans. Although individual species, and particularly the mixture of species present, vary greatly from one locality to the next in this huge region, there is a general faunal theme that pervades. Nearly all families and many genera are widely distributed throughout the region. Also, the dominant families in terms of number of species tend to be the same regardless of locality. Dominant groups across this region usually include such families as gobies, wrasses, damselfishes, rockcods, moray eels, cardinalfishes and surgeonfishes.

The reason for the region's relative homogeneity in faunal composition is at least partly explained by examining the life cycle of reef fishes. With few exceptions most species have a pelagic larval stage which is transported by ocean currents for variable distances depending on hydrological conditions and duration of the larval period. Until recently the length of larval life for most fishes was an unknown factor, but thanks to otolith aging techniques our knowledge in this area is rapidly expanding. Essentially, this technique consists of counting daily microscopic growth rings that appear on the bones of the inner ear (otoliths). We now know that the larval duration is highly variable, ranging from just a few days up to nearly two months, with an average length of about 3–4 weeks. Although the adults of most reef fishes are highly home-ranging or territorial, a homogeneous gene-pool is maintained over a broad area by the dispersal capabilities of the larval stage.

Many Indo-Australian reef fishes are distributed widely across the Indian, and west and central Pacific Oceans. Species such as the Racoon Butterflyfish (Plate **55.11**) and Pacific Gregory (Plate **66.12**) range from the shores of eastern Africa

A wealth of fish species inhabit the region's coral reefs.
(Jones/Shimlock, Secret Sea Visions).

to the Hawaiian Islands and a few others, such as the Moorish Idol (Plate **94.9**) and Longnose Hawkfish (Plate **67.18**), extend even farther, to the coast of the Americas. Indeed, throughout the Indo-Pacific region a significant segment of the fauna consists of similar widespread species. Another important component of the fauna consists of species that have more limited regional distributions. A number of species such as the Honeyhead Damsel (Plate **61.8**) and Rainbow Monocle-Bream (Plate **50.7**) are mainly confined to what biogeographers refer to as the Indo-Australian Archipelago, which encompasses the Malay Peninsula, Indonesia, Philippines, northern Australia and Melanesia. At the bottom end of the scale, a few species such as the Banggaii Cardinalfish (Plate **34.7**) have an extremely limited range. It is only found among a small group of islands off central-east Sulawesi. This fish and others that are similarly restricted usually lack a pelagic larval stage, which prevents their dispersal.

BIOLOGY OF REEF FISHES

The region's tremendous diversity of inshore fishes is reflected in a wide variety of reproductive habits and life history strategies. The following discussion is intended to give an overview of the most common patterns. More detailed information is available in the scientific literature or semi-popular works such as Thresher's (1984) *Reproduction in Reef Fishes*. The majority of reef fishes are egg layers that employ external fertilisation. Relatively few species bear live young that are prepared to fend for themselves at birth. Included in the latter category are sharks, rays and cusk eels. Basically, two patterns of oviparous or egg-laying reproduction are evident in most reef species. Females of many fishes, including the highly visible wrasses and parrotfishes, scatter relatively large numbers of small, positively buoyant eggs into open water where they are summarily fertilised by the male. Nuptial chasing, temporary colour changes and courtship display in which fins are erected typically precede the spawning event. This behaviour is generally concentrated into a short period, often at sundown or shortly afterwards. This pattern is seen in diverse groups such as lizardfishes, angelfishes, wrasses, parrotfishes and boxfishes. Typically, either pair or group spawning occurs in which the participants make

A pair of Lyretail Basslets (*Pseudanthias squamipinnis*) exhibit very different colours, which is typical for members of this group (subfamily Anthiadinae). The male (foreground) is usually more ornate and often displays an elongated fin filament (G. Allen).

Bicolor Parrotfish (*Cetoscarus ocellatus*) spawning in open water (G. Allen).

a rapid dash towards the surface, releasing their gonadal products at the apex of the ascent.

The fertilised eggs float near the surface and are dispersed by waves, winds and currents. Hatching occurs within a few days and the young larvae are similarly at the mercy of the elements. Recent studies of the daily growth rings found on the ear bones (otoliths) of reef fishes indicate that the larval stage generally varies from about 1–8 weeks depending on the species involved. The extended larval period no doubt accounts for the wide dispersal of many reef species. For example, many fishes that occur in our region have geographic ranges that extend from East Africa to Polynesia.

A second reproductive pattern involves species that lay their eggs on the bottom, frequently in rocky crevices, empty shells, sandy depressions, or on the surface of invertebrates such as sponges, corals, or gorgonians. Among the best known fishes in this category are the damselfishes, anemonefishes, gobies and triggerfishes. These fishes often prepare the surface prior to egg deposition by cleaning away detritus and algal growth. Bottom spawners also exhibit elaborate courtship rituals which involve much aggressive chasing and displaying. This behaviour has probably

A pair of anemonefish (*Amphiprion percula*) protecting their bottom-layed eggs (G. Allen).

Butterflyfish (*Chaetodon kleinii*) feeding on bottom-layed eggs (G. Allen).

A male Bangaii Cardinalfish (*Pterapogon kauderni*) brooding eggs in its mouth off central-eastern Sulawesi, Indonesia (G. Allen).

been best studied amongst the damselfishes. In addition, one or both parents may exhibit a certain degree of nest-guarding behaviour in which the eggs are kept free of debris and guarded from potential egg feeders such as wrasses and butterflyfishes.

A very specialised mode of parental care is seen in cardinalfishes, in which the male broods the egg mass in its mouth. Similarly, male pipefishes and seahorses brood their eggs on a highly vascularised region of the belly or underside of the tail. As a rule the eggs of benthic nesting fishes are more numerous, larger, have a longer incubation period and are at a more advanced developmental stage when hatched, compared to the eggs and larvae of pelagic spawning fishes. Hatching may require up to one week (in anemonefishes for example) and the larvae then lead a pelagic existence for up to several weeks before settling on the bottom in a suitable reef habitat.

There is very little information on the longevity of most reef fishes. Perhaps one of the longest life spans is that of the Lemon Shark which may reach 50 years or more. Most of the larger reef sharks probably live at least to an age of 20–30 years. In general, the larger reef fishes such as rockcods, snappers and emperors tend to live longer than smaller species. Otolith aging techniques indicate that large rockcods may live at least 25 years and some snappers approximately 20 years. Most of our knowledge of smaller reef fishes has resulted from aquarium studies. The values obtained from captive fishes may exceed the natural longevity due to lack of predation and the protective nature of the artificial environment. Batfishes (*Platax* species) are known to survive for 20 years and even small species such as damselfishes and angelfishes may reach an age of 10 years or more. Tiny gobies (genus *Eviota*) completer their entire life cycle within 60 days, which is the shortest known life span of any vertebrate.

BEHAVIOUR OF REEF FISHES

The behaviour of reef fishes is a fascinating subject that researchers are still striving to understand. Quantum advances in our knowledge of behaviour in the natural habitat is a relatively recent development, thanks to parallel advances in diving technology and underwater photographic techniques. Fish behaviour is a complex subject with myriad variations that mirror the huge biodiversity that inhabits the reefs. Generally, the behaviour of all reef fishes is dictated by the basic needs for shelter, food, and finding mates for reproduction. The majority of

Large numbers of Blue-Green Pullers (*Chromis viridis*) shoal together for protection (G. Allen).

reef fishes are diurnally active, but there is also a significant number of nocturnal species that emerge from crevices and caves shortly after sunset. Prominent nocturnal families include the Holocentridae (squirrelfishes and soldierfishes) and Apogonidae (cardinalfishes). Additionally, larger predators such as morays (Muraenidae), sweetlips (Haemulidae) and snappers (Lutjanidae) take advantage of darkness to stalk their invertebrate and small fish prey.

TWILIGHT CHANGEOVER

Reef fishes interact with their own species and others in a variety of intriguing ways. Social behaviour is often associated with modes of feeding, avoidance of predators, and reproductive activities. This may vary within a given species, depending on food supply, time of day, and seasons of the year. Plankton-feeding species, especially damselfishes, fusiliers, fairy basslets, and a variety of small wrasses, form midwater shoals containing thousands of individuals. This behaviour is efficient for maximum exploitation of the food supply and also increases an individual's chances against predators, relying on the 'safety in numbers' axiom. These legions of small fishes gradually descend closer to the bottom as darkness approaches, eventually settling into crevices for the night.

The twilight periods of dusk and dawn, present great opportunities for viewing fish behaviour, especially predation and reproductive behaviour. Barracudas, trevallies, and snappers are just a few of the reef's hunters that are particularly active during this period. Predators gain an advantage over their adversaries due to lowered light levels. They are less likely to be detected when making rapid sneak attacks. In addition, small fishes are much more vulnerable due to the temporary mass confusion that reigns during the changeover — at dusk when nocturnal fishes are emerging from the shadows and daytime fishes are jostling for night resting places, or at dawn when just the opposite occurs. Many species undergo colour changes during the changeover period, with bright daylight patterns being replaced by muted nocturnal shades. Conversely, some nocturnally active cardinalfishes show bright neon colours that disappear during the day.

The Spinyhead Cardinalfish (*Pristiapogon kallopterus*) displaying its day [top] and night [bottom] colourations (G. Allen).

TERRITORIALITY

Most reef fishes are restricted to circumscribed areas that are highly variable depending on the species. For large roving predators such as trevallies and sharks, the 'home range' may extend for hundreds of meters, but the world of most reef fishes is considerably smaller, often less than a few square meters or a single small coral formation. For some herbivorous species, the size of the territory is dictated by the availability of an algae food supply. For example certain damselfishes of the genus *Stegastes* and the colourful Bluelined Surgeonfish (*Acanthurus lineatus*) (Plate **96.4**) aggressively protect their small territories, sometimes even chasing divers. Nest-guarding damsel and anemonefishes, exhibit similar highly aggressive behaviour, especially towards egg-marauding wrasses and butterflyfishes. Small gobies and blennies are also highly restricted to a territory that is often centered around a sandy burrow or rocky crevice, into which they retreat when danger threatens. Garden-eels (family Congridae) (Plate 10) live in colonies that sometimes contain hundreds of individuals. Each member of the colony never leaves its burrow entirely, but extends nearly the full extent of its body to feed on plankton in the passing current. Spawning only occurs with partners in adjacent burrows and is accomplished by intertwining their bodies while still anchored in their respective burrows.

The Bluelined Surgeonfish (*Acanthurus lineatus*) aggressively guards its territory against other algal-feeding fishes (G. Allen).

A Redspotted Rockskipper (*Blenniella chrysospilos*) appearing from the protection of its rocky burrow (E. Daniels).

A colony of Garden-eels (*Gorgasia barnesi*) extending from their burrows to feed on passing plankton (G. Allen).

SYMBIOSIS

Symbiosis is defined as two dissimilar organisms living together in close association for the benefit of one (commensalism) or both (mutalism) partners. There are many fascinating examples of this phenomenon on coral reefs, but none as well documented as the relationship between anemonefishes (*Amphiprion* and *Premnas* species) and their invertebrate hosts (see page 190). Equally intriguing are the many examples of symbiosis that occur in the goby family. First and foremost is the mutualistic association between certain gobies and shrimps, which live together in sandy burrows. The shrimp provides a home and nesting chamber for both partners by excavating the burrow and continually maintaining it, appearing at the entrance regularly with a load of pebbles and debris. The goby maintains an alert vigil near the entrance and is in nearly constant contact with the shrimp's antennae, giving a wiggle of its tail as a signal when it is safe to emerge. Lab experiments have shown that the shrimp has very poor vision and depends on the acute visual and lateral-line sensory mechanisms of its fish partner to warn it of approaching danger.

A Yellow Shrimpgoby (*Cryptocentrus cinctus*) and Tiger Pistol Shirimp (*Alpheus bellulus*) at their burrow entrance (G. Allen).

A Clowngoby (*Gobiodon okinawae*) living among the brances of an *Acropora* coral (G. Allen).

There is also a suite of tiny gobies that form symbiotic relationships with a variety of sessile invertebrates. In some cases the commensalism is host specific, but often there may be a number of potential hosts involved for each fish species. Members of the gobiid genera *Bryaniops, Phyllogobius, Pleurosicya* and a few others are closely associated with seawhips, gorgonian fans, tunicates, sponges, algae, and corals, both hard and soft. Fish inhabitants are very small and largely transparent, and therefore difficult to detect as they blend in remarkably well with the texture of the host invertebrate. The invertebrate host functions as an effective home shelter and nesting site for the fish and also serves the very useful function of providing safe access to current-borne planktonic food items. This is particulary evident for fishes associated with sea whips, large sponges, and gorgonian fans. Branching hard corals, especially *Acropora* species, form a safe haven for species of *Gobiodon* and *Paragobiodon*. The fishes are usually difficult to observe unless they are deliberately searched for deep among the branches.

The predatory False Cleanerfish (*Aspidontus taeniatus*) [left] appears almost identical in colour pattern and shape to the Common Cleanerfish (*Labroides dimidiatus*) [right] (G. Allen).

CAMOUFLAGE AND MIMICRY

Many fishes rely on excellent camouflage colours to either avoid predators or to gain an advantage when stalking prey. The best examples of the latter group are provided by scorpionfishes (family Scorpaenidae) and anglerfishes (family Antennariidae), which often display patterns that are difficult to distinguish from the background. Their ability to deceive prey is further enhanced by a chameleon-like capability to change colours that perfectly matches the background, whether it is colourful sponge or multi-hued rock. Several fishes have clever disguises that mimic the colour patterns of other species. The False Cleanerfish (Plate **86.2**) sports a shape and colour pattern that perfectly mimics parasite-removing wrasses of the genus *Labroides* (Plate 79). The disguise is used to fool other fishes and allows easy access for this mischievous species to inflict a painful bite, removing tissue, scales and fin parts in the process. Other fishes, including some monocle-bream (Plates 50–51) and leatherjackets such as the Blacksaddle Filefish *Paraluteres prionurus* (Plate **103.18**), mimic certain species that have poisonous bites or toxic flesh and are therefore avoided by predators.

The ability of this Anglerfish (*Antennarius pictus*) [top] and Scorpionfish (*Scorpaenopsis papuensis*) [bottom] to disguise themselves gives them a great advantage while stalking prey (G. Allen).

Kri Island in West Papua's Raja Ampat. Cool upwellings in the nearby Dampier Strait are partly responsible for the areas unsurpassed fish diversity. Over 300 species can be observed around this small island (G. Allen).

ECOLOGY OF REEF FISHES

The majority of fishes included in this book are generally considered to be inhabitants of coral reefs. However, reefs are highly complex systems, consisting of numerous microhabitats. In general, coral reef fishes are finely synchronised to their environment. Each species exhibits very precise habitat preferences that are dictated by a combination of factors including the availability of food and shelter and various physical parameters such as depth, water clarity, currents and wave action. The huge number of species found on coral reefs is a direct reflection of the high number of habitat opportunities afforded by this environment.

Coral reef fishes generally exhibit a higher degree of habitat partitioning than do fishes from cooler seas. A good example of the fine scale on which this principle operates is the Striped Clingfish *Diademichthys lineatus* (Plate **12.6**). It is usually found amongst the spines of *Diadema* sea urchins or nearby branching corals, and feeds primarily on the tube feet of its host urchin or on coral-burrowing molluscs. The coral reef offers numerous examples of fishes that have similar narrow habitat

The habitat of reef fishes such the Striped Clingfish (*Diademichthys lineatus*) [top] (C. Bryce) and the anemonefish *Amphiprion clarkii* [bottom] rarely extend far beyond the safety of their hosts (G. Allen).

Mangrove and coral reef habitat at the Raja Ampat Islands, West Papua, Indonesia (Jones/Shimlock, Secret Sea Visions).

Sheltered reefs of Kimbe Bay, Papua New Guinea provide a haven for numerous coastal fishes (R. Steene).

and feeding requirements. Water depth is also an important partitioning factor and again there are numerous examples of coral reef fishes that have well-defined depth ranges. In the very broadest sense there are three main depth categories for reef fishes: shallow (0–4 m), intermediate (5–19 m) and deep (20 m+). The depth limits of these zones may vary locally, depending largely on the degree of shelter and sea conditions. The shallow environment is typified by wave action, which in highly protected areas such as coastal bays or lagoons may exert its effect down to only a few centimetres. On the contrary, in exposed outer reef structures the effect of surface waves may sometimes be felt below 10 m. The intermediate zone harbours the greatest abundance of fishes and live corals. Here wave action is minimal, although currents are often strong and sunlight is optimal for reef-building corals. The deep outer reef slope is characterised by reduced light levels, hence fewer corals and fishes. Although species numbers are reduced, the species that occur in this habitat are among the most interesting of coral reef fishes. A high percentage of the new fishes that have been discovered on coral reefs in the past three decades were collected on deep reefs by SCUBA-diving scientists.

The region's reef environments can be broadly classified into two major categories: sheltered inshore reefs or lagoons, and outer reefs. Under optimum conditions both of these environments can support extensive beds of nearly

Extreme low tide on Queensland's Great Barrier Reef (R. Steene).

Plankton-feeding fishes, including fairy basslets (*Pseudanthias*) and damselfishes (*Chromis*), are predominant members of the outer reef fish community (R. Steene).

100 per cent coral cover. Inshore or coastal reefs may be strongly influenced by freshwater runoff and resultant siltation. Underwater visibility on these reefs is often greatly reduced, particularly during the wet season when rivers are flowing at their maximum. Coastal reefs and lagoons are further characterised by extensive sand or silt-bottom areas that may support broad seagrass beds. In most coastal reef or lagoon situations the maximum depth seldom exceeds 25 m, and due to heavy siltation coral growth is usually sparse below 15 m depth.

Outer reefs often have a classical reef structure consisting of a broad shallow reef flat, a raised algal ridge, reef-front zone of surge channels and a steep outer slope. But on some islands the bottom plunges into the depths directly from the rocky shore. The clearest waters are found on outer reef slopes where underwater visibility may sometimes exceed 30 m. Coral growth is most abundant at about 5–15 m depth, although in some areas appreciable growth may extend well below this limit. In shallower water, corals are inhibited by the pounding surge and in deeper water, by the much-reduced penetration of light. Although most reef-building corals do not thrive below 30–40 m, certain reef fishes may penetrate well below these depths. Observations made in research submarines at Hawaii and Enewetak Atoll indicate that reef species, including some damselfishes, butterflyfishes and squirrelfishes, may occur to depths approaching 200 m.

Neon Fusiliers (*Pterocaesio tile*) swarm above the reef at Indonesia's Raja Ampat Islands (Jones/Shimlock, Secret Sea Visions).

CLASSIFICATION OF FISHES

Although the fundamentals of biological nomenclature and classification are common knowledge to many, it is my experience that the average non-biologist frequently has little idea of the basis of scientific names or how fishes are classified. It therefore seems worthwhile to include a brief section on the rudiments of this subject.

Every described organism, be it a single-celled amoeba, crab, bird, fish or mammal has a scientific or Latin name. It is composed of two parts and is generally italicised. The first part is the genus or generic name and the second is the species or specific name. For example the Fiveline Snapper is *Lutjanus quinquelineatus*. The generic name *Lutjanus* pertains to a group of closely related species which share a number of common features related to general shape, scalation, type of teeth, fin-ray counts, etc. The specific name *quinquelineatus* applies only to a single entity that is distinguished from its relatives by a unique set of characteristics, often including colour pattern. Related genera (plural of genus) are grouped together in a family, the spelling of which always ends in 'idae'. An illustrated guide to families is presented on pages 47–63. Worldwide there are about 440 families — at least 300 are represented in Australia and surrounding regions. A group of similar families is placed in one of the 71 orders of fishes currently recognised worldwide, the spelling of which always ends in 'iformes'. The highest rungs on the 'ladder' of classification are the class and phylum. The class Myxini contains the jawless hagfishes and lampreys (no species included in this book); Elasmobranchii and Holocephali contain sharks and rays; and the class Actinopteri contains the majority of bony fishes. All fishes, as do other higher animals including amphibians, reptiles, birds and mammals, belong to the phylum Chordata. Therefore, in summary the classification of the Fiveline Snapper can be represented as follows:

Phylum — Chordata (all animals with a notochord)

Class — Actinopteri (bony, ray-finned fishes)

Order — Perciformes (most reef fishes)

Family — Lutjanidae (Tropical snappers and relatives)

Genus — *Lutjanus* (closely related snappers)

Species — *quinquelineatus* (Fiveline Snapper)

Characters that are most often used to separate species and often genera include external features such as the number of fin-rays, size and number of scales, ratio of various body proportions and colour pattern. For higher classification at levels above genus, internal structures, particularly those pertaining to skeletal elements, are often indicative of relationships.

Many species previously unknown to science have been found in our region over the past few decades. When a new fish is discovered it is given a scientific name by the researcher, who formally publishes a detailed description in a recognised scientific journal. Scientific names are frequently descriptive. For example, *quinquelineatus* is Latin for five lines and is therefore appropriate for the Fiveline Snapper (Plate **42.7**). New fishes are sometimes named after the locality from where they are collected, for example *japonicus* (Japan) or *novaeguineae* (New Guinea). A third category of specific names is based on the names of people, often the person who first discovers the fish (respectable researchers never name fishes after themselves). Fishes named after a male end in 'i', those after females in 'ae'.

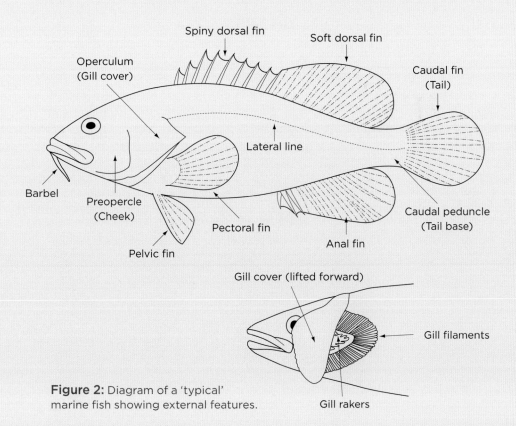

Figure 2: Diagram of a 'typical' marine fish showing external features.

FISH OR FISHES?

Confusion is frequently expressed over the use of the words fish and fishes. The term 'fish' in particular is often used inappropriately. It is grammatically correct to use 'fish' when referring to a single individual or more than one individual if only a single species is involved. For example, one might say 'there were 100 fish in that school of Spanish Mackerel'. The term 'fishes' is a plural form that is used when referring to two or more different species. For example, 'We saw hundreds of fishes while diving on the reef.'

DANGEROUS FISHES

The region's seas are generally safe for normal swimming and wading activities, but there are a number of fishes potentially capable of causing injury. They can be divided into several broad categories including species that bite or sting, or which may cause poisoning if consumed.

BITERS

First and foremost in this category are the whaler sharks and their relatives (Plates 1–3). In addition there are a number of smaller reef fishes which, although they pose no threat to swimmers, can inflict painful bites if handled carelessly by anglers. For example, barracudas (Plate 69), razorfishes (Plates 80–81) and triggerfishes (Plates 102–103) are notorious in this respect. As a rule of thumb any fish with large, obvious teeth should be handled with care.

STINGERS

Virtually any fish which possesses rigid fin spines is capable of inflicting wounds if handled carelessly. Most are non-venomous and can be treated in the same manner as any puncture wound. Surgeonfishes (Plates 95–97) are equipped with scalpel-like spines that are either fixed in an erect position or fold into a groove along the base of the tail. Spearfishermen in particular need to exercise special care when removing these fish from spears as large specimens can sever a finger. The most dangerous category of stingers includes fishes which have venomous spines — these are indicated with **VENOMOUS** in the species descriptions. The best known of these are stingrays (Plates 4–5), catfishes (Plate 11), scorpionfishes (Plates 18–20) and spinefeet (Plates 94–95). For all of these fishes the recommended first-aid procedure is to immerse the injured area in hot water (as hot as bearable), repeating until the pain subsides. Apparently the protein base of the toxin is denatured by heat, and relief is sometimes immediate. In cases where the victim is stung by several spines, or if the wound is deep, medical assistance should be obtained. Firefishes, lionfishes and stonefishes (Plates 18–19) have very potent venom in all fin spines. Several deaths have occurred as a result of people failing to receive immediate first aid after treading on stonefishes.

ELECTRIC FISHES

Fishes deemed to be electrogenic have the ability to generate an electric discharge that is strong enough to stun or kill prey and potential predators. Often referred to as numbfish, electric rays (Plate 4) should be handled or approached with great care both in and out of the water.

POISONOUS FISHES

There are two main types of fishes in this category. The first includes species that have naturally occurring poisons, either in their external mucus or in some internal organs, frequently the viscera or gonads — these are indicated with **POISONOUS** in the species descriptions. The best-known examples are pufferfishes, porcupinefishes and boxfishes (Plates 105–107). Although these fishes are eaten by the Japanese when specially prepared by licensed chefs, they are considered extremely dangerous and specimens from local waters should never be eaten. The second group of poisonous fishes includes species that acquire toxic properties during their life cycle by accumulating a dinoflagellate that lives on dead coral or among algae, and is first consumed by herbivorous fishes which are eventually eaten by larger predatory fishes. The toxin known as ciguatera is accumulative and large fishes such as the Red Bass (Plate **41.12**) and Great Barracuda (Plate **69.12**) are potentially the most dangerous. The symptoms from eating ciguatoxic fish appear from 1–10 hours later and range from mild dizziness, diarrhoea and a numb sensation of the lips, hands and fingers, to extreme nausea, coma and total respiratory failure. The degree of poisoning depends on the amount of fish that is consumed and the concentration of toxin it contains. As a matter of safe practice it would be wise to avoid eating large barracuda, Red Bass, or extraordinarily large groupers, all of which have been implicated in ciguatera poisonings in other regions.

PRESERVING FISHES

It is sometimes desirable to preserve specimens, particularly if a positive identification by museum authorities is required. Also, small, unusual or rare fishes can be kept as curios or as teaching aids for children. The recommended method of preservation in any case is exactly the same one as that employed by fish biologists in museums. The basic ingredient is full-strength formalin, which can be obtained from a pharmacy. Using gloves, the preserving solution is made by diluting one part of formalin with nine parts of water. The fish should be fully immersed in the solution. If larger than about 15–20 cm, a slit along the side of the belly will facilitate preservation of the internal organs. For long-term storage it is desirable to transfer the specimen to a 70 per cent ethyl alcohol solution (70 per cent ethanol, 30 per cent water) after the fish is fully fixed in formalin (i.e. after several weeks). However, the fish may be held in the initial formalin solution for several years without deleterious effects.

Unfortunately colours fade rapidly in preservative. Therefore photography is a valuable method of accurately recording the colour pattern.

SENDING SPECIMENS TO THE MUSEUM

Although most of the specimens in the reference collections of the various museums around Australia and South-East Asia are collected on special expeditions by museum staff, occasionally valuable fishes are donated by the public. It may also be desirable for people living far from their local museum to send specimens in for identification, particularly if the fish in question is suspected to represent a new record for the area or perhaps is very rare. Members of the public may also have the opportunity to collect fishes in remote areas that are not easily reached by museum scientists. For example, several years ago a medical officer aboard an experimental offshore drilling platform obtained a valuable collection of deep-reef fishes on Australia's North West Shelf that were accidentally captured when the drill was brought up from 120 m depth. In this case none of the fishes were recognised by the crew, which included several anglers. The specimens were wisely preserved and sent to the Western Australian Museum. Several species from this collection proved to be previously unknown to science.

Specimens can easily be sent to museums via parcel post if first properly preserved. They should be removed from the preserving solution, rinsed and wrapped in moist cloth (cheesecloth is ideal) or newspaper, then sealed in several layers of plastic bags. The bags can then be packed in a well-padded cardboard box. In Australia fishes can be sent to any of the following institutions depending on their state of origin:

Western Australian Museum
Department of Aquatic Zoology
Locked Bag 49, Welshpool DC, Western Australia 6986.

Northern Territory Museum
Department of Ichthyology
PO Box 4646, Darwin, Nortthern Territory 0801.

Queensland Museum
Department of Ichthyology
PO Box 3300, South Brisbane, Queensland 4101.

FISH PHOTOGRAPHY

Nearly everyone carries a camera on fishing and diving expeditions these days. Good photographs can be valuable in determining the identification of a questionable fish, particularly if the catch has already been eaten. Anglers frequently rely on hastily taken snapshots in order to later identify their catch. Their usefulness is sometimes diminished when little care is taken in preparing the fish. The following steps will ensure the photos are of good diagnostic quality: (1) The specimen should be photographed when fresh as live colours fade rapidly after death. (2) An attempt should be made to spread out the fins. With small fishes you can hold the fins erect with sewing pins on a piece of flat styrofoam or cardboard. (3) Wet fish should be blotted dry with a cloth or paper to prevent harsh glare when photographed. (4) The specimen should be placed on a suitable contrasting background and photographed as close as the lens will allow for sharp focus, attempting to fill the frame. (5) It is helpful if a ruler or some other object of known length can be placed beside the fish when it is photographed in order to determine its length later on.

Underwater photography is a fascinating hobby and will add a new dimension to your diving activities. Fish photography, if done on a regular basis, is an excellent method of learning the fishes of an area. Most beginners start out with a digital point-and-shoot camera in a relatively inexpensive plastic housing. However, to obtain high quality-fish portraits it is advisable to use an SLR digital camera housed in a special case made of perspex or aluminum alloy. In addition, strobe lighting is a must. The cost of the basic outfit ranges from about $4,000–$6,000, so only the serious photographer will consider this alternative. Even for accomplished divers, it requires much practice and patience before good results are obtained. The combination of a moving subject on variable backgrounds present, a great challenge.

HOW TO USE THIS BOOK

This book is designed as a pictorial guide that relies on visual comparison between the painted illustrations and actual specimens, photographs, or underwater observations. Distinguishing features are highlighted in the text accompanying each plate, in most cases referring to colour pattern or the shape of the body or fins. These features are useful for differentiating the species in question from its close relatives, or species it is likely to be confused with. A guide to families based on outline drawings precedes the fish plate section. When attempting to place a fish in the proper family, particular attention should be given to the head and body shape, number of dorsal fins, placement of fins and their positions relative to one another, and the presence or absence of spiny elements in dorsal and anal fins in particular. The use of technical scientific words is deliberately avoided, but a few terms relating to the external features of fishes are useful for identification and are illustrated below.

Each species account appearing on the page opposite the corresponding plate includes the common name and scientific name followed by the name of the person who first described it and the date of description. If the person's name appears in parentheses it indicates that the species was originally placed in a genus different from its presently recognised one.

Common names are invariably contentious in that species that range widely often have several common names according to locality. This problem is greatly compounded in South-East Asia because of the huge number of languages and dialects spoken. Because of this problem, it is unfortunately not possible to use local names. Therefore Australian common names are utilised. Numerous name changes, affecting both the scientific Latin names and common names have occurred since printing of the first three editions. Only a few of these involve scientific names, but in all cases these have been made to reflect the current universally accepted nomenclature. Those familiar with previous editions may be surprised to see a wholesale change of common names. Sincere apologies are offered for what might at first appear to be gross inconsistency. However, the common names used in this book are the result of a recent, major initiative taken by the Australian Government and Seafood Services Australia. For decades a situation existed where there were often several common names used for the same fish depending on geography or even growth stage. In an attempt to stabilise common nomenclature, an initial workshop was convened in Adelaide in 2004 that was attended by representatives from the scientific community, seafood trade and the aquarium industry. Then after a circuitous two-year process an approved list of names was formulated and finally published in October 2006 (*Standard Names of Australian Fishes*, edited by G.K. Yearsley, P.R. Last and D.F. Hoese; CSIRO Marine and Atmospheric Research Paper 009). Hopefully, the new names will be gradually accepted by the public, therefore eliminating the considerable instability and confusion that has existed in the past.

The text for each species contains general information on habitat, feeding habits, distinguishing features and geographic distribution. Several of the distributional terms need to be explained in more detail: 'Indo-E. Pacific' refers to a distribution that extends from East Africa to the Americas; 'E. Indian Ocean and W. Pacific' is generally from the Maldives eastward to the western fringe of the Pacific, including Micronesia and Melanesia; 'W. and C. Pacific' refers to the area encompassing the western fringe of the Pacific from Japan to Australia and extending eastward to embrace much of Oceania, often to Samoa, Tuamotus, or Society Islands south of the equator and the Line Islands (and sometimes Hawaii) north of the equator; 'Indo-Australian Archipelago' embraces the region that includes the Malay Peninsula, Indonesia, Philippines, northern Australia and the islands of Melanesia.

The maximum known total length, measured from snout tip to the end of the tail is given at the end of each species account, and for a few exceptionally large fishes the maximum recorded weight is also given. I have purposely omitted information on relative abundance (e.g. common, rare, etc.) as this parameter is subject to considerable local variation depending on availability of suitable habitat, and in the case of migratory species, the time of year.

In addition to the individual species accounts, 'boxes' of text are included for most plates which contain general information for families, pertaining to such topics as number of species worldwide, ecology including food habits, and any noteworthy behavioural or morphological characteristics.

COLOUR PATTERNS

A major shortcoming of any field guide to fishes is that it is virtually impossible to illustrate all of the variations in colour that commonly occur within a single species. With a few exceptions the colours shown here are the 'normal' or average ones displayed by live fish in their natural habitat. Anglers especially will be well aware that many fishes can drastically alter their colouration after being caught.

Variation in colour pattern within individual species may also be related to age, sex, environmental conditions or geography. Angelfishes (Plates 58–60), damselfishes (Plates 61–67), wrasses (Plates 70–81) and parrotfishes (Plates 82–84) are particularly notorious for dramatic changes in livery between the juvenile and adult stages. Wrasses and parrotfishes are also well known for their often different male and female patterns. It was not possible to illustrate all the variations related to sex and age, but they are included for a number of the more common species.

Figure 3: Some of the many colour variations of the anemonefish *Amphiprion clarkii* based on geography.

EDIBILITY RATINGS

Star symbols that give an indication of the eating qualities of a particular fish appear at the bottom right of each species account unless the fish is too small for human consumption, or if there is no available information.

Symbols are as follows:

☆ . . . . poor eating
☆☆ . . . . fair eating
☆☆☆ . . . . . . good eating
☆☆☆☆ . . . . excellent eating

   The star symbols are intended as approximate guides only. Wide variation in the edibility of a given species may be caused by a number of factors, of which degree of freshness and method of preparation are particularly important.

ACKNOWLEDGEMENTS

I thank the Chief Executive Officer and Board of Trustees of the Western Australian Museum for their continued support of this book project. I am also indebted to Sue Morrison, former technical officer in the fish section of the Museum's Department of Aquatic Zoology for her assistance.

   Fieldwork in north-western Australia was greatly assisted by the following people: Tony and Avril Ayling, John Braun, Norrie Cross, Eve and Bill Curry, Craig Howson, Hugh Morrison, Ian Parker, Neil Sarti and Barry Wilson. I am particularly grateful for the assistance and companionship of the museum's marine biological group (past and present) including Paddy Berry, Clay Bryce, Ray George, Barry Hutchins, Diana Jones, Loisette Marsh, Gary Morgan, Shirley Slack-Smith and Fred Wells.

   Roger Steene of Cairns, Queensland, formerly an honorary associate of the Western Australian Museum's Department of Aquatic Zoology, accompanied me on numerous field trips throughout the region and was particularly helpful in providing collecting assistance and photographic coverage of numerous fishes featured in this book.

   Walter Starck, former owner of the research vessel *El Torito*, graciously offered the use of his ship for fieldwork at Papua New Guinea, Solomon Islands and on the Great Barrier Reef. Walter first introduced me to the underwater realm of this fascinating region nearly 50 years ago.

I am particularly grateful to the following owners and dive managers, past and present, of various resorts in the South-East Asian region for providing accommodation, diving facilities and boat transport: Max Ammer (Sorido Bay Resort, West Papua), Bruce Moore (Black Sands Resort, Sulawesi), Andy and Marit Miners (Misool Eco Resort, Indonesia), Alan Raabe, Max and Cecilie Benjamen (Walindi Plantation Resort and MV *Febrina*, New Britain), Lauren Siba and Sascha Jansen (Lembeh Resort, Sulawesi, Indonesia), Danny and Angelique Charlton (Critters @ Lembeh, Sulawesi, Indonesia), Ron Holland, Jenny Majalup, Graham and Donna Taylor, (Borneo Divers, Sabah), Anton Saksono (Pulau Putri Island Resort, Java Sea), Kal Müller (Komodo Tour and Travel), Hanny and Inneke Batuna (Manado Murex Resort, Sulawesi), Frans Seda (Sao Wisata Resort, Maumere, Flores), and Mark Eckenbarger (Kungkungan Bay Resort, N. Sulawesi).

Dive guide, Wally Sagian of Denpasar, Bali, assisted with collecting and photography on Bali, Komodo and Flores. Rudie Kuiter and Roger Steene also provided diving companionship and assistance on numerous field trips. Phil Munday offered similar assistance at Kimbe Bay, New Britain. Craig Howson and his efficient staff of the *True North*, provided wonderful diving opportunities at the Rowley Shoals, Indonesia, and Papua New Guinea. Special thanks are also due to Rob Vanderloos and the crew of MV *Chertan* (Alotau, Papua New Guinea) and Patti Seery and the crew of MV *Silolona* (Bali, Indonesia) for many memorable cruises. Burt Jones and Maurine Shimlock (Washington, USA) provided valuable opportunities to join them on their Indonesian dive cruises and generously donated their excellent photographs.

Excellent facilities for extensive fieldwork and research on coral reef fishes was provided by the Christensen Research Institute, Madang, Papua New Guinea under the past directorships of Matthew Jebb and Larry Orsak. I am also grateful to Diane Christensen and the Board of Directors of CRI for providing funding and research opportunities. My son, Mark Allen, who is a keen diver and now Fish Collection Manager at the Western Australian Museum, capably assisted with fieldwork. I am also indebted to Glenn Moore, Curator of Fishes at Western Australian Museum, for his continued support and access to the collection facilities. During the past 10 years my research activities have been generously supported by the Paine Family Trust (USA). Also during this period, I have been extremely fortunate to travel and dive throughout the region with Mark Erdmann (Conservation International).

Colourful shoals of fairy basslets (*Pseudanthias dispar*), as seen here at Madang, Papua New Guinea, are integral members of the Indo-Pacific reef fish community (R. Steene).

Numerous scientists in Australia and overseas have contributed taxonomic knowledge resulting in a better understanding of the region's fish fauna, either through publications or by direct assistance with problematical identifications.

Those particularly helpful in this regard included Mark McGrouther, Doug Hoese, Jeff Leis and John Paxton (Australian Museum), Rudie Kuiter and Martin Gomon (Museum of Victoria), Michael Hammer, Barry Russell and Helen Larson (Northern Territory Museum), Jeff Johnson and Rolly McKay (Queensland Museum), Peter Last and Will White (CSIRO Fisheries, Hobart, Tasmania), Tony Gill (University of Sydney), Ronald Fricke (Natural History Museum, Stuttgart), William Eschmeyer, David Greenfield, and John McCosker (California Academy of Sciences), Ed Murdy, Jeff Williams and Victor Springer (Smithsonian Institution), Theodore Pietsch (University of Washington), Stuart Poss (Gulf Coast Research Lab, USA), Jack Randall, Richard Pyle and Arnold Suzimoto (Bishop Museum, Honolulu), Bill Smith-Vaniz (National Biological Science Centre, Gainesville, Florida), and Richard Winterbottom (Royal Ontario Museum).

We are grateful to Burt Jones and Maurine Shimlock (Secret Sea Visions) for allowing us to reproduce their excellent photographs.

Finally, this guide to the region's fishes would not have been possible without the wonderful artwork of Jill Ruse and Roger Swainston. It has been a great pleasure working with both of these highly talented artists.

GUIDE TO FAMILIES

The following section contains outline drawings of typical members of the families featured in this book. The family and corresponding plate numbers and are indicated above each drawing.

Classification of the orders and families of featured fishes in the region of Australia and South-East Asia (after Eschmeyer and Fong, 2018).

Class: Elasmobranchii	
Carcharhiniformes (whaler, hammerhead, cat sharks)	
Scyliorhinidae	50
Carcharhinidae	50
Sphyrnidae	50
Heterodontiformes (bullhead sharks)	
Heterodontidae	50
Hexanchiformes (cow sharks)	
Hexanchidae	50
Lamniformes (thresher, grey nurse, mako sharks)	
Odontaspididae	50
Alopiidae	50
Lamnidae	50
Orectolobiformes (carpet, leopard, nurse, whale sharks)	
Rhincodontidae	50
Stegostomatidae	50
Ginglymostomatidae	50
Hemiscyllidae	50
Orectolobidae	50
Pristiophoriformes (sawsharks)	
Pristidae	50
Myliobatiformes (eagle, manta, stingrays)	
Urolophidae	51
Dasyatidae	51
Mobulidae	51
Gymnuridae	51
Myliobatidae	51

CLASS/ORDER	PAGE
Rajiformes (skates)	
Rajidae	51
Squatiniformes (angel sharks)	
Squatinidae	51
Rhinopristiformes (shovelnose sharks, guitarfishes)	
Rhinobatidae	50
Rhininidae	51
Glaucostegidae	51
Trygonorrhinidae	51
Torpediniformes (electric rays)	
Narcinidae	51
Hypnidae	51
Class: Holocephali	
Chimaeriformes (ghost sharks)	
Chimaeridae	51
Class: Actinopteri	
Albuliformes (bonefishes)	
Albulidae	52
Anguilliformes (eels)	
Muraenidae	52
Congridae	52
Ophichthidae	52
Atheriniformes (hardyheads)	
Atherinidae	53
Aulopiformes (lizardfishes)	
Synodontidae	52

ELASMOBRANCHII AND HOLOCEPHALI
(cartilaginous fishes)

ORECTOLOBIFORMES
Rhincodontidae
(1)

Stegostomatidae
(1)

Ginglymostomatidae
(1)

Hemiscyllidae
(1)

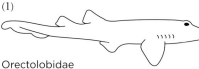

Orectolobidae
(1)

LAMNIFORMES
Odontaspididae
(1)

Alopiidae
(1)

Lamnidae
(1)

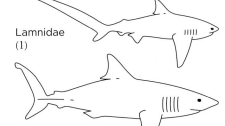

HETERODONTIFORMES
Heterodontidae
(1)

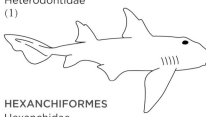

HEXANCHIFORMES
Hexanchidae
(1)

CARCHARHINIFORMES
Scyliorhinidae
(1)

Carcharhinidae
(2–3)

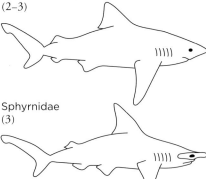

Sphyrnidae
(3)

Sphyrnidae image included above

PRISTIOPHORIFORMES
Pristidae
(3)

RHINOPRISTIFORMES
Rhinobatidae
(3)

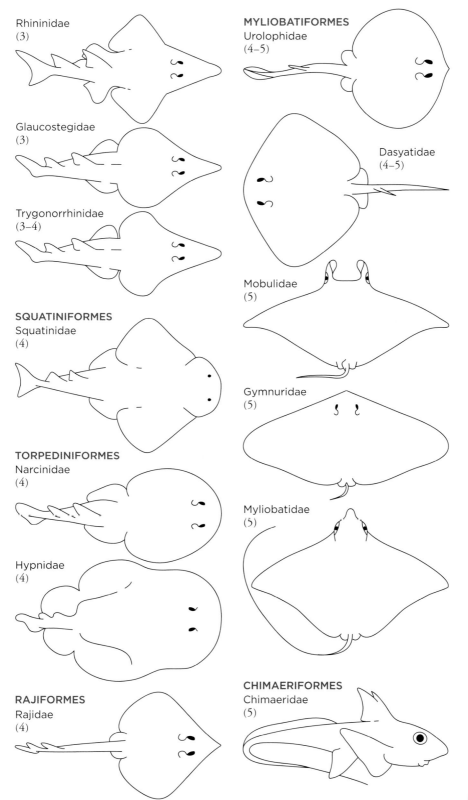

Rhininidae
(3)

Glaucostegidae
(3)

Trygonorrhinidae
(3–4)

SQUATINIFORMES
Squatinidae
(4)

TORPEDINIFORMES
Narcinidae
(4)

Hypnidae
(4)

RAJIFORMES
Rajidae
(4)

MYLIOBATIFORMES
Urolophidae
(4–5)

Dasyatidae
(4–5)

Mobulidae
(5)

Gymnuridae
(5)

Myliobatidae
(5)

CHIMAERIFORMES
Chimaeridae
(5)

ACTINOPTERI
(bony, ray-finned fishes)

ELOPIFORMES
Elopidae (6)

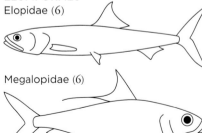

Megalopidae (6)

ALBULIFORMS
Albulidae (6)

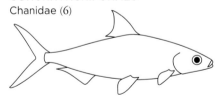

GONORHYNCHIFORMES
Chanidae (6)

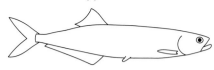

CLUPEIFORMES
Chirocentridae (6)

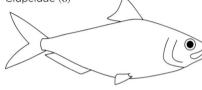

Clupeidae (6)

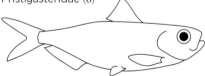

Pristigasteridae (6)

Engraulidae (6)

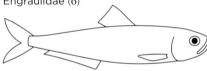

ANGUILLIFORMES
Muraenidae (7–8)

Congridae (9–10)

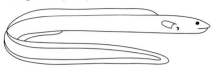

Ophichthidae (9–10)

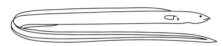

SILURIFORMES
Ariidae (11)

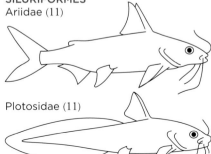

Plotosidae (11)

AULOPIFORMES
Synodontidae
• Subfamily Synodontinae (11)

• Subfamily Harpodontinae (11)

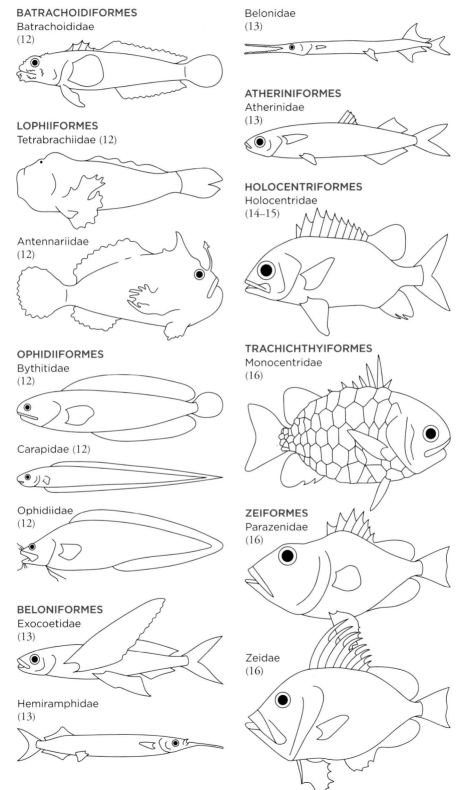

BATRACHOIDIFORMES
Batrachoididae
(12)

LOPHIIFORMES
Tetrabrachiidae (12)

Antennariidae
(12)

OPHIDIIFORMES
Bythitidae
(12)

Carapidae (12)

Ophidiidae
(12)

BELONIFORMES
Exocoetidae
(13)

Hemiramphidae
(13)

Belonidae
(13)

ATHERINIFORMES
Atherinidae
(13)

HOLOCENTRIFORMES
Holocentridae
(14–15)

TRACHICHTHYIFORMES
Monocentridae
(16)

ZEIFORMES
Parazenidae
(16)

Zeidae
(16)

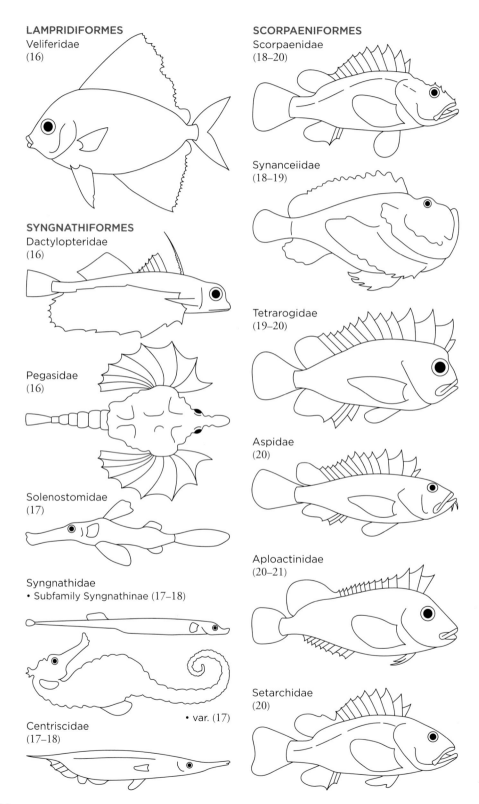

LAMPRIDIFORMES
Veliferidae
(16)

SYNGNATHIFORMES
Dactylopteridae
(16)

Pegasidae
(16)

Solenostomidae
(17)

Syngnathidae
• Subfamily Syngnathinae (17–18)

• var. (17)

Centriscidae
(17–18)

SCORPAENIFORMES
Scorpaenidae
(18–20)

Synanceiidae
(18–19)

Tetrarogidae
(19–20)

Aspidae
(20)

Aploactinidae
(20–21)

Setarchidae
(20)

Triglidae
(21)

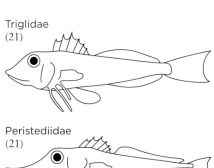

Aulostomidae
(16)

Peristediidae
(21)

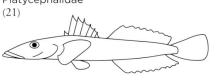

Hoplichthyidae
(16)

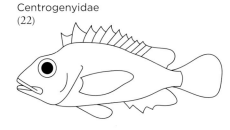

Platycephalidae
(21)

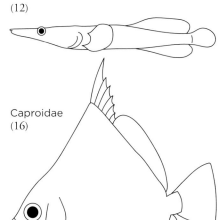

Centrogenyidae
(22)

PERCIFORMES
Gobiesocidae
(12)

Serranidae
• Subfamily Anthiadinae (22, 27–29)

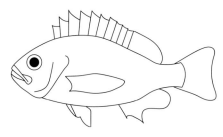

Caproidae
(16)

• Subfamily Epinephelinae
(22–26, 29)

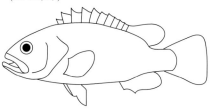

• Subfamily Grammistinae
(28–29)

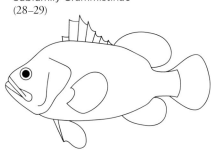

Fistulariidae
(16)

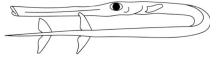

Plesiopidae
• Subfamily Plesiopinae (28–29)

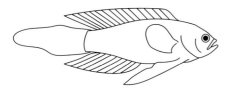

• Subfamily Acanthoclininae (28)

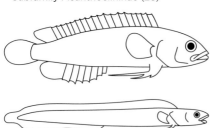

• var. (68)

Pseudochromidae
• Subfamily Pseudochrominae (28–29)

• Subfamily Congrogadinae (68)

Latidae
(30)

Ambassidae
(30)

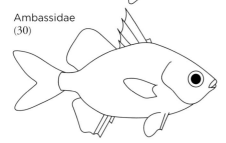

Glaucosomatidae
(30)

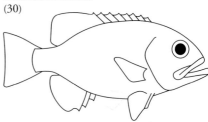

Terapontidae
(30)

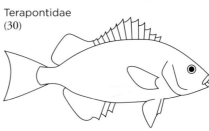

Sillaginidae
(30)

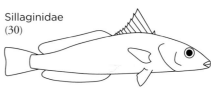

Priacanthidae
(31)

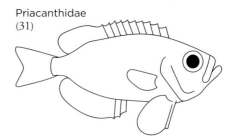

Apogonidae
(31–36)

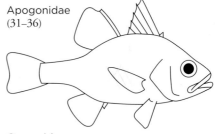

Carangidae
(37–40)

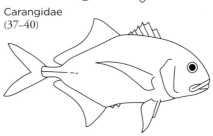

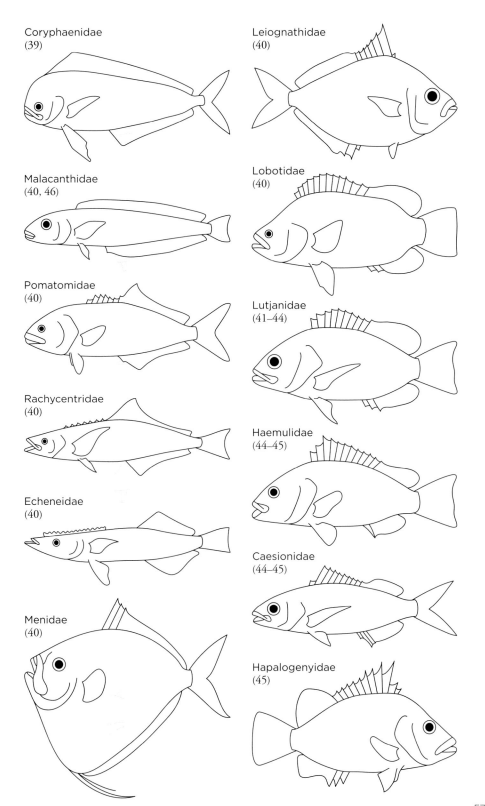

Coryphaenidae
(39)

Malacanthidae
(40, 46)

Pomatomidae
(40)

Rachycentridae
(40)

Echeneidae
(40)

Menidae
(40)

Leiognathidae
(40)

Lobotidae
(40)

Lutjanidae
(41–44)

Haemulidae
(44–45)

Caesionidae
(44–45)

Hapalogenyidae
(45)

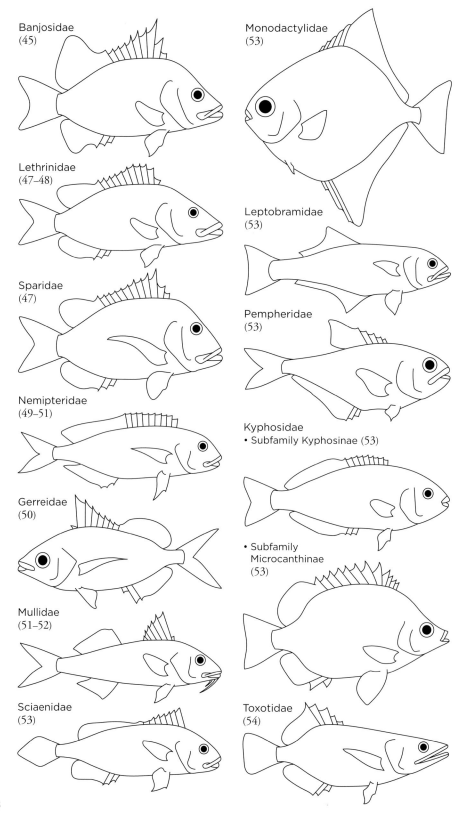

Banjosidae
(45)

Monodactylidae
(53)

Lethrinidae
(47–48)

Leptobramidae
(53)

Sparidae
(47)

Pempheridae
(53)

Nemipteridae
(49–51)

Kyphosidae
• Subfamily Kyphosinae (53)

Gerreidae
(50)

• Subfamily
  Microcanthinae
  (53)

Mullidae
(51–52)

Sciaenidae
(53)

Toxotidae
(54)

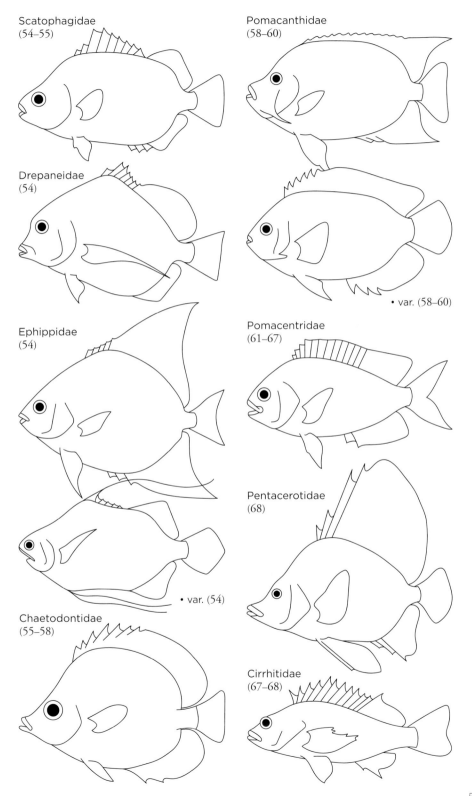

Scatophagidae
(54–55)

Drepaneidae
(54)

Ephippidae
(54)

• var. (54)

Chaetodontidae
(55–58)

Pomacanthidae
(58–60)

• var. (58–60)

Pomacentridae
(61–67)

Pentacerotidae
(68)

Cirrhitidae
(67–68)

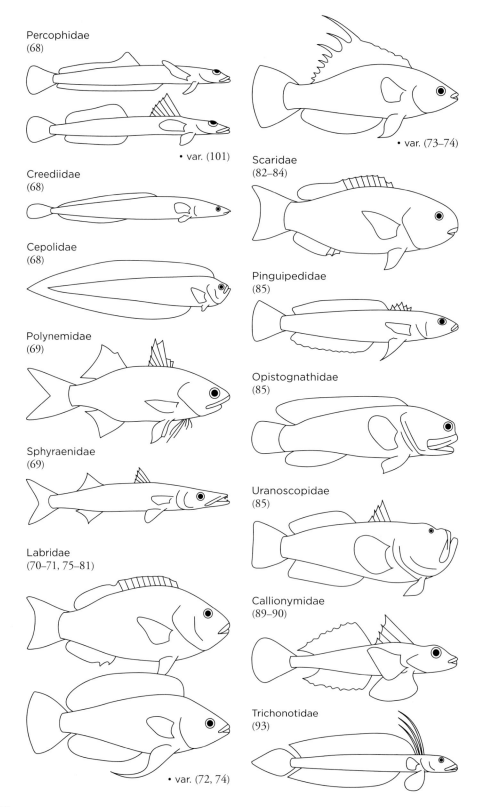

Percophidae
(68)

• var. (101)

Creediidae
(68)

Cepolidae
(68)

Polynemidae
(69)

Sphyraenidae
(69)

Labridae
(70–71, 75–81)

• var. (72, 74)

• var. (73–74)

Scaridae
(82–84)

Pinguipedidae
(85)

Opistognathidae
(85)

Uranoscopidae
(85)

Callionymidae
(89–90)

Trichonotidae
(93)

Zanclidae
(94)

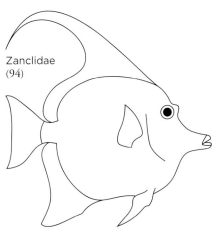

Siganidae
(94–95)

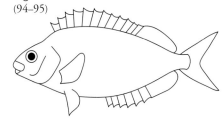

Acanthuridae
(95–97)

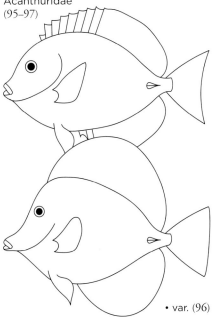

• var. (96)

MUGILIFORMS
Mugilidae
(69)

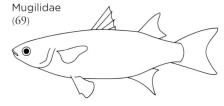

BLENNIIFORMES
Blenniidae
(86–88)

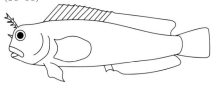

Tripterygiidae
(89)

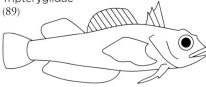

GOBIIFORMES
Gobiidae
• Subfamily Gobiinae (89–93)

• Subfamily Gobionellinae
(89–90)

• Subfamily Oxudercinae (94)

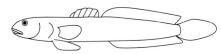

• Subfamily Amblyopinae (94)

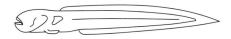

Microdesmidae
(92–93)

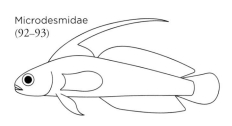

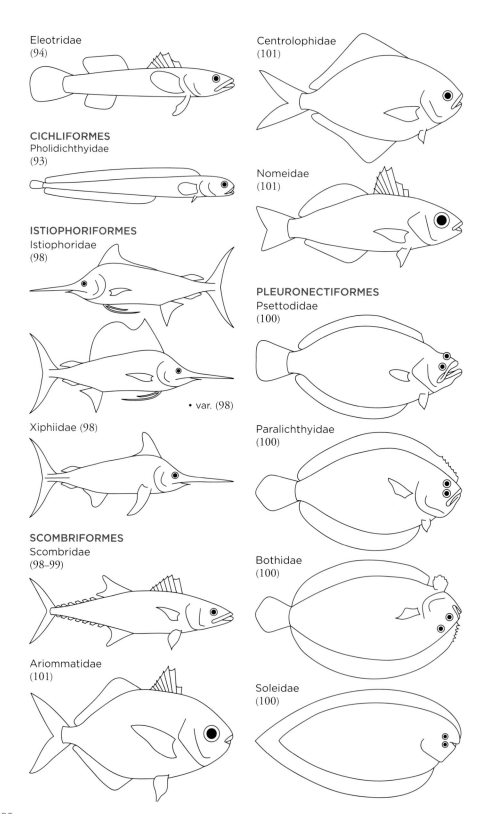

Eleotridae
(94)

CICHLIFORMES
Pholidichthyidae
(93)

ISTIOPHORIFORMES
Istiophoridae
(98)

• var. (98)

Xiphiidae (98)

SCOMBRIFORMES
Scombridae
(98–99)

Ariommatidae
(101)

Centrolophidae
(101)

Nomeidae
(101)

PLEURONECTIFORMES
Psettodidae
(100)

Paralichthyidae
(100)

Bothidae
(100)

Soleidae
(100)

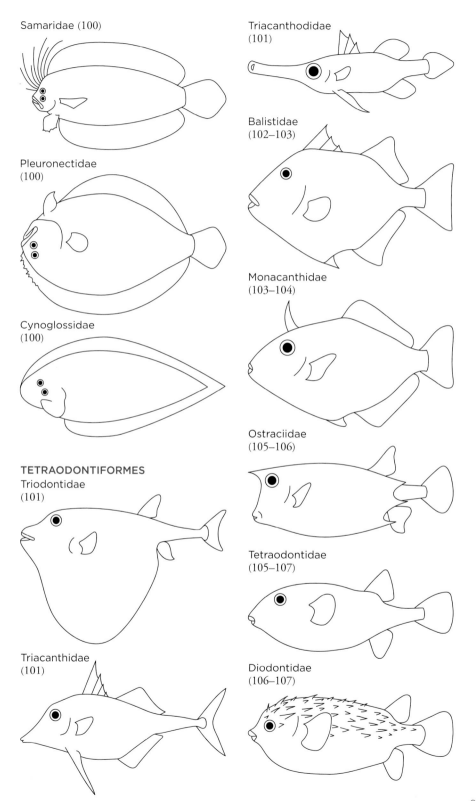

Samaridae (100)

Pleuronectidae
(100)

Cynoglossidae
(100)

TETRAODONTIFORMES
Triodontidae
(101)

Triacanthidae
(101)

Triacanthodidae
(101)

Balistidae
(102–103)

Monacanthidae
(103–104)

Ostraciidae
(105–106)

Tetraodontidae
(105–107)

Diodontidae
(106–107)

PLATE 1: SHARKS

RHINCODONTIDAE
1. WHALE SHARK
Rhincodon typus Smith, 1828
Inhabits coastal waters, also occurs well offshore; distinguished by huge size and pattern of white spots; world's largest fish, but harmless plankton feeder; rarely seen but sightings off North West Cape, Western Australia during March–April are a regular occurrence; found throughout the region; worldwide temperate and tropical seas; possibly to 18 m but seldom above 12 m.

STEGASTOMATIDAE
2. ZEBRA SHARK
Stegostoma fasciatum (Hermann, 1783)
Inhabits coastal waters and offshore areas in the vicinity of coral reefs, may be seen resting on the bottom; distinguished by large tail, dark spots and ridges on side; also known as Leopard Shark; harmless; found throughout the region; Indo-W. Pacific; to 350 cm.

GINGLYMOSTOMATIDAE
3. TAWNY SHARK
Nebrius ferrugineus (Lesson, 1831)
Inhabits shallow reefs; distinguished by brown colour; equal-sized dorsal fins and moderately long barbels on snout; harmless; found throughout the region; Indo-W. Pacific; to 320 cm.

ODONTASPIDAE
4. GREYNURSE SHARK
Carcharias taurus Rafinesque, 1810
Inhabits coastal waters, often occurs near the bottom in small schools, distinguished by pair of dorsal and anal fins nearly of equal size, long curved fang-like teeth and lack of barbels on snout; usually harmless, but will attack if provoked; subtropical Australian seas; Atlantic and Indo-W. Pacific; to 360 cm.

ALOPIIDAE
5. PELAGIC THRESHER
Alopias pelagicus Nakamura, 1935
Inhabits oceanic waters, but occasionally caught near shore; distinguished by very long upper tail lobe (used to stun schools of fish); harmless; found throughout the region; Indo-E. Pacific; to 330 cm.

HETERODONTIDAE
6. ZEBRA HORNSHARK
Heterodontus zebra (Gray, 1831)
Inhabits flat bottoms on the continental shelf to at least 50 m depth; distinguished by barred pattern and sharp spine at front of both dorsal fins; harmless although dorsal spines can cause painful wound; found throughout the region; mainly W. Pacific; to 122 cm.

LAMNIDAE
7. SHORTFIN MAKO
Isurus oxyrinchus Rafinesque, 1810
Inhabits oceanic waters usually well offshore, but sometimes visits coastal areas; distinguished by slender shape, equal-sized tail fin lobes and slender dagger-like teeth; also known as Blue Pointer; dangerous; found throughout the region; worldwide temperate and tropical seas; to 400 cm.

HEXANCHIDAE
8. BLUNTNOSE SIXGILL SHARK
Hexanchus griseus (Bonnaterre, 1788)
Inhabits coastal waters, also occurs well offshore in deeper waters of the continental shelf; distinguished by absence of second dorsal fin; found throughout the region; worldwide tropical seas; to 180 cm.

HEMISCYLLIDAE
9. SPECKLED CARPETSHARK
Hemiscyllium trispeculare Richardson, 1843
Inhabits shallow coral reefs; distinguished by pale-edged black spot partially surrounded by smaller black spots just behind gill slits; N.W. Australia and Aru Islands; to 65 cm.

10. EPAULETTE SHARK
Hemiscyllium ocellatum (Bonaterre, 1788)
Inhabits shallow coral reefs; similar to *H. trispeculare* (**9**), but lacks smaller black spots adjacent to large spot behind gill slits; harmless; N.E. Australia only; to 107 cm.

11. GREY CARPETSHARK
Chiloscyllium punctatum Müller & Henle, 1838
Inhabits shallow coral reefs; distinguished by strongly barred pattern and barbels on snout; harmless; found throughout the region; E. Indian Ocean and W. Pacific; to 104 cm.

SCYLIORHINIDAE
12. MARBLED CATSHARK
Atelomycterus macleayi Whitley, 1939
Inhabits coastal waters on sand or rocky bottoms; distinguished by small size, slender shape, no barbels on snout and pattern of black spots and faint, broad, dark bars; N. Australia only; to 60 cm.

13. RETICULATE SWELLSHARK
Cephaloscyllium fasciatum Chan, 1966
Inhabits deeper waters of the continental shelf; distinguished by rounded, inflatable stomach, blunt snout, narrow eye-slits and pattern of spots and lines; harmless; found throughout the region; N. Australia and S.E. Asia; to 80 cm.

ORECTOLOBIDAE
14. BANDED WOBBEGONG
Orectolobus ornatus (De Vis, 1883)
Inhabits shallow coastal reefs frequently on sand or weed bottoms; distinguished by ornate colour pattern and numerous skin flaps on mouth and lower part of head; harmless, but will bite if accidentally trod on; entire Australian coastline and New Guinea; to 300 cm.

15. NORTHERN WOBBEGONG
Orectolobus wardi Whitley, 1939
Inhabits coastal waters; distinguished by pale-edged dark saddles and bands; frequently has black spots on edge of dorsal fins and tail, skin flaps on head not as well developed as in *O. ornatus* (**14**); harmless; N. Australia only; to 100 cm.

16. TASSELLED WOBBEGONG
Eucrossorhinus dasypogon (Bleeker, 1867)
Inhabits coral reefs; distinguished by numerous branched skin flaps on both chin and side of head (absent on chin in *Orectolobus ornatus* (**14**) and *O. wardi* (**15**) and very broad, rounded head; harmless; N. Australia and New Guinea; to 350 cm.

SHARK TEETH

Sharks typically have an outer row of well-developed, upright teeth and several inner rows of teeth in various stages of development which are folded downward. Teeth are continuously produced throughout the life of the shark and each row moves forward to replace the next row every few weeks. The teeth are a valuable means of identifying species, particularly among the whalers illustrated on Plate 2. Typical examples from the upper and lower jaw of a number of sharks are included opposite.

PLATE 2: SHARKS

CARCHARHINIDAE

1. SILVERTIP SHARK
Carcharhinus albimarginatus (Rüppell, 1837)
Inhabits offshore coral reefs, usually below 20 m depth on outer edge of reefs; distinguished by white tips on dorsal, tail and pectoral fins; dangerous; found throughout the region; Indo-E. Pacific; to 300 cm.

2. BIGNOSE SHARK
Carcharhinus altimus (Springer, 1950)
Inhabits coastal waters; distinguished by long rounded or bluntly pointed snout when viewed from above, no conspicuous fin markings or skin ridge between dorsal fins; potentially dangerous; found throughout the region; worldwide tropical seas; to 300 cm.

3. GREY REEF SHARK
Carcharhinus amblyrhynchos (Bleeker, 1856)
Inhabits inshore and offshore coral reefs; usually seen adjacent to drop-offs on the outer edge of reefs; distinguished by black margin on tail and lack of skin ridge between dorsal fins; dangerous; found throughout the region; Indo-W. Pacific; to 255 cm.

4. PIGEYE SHARK
Carcharhinus amboinensis (Müller & Henle, 1839)
Inhabits coastal waters, sometimes entering estuaries and rivers; a large, stout, grey shark without distinguishing marks, has a large dorsal fin and lacks a skin ridge between the dorsal fins; dangerous; found throughout the region; Indo-W. Pacific; to 280 cm.

5. BRONZE WHALER
Carcharhinus brachyurus (Günther, 1870)
Inhabits coastal waters; often confused with *C. obscurus* (13), but has narrower upper teeth and no skin ridge between dorsal fins; dangerous; subtropical and temperate Australian seas; worldwide temperate and tropical seas; to 325 cm.

6. SPINNER SHARK
Carcharhinus brevipinna (Müller & Henle, 1839)
Inhabits coastal waters, often occurs in schools; distinguished by black tips on most fins, but lacks white margins around black areas as found in *C. melanopterus* (11); potentially dangerous; also known as Smooth-fanged or Inky-tail Shark; found throughout the region; Atlantic and Indo-W. Pacific; to 300 cm.

7. BULL SHARK
Carcharhinus leucas (Valenciennes, 1839)
Inhabits coastal waters, enters estuaries and rivers; landlocked freshwater populations occur in some areas outside Australia; a large, stocky shark with short, blunt snout when viewed from above; broad triangular teeth and lacks skin ridge between dorsal fins; dangerous; also known as River Whaler and Estuary Whaler; found throughout the region; worldwide temperate and tropical seas; to 340 cm.

8. SILKY SHARK
Carcharhinus falciformis (Müller & Henle, 1839)
Inhabits oceanic waters, usually well offshore; a large, slender grey shark with a moderately long rounded snout, short first dorsal fin and elongate tips on anal and second dorsal fins; potentially dangerous; found throughout the region; worldwide temperate and tropical seas; to 330 cm.

9. WHITECHEEK SHARK
Carcharhinus dussumieri (Müller & Henle, 1839)
Inhabits coastal waters; see remarks for the *C. sealei* (15); harmless; N.W. Australia and S.E. Asia; N. Indian Ocean and W. Pacific; to 100 cm.

10. COMMON BLACKTIP SHARK
Carharhinus limbatus (Müller & Henle, 1839)
Inhabits coastal waters; similar to *C. brevipinna* (6), but more black on fin tips and has black spot on pelvic fin; potentially dangerous; found throughout the region; worldwide temperate and tropical seas; to 255 cm.

11. BLACKTIP REEF SHARK
Carcharhinus melanopterus (Quoy & Gaimard, 1824)
Inhabits reef flats and coral reef lagoons; distinguished from other black-tipped sharks by white margin around black areas, especially noticeable on first dorsal fin; usually not dangerous unless cornered; found throughout the region; Indo-W. Pacific; to 180 cm.

12. OCEANIC WHITETIP SHARK
Carcharhinus longimanus (Poey, 1861)
Inhabits oceanic waters, usually well offshore; distinguished by over-sized pectoral fin and broad, rounded dorsal fin, both of these fins broadly white tipped; dangerous; found throughout the region; worldwide temperate and tropical seas; to 396 cm.

13. DUSKY WHALER
Carcharhinus obscurus (Lesueur, 1818)
Inhabits coastal waters, also found well offshore; similar to the Bronze Whaler *C. brachyurus* (5), but has wider, more triangular teeth in upper jaw and a low skin ridge between dorsal fins; dangerous; also known as Dusky Shark; subtropical and tropical Australia; worldwide temperate and tropical seas; to 362 cm.

14. SANDBAR SHARK
Carcharhinus plumbeus (Nardo, 1827)
Inhabits coastal waters; distinguished by very tall first dorsal fin that rises above rear base of pectoral fin; dangerous; also known as Sand or Thickskin Shark and Northern Whaler; found throughout the region; worldwide temperate and tropical seas; to 300 cm.

15. BLACKSPOT SHARK
Carcharhinus sealei (Pietschmann, 1913)
Inhabits coastal waters; similar to the *C. dussumieri* (9), but has falcate rather than triangular first dorsal fin; harmless; found throughout the region; Indo-W. Pacific; to 95 cm.

16. SPOT-TAIL SHARK
Carcharhinus sorrah (Müller & Henle, 1839)
Inhabits coastal waters in the vicinity of coral reefs; distinguished by conspicuous black tips on pectoral and second dorsal fins and lower lobe of tail; dangerous; found throughout the region; Indo-W. Pacific; to 160 cm.

SHARK ATTACK!

The sharks illustrated in Plate 2 are members of the family Carcharhinidae, commonly known as whalers. Although many of the species have never been implicated in attacks on humans, the family contains several which have a bad reputation. All should be handled with respect when removing hooks and none should be deliberately provoked by spearing fishes or offering food when diving in their company.

PLATE 3: SHARKS AND RAYS

CARCHARHINIDAE

1. TIGER SHARK ☆☆☆
Galeocerdo cuvier (Péron & Lesueur, 1822)
Inhabits deeper offshore areas, frequently near reefs, distinguished by blunt (when viewed from above) snout, stripes on side (faint or absent in large adults), keel on side of tail base and strongly curved teeth; very dangerous; found throughout the region; worldwide temperate and tropical seas; to 650 cm and 520 kg.

2. SLITEYE SHARK ☆☆☆
Loxodon macrorhinus Müller & Henle, 1839
Inhabits continental shelf waters between 7–80 m depth; distinguished by notch or slit on rear edge of eye socket, long slender snout and large eye; harmless; found throughout the region; Indo-W. Pacific; to 91 cm.

3. LEMON SHARK ☆☆☆
Negaprion acutidens (Rüppell, 1837)
Inhabits inshore waters, in bays, estuaries and coral reef lagoons; distinguished by yellow-brown colour, short snout and stocky body with 2 dorsal fins about equal size; generally harmless to divers but potentially dangerous; found throughout the region; Indo-W. Pacific; to 335 cm and 91 kg.

4. BLUE SHARK ☆☆☆
Prionace glauca (Linnaeus, 1758)
Inhabits surface waters, usually well offshore; similar to *Isurus oxyrinchus* (Plate **1.7**), at least in colour, but has smaller gill slits; longer pectoral fins and serrated teeth; also called Blue Whaler; dangerous; found throughout the region; worldwide temperate and tropical seas; to 380 cm and 140 kg.

5. WHITETIP REEF SHARK ☆☆
Triaenodon obesus (Rüppell, 1837)
Inhabits coral reefs, frequently seen resting on the bottom in caves or in the open; distinguished by slender shape and white tips on first dorsal and caudal fin; usually harmless, but has attacked humans; found throughout the region; Indo-E. Pacific; to 215 cm.

6. MILK SHARK ☆☆
Rhizoprionodon acutus (Rüppell, 1837)
Inhabits coastal bays and off sandy beaches, also offshore areas to 200 m depth; similar to *Loxodon macrorhinus* (**2**), but lacks notch on rear edge of eye socket; harmless; found throughout the region; E. Atlantic and Indo-W. Pacific; to 178 cm.

SPHYRNIDAE

7. SCALLOPED HAMMERHEAD ☆☆
Sphyrna lewini (Griffith & Smith, 1834)
Inhabits coastal waters and also encountered well offshore, frequently near the surface; distinguished from other hammerheads in the region by an indentation in the middle of the front edge of the head; dangerous; found throughout the region; worldwide temperate and tropical seas; to 420 cm and 76 kg.

8. WINGHEAD SHARK ☆☆
Eusphyra blochii (Cuvier, 1816)
Inhabits shallow coastal waters; distinguished by huge wing-shaped head (nearly a half length of the body); considered harmless; found throughout the region; N. Indian Ocean and Indo-Australian Archipelago; to 152 cm.

9. GREAT HAMMERHEAD ☆☆
Sphyrna mokarran (Rüppell, 1837)
Inhabits coastal waters and also found well offshore; distinguished by very flat front edge of head and tall, sail-like first dorsal fin with pointed tip, otherwise body shape similar to *S. lewini* (**7**); dangerous; found throughout the region; worldwide temperate and tropical seas; to 610 cm.

10. SMOOTH HAMMERHEAD ☆☆
Sphyrna zygaena (Linnaeus, 1758)
Inhabits coastal waters and also found well offshore; distinguished from other hammerheads in the region by smooth front edge of head; dangerous; found throughout the region; worldwide temperate and tropical seas; to 400 cm and 96 kg.

PRISTIDAE

11. GREEN SAWFISH ☆☆
Pristis zijsron Bleeker, 1851
Inhabits mud bottoms, entering estuaries; distinguished by relatively long saw-like snout; similar to *Anoxypristis cuspidatus* (**12**), but has 24–28 pairs of teeth extending along entire edge of snout; not dangerous unless cornered; found throughout the region; Indo-W. Pacific; usually to 600 cm, but reported to attain 730 cm.

12. NARROW SAWFISH ☆☆
Anoxypristis cuspidatus (Latham, 1794)
Inhabits mud bottoms inshore to about 40 m depth; similar in general appearance to *Pristis zijsron* (**11**), but body not as stout and has very long, narrow snout with 18–22 pairs of lateral teeth, but teeth absent on rear part; found throughout the region; N. Indian Ocean and Indo-Australian Archipelago; to 350 cm.

13. FRESHWATER SAWFISH ☆☆
Pristis pristis (Linnaeus, 1758)
Inhabits mud bottoms of bays and estuaries, also enters large rivers and goes well upstream; similar to *P. zijsron* (**11**), but has shorter, broader snout with 18–23 (usually 20–22) pairs of lateral teeth; also known as Wide Sawfish; found throughout the region; Indo-W. Pacific; usually to about 200 cm, but reputed to reach 700 cm.

RHINOBATIDAE

14. SHARK RAY ☆☆
Rhina ancylostoma Bloch & Schneider, 1801
Inhabits coastal waters, on mud or sand bottoms; distinguished from *Rhynchobatus australiae* (**15**) by rounded head and granular patches or ridges above each eye and on middle of forehead; found throughout the region; Indo-W. Pacific; to 260 cm.

RHINIDAE

15. WHITESPOTTED GUITARFISH ☆☆☆
Rhynchobatus australiae Whitley, 1939
Inhabits sandy areas, sometimes seen resting motionless; distinguished from *Rhina ancylostoma* (**14**) by pointed head and black spot above pectoral fin base; sometimes incorrectly referred to as Shovelnose Shark; found throughout the region; Indo-W. Pacific; to 300 cm and 75 kg.

TRYGONORRHINIDAE

16. SPOTTED SHOVELNOSE RAY ☆☆
Aptychotrema timorensis Last, 2004
Inhabits coastal waters on sand bottoms; similar to *Glaucostegus typus* (**17**), but has broad brown margin around white spots; known only from the Timor Sea, off Melville I., Northern Territory; to 120 cm.

GLAUCOSTEGIDAE

17. GIANT SHOVELNOSE RAY ☆☆
Glaucostegus typus (Bennett, 1830)
Inhabits coastal waters; similar to *Aptychotrema timorensis* (**16**), but lacks spots and snout is broader with more rounded tip; found throughout the region; E. Indian Ocean and Indo-Australian Archipelago; to at least 270 cm.

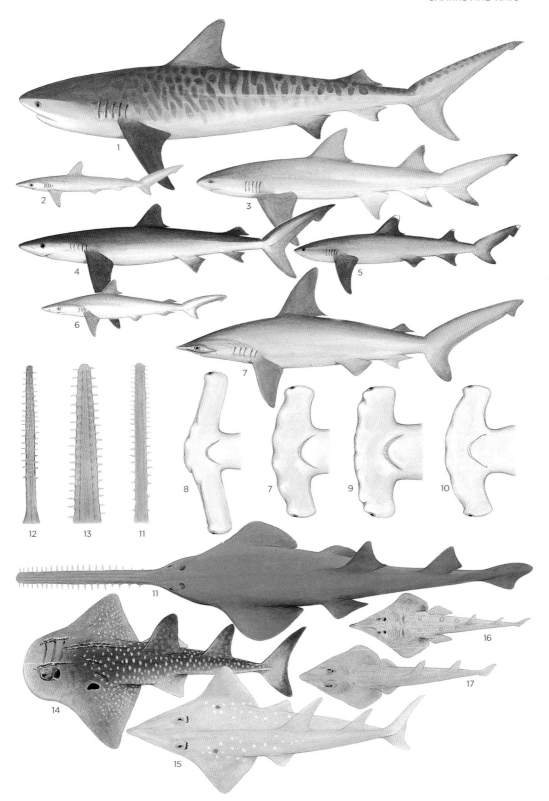

PLATE 4: SHARKS AND RAYS

SQUATINIDAE

1. WESTERN ANGEL SHARK ☆☆
Squatina pseudocellata Last & White, 2008
Inhabits deep (150–310 m) trawling grounds; a ray-like shark with distinctive shape; has greatly enlarged pectoral fins that are not entirely fused to the head and body as in rays; also has bilobed tail and 2 small dorsal fins; W. Australia between Shark Bay and Broome; to at least 64 cm.

TRYGONORRHINIDAE

2. YELLOW SHOVELNOSE RAY ☆☆
Aptychotrema vincentiana (Haacke, 1885)
Inhabits sand bottoms; similar to *A. timorensis* (Plate **3.16**), but lacks spots and snout is blunter; continental shelf of N.W. Australia; to at least 65 cm.

UROLOPHIDAE

3. BROWN STINGAREE VENOMOUS ☆☆
Urolophus westraliensis Last & Gomon, 1987
Inhabits sand bottoms in depths of 150–210 m; distinguished by sharply pointed snout tip, at least one serrated spine on tail, similar to *U. mitosis* (**4**) and *U. flavomosaicus* (Plate **5.7**), but is plain brown without markings or has 3 indistinct bars on disc; N.W. Australia between Dampier and Buccaneer Archipelago; to at least 36 cm.

4. MITOTIC STINGAREE VENOMOUS ☆☆
Urolophus mitosis Last & Gomon, 1987
Inhabits sand bottoms to depths of 200 m; similar to *U. westraliensis* (**3**) and *U. flavomosaicus* (Plate **5.7**), but has pale elongate blotches and lines that surround clusters of dark spots; N.W. Australia, known thus far only from off Port Hedland; to at least 29 cm.

NARCINIDAE

5. BANDED NUMBFISH
Narcine westraliensis McKay, 1966
Inhabits sand bottoms; distinguished by flattened 'tadpole' shape, large round head and 2 small dorsal fins; colour ranges from plain to spotted; capable of producing mild electrical shock; N.W. Australia only; to 28 cm.

6. ORNATE NUMBFISH
Narcine ornata Carvalho, 2008
This small species has often been confused with Banded Numbfish. It only occurs in the Gulf of Carpentaria; to 17 cm.

HYPNIDAE

7. COFFIN RAY
Hypnos monopterygium (Shaw, 1795)
Inhabits sand-weed areas; distinguished by round body with smaller rounded pelvic lobe at rear which bears the tail and 2 small dorsal fins; colour varies from light brown to blackish; can produce strong electrical shock if handled or accidentally trod on; also known as Numbfish; St Vincents Gulf, S. Australia to Broome, W. Australia and S. Queensland to S. New South Wales; Australia only; to 69 cm.

RAJIDAE

8. FALSE ARGUS SKATE VENOMOUS
Dentiraja falloarga (Last, 2008)
Inhabits sand bottoms of continental shelf in 60–200 m depth; distinguished by pointed snout, bilobed pelvic fins, single row of thorns or small spines down middle of tail and 2 small dorsal fins near end of tail; also has fragmented ocellus-type markings on each side of back; continental shelf of N.W. Australia; to at least 20 cm width.

9. WESTERN ROUND SKATE
Irolita westraliensis Last & Gladhill, 2008
Inhabits sand bottoms of continental shelf in 150–200 m depth; distinguished by round shape, bilobed pelvic fins, short spines or thorns in 1 or more rows on tail and 2 small dorsal fins near end of tail, also has blue-grey spots or blotches scattered on back; N.W. Australia from Shark Bay to Port Hedland; to 42 cm.

DASYATIDAE

10. PLAIN MASKRAY VENOMOUS ☆☆
Dasyatis annotata Last, 1987
Inhabits sand bottoms in 40–65 m depth; distinguished by kite-shape and 2 long serrated spines on tapering tail; similar to *D. leylandi* (**11**), but is plain grey-brown without markings and has a more pointed snout; Timor and Arafura seas off N. Australia; to at least 24 cm width and 45 cm length.

11. PAINTED MASKRAY VENOMOUS ☆☆
Dasyatis leylandi Last, 1987
Inhabits sand bottoms; two distinct colour forms are known, one with numerous irregular pale blotches and another with pepper-like spotting, both have broad dark band or 'mask' between eyes; also known as Brown Reticulated Stingray; N. Australia and S. New Guinea; to at least 25 cm width.

12. BLUESPOTTED MASKRAY VENOMOUS ☆☆
Neotrygon kuhlii (Müller & Henle, 1841)
Inhabits sand bottoms, frequently in the vicinity of coral reefs; sometimes buries itself with only the eyes protruding above the sand; distinguished by blue spots and frequently has scattered black spots on disc; found throughout the region; Indo-W. Pacific; maximum width about 45 cm; length to 70 cm.

SHARK FACTS

Sharks and their cousins, the rays, are very specialised fishes that represent a primitive stage of evolutionary development. The sharks represent an extremely ancient lineage. They were known in Devonian seas, over 350 million years ago. Many of the present genera of sharks, skates and rays date back more than 100 million years. Over 350 species of sharks are currently known. Only a small number of these are considered dangerous. Sharks represent an extremely diverse assemblage, occurring in all seas and in a variety of depths ranging from shallow intertidal pools to deep oceanic trenches, kilometres below the surface.

RAYS AND RELATIVES

Rays and their relatives are classified in the Order Rajiformes. Both sharks and rays are characterised by a cartilaginous skeleton. Other typical features of rays include a greatly flattened body that is often disc shaped and the presence of five, ventrally located gill openings. Most species bear their young alive except the Rajidae, which deposit egg cases. Many rays have venomous spikes or spines on the tail base that are capable of inflicting painful wounds. The members of the family Torpedinidae possess powerful electric organs situated in the head region. Rays dwell in a variety of habitats, ranging from oceanic depths to shallow reefs, estuaries and even freshwater streams. They range in size from about 30–40 cm disc-width (some skates) to more than 4 m (manta rays).

PLATE 5: RAYS AND GHOST SHARKS

DASYATIDAE

1. BLACK STINGRAY   VENOMOUS ☆☆
Bathytoshia lata (Garman, 1880)
Inhabits coastal waters off beaches and over sand or mud bottoms to at least 300 m depth; distinguished by blue-grey to blackish colour and short tubercles on top of head and over middle of back; has a pair of spines on tail that can inflict serious wounds; temperate and subtropical Australia northward to Shark Bay in the west and Coff's Harbour in the east; Indo-Pacific and E. Atlantic; to 180 cm disc width, 400 cm total length and 65 kg.

2. COWTAIL STINGRAY   VENOMOUS ☆☆
Pastinachus sephen (Forsskål, 1775)
Inhabits flat sand or mud bottoms near shore, also common in brackish mangrove estuaries and in the lower reaches of rivers; distinguished by grey-brown colour and broad flap of skin on lower edge of tail; large specimens may have tubercles on back similar to *Bathytoshia lata* (1); has 2 dangerous spines on tail; found throughout the region; Indo-W. Pacific to 180 cm disc width.

3. BLOTCHED FANTAIL RAY   VENOMOUS ☆☆
Taeniurops meyeni (Müller & Henle, 1841)
Inhabits sandy bottoms in the vicinity of coral reefs; distinguished by round shape and dense pattern of black spots; has pair of dangerous spines on tail; found throughout the region; Indo-W. Pacific; to 180 cm disc width and 330 cm total length.

4. BLUESPOTTED FANTAIL RAY   VENOMOUS
Taeniura lymma (Forsskål, 1775)
Inhabits flat sand bottoms in the vicinity of coral reefs; distinguished by kite shape and pattern of bright blue spots; has 1–2 dangerous spines on tail; found throughout the region; Indo-W. Pacific; to at least 30 cm disc width and 70 cm total length.

5. BLACKSPOTTED WHIPRAY   VENOMOUS ☆☆
Maculabatis toshi (Whitley, 1939)
Inhabits sandy beaches, sand flats near reefs, or shallow mangrove estuaries; distinguished by very long, whip-like tail and pattern of small black spots; has pair of dangerous spines on tail (sometimes missing); N. Australia and S. New Guinea; to at least 70 cm disc width and 180 cm total length.

6. LEOPARD WHIPRAY   VENOMOUS ☆☆
Himantura undulata (Bleeker, 1852)
Inhabits sandy beaches, sand flats near reefs, or shallow mangrove estuaries; distinguished by very long, whip-like tail and leopard-like spot pattern; has dangerous spine on tail; *H. uarnak* (not shown) is a similar species also found throughout the region — it has a reticulate, maze-like pattern; N. Australia and S. New Guinea; to at least 70 cm disc width and 180 cm total length.

7. PATCHWORK STINGAREE   VENOMOUS ☆☆
Urolophus flavomosaicus Last & Gomon, 1987
Inhabits coastal waters on flat sand bottoms; similar to *U. westraliensis* (Plate **4.3**) and *U. mitosis* (Plate **4.4**), but has ornate pattern of white spots and reticulated white and brown lines; found throughout the region; central W. Australia and southern half of Queensland; to 60 cm.

MOBULIDAE

8. OCEANIC MANTA RAY   ☆☆☆
Mobula birostris (Walbaum, 1792)
Inhabits coastal waters and the vicinity of offshore reefs; distinguished by large size, pair of protruding flaps at front of head and short tail; one of the largest of all fishes, it is a harmless plankton feeder well known for its ability to make spectacular leaps above the water surface; found throughout the region; worldwide circumtropical; to 700 cm disc width and over 2 tons in weight. The Reef Manta (*M. alfredi*), a slightly smaller, but similar species (not shown) also occurs in the region.

GYMNURIDAE

9. AUSTRALIAN BUTTERFLY RAY
Gymnura australis (Ramsay & Ogilby, 1886)
Inhabits shallow coastal waters; distinguished by broad triangular 'wings' and very short rat-like tail; northern half of Australia and S. New Guinea; to at least 80 cm disc width.

MYLIOBATIDAE

10. BANDED EAGLE RAY   VENOMOUS
Aetomylaeus nichofii (Bloch & Schneider, 1801)
Inhabits coastal waters in the vicinity of reefs; distinguished by bulging head and protruding snout similar to *Aetobatus ocellatus* (**11**), but lacks white spots and has pale blue cross-bands on back; found throughout the region; C. and E. Indian Ocean to W. Pacific; to 58 cm disc width and about 100 cm total length.

11. WHITESPOTTED EAGLE RAY   VENOMOUS ☆☆
Aetobatus ocellatus (Kuhl, 1823)
Inhabits coastal waters in the vicinity of reefs; similar to *Aetomylaeus nichofii* (**10**), but has white spots on back and 2–6 barbed spines on base of tail; found throughout the region; worldwide circumtropical; to at least 300 cm disc width and 880 cm total length.

CHIMAERIDAE

12. BLACKFIN GHOSTSHARK
Hydrolagus lemures (Whitley, 1939)
Inhabits deeper offshore waters of continental shelf in 200–500 m depth; distinguished by 'rodent-like' head with small mouth below eye, large pectoral fins, long tapering tail; several similar species found in region, but lack dark edge on first dorsal fin; widespread along most of the Australian continental shelf; to 30 cm.

BEWARE OF SPINES

Many of the rays illustrated on Plates 4 and 5 are characterised by one or more venomous spines on the tail. Stings inflicted by these spines are extremely painful and fatalities have occurred when either heart, abdomen or lungs were badly perforated. Caution should be exercised when wading on sandy bottoms. It is advisable to use a walking stick to probe just ahead or at least walk with a shuffling gait rather than in normal strides. This sort of movement will often prevent treading directly on the back of a partially buried ray. If a ray is stepped on it has the ability to thrust its tail upward and forward, impaling the victim with remarkable speed. Pain is immediate and intense and may persist for several days. Immersion in hot water (about 50°C) for 30–90 minutes may dramatically relieve the pain as the venom is a protein which is heat labile. Medical assistance should always be obtained as the wound may be far more serious than it appears.

PLATE 6: HERRINGS AND RELATIVES

ELOPIDAE

1. HAWAIIAN GIANT HERRING ☆
Elops hawaiensis Regan, 1909
Inhabits coastal waters and mangrove areas; distinguished by slender body and relatively large mouth; found throughout the region; Indo-C. Pacific; to 120 cm.

ALBULIDAE

2. BONEFISH ☆
Albula argentea (Forster, 1801)
Inhabits estuaries and mudflats; distinguished by protruding snout; found throughout the region; Indo-W. Pacific; to 110 cm.

CHANIDAE

3. MILKFISH ☆
Chanos chanos (Forsskål, 1775)
Inhabits coastal waters near reefs; distinguished by small mouth and scissor-like tail; found throughout the region; Indo-W. Pacific; to 120 cm and 10.6 kg.

MEGALOPIDAE

4. OXEYE HERRING ☆
Megalops cyprinoides (Broussonet, 1782)
Inhabits coastal waters and mangrove areas; distinguished by large eye and mouth, and filament at end of dorsal fin; found throughout the region; Indo-W. Pacific; to 150 cm and 2.3 kg.

CHIROCENTRIDAE

5. DORAB WOLF HERRING ☆
Chirocentrus dorab (Forsskål, 1775)
Inhabits coastal waters; distinguished by large fangs; found throughout the region; Indo-W. Pacific; to 140 cm.

CLUPEIDAE

6. SMOOTHBELLY SARDINE ☆☆
Amblygaster leiogaster (Valenciennes, 1847)
Inhabits coastal waters in large schools; similar to *Dussumieria elopsoides* (**8**), but pelvic and anal fins farther apart; N.W. Australia and Indo-Malay Archipelago; Indo-W. Pacific; to 25 cm.

7. SPOTTED SARDINE ☆☆
Amblygaster sirm (Walbaum, 1792)
Inhabits coastal waters; distinguished by row of spots on side; N.W. Australia to Gulf of Carpentaria and throughout S.E. Asia; Indo-W. Pacific; to 22 cm.

8. SLENDER SARDINE ☆☆
Dussumieria elopsoides Bleeker, 1849
Inhabits coastal waters; similar to *Amblygaster leiogaster* (**6**), but pelvic and anal fins closer together; N.W. Australia to Gulf of Carpentaria and throughout S.E. Asia; Indo-W. Pacific; to 25 cm.

9. GOLDSPOT HERRING ☆☆
Herklotsichthys quadrimaculatus (Rüppell, 1837)
Inhabits coastal waters; distinguished from all other plain-coloured herrings on this page by a pair of fleshy outgrowths on margin of gill cover; found throughout the region; Indo-W. Pacific; to 16 cm.

10. LARGESPOTTED HERRING ☆☆
Herklotsichthys koningsbergeri (Weber & de Beaufort, 1912)
Inhabits beaches and inlets; distinguished by double row of spots on side; found throughout the region; N.W. Australia to Gulf of Carpentaria and S. New Guinea; to 15 cm.

11. GIZZARD SHAD ☆☆
Anodontostoma chacunda (Hamilton-Buchanan, 1822)
Inhabits coastal waters and mangrove areas; similar to *Nematalosa come* (**12**), but lacks filament at rear of dorsal fin; found throughout the region; N.W. Australia to Gulf of Carpentaria and throughout S.E. Asia; Indo-Australian Archipelago and N. Indian Ocean: to 20 cm.

12. HAIRBACK HERRING ☆☆
Nematalosa come (Richardson, 1846)
Inhabits coastal bays and estuaries; similar to *Anodontostoma chacunda* (**11**), but has filament at end of dorsal fin; found throughout the region; mainly Indo-Australian Archipelago north to E. China Sea; to 23 cm.

13. SLENDER SPRAT ☆☆
Spratelloides gracilis (Temminck & Schlegel, 1846)
Inhabits coastal waters; distinguished by slender shape and silvery stripe on sides; found throughout the region; Indo-C. Pacific; to 11 cm.

14. BLUE SPRAT ☆☆
Spratelloides robustus Ogilby, 1897
Inhabits coastal waters and estuaries; distinguished by bluish-back and lack of silver stripe on sides; Australia only (W. Australia and New. S. Wales); to 9 cm.

15. GOLDSTRIPE SARDINELLA ☆☆
Sardinella gibbosa (Bleeker, 1849)
Inhabits coastal waters, distinguished by thin gold-coloured stripe on sides; N.W. Australia and throughout S.E. Asia; Indo-W. Pacific; to 19 cm.

PRISTIGASTERIDAE

16. BANDED ILISHA ☆☆
Ilisha striatula Wongratana, 1983
Inhabits coastal waters; similar to *Pellona ditchela* (**17**), but has faint stripe along middle of side (not shown) and lacks dark spot behind gill cover; N.W. Australia and Indonesia; mainly N. Indian Ocean: to 22 cm.

17. DITCHELEE ☆☆
Pellona ditchela Valenciennes, 1847
Inhabits coastal bays and estuaries; similar to *Ilisha striatula* (**16**), but lacks stripe on sides and has dark spot behind gill cover; found throughout the region; Indo-W. Pacific; to 18 cm.

ENGRAULIDAE

18. BAREBACK ANCHOVY ☆☆
Papuengraulis micropinna Munro, 1964
Inhabits coastal bays and estuaries; distinguished by threadlike dorsal fin; N. Australia and S. New Guinea; to 15 cm.

19. INDIAN ANCHOVY ☆☆
Stolephorus indicus (van Hasselt, 1823)
Inhabits coastal waters; distinguished by rounded snout and broad silvery stripe on sides; found throughout the region; Indo-W. Pacific; to 16 cm.

20. COMMON HAIRFIN ANCHOVY ☆☆
Setipinna tenuifilis (Valenciennes, 1848)
Inhabits coastal waters; similar to *Papuengraulis micropinna* (**18**), but has normal dorsal fin; N.W. Australia and S. New Guinea; E. Indian Ocean and W. Pacific; to 20 cm.

21. HAMILTON'S THRYSSA ☆☆
Thryssa hamiltonii (Gray, 1835)
Inhabits estuaries and mudflats; distinguished by rounded snout, large mouth and spot behind gill cover; *Thryssa setirostris* (not shown) is similar, but with extremely long posterior extension of upper jaw; found throughout the region except E. Queensland; N. Indian Ocean and W. Pacific; to 25 cm.

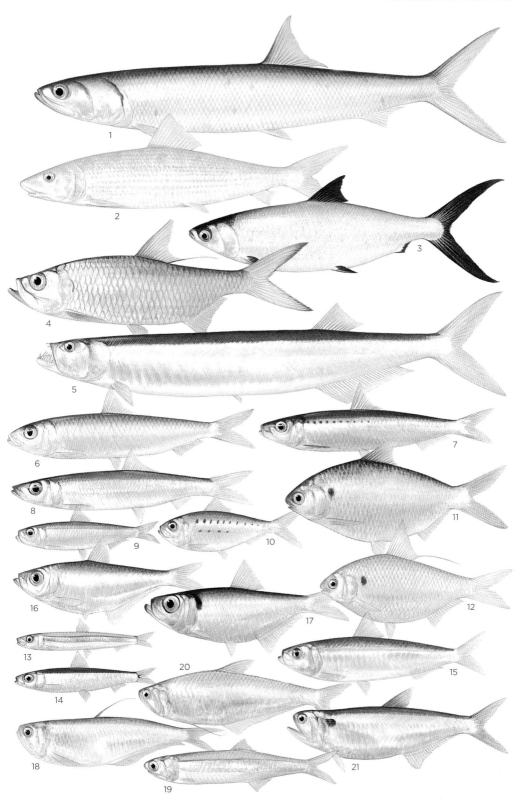

PLATE 7: MORAY EELS

MURAENIDAE

1. STARRY MORAY
Echidna nebulosa (Ahl, 1789)
Inhabits shallow coral reefs; distinguished by whitish body with 2 longitudinal rows of darkish, pale-centred blotches and lacks sharp fangs; also known as Clouded Reef Eel; found throughout the region; Indo-E. Pacific; to 70 cm.

2. GIRDLED MORAY
Echidna polyzona (Richardson, 1845)
Inhabits shallow coral reefs, often exposed to surge; distinguished by alternating light and dark bars of approximately equal width and lacks sharp fangs; N.W. Australia, E. Queensland and throughout S.E. Asia; Indo-W. Pacific; to 60 cm.

3. ZEBRA MORAY
Gymnomuraena zebra (Shaw, 1797)
Inhabits shallow coral reefs, often exposed to surge; distinguished by narrow pale bands encircling head and body and lacks sharp fangs; N.W. Australia, E. Queensland and throughout S.E. Asia; Indo-E. Pacific; to 150 cm.

4. LATTICETAIL MORAY
Gymnothorax buroensis (Bleeker, 1857)
Inhabits offshore coral reefs; distinguished by brown colour on front of body and blackish colour on posterior part with pale spotting; N.W. Australia, E. Queensland and throughout S.E. Asia; Indo-E. Pacific; to 31 cm.

5. STOUT MORAY
Gymnothorax eurostus (Abbot, 1860)
Inhabits coral reef crevices; distinguished by numerous small yellowish spots becoming larger on rear part of body; also dark spots or blotches evident mainly on front half; N.W. Australia, E. Queensland and throughout S.E. Asia; Indo-E. Pacific; to 40 cm and 0.23 kg.

6. SIEVE MORAY
Gymnothorax criboris Whitley, 1932
Inhabits coral reef crevices; distinguished by several dark spots behind eye; network of fine interconnected lines on front half of body and network of darker brown surrounding pale blotches on posterior half; also known as Brown-flecked Moray; N. Australia southward to Sydney; to 75 cm.

7. TESSELLATE MORAY
Gymnothorax favagineus Bloch & Schneider, 1801
Inhabits coral reef crevices; distinguished by bold spot pattern; one of the largest of moray eels, but usually harmless unless provoked; its sharp fangs can cause serious injury; also known as Giraffe Eel; found throughout the region; Indo-W. Pacific; to 300 cm.

8. YELLOWMARGIN MORAY
Gymnothorax flavimarginatus (Rüppell, 1830)
Inhabits coral reef crevices; generally yellow-brown in colour with fine dark spotting on head and body, and black patch at gill opening; juveniles are dark brown with fine yellow-green margin on dorsal and anal fins; also known as Leopard Eel; N.W. Australia, E. Queensland and throughout S.E. Asia; Indo-E. Pacific; to 50 cm.

9. FIMBRIATE MORAY
Gymnothorax fimbriatus (Bennett, 1832)
Inhabits coral reef crevices; distinguished by tan or light brown colour with loose network of branched dark bands; N.W. Australia, E. Queensland and throughout S.E. Asia; Indo-W. Pacific; to 80 cm.

10. GIANT MORAY
Gymnothorax javanicus (Bleeker, 1859)
Inhabits offshore coral reef, distinguished by yellow-brown head with small dark spots and large dark patch at gill opening; adults have leopard-like spotting on body; a large eel that can be dangerous if provoked; several attacks have been reported; found throughout the region; Indo-W. Pacific; to 250 cm.

11. PEARLY MORAY
Gymnothorax margaritophorus Bleeker, 1864
Inhabits coral reef crevices; distinguished by series of dark blotches just behind eye, pale chin and breast on body and 'lattice' pattern on rear part of body; N.W. Australia, E. Queensland and throughout S.E. Asia; Indo-W. Pacific; to 40 cm.

12. UNDULATE MORAY
Gymnothorax undulatus (Lacepède, 1803)
Inhabits coral reef crevices, distinguished by 'chain-link' pattern of narrow pale bands; juvenile with diffuse vertical bars most noticeable towards tail; found throughout the region; Indo-E. Pacific; to 150 cm.

13. BARTAIL MORAY
Gymnothorax zonipectis Seale, 1906
Inhabits coral reef crevices; distinguished by white spots on upper and lower jaw; dark spots on body and distinct dark bars on rear portion of dorsal and anal fins; N.W. Australia, E. Queensland and throughout S.E. Asia; Indo-W. Pacific; to 32 cm.

14. PAINTED MORAY
Gymnothorax pictus (Ahl, 1789)
Inhabits shallow reef flats and tide pools; sometimes seen entirely out of water at low tide; distinguished by white colouration with numerous small dark spots; also known as Peppered Moray; found throughout the region; Indo-E. Pacific; to 68 cm.

15. GREYFACE MORAY
Gymnothorax thyrsoideus (Richardson, 1845)
Inhabits shallow coral reefs; distinguished by light brown or tan-coloured body (with faint mottlings), white to bluish snout and silvery eyes; found throughout the region; Indo-W. Pacific; to 35 cm.

MORAY EELS

The eels featured on this plate are all members of the family Muraenidae, commonly known as morays. Most are equipped with needle-sharp teeth that have given them a largely undeserved reputation of being dangerous. While it is true that some larger eels, for example the Giant Moray *Gymnothorax javanicus* (**10**), have attacked humans, in most cases the eel had been provoked in some manner. Large eels should definitely not be teased with offerings of dead or struggling fish either handheld or on the end of a spear. Exceptions are morays that hang out at popular tourist dive sites and are relatively tame. In this case trust your local guide for advice, but always be cautious! Species in the genus *Echidna* have blunt teeth in contrast to most other eels. This is an adaptation for feeding on shelled molluscs and crustaceans. They exhibit striking colour patterns and are sometimes kept as aquarium pets. The Painted Moray *G. pictus* (**14**) sometimes frightens beachcombers. It occurs in very shallow pools at low tide or is occasionally found high and dry under rocks.

PLATE 8: MORAY EELS

MURAENIDAE

1. SPOTTED MORAY
Gymnothorax isingteena Richardson, 1845
Inhabits coral reef crevices; distinguished by bold black spots on white background, with many of the spots u-shaped; throughout central Indonesia northward to Hong Kong and Taiwan; to 180 cm.

2. LONGFANG MORAY
Enchelynassa canina (Quoy & Gaimard, 1824)
Inhabits coral reef crevices; distinguished by bilobed flap on front nostril, hooked jaws, wrinkled appearance of head, extremely long canine teeth at front of mouth and several white spots on lower jaw; Great Barrier Reef and throughout S.E. Asia; Indo-E. Pacific; to 150 cm.

3. WHITE-MARGINED MORAY
Enchelycore schismatorhynchus (Bleeker, 1853)
Inhabits coral reef crevices; distinguished by hooked jaws, large fangs and white margin on dorsal fin; throughout S.E. Asia; Indo-C. Pacific; to 120 cm.

4. HOOKJAW MORAY
Enchelycore bayeri (Schultz, 1953)
Inhabits coral reef crevices; distinguished by plain brown colour, large fangs and hooked jaws; a relatively small harmless species; Great Barrier Reef, offshore reefs of W. Australia and throughout S.E. Asia; Indo-C. Pacific; to 70 cm.

5. DRAGON MORAY
Enchelycore pardalis (Temminck & Schlegel, 1846)
Inhabits coral reef crevices; distinguished by highly ornate pattern of bars and spots and long tube-like rear nostrils above front part of eyes; throughout S.E. Asia; Indo-C. Pacific; to 80 cm.

6. WHITEMOUTH MORAY
Gymnothorax meleagris (Shaw, 1795)
Inhabits coral reef crevices; distinguished by network of small white spots on dark ground colour, also inside of mouth is white; Great Barrier Reef and throughout S.E. Asia; Indo-C. Pacific; to 100 cm.

7. MOLUCCAN MORAY
Gymnothorax moluccensis (Bleeker, 1864)
Inhabits coral reef crevices; plain brown colour without distinguishing marks; throughout S.E. Asia; W. Pacific; to at least 50 cm.

8. YELLOWMOUTH MORAY
Gymnothorax nudivomer (Günther, 1867)
Inhabits coral reef crevices; distinguished by yellow colour on inside of mouth, network of fine whites spots on head and much larger white spots over much of body; Great Barrier Reef and throughout S.E. Asia; Indo-C. Pacific; to 180 cm.

9. TIGER MORAY
Gymnothorax enigmaticus McCosker & Randall, 1982
Inhabits coral reef crevices; distinguished by black bars over entire length of body; similar to *G. rueppellii* (**15**), but bars on head completely encircle body and no yellow present on head; Great Barrier Reef, offshore reefs of W. Australia and throughout S.E. Asia; Indo-C. Pacific; to 58 cm.

10. HIGHFIN MORAY
Gymnothorax pseudothrysoideus (Bleeker, 1852)
Inhabits coral reef crevices; distinguished by spotted pattern and relatively well-developed dorsal fin; Great Barrier Reef and throughout S.E. Asia; W. Pacific; to 80 cm.

11. RICHARDSON'S MORAY
Gymnothorax richardsonii (Bleeker, 1852)
Inhabits coral reef crevices; a small speckled eel that is frequently found under rocks on shallow reef flats, often in weedy areas; throughout S.E. Asia; W. Pacific; to at least 30 cm.

12. SLENDERTAIL MORAY
Gymnothorax gracilicauda Jenkins, 1903
Inhabits coral reef crevices; distinguished by vertically elongate, branching dark blotches, forming definite bars on anterior half of body, but in several interconnected rows on posterior half; offshore reefs of W. Australia, Great Barrier Reef and throughout Oceania; to 32 cm.

13. DWARF MORAY
Gymnothorax melatremus Schultz, 1953
Inhabits coral reef crevices; distinguished by small size, black rim around eye and prominent black mark around gill opening; general colour ranges from brown to bright yellow, sometimes with network of dark markings posteriorly; Great Barrier Reef, offshore reefs of W. Australia and throughout S.E. Asia; Indo-W. and C. Pacific; to 26 cm.

14. MARBLED SNAKE MORAY
Uropterygius marmoratus (Lacepède, 1803)
Inhabits coral reef crevices; distinguished by marbled-colour pattern and complete lack of dorsal and anal fins; Great Barrier Reef, offshore reefs of W. Australia and throughout S.E. Asia; W. and C. Pacific; to 50 cm.

15. BANDED MORAY
Gymnothorax rueppellii (McClelland, 1844)
Inhabits coral reef crevices; similar to *G. enigmaticus* (**9**), but distinguished by yellowish head and dark bars on head do not encircle the body; Great Barrier Reef, offshore reefs of W. Australia and throughout S.E. Asia; Indo-C. Pacific; to 80 cm.

16. RIBBON EEL
Rhinomuraena quaesita Garman, 1888
Inhabits sand or rubble patches on the edge of coral reefs; feeds on fishes and crustaceans; males are bright blue and yellow with elaborate nostril flaps, females are yellow except for black anal fin, juveniles and sub-adults are largely black; harmless; prized as aquarium pets; Great Barrier Reef and throughout S.E. Asia; Indo-C. Pacific; to 120 cm.

17. WHITE RIBBON EEL
Pseudechidna brummeri (Bleeker, 1859)
Inhabits reef flats, sheltered coastal reefs and lagoons, usually on sand-rubble bottoms with rocky outcrops; distinguished by compressed ribbon-like body and overall pale colouration; throughout S.E. Asia; Indo-W. Pacific; to 105 cm.

RIBBON EEL

The bright-coloured Ribbon Eel *Rhinomuraena quaesita* (**16**) is aptly named. Although the head is roughly cylindrical, its body is thin and ribbon-like. Unlike most morays, it lives in sandy burrows. It is usually seen protruding its head and up to about one-third of the body length outside the burrow. Aside from colouration and shape, the most distinguishing feature is the enormously expanded nostrils, which form a membranous scoop-like structure. If threatened, for example when closely approached by a diver, the eel swiftly retreats into its burrow, waiting several minutes before emerging.

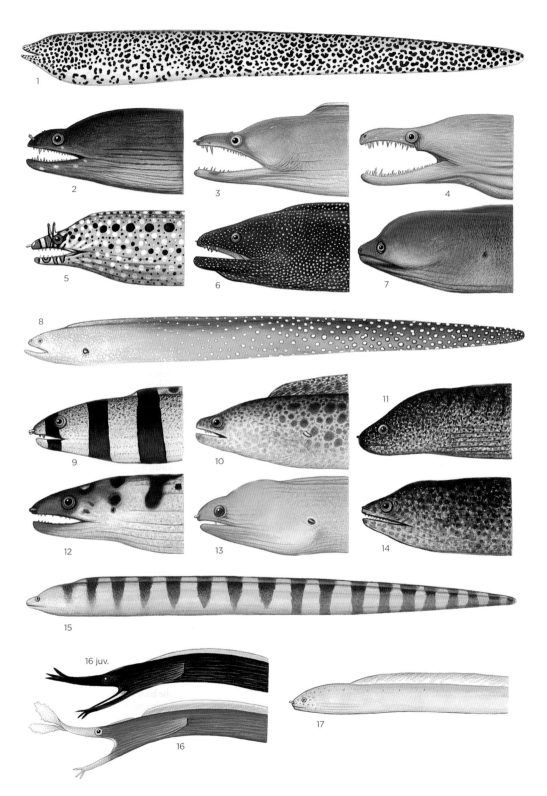

PLATE 9: SNAKE-EELS AND CONGER EELS

CONGRIDAE

1. BLACKLIP CONGER

Conger cinereus Rüppell, 1830
Inhabits coral reef crevices; distinguished by well-developed
pectoral fins, relatively tall, black-edged dorsal and anal fins,
and diagonal dark band behind mouth; found throughout
the region; Indo-C. Pacific; to 103 cm.

OPHICHTHIDAE

2. MARBLED SNAKE-EEL

Callechelys marmorata (Bleeker, 1853)
Inhabits sand bottoms near coral reefs; distinguished by
dense pattern of irregular black spots; N.W. Australia, E.
Queensland and throughout S.E. Asia; Indo-C. Pacific;
to 57 cm.

3. STARGAZER SNAKE-EEL

Brachysomaphis cirrocheilos (Bleeker, 1857)
Inhabits sand bottoms, often with eyes only protruding
above surface; distinguished by upward-directed eyes near
tip of snout, fringe of skin tentacles on lips, fang-like teeth
in jaws and roof of mouth, and overall pale colour; N.W.
Australia, E. Queensland and throughout S.E. Asia; Indo-W.
Pacific; to 125 cm.

4. SLENDER WORM EEL

Scolecenchelys gymnota (Bleeker, 1857)
Inhabits sand bottoms near coral reefs; distinguished by
small worm-like body, olive-coloured back, pale belly and
lack of pectoral fins; found throughout the region; Indo-C.
Pacific; to 17 cm.

5. FRINGELIP SNAKE-EEL

Cirrhimuraena calamus (Günther, 1870)
Inhabits sand bottoms; distinguished by fringe of skin
tentacles on upper lip, small pectoral fin, brownish colour of
back and abrupt transition to pale on lower half; W. Australia
only from Geographe Bay northwards; to 62 cm.

6. SADDLED SNAKE-EEL

Leiuranus semicinctus (Lay & Bennett, 1839)
Inhabits sand bottoms; distinguished by series of black
saddles on upper two-thirds of body; found throughout the
region; Indo-C. Pacific; to 60 cm.

7. HARLEQUIN SNAKE-EEL

Myrichthys colubrinus (Boddaert, 1781)
Inhabits sand bottoms; similar to *Leiuranus semicinctus* (**6**),
but black bars completely or nearly encircle body; N.W.
Australia, E. Queensland and throughout S.E. Asia; Indo-C.
Pacific; to 88 cm.

8. FLAPPY SNAKE-EEL

Phyllophichthus xenodontus Gosline, 1951
Inhabits sand bottoms near reefs; distinguished by long
pointed snout, leaf-like skin flap at each anterior nostril (near
snout tip) and small pectoral fins; found throughout the
region; N.W. Australia, E. Queensland and throughout S.E.
Asia; Indo-C. Pacific; to 42 cm.

9. BLACKSADDLE SNAKE-EEL

Ophichthus cephalozona Bleeker, 1864
Inhabits sand bottoms; distinguished by white-edged black
saddle on middle of head; N.W. Australia, E. Queensland
and throughout S.E. Asia; mainly W. Pacific; to 80 cm.

10. OLIVE SNAKE-EEL

Ophichthus rutidoderma (Bleeker, 1853)
Inhabits sand bottoms; distinguished by nondescript pattern,
pointed snout, pointed teeth and pectoral fin base on upper
half of gill opening; N.W. Australia and Indonesia; mainly
Indo-Australian Archipelago; to 68 cm.

11. BLACKFINNED SNAKE-EEL

Ophichthus altipennis (Kaup, 1856)
Inhabits sand bottoms near coral reefs; distinguished by
black edge on dorsal fin, also pectoral fins sometimes entirely
or partly black; N.W. Australia and throughout S.E. Asia;
Indo-C. Pacific; to 80 cm.

12. ESTUARY SNAKE-EEL

Pisodonophis boro (Hamilton-Buchanan, 1822)
Inhabits sand or mud bottoms, often in estuaries or
freshwater streams; distinguished by nondescript pattern,
granular teeth, pectoral fin broad-based (not restricted to
upper half of gill opening) and dorsal fin begins behind end
of pectoral fins; N.W. Australia and throughout S.E. Asia;
Indo-W. Pacific; to 100 cm.

13. BURROWING SNAKE-EEL

Pisodonophis cancrivorous (Richardson, 1848)
Inhabits sand bottoms distinguished by blunt snout (jaws
equal in length), granular teeth, pectoral fin broad-based and
dorsal fin begins above pectoral fins; N.W. Australia, E.
Queensland and throughout S.E. Asia; Indo-C. Pacific;
to 75 cm.

14. VULTURE EEL

Ichthyapus vulturis (Weber & de Beaufort, 1916)
Inhabits sand bottoms near coral reefs; distinguished by
general pale colouration, long pointed snout, very small eye
and no pectoral fins; N.W. Australia and throughout S.E.
Asia; Indo-C. Pacific; to 50 cm.

SNAKE-EELS

All of the species on this plate, except the Blacklip
Conger *Conger cinereus* (**1**), are members of the family
Ophichthidae, known as Snake-Eels. Although
they are very common, most people, including
keen anglers, are unaware of their presence. This
is because they spend most of the time buried in
the sand. Most of the species have a pointed snout
to aid in burrowing. In addition, many have a
bony, sharp tail and are equally adept at burrowing
forward or backward. The diet of most Snake-
Eels consists of small fishes, crabs and prawns.

A few species, particularly those with banded patterns,
are sometimes mistaken for sea snakes, but they are
easily distinguished by the lack of scales and possession
of a pointed tail (paddle-like in snakes). The Blacklip
Conger (**1**) belongs to the family Congridae. It is found
in rocky areas and amongst coral reef crevices. In some
parts of the Indo-Pacific region its flesh is considered a
delicacy. Neither conger nor Snake-Eels are dangerous.

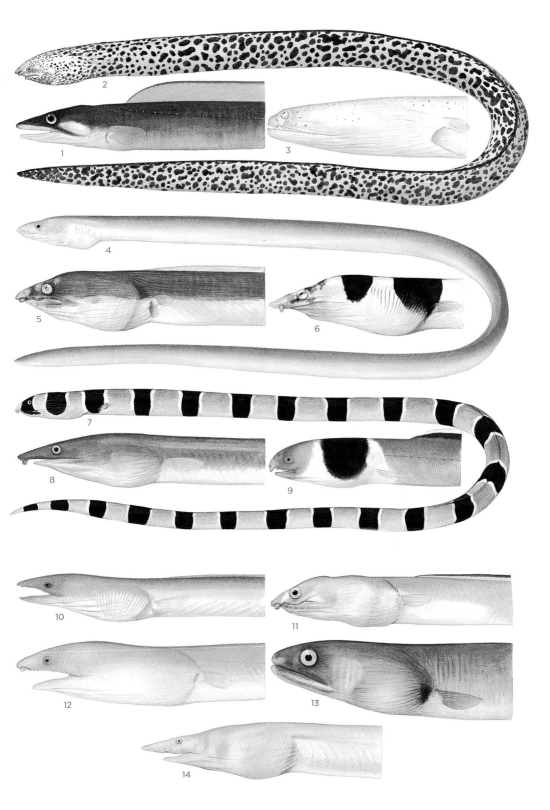

PLATE 10: SNAKE-EELS AND GARDEN-EELS

OPHICHTHIDAE

1. SHARPSNOUT SNAKE-EEL
Apterichtus klazingai (Weber, 1913)
Inhabits sand bottoms near coral reefs, buries in sand and is seldom seen; distinguished by pointed snout and white colour, and numerous small light-brown spots; Great Barrier Reef and throughout S.E. Asia; Indo-W. Pacific; to 40 cm.

2. PURPLEBANDED SNAKE-EEL
Ophichthus bonaparti (Kaup, 1856)
Inhabits sand bottoms near coral reefs, buries in sand (sometimes seen with head protruding); Indonesia and Philippines; to 60 cm.

3. CROCODILE SNAKE-EEL
Brachysomophis crocodilinus (Bennett, 1833)
Inhabits sand bottoms near coral reefs, buries in sand (sometimes seen with head protruding); distinguished by numerous skin flaps lining mouth; similar to *B. cirrocheilos* (Plate **9.3**), but has smaller pectoral fins (their length fits about 10–12 times into head length instead of only 4–5 times); Great Barrier Reef and throughout S.E. Asia; Indo E. Pacific; to 110 cm.

4. BLACKSTRIPED SNAKE-EEL
Callechelys catostoma (Forster, 1801)
Inhabits sand bottoms near coral reefs, buries in sand and seldom seen; distinguished by broad black stripe; *C. melanotaenia* is a synonym; Great Barrier Reef, offshore reefs of N.W. Australia and throughout S.E. Asia; to 60 cm.

5. OCELLATE SNAKE-EEL
Myrichthys maculosus (Cuvier, 1816)
Inhabits sand bottoms near coral reefs, buries in sand, but sometimes seen entirely exposed; distinguished by row of large dark spots; Great Barrier Reef, offshore reefs of N.W. Australia and throughout S.E. Asia; to 50 cm.

CONGRIDAE

6. GARDEN-EEL
Heteroconger cobra Böhlke and Randall, 1981
Inhabits sand bottoms near coral reefs; mainly covered with brown spots, but distinguished by large dark blotch surrounding U-shaped white marking on head; New Guinea and Solomon Islands; to 40 cm.

7. BLACK GARDEN-EEL
Heteroconger perissodon (Böhlke & Randall, 1981)
Inhabits sand bottoms near coral reefs; distinguished by white blotch on side of head; Philippines and Indonesia; to 60 cm.

8. SPLENDID GARDEN-EEL
Gorgasia preclara Böhlke & Randall, 1981
Inhabits sand bottoms near coral reefs; distinguished by bold brown and white pattern of bars; Philippines and Indonesia, also Maldive Islands; to 60 cm.

9. SPOTTED GARDEN-EEL
Heteroconger hassi (Klausewitz & Eibl-Eibesfeldt, 1959)
Inhabits sand bottoms near coral reefs; distinguished by fine spotting and pair of large black spots on anterior third of body; Great Barrier Reef, offshore reefs of N.W. Australia and throughout S.E. Asia; Indo-C. Pacific; to 60 cm.

10. TAYLOR'S GARDEN-EEL
Heteroconger taylori Castle & Randall, 1995
Inhabits sand bottoms near coral reefs; distinguished by leopard-like black spots; Indonesia and New Guinea; to 40 cm.

11. BARNES' GARDEN-EEL
Gorgasia barnesi Robison & Lancraft, 1984
Inhabits sand bottoms near coral reefs; distinguished by fine brown speckling and dark lips; Indonesia (Flores to Banda); to 100 cm.

12. SPECKLED GARDEN-EEL
Gorgasia galzini Castle & Randall, 1999
Inhabits sand bottoms near coral reefs; distinguished by fine brownish-yellow speckling; Great Barrier Reef and Coral Sea; W. Pacific; to 46 cm.

EEL GARDENS

Garden-eels (**6–12**) are easy to miss, even though they are frequently abundant. The reason for their apparent scarcity is that they live on flat or sloping sand bottoms — boring terrain for most divers or snorklers, who generally prefer the excitement of coral reefs. These unusual animals do not take a baited hook and were unknown to the scientific world, until the advent of scuba diving a few decades ago. However, their unusual and interesting habits offer great rewards for the observant diver and underwater photographer. Although small groups are occasionally encountered, they usually reside in colonies composed of many individuals, sometimes hundreds or even thousands! The eels live in sandy burrows, which they construct. They seldom leave the burrow, but while feeding in the passing current they rise out of their retreat — exposing up to two-thirds of the body length. Zooplankton is their primary food source. The eels even stay in their burrows when spawning — by stretching over to their mate's adjacent burrow and entwining bodies.

When disturbed the eels retreat backward into the opening of their lair. If a diver swims through the colony a wave 'effect' is created — directly ahead the eels gradually disappear into the sand, while those in the diver's wake gradually reappear. The common name of these creatures is derived from the appearance of the colonies when all the members are feeding in an extended position — from a distance they resemble a bed of plant stalks.

These animals offer a real challenge to underwater photographers. A telephoto lens is required, either 105 or 210 mm. In spite of the magnification advantage of these lenses, it is still necessary to have lots of patience. The best shots result when one can hide behind adjacent reef and hold breaths for long periods — encouraging the eel to rise high into the water column.

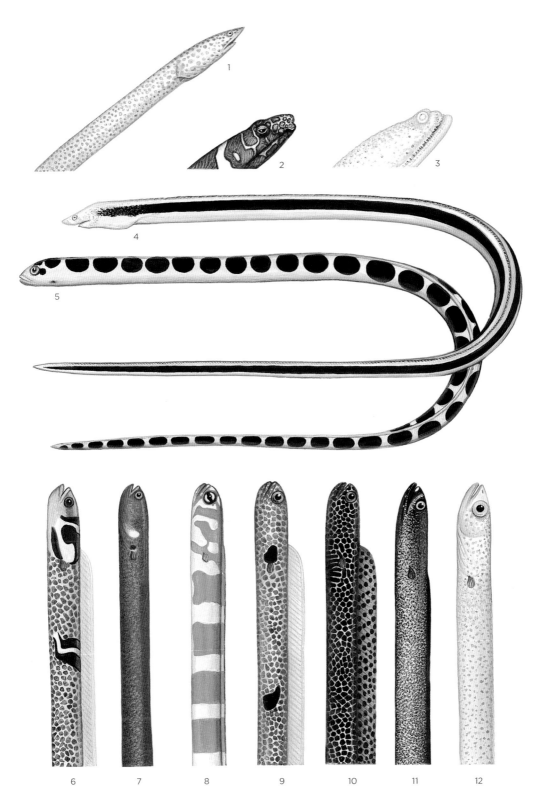

PLATE 11: CATFISHES AND LIZARDFISHES

ARIIDAE

1. GIANT SEA CATFISH VENOMOUS ☆ ☆
Netuma thalassina (Rüppell, 1837)
Inhabits coastal waters; there are about 8 species of salmon catfishes in northern waters which are difficult to identify even for experts; *N. thalassinus* is the largest species and has 6 patches of teeth on roof (palate) of mouth (versus 2–4 in others); found throughout the region; Indo-C. Pacific; to 185 cm.

2. BLUE CATFISH VENOMOUS ☆ ☆ ☆
Neoarius graeffei (Kner & Steindachner, 1867)
Inhabits coastal waters, estuaries and freshwater streams; difficult to identify, but has gill raker-like processes on back of all gill arches, 4 oval patches of teeth on roof of mouth and barbel on upper jaw not reaching farther than beginning of dorsal fin; N. Australia and S. New Guinea only; to 50 cm.

PLOTOSIDAE

3. NAKEDHEAD CATFISH VENOMOUS
Euristhmus nudiceps (Günther, 1880)
Inhabits coastal waters; similar to *E. lepturus* (**4**), but is more slender with greatest depth of body (i.e. height of body below first dorsal fin) fitting about 10–13 times in total length; N. Australia and New Guinea only; to 33 cm.

4. LONGTAIL CATFISH VENOMOUS
Euristhmus lepturus (Günther, 1864)
Inhabits coastal waters; similar to *E. nudiceps* (**3**), but not as slender, with greatest depth of body (i.e. height of body below first dorsal fin) fitting about 8 or 9 times in total length; N. Australia and S. New Guinea only; to 46 cm.

5. STRIPED CATFISH VENOMOUS
Plotosus lineatus (Thunberg, 1787)
Inhabits coastal waters, frequently in the vicinity of coral reefs; juveniles may form tightly packed aggregations containing up to several hundred fish; found throughout the region; Indo-C. Pacific; to 32 cm.

6. WHITELIP CATFISH VENOMOUS ☆ ☆ ☆
Paraplotosus albilabris (Valenciennes, 1840)
Inhabits coastal reefs, frequently found amongst weed; distinguished from *P. butleri* (**7**) by lighter colour and much shorter dorsal fin; found throughout the region; mainly Indo-Australian Archipelago; to 134 cm.

7. SAILFIN CATFISH VENOMOUS
Paraplotosus butleri Allen, 1998
Inhabits coastal reefs, usually in the vicinity of coral reefs; distinguished by black colour and tall dorsal fin; N.W. Australia south to Point Quobba; also Aru Islands; to 30 cm.

SYNODONTIDAE

8. INDIAN LIZARDFISH
Synodus indicus (Day, 1873)
Inhabits trawling grounds; distinguished by overall light colour with faint stripes on back and 2 dark streaks on upper corner of gill cover; N.W. Australia and throughout S.E. Asia; Indian Ocean and Indo-Australian Archipelago; to 21 cm.

9. TAILSPOT LIZARDFISH
Synodus jaculum Russell & Cressey, 1979
Inhabits the vicinity of coral reefs; distinguished by black spot at base of tail; Ningaloo Reef northwards; N.W. Australia, E. Queensland and throughout S.E. Asia; Indo-C. Pacific; to 13 cm.

10. BLACK LIZARDFISH
Synodus kaianus (Günther, 1880)
Inhabits trawling grounds; distinguished by overall dark colouration; N.W. Australia and Indonesia; mainly W. Pacific: to 22 cm.

11. TRIPLECROSS LIZARDFISH
Synodus macrops Tanaka, 1917
Inhabits trawling grounds; distinguished by large size of eye and 3 large dark blotches on side; N.W. Australia and Indonesia; Andaman Sea and W. Pacific; to 20 cm.

12. BLACKSHOULDER LIZARDFISH
Synodus hoshinonis Tanaka, 1917
Inhabits trawling grounds; distinguished by prominent black area on upper edge of gill cover; N.W. Australia, E. Queensland and throughout S.E. Asia; Indo-W. Pacific; to 22 cm.

13. FISHNET LIZARDFISH
Synodus sageneus Waite, 1905
Inhabits trawling grounds; distinguished from other lizardfishes by the absence or reduced size of the adipose fin (small fin on back between dorsal fin and tail); also known as Netted Lizardfish; N. Australia and S. New Guinea; to 26 cm.

14. VARIEGATED LIZARDFISH
Synodus variegatus (Lacepède, 1803)
Inhabits sand rubble areas in the vicinity of coral reefs; distinguished by mottled appearance with series of dark bars on side; N.W. Australia, E. Queensland and throughout S.E. Asia; Indo-C. Pacific; to 25 cm.

15. PAINTED GRINNER ☆ ☆
Trachinocephalus myops (Forster, 1801)
Inhabits coastal waters and trawling grounds; distinguished by pug-headed appearance, yellowish colour and bluish stripes on side; found throughout the region; Indo-C. Pacific; to 66 cm.

16. GRACILE SAURY ☆ ☆
Saurida gracilis (Quoy & Gaimard, 1824)
Inhabits sandy areas, frequently near coral reefs; similar to *Synodus sageneus* (**13**), but teeth not covered by lips when mouth is closed; N.W. Australia, E. Queensland and throughout S.E. Asia; Indo-C. Pacific; to 28 cm.

17. LARGESCALE SAURY ☆ ☆
Saurida undosquamis (Richardson, 1848)
Inhabits trawling grounds; distinguished by small black spots along upper edge of tail; also known as Chequered Lizardfish; found throughout the region; Indo-W. Pacific; to 45 cm.

18. COMMON SAURY ☆ ☆
Saurida tumbil (Bloch, 1795)
Inhabits trawling grounds; distinguished by lack of markings and dark lower lobe of tail; found throughout the region; Indo-W. Pacific; to 43 cm.

19. GLASSY BOMBAY DUCK ☆
Harpodon translucens Saville-Kent, 1889
Inhabits bays and estuaries; distinguished by large curved teeth and flaccid semi-transparent appearance; N. Australia and S. New Guinea only; to 70 cm.

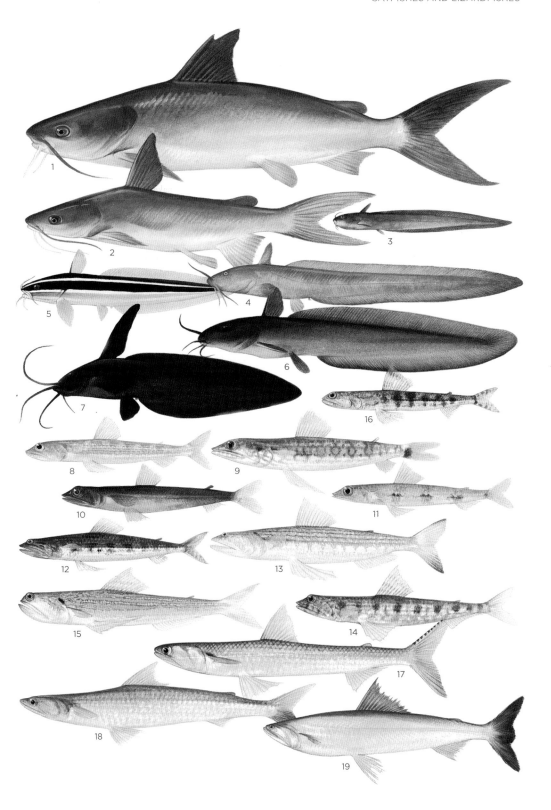

PLATE 12: FROGFISHES, ANGLERFISHES, CLINGFISHES AND CUSKEELS

BATRACHOIDIDAE

1. DAHL'S FROGFISH
Batrachomoeus dahli (Rendahl, 1922)
Inhabits shallow reefs; distinguished by gill slit extending along entire pectoral fin base and marbled pattern without distinctive cross-bars; N.W. Australia only; to 20 cm.

2. WESTERN FROGFISH
Batrachomoeus occidentalis Hutchins, 1976
Inhabits offshore trawling grounds; distinguished by gill slit extending along entire pectoral base and distinct cross-bars on side; Rottnest Island to Exmouth Gulf, W. Australia; to 20 cm.

3. THREESPINE FROGFISH
Batrachomoeus trispinosus (Günther, 1861)
Inhabits coastal reefs; similar to *B. dahli* (**1**), but has relatively distinct cross-bars on side and well-contrasted markings on dorsal surface of head; found throughout the region; N. Australia and New Guinea; to 30 cm.

4. BANDED FROGFISH
Halophryne diemensis (Lesueur, 1824)
Inhabits reef crevices; distinguished by gill slit extending only half to two-thirds of pectoral fin base and lacks small dark-edged white spots on side; found throughout the region; Indo-Australian Archipelago; to 26 cm.

5. OCELLATE FROGFISH
Halophryne ocellatus Hutchins, 1974
Inhabits offshore trawling grounds, may enter craypots; distinguished by restricted gill slit as in *H. diemensis* (**4**), but has small dark-edged white spots on side; Fremantle to Broome, W. Australia; to 26 cm.

GOBIESOCIDAE

6. STRIPED CLINGFISH
Diademichthys lineatus (Sauvage, 1883)
Inhabits coral reefs amongst spines of sea urchins or in branching corals; distinguished by peculiar shape with pale stripe on middle of side; found throughout the region; Indo-W. Pacific; to 5 cm.

7. BRIDLED CLINGFISH
Lepadichthys frenatus Waite, 1904
Inhabits trawling grounds; distinguished by red to brown colour, dark stripe behind eye and peculiar shape; N. Australia; W. Pacific; to 5 cm.

TETRABRACHIIDAE

8. HUMPBACK ANGLERFISH
Tetrabrachium ocellatum Günther, 1880
Inhabits offshore trawling grounds; distinguished by amorphous appearance, low dorsal and anal fins, small eyes and mouth and numerous white spots; N. Australia and New Guinea; to 8.5 cm.

ANTENNARIIDAE

9. STRIATE ANGLERFISH
Antennarius striatus (Shaw, 1794)
Inhabits inshore reefs, often in weeds; distinguished by narrow dark streaks and elongate blotches on body and fins; also entirely black variety; found throughout the region; Indo-W. Pacific; to 22 cm.

10. SPOTFIN ANGLERFISH
Antennarius nummifer (Cuvier, 1817)
Inhabits inshore reefs; similar to *A. coccineus* (**11**), but has distinct tail base and usually a dark spot at base of dorsal fin; found throughout the region; Indo-W. Pacific; to 13 cm.

11. FRECKLED ANGLERFISH
Antennarius coccineus (Lesson, 1831)
Inhabits offshore coral reefs; similar to *A. nummifer* (**10**), but lacks distinct tail base and black spot on dorsal fin base; found throughout the region; Indo-E. Pacific; to 13 cm.

12. SHAGGY ANGLERFISH
Antennarius hispidus (Bloch & Schneider, 1801)
Inhabits coastal reefs; distinguished by scattered dark blotches on side and fins and diagonal, elongate streaks and blotches on dorsal fin; found throughout the region; Indo-W. Pacific; to 20 cm.

13. PAINTED ANGLERFISH
Antennarius pictus (Shaw, 1794)
Inhabits coastal reefs; distinguished by scattered dark spots (some pale-edged) and with light patches on nape, cheek and pectoral regions; found throughout the region; Indo-W. Pacific; to 24 cm.

14. SPOT-TAIL ANGLERFISH
Lophiocharon trisignatus (Richardson, 1844)
Inhabits coastal reefs, also found under wharves; distinguished by dark-edged pale spots on tail; Indo-Australian Archipelago; to 18 cm.

15. SARGASSUM FISH
Histrio histrio (Linnaeus, 1758)
Usually found in clumps of floating sargassum weed; distinguished by smooth skin (most other anglerfishes have prickles), often with skin flaps and filaments on head and body; found throughout the region; worldwide temperate and tropical seas; to 16 cm.

BYTHITIDAE

16. RED CUSKEEL
Diancistrus alleni Schwarzhans, Møller & Nielsen, 2005
Inhabits coral reef crevices; distinguished by yellow to orange colour; elongate, tapering shape, blunt snout and tail separated from dorsal and anal fins; found throughout the region; W. Pacific; to 9 cm.

CARAPIDAE

17. CUCUMBER PEARLFISH
Onuxodon margaritiferae (Rendahl, 1921)
Inhabits coastal waters, lives in the mantle cavity of oysters; other similar species found inside sea cucumbers and cushion seastars; distinguished by long, slender, transparent body; found throughout the region; Indo-W. Pacific; to 9 cm.

OPHIDIIDAE

18. BLACKEDGE CUSK
Ophidion muraenolepis (Günther, 1880)
Inhabits continental shelf and slope; distinguished by long tapering body, low, dark-edged dorsal and anal fins; no barbels, but thread-like pelvic fins just behind chin; N.W. Australia and S. Indonesia; mainly eastern Indian Ocean; to 20 cm.

19. BEARDED CUSK
Brotula multibarbata Temminck & Schlegel, 1846   ☆☆
Inhabits coastal reefs; xdistinguished by elongate body, barbels around mouth and thread-like pelvic fins; found throughout the region; Indo-C. Pacific; to 90 cm.

20. GOLDEN CUSK
Sirembo imberis (Temminck & Schlegel, 1846)
Inhabits trawling grounds; similar to *Ophidion muraenolepis* (**18**), but with broken stripes and spots on side; found throughout the region; N. Indian Ocean and W. edge of Pacific; to 20 cm.

PLATE 13: FLYING FISHES, GARFISHES, LONGTOMS AND HARDYHEADS

EXOCOETIDAE

1. FLYINGFISH ☆☆

Cypselurus sp.
Inhabits oceanic waters, frequently well offshore; several species of flyingfishes are common in the region, but only one is shown here as they are seldom caught by anglers and identification at the species level is frequently difficult; flyingfishes are distinguished by the wing-like pectoral fins and elongated lower tail lobe which facilitate long gliding flights over the sea surface; found throughout the region; to 27 cm.

HEMIRAMPHIDAE

2. SNUBNOSED GARFISH ☆☆☆

Arrhamphus sclerolepis Günther, 1866
Inhabits coastal waters, sometimes entering brackish estuaries and the lower reaches of freshwater streams; distinguished by its short snout and lack of elongated lower jaw (as in other garfishes); N. Australia and New Guinea; to 30 cm.

3. NORTHERN RIVER GARFISH ☆☆

Zenarchopterus buffonis (Valenciennes, 1847)
Inhabits coastal waters, sometimes entering estuaries; distinguished by truncate tail (forked in other genera of garfishes) and prominent dark brown stripe along midline of snout; male (shown here) has elongated and thickened anal fin; several similar species in region, usually in brackish or fresh waters; found throughout the region; Andaman Sea and Indo-Australian Archipelago; to 13 cm.

4. BLACKBARRED GARFISH ☆☆☆

Hemiramphus far (Forsskål, 1775)
Inhabits coastal waters, frequently in schools near reefs; distinguished by 4–6 prominent dark bars on side; found throughout the region; Indo-W. Pacific; to 35 cm.

5. THREE-BY-TWO GARFISH ☆☆☆

Hemiramphus robustus Günther, 1866
Inhabits coastal waters; similar to *H. far* (**4**), but lacks dark bars on side (may have a single dark blotch below dorsal fin); both these species differ from *Hyporhamphus affinis* (**6**) and *Hyporhamphus quoyi* (**7**) in lacking scales on the triangular-shaped surface of the upper jaw; also known as Robust Garfish; tropical and temperate Australia only; to 48 cm.

6. TROPICAL GARFISH ☆☆

Hyporhamphus affinis (Günther, 1866)
Inhabits coastal waters, occurring in schools; similar to *Hemiramphus far* (**4**) and *Hemiramphus robustus* (**5**), but has scales (versus no scales) on the triangular-shaped surface of the upper jaw, is more slender and lacks bars or blotches on side; found throughout the region; Indo-C. Pacific; to 25 cm.

7. LONGTAIL GARFISH ☆☆☆

Hyporhamphus quoyi (Valenciennes, 1847)
Inhabits coastal waters, occurring in schools; distinguished by the relatively short lower jaw; found throughout the region; E. Indian Ocean and W. Pacific; to 34 cm.

8. LONGFIN GARFISH ☆☆☆

Euleptorhamphus viridis (van Hasselt, 1823)
Inhabits coastal waters, but sometimes encountered well offshore; distinguished by strongly compressed ribbon-like body, very long lower jaw and wing-like pectoral fins; exhibits gliding behaviour similar to flyingfishes; found throughout the region; Indo-E. Pacific; to 60 cm.

BELONIDAE

9. BARRED LONGTOM ☆☆

Ablennes hians (Valenciennes, 1846)
Inhabits oceanic waters, often well offshore; distinguished by bars on rear part of body below dorsal fin; found throughout the region; worldwide tropical and subtropical seas; to 120 cm.

10. FLAT-TAIL LONGTOM ☆☆

Platybelone argalus (Bennett, 1832)
Inhabits offshore waters; distinguished by flattened (dorsoventrally) tail base; found throughout the region; Indo-C. Pacific; to 40 cm.

11. SLENDER LONGTOM ☆☆

Strongylura leiura (Bleeker, 1850)
Inhabits coastal waters, frequently in bays and estuaries; distinguished by elongate jaws, slender shape and black bar or streak across base of gill cover (not shown); found throughout the region; Indo-W. Pacific; to 110 cm.

12. CROCODILE LONGTOM ☆☆

Tylosurus crocodilus (Péron & Lesueur, 1821)
Inhabits coastal waters; distinguished by dark fleshy ridge on side of tail base (not shown); found throughout the region; Atlantic and Indo-C. Pacific; to 150 cm.

13. STOUT LONGTOM ☆☆

Tylosurus gavialoides (Castelnau, 1873)
Inhabits coastal waters; similar to *T. crocodilus* (**12**), but lacks fleshy ridge on side of tail base; also has more rounded snout tip (when viewed from above); found throughout the region; E. Indian Ocean and W. Pacific; to 130 cm.

ATHERINIDAE

14. SPOTTED HARDYHEAD

Craterocephalus mugiloides (McCulloch, 1912)
Inhabits coastal waters, frequently in schools off beaches; distinguished by small dark spot below pectoral fin; N. Australia only; to 6 cm.

15. FEW-RAY HARDYHEAD

Craterocephalus pauciradiatus (Günther, 1861)
Inhabits coastal waters, occurring in schools; a nondescript silvery fish which has the anus positioned close to the pelvic fin base and lacks a notch on the lower cheek margin; N.W. Australia only; to 6 cm.

16. SAMOAN HARDYHEAD

Hypoatherina temminckii (Bleeker, 1854)
Inhabits coastal waters; distinguished by slender shape, anus placed far behind pelvic fin base and prominent silvery mid-lateral stripe; found throughout the region; Indo-C. Pacific; to 10 cm.

17. ENDRACHT HARDYHEAD

Atherinomorus endrachtensis (Quoy & Gaimard, 1825)
Inhabits coastal waters; similar to *Craterocephalus mugiloides* (**14**), but no spot below pectoral fin and rear part of lower jaw only slightly elevated (versus prominently elevated — mouth must be opened widely to detect this feature); N. Australia and New Guinea; to 10 cm.

18. COMMON HARDYHEAD

Atherinomorus vaigiensis (Quoy & Gaimard, 1825)
Inhabits shallow coastal waters, including bays and estuaries, usually in schools; distinguished by dark blotch at tip of pectoral fins; found throughout the region; Australia only — W. Australia, Queensland and New South Wales; to 17 cm.

PLATE 14: SQUIRRELFISHES

HOLOCENTRIDAE

1. SHADOWFIN SOLDIERFISH ☆☆☆
Myripristis adusta Bleeker, 1853
Inhabits caves and crevices of coral reefs; distinguished by black area on outer half of dorsal and anal fins; found throughout the region; W. Australia, Great Barrier Reef and throughout S.E. Asia; Indo-W. Pacific; to 30 cm.

2. DOUBLETOOTH SOLDIERFISH ☆☆☆
Myripristis hexagona (Lacepède, 1802)
Inhabits caves and crevices of coral reefs; similar to *M. botche* (**4**) (both have 2 pairs of tooth patches on front of lower jaw, just outside of the mouth), but differs in having small scales on the inside base 'armpit' of pectoral fin; found throughout the region; Indo-W. Pacific; to 20 cm.

3. EPAULETTE SOLDIERFISH ☆☆☆
Myripristis kuntee Valenciennes, 1831
Inhabits caves and crevices of coral reefs; distinguished by broad dark band behind head to pectoral fin base and 37–44 scales in lateral line; found throughout the region; Indo-C. Pacific; to 20 cm.

4. PALE SOLDIERFISH ☆☆☆
Myripristis botche Cuvier, 1829
Inhabits caves and crevices of coral reefs; similar to *M. hexagona* (**2**), but differs in lacking small scales on the inside base 'armpit' of pectoral fin; found throughout the region; Indo-W. Pacific; to 30 cm.

5. CRIMSON SOLDIERFISH ☆☆☆
Myripristis murdjan (Forsskål, 1775)
Inhabits caves and crevices of coral reefs; distinguished by dark margin on upper part of gill cover and 27–32 scales in lateral-line; found throughout the region; Indo-C. Pacific; to 30 cm.

6. SLENDER SQUIRRELFISH ☆☆
Neoniphon sammara (Forsskål, 1775)
Inhabits patch reefs in lagoons amongst branching corals; distinguished by slender shape, silvery or pale colouration and black spot at front of dorsal fin; found throughout the region; Indo-C. Pacific; to 32 cm.

7. DEEPWATER SQUIRRELFISH ☆☆
Ostichthys kaianus (Günther, 1880)
Inhabits offshore trawling ground between about 300–650 m depth; distinguished by broad V-shaped groove at middle of snout and 12 dorsal spines; N.W. Australia and Indonesia; Indo-W. Pacific; to 30 cm.

8. ROUGH SQUIRRELFISH ☆☆
Pristilepis oligolepis (Whitley, 1941)
Inhabits offshore trawling grounds; distinguished by narrow, elongate groove at middle of snout and 12 dorsal spines; W. Australia and scattered, mainly W. Pacific localities; to 20 cm.

9. CROWN SQUIRRELFISH ☆☆
Sargocentron diadema (Lacepède, 1802)
Inhabits coral reefs to 30 m depth; distinguished by broad black margin on dorsal fin; found throughout the region; N.W. Australia, Great Barrier Reef and throughout S.E. Asia; Indo-C. Pacific; to 16 cm.

10. SPECKLED SQUIRRELFISH ☆☆
Sargocentron punctatissimum (Cuvier, 1829)
Inhabits rocky shores and reefs exposed to wave action; distinguished by pepper-like spotting on sides; N.W. Australia, Great Barrier Reef and throughout S.E. Asia; Indo-C. Pacific; to 15 cm.

11. RED SQUIRRELFISH ☆☆
Sargocentron rubrum (Forsskål, 1775)
Inhabits live and dead coral reefs, usually in protected lagoons; distinguished by red and white stripes of about equal width; found throughout the region; Indo-W. Pacific; to 28 cm.

12. SABRE SQUIRRELFISH ☆☆☆
Sargocentron spiniferum (Forsskål, 1775)
Inhabits caves and crevices of coral reefs, distinguished by overall red colouration and very long spine at lower margin of cheek; N.W. Australia, Great Barrier Reef and throughout S.E. Asia; Indo-C. Pacific; to 40 cm.

13. BLUESTRIPE SQUIRRELFISH ☆☆☆
Sargocentron tiere (Cuvier, 1829)
Inhabits mainly outer, exposed reefs to 20 m depth; distinguished by brilliant red colour and iridescent blue stripes on lower sides; N.W. Australia, Great Barrier Reef and throughout S.E. Asia; Indo-C. Pacific; to 34 cm.

14. REDFACE SQUIRRELFISH ☆☆
Sargocentron violaceum (Bleeker, 1853)
Inhabits caves and crevices of coral reefs; distinguished by overall dusky appearance; found throughout the region; Indo-W. Pacific; to 23 cm.

PREDATORS OF THE NIGHT

The fishes featured on this plate are members of the family Holocentridae, commonly known as squirrelfishes or soldierfishes. They occur in all tropical seas. Most of the approximately 90 species inhabit the Indo-Pacific region. They are characterised by rough scales, prominent fin spines, a large eye and red colouration. Another remarkable feature is their ability to produce clearly audible 'clicking' sounds, believed to function as a form of communication between members of the school. Squirrelfishes differ from soldierfishes in possessing a sharp spine at the back of each cheek, which can inflict a painful wound if handled carelessly. Therefore caution must be exercised when removing them from a hook. Although most of the species are small, the flesh is considered good eating.

Although very abundant on coral reefs, snorkelers seldom see these fishes. During the day they remain hidden deep in the shadows of caves, cracks and crevices. They begin to appear in the open shortly after sunset. Because most of the reef's fish occupants are active during the day, many invertebrates, particularly crustaceans and echinoderms, have evolved a strategy to avoid them by coming out to feed at night. Squirrelfishes have adapted night-time feeding habits to take advantage of this nocturnal food supply. They feed mainly on crustaceans, particularly small crabs and shrimps.

PLATE 15: SQUIRRELFISHES

HOLOCENTRIDAE

1. BIGSCALE SOLDIERFISH ☆☆☆
Myripristis berndti Jordan & Evermann, 1903
Inhabits coral reef caves and ledges; all *Myripristis* lack a prominent spine on the lower edge of the cheek that is found in other squirrelfishes; distinguished by 28–31 scales along lateral line, pale body with dark scale edges, yellow dorsal fin and dark edge on gill cover; Great Barrier Reef, offshore reefs of W. Australia and throughout S.E. Asia; Indo-E. Pacific; to 19 cm.

2. YELLOWFIN SOLDIERFISH ☆☆☆
Myripristis chryseres Jordan & Evermann, 1903
Inhabits coral reef caves and ledges, usually below 30 m depth; distinguished by bright yellow fins; Great Barrier Reef and Indonesia; widely scattered localities in the Indo-C. Pacific; to 25 cm.

3. BIGEYE SOLDIERFISH ☆☆☆
Myripristis pralinia Cuvier, 1829
Inhabits coral reef caves and ledges; distinguished by dark mark that ends abruptly midway on rear edge of gill cover; Great Barrier Reef, offshore reefs of W. Australia and throughout S.E. Asia; Indo-C. Pacific; to 20 cm.

4. VIOLET SOLDIERFISH ☆☆☆
Myripristis violacea Bleeker, 1851
Inhabits coral reef caves and ledges; distinguished by bluish-silver colour and broad, dark scale edges that give dusky appearance to upper sides; Great Barrier Reef, offshore reefs of W. Australia and throughout S.E. Asia; Indo-C. Pacific; to 20 cm.

5. WHITETIP SOLDIERFISH ☆☆☆
Myripristis vittata Valenciennes, 1831
Inhabits coral reef caves and ledges, usually on outer slopes below about 20 m; distinguished by bright red-orange colour and white tips on dorsal spines; Great Barrier Reef, offshore reefs of W. Australia and throughout S.E. Asia; Indo-C. Pacific; to 20 cm.

6. SILVER SQUIRRELFISH ☆☆
Neoniphon argenteus (Valenciennes, 1831)
Inhabits coral reefs, frequently amongst branching corals; distinguished by mainly silver colour with faint spots forming longitudinal lines on side and plain dorsal fin; offshore reefs of W. Australia and throughout S.E. Asia; Indo-C. Pacific; to 25 cm.

7. YELLOWSTRIPED SQUIRRELFISH ☆☆
Neoniphon aurolineatus (Liénard, 1839)
Inhabits coral reefs, under ledges and amongst corals, usually below 40 m depth; distinguished by prominent yellow stripes on side; Great Barrier Reef; scattered localities in Indo-C. Pacific; to 22 cm.

8. BLACKFIN SQUIRRELFISH ☆☆
Neoniphon opercularis (Valenciennes, 1831)
Inhabits coral reefs, under ledges and amongst corals; distinguished by broad black band through anterior dorsal fin; Great Barrier Reef, offshore reefs of W. Australia and throughout S.E. Asia; Indo-C. Pacific; to 24 cm.

9. ROUGHSCALE SOLDIERFISH ☆☆
Plectrypops lima (Valenciennes, 1831)
Inhabits coral reefs, a cryptic species that hides in deep recesses during the day and rarely ventures far from caves at night; differs from other soldierfishes in having 12 instead of 11 dorsal spines; has stocky body shape similar to *Sargocentron lepros* (**14**), but lacks spine at lower corner of cheek; Great Barrier Reef and throughout S.E. Asia; Indo-C. Pacific; to 16 cm.

10. WHITETAIL SQUIRRELFISH ☆☆
Sargocentron caudimaculatum (Rüppell, 1838)
Inhabits coral reefs, frequently in caves and under ledges, but often seen in the open; distinguished by silvery-white spot behind dorsal fin base or entire rear part of fish silvery white; Great Barrier Reef, offshore reefs of W. Australia and throughout S.E. Asia; Indo-C. Pacific; to 21 cm.

11. HORNED SQUIRRELFISH ☆☆
Sargocentron cornutum (Bleeker, 1853)
Inhabits coral reef caves and ledges; similar black marks at base of caudal, dorsal and anal fins as *S. melanospilos* (**15**), but lacks yellow colour on body and has black submarginal band on dorsal fin; Great Barrier Reef, offshore reefs of W. Australia, Indonesia, Philippines, New Guinea and Solomon Islands; to 17 cm.

12. SAMURAI SQUIRRELFISH ☆☆
Sargocentron ittodai (Jordan & Fowler, 1902)
Inhabits coral reef caves and ledges in 5–70 m depth; a red-striped squirrelfish lacking distinguishing marks, but dorsal fin is largely red with white 'windows' across the middle; Great Barrier Reef and widely scattered localities in the Indo-W. Pacific; to 17 cm.

13. PINK SQUIRRELFISH ☆☆
Sargocentron tiereoides (Bleeker, 1853)
Inhabits coral reef caves and ledges; distinguished by silvery-pink stripes between red stripes on side of body, dorsal fin red with white tips; Great Barrier Reef and throughout S.E. Asia; Indo-C. Pacific; to 16 cm.

14. SPINY SQUIRRELFISH ☆☆
Sargocentron lepros (Allen & Cross, 1983)
Inhabits coral reef caves and ledges in 15–45 m depth; distinguished by stocky body shape, similar to *Plectrypops lima* (**9**), but has sharp spine on lower edge of cheek; offshore reefs of W. Australia and scattered localities in E. Indian Ocean; to 7 cm.

15. BLACKSPOT SQUIRRELFISH ☆☆
Sargocentron melanospilos (Bleeker, 1858)
Inhabits coral reef caves and ledges; distinguished by yellow colouration and three black spots at bases of soft dorsal, anal and caudal fins; often misidentified as *S. cornutum* (**11**); Great Barrier Reef and throughout S.E. Asia; Indo-C. Pacific; to 25 cm.

16. SMALLMOUTH SQUIRRELFISH ☆☆
Sargocentron microstoma (Günther, 1859)
Inhabits coral reef caves and ledges; distinguished by slender body, very long third anal spine and alternating white and red stripes; Great Barrier Reef, offshore reefs of W. Australia and throughout S.E. Asia; Indo-C. Pacific; to 19 cm.

NIGHT SHIFT

By day the coral reef is a beehive of activity. Fishes of every description swarm over the reef. Keen observers with a mask and snorkel can effortlessly watch the fascinating drama of undersea life as the occupants of the reef engage in their daily activities. But what happens to the fishes at night? Most retire to the safety of a cave or crevice at dusk — but as darkness descends squirrelfishes (Plates 14–15), cardinalfishes (Plates 31–36) and other members of the night shift become active.

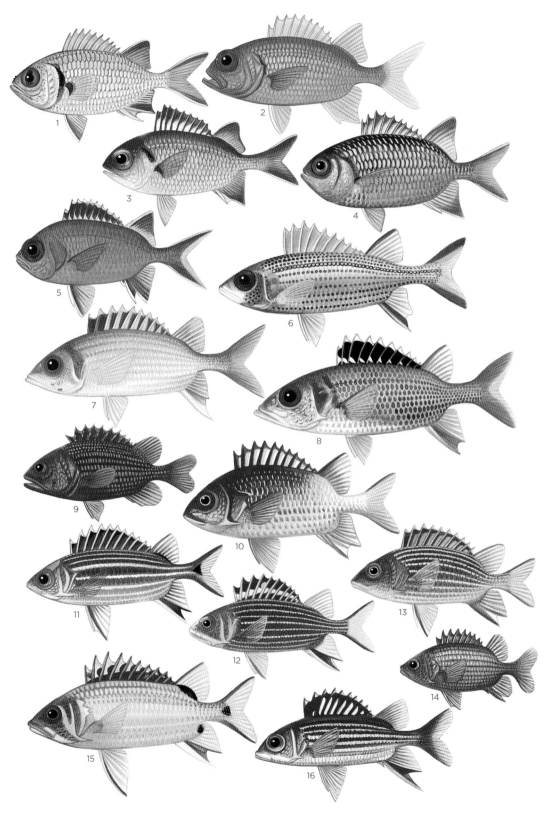

PLATE 16: KNIGHT FISHES, DORIES, FLUTEMOUTHS AND MISCELLANEOUS FAMILIES

MONOCENTRIDAE

1. AUSTRALIAN PINEAPPLEFISH

Cleidopus gloriamaris De Vis, 1882
Inhabits coastal reefs, usually in caves or under ledges; similar to *Monocentris japonica* (**2**), but has very conspicuous light-producing organ on each side of lower jaw (appearing as orange spot in daylight or a blue-green one at night) and scales are more strongly outlined by dark colouration; also known as Pineapple Fish; Australia only, mainly in subtropical and temperate waters of east and west coasts; to 28 cm.

2. JAPANESE PINEAPPLEFISH

Monocentris japonica (Houttuyn, 1782)
Inhabits deeper offshore reefs and trawling grounds; similar to *Cleidopus gloriamaris* (**1**), but light organs not as conspicuous, narrower dark margins around scales and wider gap between eye and mouth; N.W. Australia, New South Wales and scattered localites in Indo-Malay region; Indo-W. Pacific; to 20 cm.

PARAZENIDAE

3. LITTLE DORY

Cyttopsis cypho (Fowler, 1934)
Inhabits deeper trawling grounds of the continental shelf; general shape similar to *Zenopsis nebulosus* (**4**) and *Zeus faber* (**5**), but a much smaller fish lacking filamentous dorsal fin-rays; found throughout the region; mainly W. Pacific; to 18 cm.

ZEIDAE

4. MIRROR DORY ☆☆☆☆

Zenopsis nebulosus (Temminck & Schlegel, 1845)
Inhabits deeper trawling grounds of the continental shelf; similar to *Zeus faber* (**5**), but lacks scales (versus small scales present) and forehead profile distinctly concave (versus convex); found throughout the region; C. and W. Pacific; to 58 cm.

5. JOHN DORY ☆☆☆☆

Zeus faber Linnaeus, 1758
Inhabits deeper trawling grounds of the continental shelf, although sometimes found close to the coast; similar to *Zenopsis nebulosus* (**4**), but has small scales versus no scales and forehead profile is concave versus convex; Australia, mainly in temperate seas; tropical and temperate E. Atlantic and Indo-W. Pacific; to 75 cm.

CAPROIDAE

6. RHOMBOID DEEPSEA BOARFISH

Antigonia rhomboidea McCulloch, 1915
Inhabits deeper trawling grounds of the continental shelf; distinguished by diamond-shaped body; red or pink colouration with yellowish fins; Australia only — shelf areas off eastern and western coasts in tropical and temperate seas; to 15 cm.

VELIFERIDAE

7. HIGHFIN VEILFIN

Velifer hypselopterus Bleeker, 1879
Inhabits deeper trawling grounds of the continental shelf, although the young may appear in shallow coastal waters; distinguished by filamentous dorsal and anal fins and diffuse dark bars on side; shelf areas off eastern and western coasts of Australia in tropical and temperate seas, also Arafura Sea; Indo-W. Pacific; to 40 cm.

FISTULARIIDAE

8. SMOOTH FLUTEMOUTH

Fistularia commersonii Rüppell, 1838
Inhabits coastal waters in the vicinity of reefs; distinguished by long snout, trailing filament on tail and greenish-brown colour of back; found throughout the region; Indo-E. Pacific; to 163 cm.

9. ROUGH FLUTEMOUTH

Fistularia petimba Lacepède, 1803
Inhabits coastal waters, also found well offshore; similar to *F. commersonii* (**8**), but has row of bony plates along middle of back (absent in **8**) and is reddish or brownish-orange in colour (versus greenish-brown); found throughout the region; Atlantic and Indo-C. Pacific; to 185 cm.

AULOSTOMIDAE

10. TRUMPETFISH

Aulostomus chinensis (Linnaeus, 1766)
Inhabits coral reefs; roughly similar shape to *Fistularia commersonii* (**8**) and *F. petimba* (**9**), but has shorter snout, has small scales (versus no scales), row of feeble dorsal spines on back, different-shaped fins and lacks tail filament; a yellow variety is frequently seen; found throughout the region; Indo-E. Pacific; to 50 cm.

HOPLICHTHYIDAE

11. REGAN'S GHOST FLATHEAD

Hoplichthys regani Jordan, 1908
Inhabits deep offshore trawling grounds; similar to flatheads (Plate 21) in body shape (i.e. greatly flattened), but lacks scales and has filamentous dorsal fin-rays; N.W. Australia and S. Indonesia; Indo-W. Pacific; to 20 cm.

DACTYLOPTERIDAE

12. PURPLE FLYING GURNARD

Dactyloptaenia orientalis (Cuvier, 1829)
Inhabits coastal waters, usually on sand bottoms near coral reefs; distinguished by huge wing-like pectoral fins; found throughout the region; Indo-C. Pacific; to 38 cm.

PEGASIDAE

13. SLENDER SEAMOTH

Pegasus volitans Linnaeus, 1758
Inhabits sand or silt bottoms of bays and estuaries; distinguished by flattened head and tapered body encased in plate-like armour similar to seahorses and fan-like pectoral fins; often identified as *Parapegasus natans*; found throughout the region; Indo-W. Pacific; to 16 cm.

14. LITTLE DRAGONFISH

Eurypegasus draconis (Linnaeus, 1766)
Inhabits sand or silt bottoms, frequently in bays or estuaries; similar to *Pegasus volitans* (**13**), but wider body (when viewed from above), shorter snout and tail and body is more 'sculptured'; found throughout the region; Indo-C. Pacific; to 10 cm.

PLATE 17: SEAHORSES AND PIPEFISHES

CENTRISCIDAE

1. GROOVED RAZORFISH
Centriscus scutatus Linnaeus, 1758
Inhabits coastal waters; distinguished by long snout and thin (highly compressed) body composed of bony plates; Great Barrier Reef and throughout S.E. Asia; Indo-W. Pacific; to 15 cm.

SOLENOSTOMIDAE

2. ORNATE GHOSTPIPEFISH
Solenostomus paradoxus (Pallas, 1770)
Inhabits inshore reefs and weed beds, sometimes in floating seaweed; distinguished by skin flaps on head and body, stripes on body and spotted fins; N.W. Australia, Great Barrier Reef and throughout S.E. Asia; Indo-W. Pacific; to 12 cm.

3. ROBUST GHOSTPIPEFISH
Solenostomus cyanopterus Bleeker, 1854
Inhabits inshore reef areas; distinguished by yellowish to green or brown colour; general shape similar to *S. paradoxus* (**2**), but has fewer skin flaps and shorter tail base; N.W. Australia, Great Barrier Reef and throughout S.E. Asia; Indo-W. Pacific; to 16 cm.

SYGNATHIDAE

4. COMMON SEAHORSE
Hippocampus taeniopterus Bleeker, 1852
Inhabits sheltered waters; variable in colour; either yellow, brown or blackish; found throughout the region; Indo-C. Pacific; to 30 cm.

5. WESTERN SPINY SEAHORSE
Hippocampus angustus Günther, 1870
Inhabits sheltered bays; variable in colour, also has narrow lines across snout; N. Australia, except ranging south on W. coast to Augusta; to 22 cm (illustration not shown at scale).

6. SPINY SEAHORSE
Hippocampus histrix Kaup, 1856
Inhabits coastal waters; distinguished by pronounced spiny ridges on head and body; colour variable; found throughout the region; Indo-W. Pacific; to 15 cm.

7. HELEN'S PYGMY PIPEHORSE
Idiotropiscis larsonae (Dawson, 1984)
Inhabits coral reefs or amongst sargassum weed; distinguished by seahorse shape and bulbous forehead; known only from Montebello Islands, W. Australia; to 3.5 cm.

8. BRAUN'S PUGHEAD PIPEFISH
Bulbonaricus brauni (Dawson & Allen, 1978)
Inhabits coral reefs amongst organ-pipe coral; distinguished by eel-like shape; Ningaloo Reef, W. Australia and Indo-Malay region; to 6 cm.

9. MUIRON PIPEFISH
Choeroichthys latispinosus Dawson, 1978
Inhabits coral reefs; distinguished by relatively broad, elongate snout with upturned mouth and short tail; known thus far only from South Muiron Island, W. Australia; to 3 cm.

10. PACIFIC SHORTBODY PIPEFISH
Choeroichthys brachysoma (Bleeker, 1855)
Inhabits reefs and seagrass beds; distinguished by broad midsection tapering at head and tail; found throughout the region; Indo-C. Pacific; to 7 cm.

11. BANDED PIPEFISH
Dunckerocampus dactyliophorus (Bleeker, 1853)
Inhabits coral reef crevices; distinguished by prominent light and dark bands found throughout the region; Indo-W. Pacific; to 18 cm.

12. CLEANER PIPEFISH
Doryrhamphus janssi (Herald & Randall, 1972)
Inhabits coral reef crevices; distinguished by red central section of body grading to blue on rear part and fan-shaped dark tail with pale centre and pale outer margin; N.W. Australia, Great Barrier Reef and throughout S.E. Asia; mainly W. Pacific; to 13 cm.

13. LADDER PIPEFISH
Festucalex scalaris (Günther, 1870)
Inhabits trawling grounds, amongst weeds; distinguished by short snout and variegated pattern of light and dark spots, blotches and bars; central W. coast of W. Australia only; to 18 cm.

14. TIGER PIPEFISH
Filicampus tigris (Castelnau, 1879)
Inhabits sand-weed areas; distinguished by diagonal dark stripes on head, diffuse dark bars and abruptly white belly; Australia only — west and S.E. coast, also Spencer's Gulf, S. Australia; to 35 cm.

15. TASSELLED PIPEFISH
Halicampus brocki (Herald, 1953)
Inhabits coral and rocky reefs; distinguished by skin flaps and branched tassels; N.W. Australia, Great Barrier Reef and throughout S.E. Asia; mainly W. Pacific; to 11 cm.

16. SPINYSNOUT PIPEFISH
Halicampus spinirostris (Dawson & Allen, 1981)
Inhabits coral reefs; distinguished by short snout, no skin flaps and broad dark bars with narrow pale bars between them; W. Australia (Ningaloo Reef), Sri Lanka and Samoa; to 11 cm.

17. RIBBONED PIPEHORSE
Haliichthys taeniophorus Gray, 1859
Inhabits trawling grounds; distinguished by large size, elongate snout, bony knobs above eye and prominent spines or knobs on body ridges; N. Australia and New Guinea; to 30 cm.

18. BEADY PIPEFISH
Hippichthys penicillus (Cantor, 1849)
Inhabits mangrove estuaries; distinguished by relatively long snout and small pale spots on front part of body; found throughout the region; N. Indo and W. Pacific; to 18 cm.

19. HARDWICKE'S PIPEFISH
Solegnathus hardwickii (Gray, 1830)
Inhabits trawling grounds; distinguished by large size, pale colouration and dark marks along edge of back; found throughout the region; mainly W. Pacific; to 50 cm.

20. TIDEPOOL PIPEFISH
Micrognathus micronotopterus (Fowler, 1938)
Inhabits inshore reefs and tide pools; distinguished by short snout, small, usually unbranched skin flaps on head and body and 10–12 pale saddles on back; N.W. Australia to Gulf of Carpentaria, also scattered Indo-Malay localites; to 7 cm.

21. DOUBLE-END PIPEFISH
Syngnathoides biaculeatus (Bloch, 1785)
Inhabits coastal waters, amongst weeds; distinguished by large size with deep, laterally compressed snout and prehensile tail; found throughout the region; Indo-W. Pacific; to 29 cm.

22. BENTSTICK PIPEFISH
Trachyrhamphus bicoarctatus (Bleeker, 1857)
Inhabits sand, rubble or weed bottoms; distinguished by long thin tapering body and tiny tail; found throughout the region; Indo-W. Pacific; to 40 cm.

23. STRAIGHTSTICK PIPEFISH
Trachyrhamphus longirostris Kaup, 1856
Inhabits trawling grounds; similar to *T. bicoarctatus* (**22**), but has thicker snout and fewer rings or body segments (41–53 behind anus versus 55–63); found throughout the region; Indo-W. Pacific; to 32 cm.

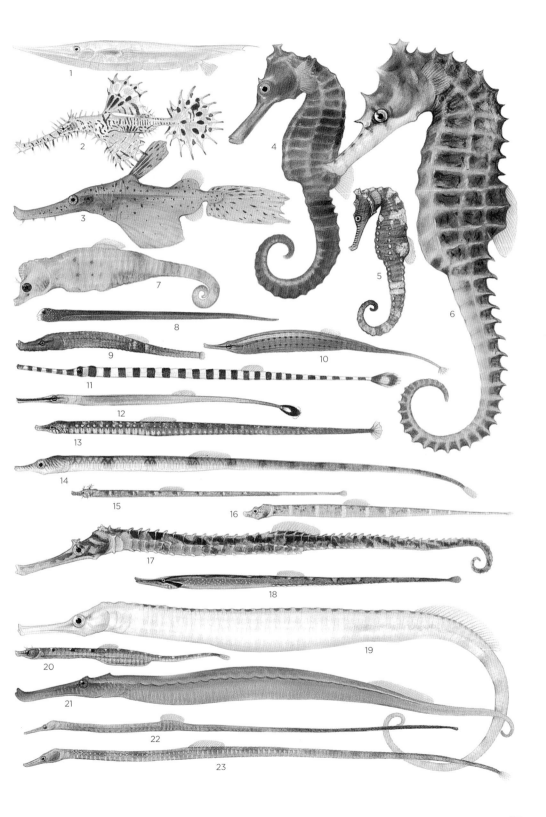

PLATE 18: PIPEFISHES, SCORPIONFISHES AND STONEFISHES

CENTRISCIDAE

1. JOINTED RAZORFISH
Aeoliscus strigatus (Günther, 1861)
Inhabits coral reefs forming schools that orient themselves vertically with head downward among branching corals or urchins; similar to *Centriscus scutatus* (Plate **17.**1), but tail has different shape; Great Barrier Reef and throughout S.E. Asia; Indo-W. Pacific; to 14 cm.

SYNGNATHIDAE

2. MANY-BANDED PIPEFISH
Dunckerocampus multiannulatus (Regan, 1903)
Inhabits coral reef crevices; similar to *D. dactyliophorus* (Plate **17.**11), but has more numerous dark bands; N.W. Australia; Indian Ocean and Red Sea; to 18 cm.

3. YELLOW-BANDED PIPEFISH
Dunckerocampus pessuliferus Fowler, 1938
Inhabits coral reef crevices; similar to *D. dactyliophorus* (Plate **17.**11), but has orange instead of white background colour; Indonesia (N. Sulawesi) and Philippines; to 15 cm.

4. BLUESTRIPE PIPEFISH
Doryrhamphus excisus Kaup, 1856
Inhabits coral reef crevices; distinguished by reddish fan-shaped tail; found throughout the region; Indo-E. Pacific; to 7 cm.

5. REEFTOP PIPEFISH
Corythoichthys haematopterus (Bleeker, 1851)
Inhabits coral reefs, usually on rubble bottoms; similar to *C. intestinalis* (**6**), but dark markings are usually less distinct on rear part of body; N.W. Australia and throughout S.E. Asia; Indo-W. Pacific; to 20 cm.

6. MESSMATE PIPEFISH
Corythoichthys intestinalis (Ramsay, 1881)
Inhabits coral reefs, usually on rubble bottoms; similar to *C. haematopterus* (**5**), but dark markings are usually more distinct on rear part of body; Great Barrier Reef, N.W. Australia and throughout S.E. Asia; mainly W. Pacific; to 16 cm.

7. SCHULTZ'S PIPEFISH
Corythoichthys schultzi Herald, 1953
Inhabits coral reefs, usually on rubble bottoms; similar to *C. haematopterus* (**5**) and *C. intestinalis* (**6**), but has much longer snout; Great Barrier Reef, offshore reefs of N.W. Australia and throughout S.E. Asia; Indo-W. Pacific; to 15 cm.

8. REDBANDED PIPEFISH
Corythoichthys amplexus Dawson & Randall, 1975
Inhabits coral reefs; distinguished by broad brown bars with narrower white bars between; Great Barrier Reef and throughout S.E. Asia; Indo-W. Pacific; to 9 cm.

9. GLITTERING PIPEFISH
Halicampus nitidus (Günther, 1873)
Inhabits coral reefs; distinguished by short snout and white background colour with numerous narrow brown bars; Great Barrier Reef, offshore reefs of N.W. Australia and throughout S.E. Asia; mainly W. Pacific; to 7.5 cm.

10. MUSHROOM-CORAL PIPEFISH
Siokunichthys nigrolineatus Dawson, 1983
Inhabits coral reefs; lives among polyps of mushroom corals; distinguished by overall white colour; Indonesia, Philippines and New Guinea; to 8 cm.

SCORPAENIDAE

11. WHITELINED LIONFISH   VENOMOUS
Pterois radiata Cuvier, 1829
Inhabits coral reef caves and ledges; distinguished by broad brown bars on body separated by narrow white lines, horizontal band on tail base and enlarged filamentous pectoral fins; offshore reefs of N.W. Australia and throughout S.E. Asia; Indo-C. Pacific; to 20 cm.

12. TWINSPOT LIONFISH   VENOMOUS
Dendrochirus biocellatus (Fowler, 1938)
Inhabits coral reef caves and ledges; distinguished by elongate 'whiskers' and pair of pale-rimmed dark spots on rear part of dorsal fin; offshore reefs of N.W. Australia and throughout S.E. Asia; Indo-C. Pacific; to 13 cm.

13. WEEDY SCORPIONFISH   VENOMOUS
Rhinopias aphanes Eschmeyer, 1973
Inhabits coral reefs; distinguished by bold maze-like pattern and filamentous tentacles on head and body; Great Barrier Reef and New Guinea; W. Pacific; to 24 cm.

14. OCELLATE SCORPIONFISH   VENOMOUS
Parascorpaena mcadamsi (Fowler, 1938)
Inhabits coral reef crevices; distinguished by 12 dorsal spines (second spine above upper jaw curves outward and hooks forward) and black spot at rear of spiny part of dorsal fin; offshore reefs of N.W. Australia and throughout S.E. Asia; Indo-W. Pacific; to 6 cm.

15. CORAL SCORPIONFISH   VENOMOUS
Scorpaenodes parvipinnis (Garrett, 1863)
Inhabits coral reef crevices; distinguished by 13 dorsal spines and relatively low spiny part of dorsal fin; Great Barrier Reef, offshore reefs of N.W. Australia and throughout S.E. Asia; Indo-C. Pacific; to 13 cm.

16. HAIRY SCORPIONFISH   VENOMOUS
Scorpaenodes hirsutus (Smith, 1957)
Inhabits coral reef crevices, usually on outer slopes; distinguished by 13 dorsal spines, dark blotch at front of dorsal fin and another on basal half of pectoral fin; Great Barrier Reef and throughout S.E. Asia; Indo-C. Pacific; to 5 cm.

17. SMALLSCALE SCORPIONFISH   VENOMOUS
Scorpaenopsis papuensis (Cuvier, 1829)
Inhabits coral reefs; rests in the open and is most commonly observed scorpionfish; similar to *S. venosa* (Plate **20.**11), but usually has 20 pectoral rays instead of 17–18; Great Barrier Reef, offshore reefs of N.W. Australia and throughout S.E. Asia; Indo-W. Pacific; to 30 cm.

18. YELLOWSPOTTED SCORPIONFISH   VENOMOUS
Sebastapistes cyanostigma (Bleeker, 1856)
Inhabits coral heads (often *Pocillopora*); distinguished by large yellow blotches and tiny pale spots on side; Great Barrier Reef, offshore reefs of N.W. Australia and throughout S.E. Asia; Indo-C. Pacific; to 7 cm.

SYNANCEIIDAE

19. REEF STONEFISH   VENOMOUS
Synanceia verrucosa Bloch & Schneider, 1801
Inhabits coral reefs, among rocks or under slabs of dead coral; wound from venomous dorsal and anal-fin spines may cause serious injury or death; similar to *S. horrida* (Plate **19.**8), but found more offshore in clear water; found throughout the region; Indo-W. Pacific; to 35 cm.

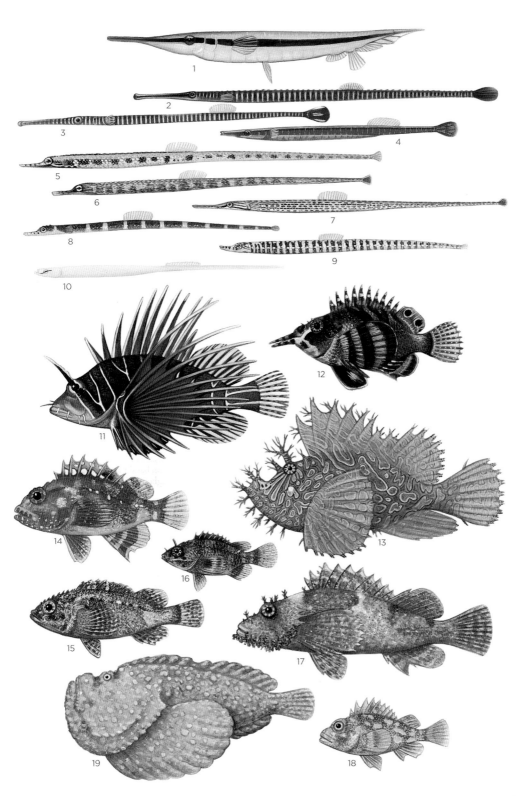

PLATE 19: SCORPIONFISHES, STONEFISHES AND WASPFISHES

SCORPAENIDAE

1. DWARF LIONFISH   VENOMOUS
Dendrochirus brachypterus (Cuvier, 1829)
Inhabits coral reefs, distinguished by large pectoral fins without elongate, free filamantous rays, similar to *D. zebra* (**2**), but has more prominent curved bands on pectoral fins and bars on side are less well defined; also known as Short-spined Scorpionfish; found throughout the region; Indo-C. Pacific; to 15 cm.

2. ZEBRA LIONFISH   VENOMOUS
Dendrochirus zebra (Cuvier, 1829)
Inhabits coral reefs; distinguished by large pectoral fins without elongate, free filamantous rays, similar to *D. brachypterus* (**1**), but bands on pectoral fins poorly defined and bars on side more distinct, also known as Butterfly Scorpionfish; found throughout the region; Indo-C Pacific; to 18 cm.

3. SPOTFIN LIONFISH   VENOMOUS
Pterois antennata (Bloch, 1787)
Inhabits coral reefs, usually in caves and crevices distinguished by white filamentous pectoral rays, row of large dark spots at base of this fin and relatively few dark bars on head; also known as Ragged-finned Firefish; found throughout the region; Indo-C. Pacific; to 30 cm.

4. FEWSPINE LIONFISH   VENOMOUS
Pterois paucispinula Matsunuma & Motomura, 2014
Inhabits offshore reefs, usually below 40 m depth; distinguished by relatively short filamentous tips on pectoral fin, which is densely spotted, and maze of dark and light bands on tail base; N.W. Australia and Indonesia; W. Pacific; to 16 cm.

5. PLAINTAIL LIONFISH   VENOMOUS
Pterois russelii Bennett, 1831
Inhabits offshore reefs, usually below 20–30 m depth; distinguished by filamentous pectoral rays and lack of spots on dorsal, anal and tail fins; found throughout the region; Indo-W. Pacific; to 30 cm.

6. COMMON LIONFISH   VENOMOUS
Pterois volitans (Linnaeus, 1758)
Inhabits coral and rocky reefs, usually in caves or crevices, distinguished by broad filamentous pectoral rays, similar to *P. russeli* (**5**), but has spots on dorsal, anal and tail fins; also known as Butterfly Cod; found throughout the region; Indo-C. Pacific; *P. andover* is a similar species found in the region (except Australia), but has dorsal fin 'pennants' and fewer dark fin spots; to 38 cm.

7. SAWCHEEK SCORPIONFISH   VENOMOUS
Brachypterois serrulifer Fowler, 1938
Inhabits deeper trawling grounds, distinguished by dusky fan-like pectoral fins without free filamentous rays, lack of distinct bars on side and faint spotting on dorsal, anal and tail fins; N.W. Australia and Timor-Arafura seas; Indo-W. Pacific; to 10 cm.

SYNANCEIIDAE

8. ESTUARINE STONEFISH   VENOMOUS
Synanceia horrida (Linnaeus, 1766)
Inhabits estuaries and inshore areas on sand or mud bottoms, amongst rocks, or sometimes under dead coral slabs; distinguished by stone-like appearance and warty projections on body; *S. verrucosa* (not shown) is a similar species occurring on coral reefs; fin spines extremely venomous; found throughout the region; E. Indian Ocean and W. Pacific; to 47 cm.

9. PACIFIC MONKEYFISH   VENOMOUS
Erosa erosa (Cuvier, 1829)
Inhabits trawling grounds; similar to *E. daruma* (**10**), but has slight hump in front of dorsal fin, white spots on outer part of pectoral fin and narrow cross-bars on tail; also known as Pitted Scorpionfish; found throughout the region; mainly W. Pacific; to 15 cm.

10. DARUMA STINGER   VENOMOUS
Erosa daruma (Whitley, 1932)
Inhabits coastal waters in the vicinity of reefs, sometimes under wharves; similar to *E. erosa* (**9**), but has rounded head profile without hump in front of dorsal tin, broad white band (instead of spots) on outer pectoral fin and a single dark bar across middle part of tail; N.W. Australia only; to 13 cm.

11. PLUMBSTRIPED STINGFISH   VENOMOUS
Minous versicolor Ogilby, 1910
Inhabits trawling grounds; distinguished by irregular stripes and blotches on upper side and wavy cross-bands on dorsal and tail fins, also has free lower-most pectoral ray; N. Australia only; to 11 cm.

12. LONGSNOUT STINGERFISH   VENOMOUS
Inimicus didactylus (Pallas, 1769)
Inhabits rubble bottoms, frequently in the vicinity of coral reefs; distinguished by large upturned mouth, free pair of rays at lowermost part of pectoral fin and prominent dorsal spines, similar to *I. sinensis* (**13**), but has yellow tail with dark submarginal bar and pale band across pectoral fin; N.W. Australia and throughout S.E. Asia; mainly Indo-Australian Archipelago; to 18 cm.

13. SPOTTED STINGERFISH   VENOMOUS
Inimicus sinensis (Valenciennes, 1833)
Inhabits rubble bottoms; similar to *I. didactylus* (**12**), but tail mainly dusky or spotted (not yellow with dark cross-bar) and lacks pale band on pectoral fin; N.W. Australia, Gulf of Carpentaria and throughout S.E. Asia; E. Indian Ocean and W. Pacific; to 25 cm.

TETRAROGIDAE

14. COCKATOO WASPFISH   VENOMOUS
Ablabys taenianotus (Cuvier, 1829)
Inhabits coastal reefs; distinguished by thin, laterally compressed body, vertical profile of snout and elevated rays at front of dorsal fin; found throughout the region; Indo-W. Pacific; to 10 cm.

15. BLACKSPOT WASPFISH   VENOMOUS
Liocranium praepositum Ogilby, 1903
Inhabits trawling grounds; similar to *Ablabys taenianotus* (**14**), but has larger eye, lacks elevated rays at front of dorsal fin and has prominent dark blotch above pectoral fin; N. Australia and Indonesia; E. Indian Ocean and W. Pacific; to 13 cm.

16. WASP ROGUEFISH   VENOMOUS
Paracentropogon vespa Ogilby, 1910
Inhabits trawling grounds; similar to *Ablabys taenianotus* (**14**) and *Liocranium praepositum* (**15**), but has large dark blotch on base of front part of dorsal fin; N. Australia only; to 9 cm.

WARNING!

The fishes of the families on Plates 18–21 possess venomous fin spines and handling of live or freshly dead specimens should be avoided. The Estuarine Stonefish *Synanceia horrida* (**8**) is amongst the most venomous of all fishes and is capable of causing death. Symptoms of scorpionfish stings range from a bee-sting type sensation to violent pain and may lead to unconsciousness or extended coma. Immersing the wound in very hot water is an effective first-aid treatment and a physician should be consulted immediately.

PLATE 20: SCORPIONFISHES, WASPFISHES AND VELVETFISHES

APISTIDAE

1. SHORTFIN WASPFISH   VENOMOUS
Apistops coloundra (De Vis, 1886)
Inhabits trawling grounds; distinguished by 5 chin barbels, diffuse dark stripes on side and spot on dorsal fin, similar to *A. carinatus* (2), but pectoral fins shorter (do not reach the rear part of anal fin); N. Australia only; to 12 cm.

2. LONGFIN WASPFISH   VENOMOUS
Apistus carinatus (Bloch & Schneider, 1801)
Inhabits trawling grounds, similar to *A. coloundra* (1), but with 3 chin barbels, no stripes on side and pectoral fins usually longer, reaching to rear part of anal fin; found throughout the region; Indo-W. Pacific; to 18 cm.

APLOACTINIDAE

3. DECEITFUL VELVETFISH   VENOMOUS
Peristrominous dolosus Whitley, 1952
Inhabits trawling grounds; distinguished by elongate brown body without distinct markings and pointed snout; N. Australia only; to 9 cm.

TETRAROGIDAE

4. YELLOW WASPFISH   VENOMOUS
Cottapistus cottoides (Linneaus, 1758)
Inhabits deep offshore reefs and trawling grounds; distinguished by forward position (over eye) of dorsal fin origin, hump on snout and very small scales; N.W. Australia, Gulf of Carpentaria and scattered localities in Indo-Malay region; mainly W. Pacific, to 12 cm.

5. WHITEBELLY ROUGEFISH   VENOMOUS
Richardsonichthys leucogaster (Richardson, 1848)
Inhabits trawling grounds; distinguished by laterally compressed body, forward position (above rear part of eye) of dorsal fin origin, relatively large eye and complete lack of scales; found throughout the region; Indo-W. Pacific; to 8 cm.

SCORPAENIDAE

6. PAINTED SCORPIONFISH   VENOMOUS
Parascorpaena picta (Cuvier, 1829)
Inhabits crevices of coral and rocky reefs; distinguished by well-camouflaged appearance with skin flaps and tentacles on head and body, 12 dorsal spines and spine above upper jaw that curves forward; found throughout the region; Indo-W. Pacific; to 16 cm.

7. GUAM SCORPIONFISH   VENOMOUS
Scorpaenodes guamensis (Quoy & Gaimard, 1824)
Inhabits coral reef crevices; distinguished by dark spot on upper part of gill cover and 13 dorsal spines; found throughout the region; Indo-C. Pacific; to 12 cm.

8. BLOTCHFIN SCORPIONFISH   VENOMOUS
Scorpaenodes varipinnis Smith, 1957
Inhabits coral reef crevices; distinguished by red colour with white blotches on head and along middle of sides, a curved dark band across pectoral fin and 13 dorsal spines; found throughout the region; Indo-W. Pacific; to 7 cm.

9. LITTLE SCORPIONCOD   VENOMOUS
Scorpaenodes sp.
Inhabits coral reef crevices, distinguished by red or brown spots on fins, pale bar across tail base, lack of dark spot on gill cover and 13 dorsal spines; possibly a colour variation of *S. scaber* (10); W. Australia; to 8 cm.

10. PYGMY SCORPIONFISH   VENOMOUS
Scorpaenodes scaber (Ramsay & Ogilby, 1886)
Inhabits coastal and estuaries reefs; similar to *Parascorpaena picta* (6), but has dark spot (darker than shown) on lower edge of gill cover instead of upper part; found throughout the region; Indo-W. Pacific; to 8 cm.

11. RAGGY SCORPIONFISH   VENOMOUS
Scorpaenopsis venosa (Cuvier, 1829)
Inhabits coral reef crevices; distinguished by skin flaps and tentacles on head and body; relatively tall dorsal fin and 12 dorsal spines, juveniles usually more ornate as shown; N.W. Australia and throughout S.E. Asia; Indo-C. Pacific; to 18 cm.

12. FALSE STONEFISH   VENOMOUS
Scorpaenopsis diabolus (Cuvier, 1829)
Inhabits coral reef crevices and rubble bottoms; distinguished by well-camouflaged appearance, humped back and bright yellow-orange patch on inner surface (not shown) of pectoral fins; often confused with the true stonefish (*Synanceia* Plates 18–19), which is far more venomous; found throughout the region; Indo-C. Pacific; to 18 cm.

13. LEAF SCORPIONFISH   VENOMOUS
Taenianotus triacanthus Lacepède, 1802
Inhabits offshore coral reefs; distinguished by thin leaf-like body and tall dorsal fin, several colour varieties encountered including ones that are predominantly reddish, yellow, or black; offshore reefs of W. Australia, Great Barrier Reef and throughout S.E. Asia; Indo-C. Pacific; to 10 cm.

SETARCHIDAE

14. DEEPWATER SCORPIONFISH   VENOMOUS
Setarches guentheri Johnston, 1862
Inhabits offshore trawling grounds, distinguished by overall red colour without distinct marks, relatively pointed snout, very stout spines on edge of cheek and 12 dorsal spines; N.W. Australia; worldwide in tropical seas; to 23 cm.

SCORPIONFISH COLOURS

The colouration of many of the scorpionfishes shown on this plate is extremely variable, depending on size, depth and habitat; it is not unusual for the same species to exhibit very different patterns at a particular locality. For example the Painted Scorpionfish *Parascorpaena picta* (6) is often mottled brown when found among rocks in shallow weedy areas and red (as shown) if seen in caves on deeper sections of the reef.

SCORPIONFISHES AND ALLIED FAMILIES

The families featured on Plates 18–20 are members of the order Scorpaeniformes. They are distinguished by a bony ridge on the cheek and the head is frequently spiny or tasseled. All are bottom-living fishes that occur in a variety of depths and habitats. They often exhibit variegated colour patterns that blend well with their surroundings.

PLATE 21: VELVETFISHES, GURNARDS AND FLATHEADS

APLOACTINIDAE

1. SANDPAPER VELVETFISH
Adventor elongatus (Whitley, 1952)
Inhabits trawling grounds; distinguished by elongate body shape and bony knobs on head, similar to *Paraploactis intonsa* (5), but dorsal fin begins further back on head; N. Australia only; to 11 cm.

2. DUSKY VELVETFISH
Aploactis aspera (Richardson, 1844)
Inhabits trawling grounds; has longer anal fin base than other velvet fishes on this page; colour sometimes brown; found throughout the region, but rare; E. Indian Ocean and W. Pacific; to 9 cm.

3. GOATEE VELVETFISH
Pseudopataceus carnatobarbatus Johnson, 2012
Inhabits trawling grounds and sandy areas near reefs; distinguished by laterally compressed body, steep forehead and tall anterior part of dorsal fin, and fleshy chin 'goatee'; similar to some scorpionfishes (Plates 19–20), but has bony knobs (versus spines) on head and body covered with prickles; N.W. Australia only; to 5 cm.

4. THREEFIN VELVETFISH
Neoaploactis tridorsalis Eschmeyer & Allen, 1978
Inhabits sand or rubble bottoms near reefs, distinguished by 3 separate dorsal fins; N. Australia only; to 5 cm.

5. BEARDED VELVETFISH
Paraploactis intonsa Poss & Eschmeyer, 1978
Inhabits trawling grounds, similar to *Adventor elongatus* (1) and *Aploactis aspera* (2), but deeper bodied, steeper forehead and dorsal fin begins above eye; *P. pulvinus* (not shown) is similar, but lacks prickles on ventral surface of lower jaw; known only from Shark Bay, W. Australia only; to 14 cm.

6. DARKFIN VELVETFISH
Erisphex aniarus (Thomson, 1967)
Inhabits continental shelf in about 200 m depth; distinguished by pale colouration except for blackish fins; N.W. Australia and E. Queensland; E. Indian Ocean and W. Pacific; to 10 cm.

TRIGLIDAE

7. EYE GURNARD
Lepidotrigla argus Ogilby, 1910
Inhabits trawling grounds; distinguished by pair of short, forward-projecting spines on snout and enlarged fan-like pectoral fins with blue and yellow markings and blue-edged black spot; N. Australia only; to 18 cm.

8. BULLHEAD GURNARD
Pterygotrigla leptacanthus (Günther, 1880)
Inhabits trawling grounds; similar to *Lepidotrigla argus* (7), but lacks scales, has longer forward projecting spines on snout and blackish pectoral fins; N.W. Australia and Arafura Sea; to 15 cm.

9. BLACKSPOTTED GURNARD
Pterygotrigla hemisticta (Temminck & Schlegel, 1843)
Inhabits trawling grounds, similar to *P. leptacanthus* (8), but has black spot on first dorsal fin and scattered brown spots on back; N.W. Australia and Indonesia; E. Indian Ocean and W. Pacific; to 25 cm.

PERISTEDIIDAE

10. ARMOURED GURNARD
Peristedion liorhynchus (Günther, 1872)
Inhabits trawling grounds, distinguished by dark margin on dorsal fins and banded pectoral fins; shape from dorsal view similar to *Satyrichthys rieffeli* (11); found throughout the region; E. Indian Ocean and W. Pacific; to 25 cm.

11. SPOTTED ARMOURED GURNARD
Satyrichthys rieffeli (Kaup, 1859)
Inhabits trawling grounds; distinguished by black spotting on head, body and dorsal fin; shape from side view similar to *Peristedion liorhynchus* (10); N.W. Australia and Indonesia; E. Indian Ocean and W. Pacific; to 20 cm.

PLATYCEPHALIDAE

12. FRINGE-EYE FLATHEAD
Cymbacephalus nematophthalmus (Günther, 1860)
Inhabits sand bottoms; distinguished by 6–9 skin tentacles above eye (versus 0–1 in most flatheads), 7–8 dusky bands across nape and back extending on to sides and strongly variegated pattern on fins; found throughout the region; Indo-Australian Archipelago; to 58 cm.

13. DWARF FLATHEAD
Elates ransonnettii (Steindachner, 1876)
Inhabits sand bottoms; distinguished by 6 dorsal spines (versus 7–9 spines for other flatheads), filamentous upper lobe of tail and semi-transparent appearance; found throughout the region; Indo-Australian Archipelago; to 19 cm.

14. HARRIS' FLATHEAD
Inegocia harrisii (McCulloch, 1914)
Inhabits sand bottoms, distinguished by overall orange-brown colour with fine brown spots on back and white below, irregular dark bars on pectoral fins and elongate dark streaks on tail; N. Australia only; to 20 cm.

15. MIDGET FLATHEAD
Onigocia spinosa (Temminck & Schlegel, 1843)
Inhabits sand bottoms; distinguished by numerous small spines on head which is very broad (when viewed from above), outer half of spiny dorsal fin dark brown; irregular brown bars across back and sides and largely blackish pelvic fins with yellowish tips; N.W. Australia and Indonesia; E. Indian Ocean and W. Pacific; to 9 cm.

16. NORTHERN SAND FLATHEAD ☆☆☆
Platycephalus endrachtensis Quoy & Gaimard, 1825
Inhabits sand bottoms; distinguished by black stripes on tail; N. Australia and Indonesia; to 45 cm.

17. YELLOWTAIL FLATHEAD ☆☆☆
Platycephalus westraliae (Whitley, 1938)
Inhabits sand bottoms; distinguished by black stripes on tail, similar to *P. endrachtensis* (16), but has fewer black stripes and a yellow blotch on upper part of tail; N. Australia, New Guinea and Java; to 26 cm.

18. RUSTY FLATHEAD ☆☆☆
Inegocia japonica (Cuvier, 1829)
Inhabits sand bottoms; a reddish-brown flathead similar to *I. harrisii* (14) in general appearance, but has definite dark spots on tail (versus elongate streaks); sometimes referred to as *S. isacathus*; found throughout the region; Indo-W. Pacific; to 20 cm.

19. TUBERCULATE FLATHEAD ☆☆☆
Rogadius tuberculata (Cuvier, 1829)
Inhabits sand bottoms; distinguished by prominent black area on outer part of pectoral fins and strongly barred pelvic fins; found throughout the region; Indo-W. Pacific; to 50 cm.

20. OLIVE-TAIL FLATHEAD ☆☆☆
Rogadius asper (Cuvier, 1829)
Inhabits sand bottoms, distinguished from other flatheads by forward directed spine on lower edge of cheek, similar in colour to *R. tuberculata* (19), but has broad dusky margin on spiny dorsal fin and lacks faint spotting on tail; found throughout the region; Indo-W. Pacific; to 17 cm.

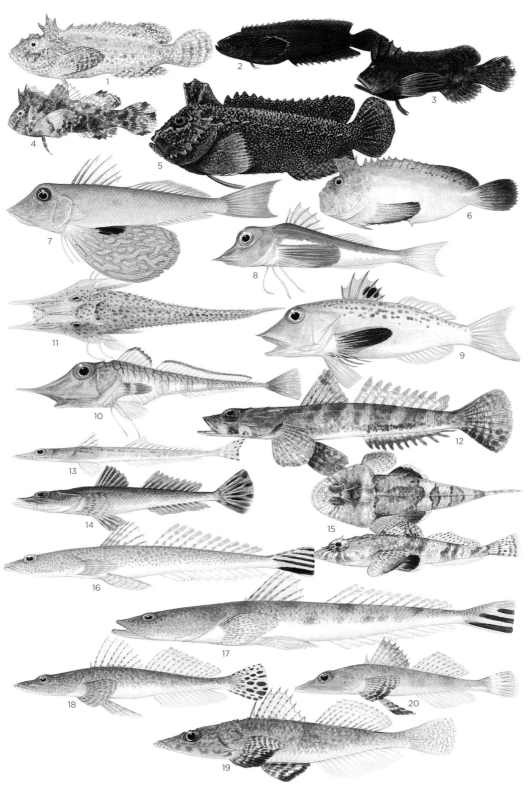

PLATE 22: ROCKCODS

CENTROGENYIDAE

1. FALSE SCORPIONFISH
Centrogenys vaigiensis (Quoy & Gaimard, 1824)
Inhabits sand and weed flats, frequently around rocky
outcrops; resembles members of scorpionfish family (Plates
18–20), but lacks numerous head spines and is not venomous
(fin spines); found throughout the region; Indo-Australian
Archipelago; to 15 cm.

SERRANIDAE

2. WHITELINED ROCKCOD ☆☆☆
Anyperodon leucogrammicus (Valenciennes, 1828)
Inhabits coral reefs; distinguished by elongate shape and
pattern of pale longitudinal stripes and numerous dark spots;
N.W. Australia, Great Barrier Reef and throughout S.E. Asia;
Indo-C. Pacific; to 50 cm.

3. BROWNBARRED ROCKCOD ☆☆
Cephalopholis boenak (Bloch, 1790)
Inhabits dead reefs in protected inshore waters; distinguished
by overall brown colour with faint dark bars on sides and
large blackish spot at rear of gill cover; formerly known as
C. pachycentron; found throughout the region; Indo-W.
Pacific; to 22 cm.

4. PEACOCK ROCKCOD ☆☆☆
Cephalopholis argus Bloch & Schneider, 1801
Inhabits caves and crevices of coral reefs; distinguished by
numerous dark-edged blue spots on head, body and fins, also
by whitish area in front of pectoral fin and 5–6 pale bars on
posterior part of body frequently present; N.W. Australia,
Great Barrier Reef and throughout S.E. Asia;
Indo-C. Pacific; to 50 cm.

5. CORAL ROCKCOD ☆☆☆
Cephalopholis miniata (Forsskål, 1775)
Inhabits caves and crevices of coral reefs; distinguished
by numerous blue spots on orange-red to red-brown
background; also known as Coral Trout; found throughout
the region; Indo-W. Pacific; to 41 cm and 1.6 kg.

6. BLUELINED ROCKCOD ☆☆☆
Cephalopholis formosa (Shaw, 1812)
Inhabits inshore coral reefs; distinguished by narrow dark
blue stripes on head, body and fins; N.W. Australia, Great
Barrier Reef and throughout S.E. Asia; Indo-W. Pacific;
to 33 cm.

7. LEOPARD ROCKCOD ☆☆
Cephalopholis leopardus (Lacepède, 1801)
Inhabits caves and crevices of coral reefs; distinguished by
oblique dark streaks on upper and lower lobe of tail, dark
patch on upper edge of tail base and dark spot at rear of gill
cover; N.W. Australia, Great Barrier Reef and throughout
S.E. Asia; Indo-C. Pacific; to 20 cm.

8. TOMATO ROCKCOD ☆☆☆
Cephalopholis sonnerati (Valenciennes, 1828)
Inhabits coral and rock reefs, adults often in deep water
(30–100 m); distinguished by orange-red to reddish brown
colour, frequently with scattered whitish blotches; brown
variety (Plate **23.12**); juveniles are pale pinkish; N.W.
Australia, Great Barrier Reef and throughout S.E. Asia;
Indo-C. Pacific; to 58 cm.

9. FLAGTAIL ROCKCOD ☆☆
Cephalopholis urodeta (Forster, 1801)
Inhabits coral reef crevices, distinguished by pale oblique
streaks on lobes of tail; found throughout the region;
Indo-C. Pacific; to 23 cm.

10. BARRAMUNDI COD ☆☆☆☆
Cromileptes altivelis (Valenciennes, 1828)
Inhabits caves and crevices of coral reefs; distinguished by
small head, laterally compressed body and polkadot pattern;
N.W. Australia, Great Barrier Reef and throughout S.E. Asia;
Indo-W. Pacific, to 70 cm and 4.8 kg.

11. RED BASSLET
Pseudanthias cooperi (Regan, 1902)
Inhabits offshore reefs to at least 160 m depth; male (shown
here) has red spot on sides and elongate filaments on pelvic,
anal and tail fins; female lacks these features and has a red
spot on the tip of each lobe of the tail; N.W. Australia, Great
Barrier Reef and throughout S.E. Asia; Indo-W. Pacific;
to 13 cm.

12. PEARLSPOT FAIRY BASSLET
Selenanthias analis Tanaka, 1918
Inhabits offshore trawling grounds; distinguished by pearly
spots on sides and black spot on anal fin; N. Australia and
Japan to Taiwan; to 16 cm.

13. CITRON PERCHLET
Plectranthias megalophthalmus Fourmanoir & Randall, 1979
Inhabits deep offshore trawling grounds to 360 m depth;
distinguished by yellow colouration; New Caledonia and
N.W. Australia; to 8 cm.

14. SPOTTED PERCHLET
Plectranthias wheeleri Randall, 1980
Inhabits deep offshore trawling grounds to 230 m;
distinguished by irregular blotches on sides; found
throughout the region; Australia and Indonesia; to 10 cm.

15. JAPANESE PERCHLET
Plectranthias japonicus (Steindachner, 1883)
Inhabits deep trawling grounds to at least 200 m;
distinguished by red-orange colouration, sometimes with
darker blotches on sides; N.W. Australia and Japan; to 15 cm.

INTRODUCTION TO ROCKCODS

Rockcods and their relatives in the grouper family
(Serranidae) are a dominant element of the fish
community on all coral reefs, particularly in the
Indo-Pacific region. The larger species are important
table fish at many localities and the small schooling
members, for instance the numerous Anthias (or
Fairy Basslets), no doubt play an important role
in the reef's food chain. Members of the genus
Cephalopholis are small- to medium-sized groupers
(also know as Cods or Rockcods in Australia) that
occur in a variety of coral reef habitats. The Coral
Rockcod *C. miniata* (**5**), with its bright red coat
studded with blue spots, is among the most colourful
species. It grows to a reported length of 41 cm and is
most often encountered in clear water of outer reefs
to depths of at least 150 m. Like most of the larger
groupers it feeds mainly on small fishes, supplemented
by crustaceans. Feeding occurs mainly during the
early morning and midafternoon. The favourite
food appears to be small, schooling Anthias, which
are skilfully captured with a quick head-on rush.

PLATE 23: ROCKCODS

SERRANIDAE

1. REDMOUTH ROCKCOD ☆☆☆
Aethaloperca rogaa (Forsskål, 1775)
Inhabits coral reefs in the vicinity of caves; distinguished by elevated shape of body, dark colourati on and white edge on tail; N.W. Australia, Great Barrier Reef and throughout S.E. Asia; Indo-W. Pacific; to 60 cm.

2. BANDED GROUPER ☆☆☆
Epinephelus amblycephalus (Bleeker, 1857)
Inhabits deeper offshore reefs; distinguished by 5 dark bars on body; N.W. Australia and throughout S.E. Asia; mainly Indo-Australian Archipelago; to 45 cm.

3. YELLOWSPOTTED ROCKCOD ☆☆☆
Epinephelus areolatus (Forsskål, 1775)
Inhabits inshore reefs, usually around small coral heads in sandy areas or among sea grass; distinguished by dense pattern of large round spots and truncate (not rounded) tail; N.W. Australia and throughout S.E. Asia; Indo-W. Pacific; to 35 cm.

4. WHITESPOTTED GROUPER ☆☆☆
Epinephelus coeruleopunctatus (Bloch, 1790)
Inhabits coral reefs, near caves and crevices; similar to *E. multinotatus* (Plate **24.2**), but spots more uniformly round and smaller; N.W. Australia, Great Barrier Reef and throughout S.E. Asia; Indo-W. Pacific; to 60 cm.

5. CORAL GROUPER ☆☆☆
Epinephelus corallicola (Valenciennes, 1828)
Inhabits shallow, silty reefs and estuaries; distinguished by round black spots on grey background; found throughout the region; W. Pacific; to 31 cm.

6. BLACKTIP ROCKCOD ☆☆☆
Epinephelus fasciatus (Forsskål, 1775)
Inhabits coral reefs and rocky bottoms to 100 m depth; distinguished by reddish bars and narrow black border on front part of dorsal fin; found throughout the region; Indo-C. Pacific; to 40 cm.

7. STRIPED GROUPER ☆☆☆
Epinephelus latifasciatus (Temminck & Schlegel, 1843)
Inhabits sand and rock bottoms on the continental shelf between 20–200 m depth; distinguished by thin dark lines (or sometimes rows of faint spots) on sides and spots on dorsal fin and tail; N.W. Australia; Indo-W. Pacific; to 70 cm.

8. FLOWERY ROCKCOD ☆☆☆
Epinephelus fuscoguttatus (Forsskål, 1775)
Inhabits coral reefs and rocky bottoms; similar to *E. polyphekadion* (**11**), but irregular brown blotches on sides generally more diffuse and spot at upper base of tail smaller; best means of separation is higher pectoral fin-ray count (18–20, usually 19); N.W. Australia, Great Barrier Reef and throughout S.E. Asia; Indo-W. Pacific; to 90 cm.

9. THREELINE ROCKCOD ☆☆☆
Epinephelus heniochus Fowler, 1904
Inhabits offshore trawling grounds to at least 80 m depth; distinguished by overall pinkish-red colour and narrow stripes (often very faint) on head; N.W. Australia to Gulf of Carpentaria, also scattered localites in S.E. Asia; W. Pacific; to 30 cm.

10. BIRDWIRE ROCKCOD ☆☆☆
Epinephelus merra Bloch, 1793
Inhabits protected inshore coral reefs; distinguished by dense network of large spots on body and fins; similar to *E. quoyanus* (**13**), but spotting denser and lacks diagonal bands on breast; N.W. Australia, Great Barrier Reef and throughout S.E. Asia; Indo-C. Pacific; to 28 cm.

11. CAMOUFLAGE GROUPER ☆☆☆
Epinephelus polyphekadion (Bleeker, 1849)
Inhabits coral reefs, often around large bommies; similar to *E. fuscoguttatus* (**8**), but has more distinct oblique bands on back and head and fewer pectoral rays (16–17, usually 17); *E. microdon* is a synonym; N.W. Australia, Great Barrier Reef and throughout S.E. Asia; Indo-C. Pacific, to 61 cm.

12. TOMATO ROCKCOD ☆☆☆
Cephalopholis sonnerati (Valenciennes, 1828)
Inhabits coral reefs in the vicinity of caves and crevices; red variety and juvenile (Plate **22.8**) sometimes seen at Ningaloo Reef, W. Australia in 12–20 m depth; N.W. Australia, Great Barrier Reef and throughout S.E. Asia; Indo-C. Pacific; to 58 cm.

13. LONGFIN ROCKCOD ☆☆☆
Epinephelus quoyanus (Valenciennes, 1830)
Inhabits silty inshore reefs; similar to *E. merra* (**10**), but spotting is less dense and has oblique dark bands just below and slightly in front of pectoral fin base; found throughout the region; mainly W. Pacific; to 35 cm.

14. CHINAMAN ROCKCOD ☆☆☆
Epinephelus rivulatus (Valenciennes, 1830)
Inhabits inshore coral and rock reefs, usually around small coral heads or among weed; distinguished by oblique brown bars on sides and white blotches on head; W. and E. coasts of Australia and scattered locations in S.E. Asia; Indo-W. Pacific; to 35 cm.

15. RADIANT ROCKCOD ☆☆☆
Epinephelus radiatus (Day, 1868)
Inhabits sand and rock bottoms, usually trawled between 80–160 m depth; distinguished by broad diagonal bands on head and body; N.W. Australia and outer edge of N. Great Barrier Reef; Indo-W. Pacific; to 70 cm.

SEX CHAMELEONS

Groupers are noted for their ability to change sex. Although relatively few species have been studied, groupers appear to be protogynous hemaphrodites. This is a fancy way of saying that an individual can function as an egg-producing female for one or more years, then change sex and function as a male. Adult fish are generally solitary in habit, but there are limited observations for a few species, which indicate they may aggregate at spawning times. Some species are known to migrate to specific spawning sites from distances of up to several kilometres. Unfortunately, they are highly vulnerable to overfishing at this time. Individual males may spawn several times during each reproductive period, which generally last one or two weeks. However, females only spawn once. The tiny (0.7–1.2 mm diameter) eggs float at the surface until hatching. The larvae have a characteristic kite-shaped body, imparted by the very elongate second dorsal spine and a pelvic spine, which is nearly as long. The larval stage lasts for about 1 or 2 months depending on the species involved. During this period the young fish, which have limited swimming powers, are dispersed by surface currents.

PLATE 24: ROCKCODS

SERRANIDAE

1. FROSTBACK ROCKCOD ☆☆☆
Epinephelus bilobatus Randall & Allen, 1987
Inhabits inshore coral reefs, usually where there is some sand;
distinguished by white area on upper back and dark spots
along base of dorsal fin; N.W. Australia and W. Papua;
to 40 cm.

2. RANKIN COD ☆☆☆
Epinephelus multinotatus (Peters, 1877)
Inhabits inshore coral reefs and deeper offshore trawling
grounds; distinguished by irregular white blotches; also
known as Rankin's Rockcod; coast of W. and N.W.
Australia; mainly W. Indian Ocean; to 100 cm
and 9 kg.

3. SIXBAR GROUPER ☆☆☆
Epinephelus sexfasciatus (Kuhl & van Hasselt, 1828)
Inhabits offshore trawling grounds to 70 m depth;
distinguished by combination of bars on sides and spotted
tail; found throughout the region; Indo-Australian
Archipelago; to 26 cm.

4. GOLDSPOTTED ROCKCOD ☆☆☆
Epinephelus coioides (Hamilton, 1822)
Inhabits inshore coral reefs and estuaries; distinguished by
oblique bands on sides overlaid with red-brown spotting;
frequently misidentified as *E. malabaricus* or *E. tauvina*; also
known as Greasy Cod; found throughout the region;
Indo-W. Pacific; to at least 95 cm.

5. POTATO ROCKCOD ☆☆☆
Epinephelus tukula Morgans, 1959
Inhabits coral reefs in the vicinity of caves and crevices;
distinguished by large ovate spots; offshore reefs of N.W.
Australia, Great Barrier Reef and throughout S.E. Asia;
Indo-W. Pacific, to 140 cm.

6. OVAL ROCKCOD ☆☆☆
Triso dermopterus (Temminck & Schlegel, 1843)
Inhabits offshore trawling grounds; distinguished by 11
dorsal spines, rounded tail, 2 short canine teeth on each side
at front of jaws and ctenoid scales (i.e. rough to the touch);
N.W. Australia and C. Queensland; Australia and Japan to
Taiwan; to 45 cm.

7. COMMON CORAL TROUT ☆☆☆☆
Plectropomus leopardus (Lacepède, 1802)
Inhabits coral reefs; distinguished by numerous small round
spots on head and body; also known as Leopard Cod; N.W.
Australia, Great Barrier Reef and throughout most of S.E.
Asia; mainly W. Pacific; to 75 cm and 15.5 kg.

8. PASSIONFRUIT CORAL TROUT ☆☆☆
Plectropomus areolatus (Rüppell, 1830)
Inhabits coral reefs; distinguished by numerous dark-edged
round spots on head and body; N.W. Australia, Great
Barrier Reef and throughout S.E. Asia; Indo-W. Pacific;
to 70 cm.

9. BARCHEEK CORAL TROUT ☆☆☆
Plectropomus maculatus (Bloch, 1790)
Inhabits coral reefs; similar to *P. leopardus* (**7**), but has fewer,
more widely-spaced spots and those on head are elongate in
shape; also known as Coral Cod; found throughout the
region; Indo-Australian Archipelago; to 70 cm and 6 kg.

10. VERMICULAR COD ☆☆☆
Plectropomus oligacanthus (Bleeker, 1854)
Inhabits offshore coral reefs; distinguished by bright
pinkish-red colour, blue spots (some of which are elongated)
on body and fins and relatively tall dorsal (posterior half)
and anal fins; offshore reefs of N.W. Australia, Great
Barrier Reef and throughout S.E. Asia; mainly W. Pacific;
to 56 cm.

11. YELLOWEDGE CORONATION TROUT ☆☆☆
Variola louti (Forsskål, 1775)
Inhabits inshore coral reefs and deeper offshore reefs to 100
m; distinguished by bright colour pattern and distinct lunar
shaped tail; *V. albimarginata* (not shown) is a similar species
occurring in the region, but has a narrow white margin on
the tail instead of a relatively broad yellow one; N.W.
Australia, Great Barrier Reef and throughout S.E. Asia;
Indo-C. Pacific; known to cause ciguatera poisoning
in some areas; to 80 cm.

12. QUEENSLAND GROPER ☆☆☆
Epinephelus lanceolatus (Bloch, 1790)
Inhabits coral reefs and rocky areas, often in the vicinity of
caves; mainly distinguished by its huge size, is one of the
largest bony fishes; placed in the genus *Promicrops* by some
authors; N.W. Australia, Great Barrier Reef and throughout
S.E. Asia; Indo-W. Pacific; to 270 cm.

GIANTS OF THE REEF

Although most of the serranid fishes featured on
Plates 22–26 have a maximum size well under 1 m,
3 of the species featured on this plate are giants by
comparison. The Queensland Groper *Epinephelus
lanceolatus* (**12**) holds the distinction of being the
largest of all bony fishes (which excludes sharks and
rays) occurring on coral reefs. There are reports of
particularly huge individuals weighing as much as
400 kg and measuring nearly 3 metres. Although
its common name suggests a limited distribution,
it is actually found over a huge area of the tropical
Indo-Pacific, extending from East Africa to the
islands of the central Pacific Ocean. These monsters
are usually just curious towards divers. They either
approach at close range for a brief moment, or may
spend several minutes following them from a safe
distance. Although the details are vague and none
are fully documented, there are a few reports of fatal
attacks on humans. One precaution that divers must
take is to never try and handfeed large individuals. At
least one person learned this lesson the hard way on
Australia's Great Barrier Reef. A young man offered a
struggling fish he had just speared. The Queensland
Groper's response was lightning quick — the fish was
literally inhaled, along with the man's arm. Luckily he
managed to jerk his arm out of the mouth, but in the
process it was severely lacerated by the numerous rows
of small, sharp teeth. Although not as formidable as
the giant Queensland Groper, other large species that
grow over 1 metre include the Goldspotted Rockcod
E. coioides (**4**), Potato Rockcod *E. tukula* (**5**) and
Blackspotted Rockcod *E. malabaricus* (Plate **25.1**).

PLATE 25: ROCKCODS

SERRANIDAE

1. BLACKSPOTTED ROCKCOD ☆☆☆
Epinephelus malabaricus (Bloch & Schneider, 1801)
Inhabits coral or rocky reefs, estuaries, mangrove swamps, tidepools and sand-mud bottoms to depths of 150 m; similar to *E. coioides* (Plate **24.4**), but has dark brown or black spots with irregular white spots or blotches (orange or reddish brown spots and no white spots on *E. coioides*); found throughout the region; Indo-W. Pacific; to 115 cm and at least 25 kg.

2. BLACKDOTTED GROUPER ☆☆☆
Epinephelus stictus Randall & Allen, 1987
Inhabits continental shelf on mud or sand bottoms at depths between 60–142 m; distinguished by light brown colouration and small dark spots on back; N.W. Australia, Java and Vietnam to S. Japan; to 41 cm.

3. YELLOWSPOTTED GROUPER ☆☆☆
Epinephelus timorensis Randall & Allen, 1987
Inhabits continental shelf or over sand-mud bottoms at depths between 73–210 m; distinguished by irregular bars on body and yellow spots on head; known only from W. Australia, Samoa and Phoenix Islands; to 32 cm.

4. PLUMP GROUPER ☆☆☆
Epinephelus trophis Randall & Allen, 1987
Inhabits continental shelf on sand-mud bottoms to depths of at least 130 m; a plain charcoal-coloured fish without distinguishing marks; known on the basis of only 2 specimens collected from the base of an experimental drilling rig at Dillon Shoals in the Timor Sea; to at least 15 cm.

5. DUSKYTAIL GROUPER ☆☆☆
Epinephelis bleekeri (Vaillant, 1878)
Inhabits rocky banks on the continental shelf at depths between 30–104 m; distinguished by dusky tail and reddish, orange or yellow spots covering head and body; N.W. Australia, Northern Territory and throughout S.E. Asia; Indo-W. Pacific; to 76 cm.

6. NETFIN GROUPER ☆☆☆
Epinephelus miliaris (Valenciennes, 1830)
Inhabits coral reefs, but juveniles found in seagrass beds, mangroves, or on mud bottoms; distinguished by pattern of fine spots on body and mesh-like spotting of fins; offshore reefs of N.W. Australia; Indo-W. Pacific, usually around oceanic islands; to 53 cm.

7. SPECKLED GROUPER ☆☆☆
Epinephelus magniscuttis Postel, Fourmanoir & Guézé, 1963
Inhabits continental shelf and deep reefs around islands at depths between 128–300 m; N. Queensland, New Guinea and Philippines; Indo-W. Pacific; to 150 cm and 50 kg.

8. COMET GROUPER ☆☆☆
Epinephelus morrhua (Valenciennes, 1833)
Inhabits deep reefs of continental shelf and oceanic islands between depths of 80–370 m; distinguished by broad, curved bands on sides and diagonal bands on head; Queensland and a few scattered localities in Indo-Malay Archipelago; Indo-C. Pacific; to 80 cm.

9. SMALLSCALED GROUPER ☆☆☆
Epinephelus polylepis Randall & Heemstra, 1991
Inhabits continental shelf on flat sand-rubble bottoms at depths between 30–100 m; distinguished by network of small, close-set, dark brown spots and several faint dark bars on side; N.W. Australia; Indian Ocean; to at least 61 cm.

10. SPECKLEFIN GROUPER ☆☆☆
Epinephelus ongus (Bloch, 1790)
Inhabits shallow coral reefs; distinguished by general brown colouration and pattern of undulating lines on sides and large white blotches; *E. summana* is a synonym; found throughout the region; Indo-W. Pacific; to 40 cm.

11. MAORI ROCKCOD ☆☆☆
Epinephelus undulatostriatus (Peters, 1866)
Inhabits coral and rocky reefs, usually at depths between 25–80 m; distinguished by pattern of undulating and slanting fine bands on side; S. Queensland and NSW; to 55 cm.

12. BLUESPOTTED CORAL TROUT ☆☆☆
Plectropomus laevis (Lacepède, 1801)
Inhabits coral reefs, both in lagoons and on outer reefs; distinguished by white colouration, yellow fins and prominent black bars or saddles; another commonly observed variety has numerous small dark-edged spots on the head and body with greyish bars and fins; Great Barrier Reef, offshore reefs of W. Australia and throughout S.E. Asia; Indo-W. Pacific; to 100 cm.

PLATE 26: ROCKCODS

SERRANIDAE

1. THINSPINE GROUPER ☆☆☆
Gracila albomarginata (Fowler & Bean, 1930)
Inhabits outer slopes in 15–100 m; usually swims a short distance above the bottom; distinguished by large squarish white blotch on upper side and black spot at base of tail; juveniles plain with brilliant red markings on fins; Great Barrier Reef, offshore reefs of W. Australia and throughout S.E. Asia; Indo-C. Pacific. to 40 cm.

2. DOT-HEAD ROCKCOD ☆☆
Cephalopholis microprion (Bleeker, 1852)
Inhabits inshore reefs, common on shallow silty reefs; distinguished by plain brown body and numerous small blue spots on head and breast; N. Great Barrier Reef and throughout S.E. Asia; W. Pacific to Andaman Sea; to 23 cm.

3. GOLDBAR GROUPER ☆☆☆
Cephalopholis igarashiensis Katayama, 1957
Inhabits deeper reef areas, generally between 60–250 m; distinguished by bright pattern of yellow, red and orange bars; S.E. Asia; W. Pacific; to 43 cm.

4. STRAWBERRY ROCKCOD
Cephalopholis spiloparaea (Valenciennes, 1828)
Inhabits steep outer reef slopes, usually in about 15–100 m depth; appears plain grey brown underwater, but is actually bright red orange with diagonal white markings near edge of tail; Great Barrier Reef, offshore reefs of W. Australia and throughout S.E. Asia; Indo-C. Pacific; to 22 cm.

5. SIXBAND ROCKCOD ☆☆☆
Cephalopholis sexmaculata (Rüppell, 1830)
Inhabits caves and ledges, usually seen on outer reef slopes below 10 m depth; distinguished by combination of bright red colouration, brilliant blue spots and lines, and series of dark bars on side that are darkest on upper back; Great Barrier Reef, offshore reefs of W. Australia and throughout S.E. Asia; Indo-C. Pacific; to 47 cm.

6. BLUESPOTTED ROCKCOD ☆☆☆
Cephalopholis cyanostigma (Valenciennes, 1828)
Inhabits coral reefs, often in lagoons or seagrass beds; distinguished by brown or orange-brown colouration with numerous blue spots on head, body and fins, a white 'halo' surrounding each spot on body; juveniles are plain grey-brown with yellow fins; Great Barrier Reef, offshore reefs of W. Australia and throughout S.E. Asia; W. Pacific; to 35 cm.

7. HIGHFIN GROUPER ☆☆☆
Epinephelus maculatus (Bloch, 1790)
Inhabits coral reefs, usually seen around coral bommies in lagoons; distinguished by overall dark grey colouration, pattern of dark spotting and white saddles on forehead, middle of dorsal fin and sometimes on upper tail base; Great Barrier Reef, offshore reefs of W. Australia and throughout S.E. Asia; W. Pacific to Samoa and Marshall Islands; to 50 cm.

8. PURPLE ROCKCOD ☆☆☆
Epinephelus cyanopodus (Richardson, 1846)
Inhabits sandy areas near coral reefs, usually in protected lagoons; distinguished by general pale colouration and numerous small dark spots on head, body and fins; juveniles mainly yellow with blue-grey wash on head and front of body; Great Barrier Reef, offshore reefs of W. Australia and throughout S.E. Asia; Indo-C. Pacific; to 100 cm.

9. WIRENET ROCKCOD ☆☆☆
Epinephelus hexagonatus (Forster, 1801)
Inhabits coral reefs, usually found in exposed outer reef areas in shallow water; distinguished by numerous brown spots separated by pale hexagonal 'wire-netting' pattern; Great Barrier Reef, offshore reefs of W. Australia and throughout S.E. Asia; Indo-C. Pacific; to 30 cm.

10. SNUBNOSE GROUPER
Epinephelus macrospilos (Bleeker, 1855)
Inhabits coral reefs to depths of at least 44 m; distinguished by pattern of dark brown spots, which are very large and roughly hexagonal-shaped in juveniles and subadults, but become more numerous, smaller and rounded in adults; Great Barrier Reef, offshore reefs of W. Australia and throughout S.E. Asia; Indo-C. Pacific; to 43 cm.

11. GREASY ROCKCOD
Epinephelus tauvina (Forsskål, 1775)
Inhabits coral reefs in clear water; distinguished by pattern of brown spots on a whitish background; similar to *E. macrospilos* (**10**), but spots are larger and more widely spaced; Great Barrier Reef, northern W. Australia and throughout S.E. Asia; Indo-C Pacific; to 70 cm.

RAINBOWS OF THE REEF

Perhaps no other group of coral reef fishes exhibits such a myriad of dazzling colours as the members of the genus *Pseudanthias* (Plate 27), often commonly referred to as Anthias or Basslets. The vivid neon lustre of these fishes is greatly enhanced by their habit of forming large aggregations. Particularly notable in this respect is the Purple Queen *P. tuka* (Plate **27.10**) which forms huge schools adjacent to outer reef dropoffs. Surprisingly, these graceful fishes are members of the family Serranidae, which also contains the rockcods and coral trout. They constitute a separate subfamily, Anthiadinae, which contains more than 100 species in tropical and subtropical seas. Most of these occur in the Indo-W. Pacific region.

One of the most interesting aspect of the biology of Anthias is their reproductive behaviour. They exhibit a harem-type social structure. Each male reigns supreme over a group of females which may include up to 10 or more fishes. Among the females there is a 'peck-order' hierarchy of social dominance. If something should happen to the male fish, for example if it is eaten by a predator or experimentally removed, the highest ranking female changes sex and assumes control of the harem. The sex change is relatively rapid, beginning within about 3–10 days, and is completed within two weeks. The sex change is accompanied by a change in colouration. It is facilitated by the presence of both ovarian and testicular tissue within the gonads. During the initial or female phase of the sexual cycle only the ovarian tissue is functional; the assumption of social dominance triggers a hormonal reaction that stimulates the testicular tissue.

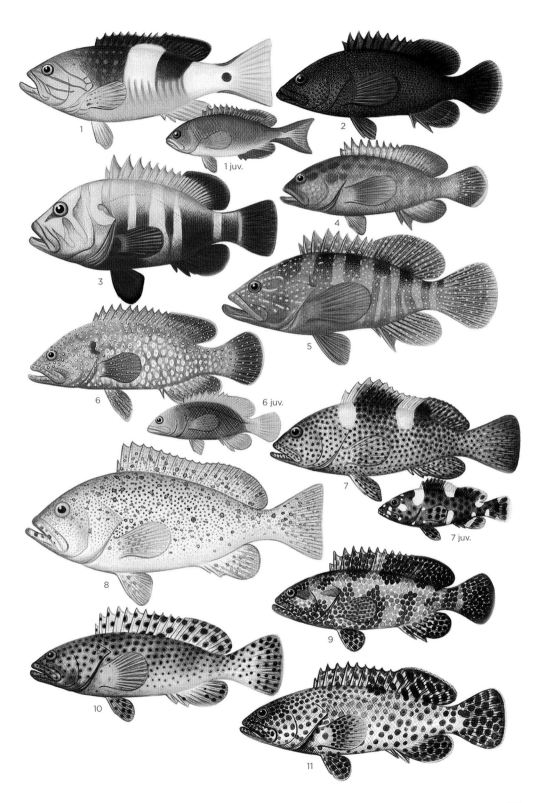

PLATE 27: BASSLETS

SERRANIDAE

1. PRINCESS BASSLET
Pseudanthias smithvanizi (Randall & Lubbock, 1981)
Inhabits outer reef slopes, usually seen below depths of 25–30 m; occurs in aggregations; distinguished by small size, swollen upper lip (males), prolonged 3rd dorsal fin spine (males), numerous yellow spots on upper half of body and strongly forked tail; Great Barrier Reef, offshore reefs of W. Australia and throughout S.E. Asia; Indo-C. Pacific; to 9.5 cm.

2. LORI'S BASSLET
Pseudanthias lori (Lubbock & Randall, 1976)
Inhabits outer reef slopes, usually seen in aggregations at depths between 25–60 m; distinguished by bright red bars on back and broad red band on tail base; Great Barrier Reef, offshore reefs of W. Australia and throughout S.E. Asia; C.-W. Pacific and E. Indian Ocean; to 12 cm.

3. PACIFIC BASSLET
Pseudanthias huchtii (Bleeker, 1857)
Inhabits coral reefs; a common inhabitant of lagoons, passes and upper edge of outer reef slopes; similar to *P. squamipinnis* (4), but less brilliantly coloured, males have reddish rather than orange band across cheek and lack large dark spot on pectoral fin, females are greenish yellow rather than orange; Great Barrier Reef and throughout S.E. Asia; Philippines to N.E. Australia and Vanuatu: to 12 cm.

4. ORANGE BASSLET
Pseudanthias squamipinnis (Peters, 1855)
Inhabits coral reefs, a common inhabitant of lagoons, passes and upper edge of outer reef slopes; males distinguished by purple colouration, red spot on pectoral fins and elongated 3rd dorsal spine, females bright yellow-orange with diagonal bar across cheek; Great Barrier Reef, offshore reefs of W. Australia and throughout S.E. Asia; Indo-W. Pacific; to 15 cm.

5. LUZON BASSLET
Pseudanthias luzonensis (Katayama & Masuda, 1983)
Inhabits steep outer reef slopes, usually seen below 25–30 m depth; males distinguished by elongate 3rd dorsal spine, red spot on front half of dorsal fin and somewhat oblique rows of small orange spots on sides, females are pinkish, both males and females have diagonal orange stripe across cheek to pectoral fin base; Philippines and Indonesia to N.E. Australia and New Guinea; to 14.5 cm.

6. FAIRY BASSLET
Pseudanthias dispar (Herre, 1955)
Inhabits coral reefs, usually seen on the upper edge of outer reef slopes or passes in 1–15 m depth; forms aggregations which alternately feed on plankton or swarm into crevices in the reef; males distinguished by bright red dorsal fin, swollen protuberance on upper lip and yellowish hue, females are delicate pinkish orange and always outnumber males; Great Barrier Reef, offshore reefs of W. Australia and throughout S.E. Asia; W. and C. Pacific; to 9.5 cm.

7. PYGMY BASSLET
Luzonichthys waitei (Fowler, 1931)
Inhabits coral reefs, usually seen in aggregations on outer reef slopes in 10–50 m depth; several similar species in this genus occurring in the region; distinguished from similar coloured Anthias (genus *Pseudanthias*) by two instead of a single dorsal fin; Great Barrier Reef, offshore reefs of W. Australia and throughout S.E. Asia; Indo-W. Pacific; to 7 cm.

8. RANDALL'S FAIRY BASSLET
Pseudanthias randalli (Lubbock & Allen, 1978)
Inhabits steep outer reef dropoffs in 20–70 m depth, usually seen in small groups; distinguished by broad stripes of magenta and orange on body and dorsal fin, female is mainly yellow; Indo-Malay Archipelago to Marshall Islands and north to Yaeyama Islands; to 7 cm.

9. SAILFIN QUEEN
Pseudanthias pascalus (Jordan & Tanaka, 1927)
Inhabits coral reefs, usually seen in aggregations on outer reef slopes in 5–45 m depth; distinguished by bright purple colouration of both males and females; males have swollen protuberance on upper lip and elongated soft dorsal rays with red colour on outer part of fin; Great Barrier Reef; French Polynesia west to Queensland and in the N. Pacific from the Marshall Islands to S. Japan; to 17 cm.

10. PURPLE QUEEN
Pseudanthias tuka (Herre & Montalban, 1927)
Inhabits coral reefs, usually seen in spectacular large aggregations on the upper edge of outer reef slopes or in lagoon passes; distinguished by bright purple colouration; males have swollen protuberance on upper lip and elongated soft dorsal rays, females characterised by yellow stripe along back and yellow margins on tail; also known as Purple Anthias; Great Barrier Reef, offshore reefs of W. Australia and throughout S.E. Asia; Philippines to N.E. Australia; to 12 cm.

11. YELLOWBACK BASSLET
Pseudanthias bicolor (Randall, 1979)
Inhabits coral reefs, usually seen in deeper lagoon channels or on outer reef slopes below 20 m depth; forms aggregations over isolated coral formations; distinguished by elongate dorsal spines and 'two-tone' colour of body which is readily apparent when viewed underwater; male and female are similar; Great Barrier Reef and throughout S.E. Asia; Indo-C. Pacific; to 13 cm.

12. MIRROR BASSLET
Pseudanthias pleurotaenia (Bleeker, 1857)
Inhabits steep outer reef slopes, usually found below 20 m depth; males distinguished by large, squarish violet area above pectoral fin and prolonged 3rd dorsal spine, females are bright yellow with a pair of violet bands running across cheek and continuing along ventral part of body; Great Barrier Reef and throughout S.E Asia, replaced by the similar *P. sheni* at offshore reefs of W. Australia; W. Pacific to Marshall islands; to 20 cm.

13. LONGFIN BASSLET
Pseudanthias ventralis (Randall, 1979)
Inhabits outer slopes between 26–68 m depth, usually seen in small aggregations; males distinguished by irregular magenta and yellow streaks, females are more uniform in appearance with yellow back and fins; Great Barrier Reef; C. and W. Pacific, usually around islands or oceanic reefs; to 7 cm.

14. PINK BASSLET
Pseudanthias hypselosoma Bleeker, 1878
Inhabits coral reefs, usually seen on sheltered inshore reefs or in lagoon passes; typical habitat consists of sand bottom or rubble areas where it congregates around isolated coral outcrops or wreckage; male is distinguished by rounded profile of dorsal fin and elongate reddish blotch on anterior half of this fin, females are pinkish red with red tips on the tail; Great Barrier Reef and throughout S.E. Asia; Samoa to Maldives; to 19 cm.

15. REDSTRIPE BASSLET
Pseudanthias fasciatus (Kamohara, 1954)
Inhabits coral reefs, usually on outer slopes between 20–68 m depth; distinguished by yellow body with bright red stripe on middle of side; Great Barrier Reef northward to S. Japan; to 21 cm.

16. TWOSPOT BASSLET
Pseudanthias bimaculatus (Smith, 1955)
Inhabits outer reef slopes; 2 orange to yellow bands bordered with lavender to purple extend from eye to pectoral fin, tips of tail lobes bluish; widespread Indian Ocean from E. Africa to Java and Bali, Indonesia; to 9 cm.

PLATE 28: LONGFINS, DOTTYBACKS AND RELATIVES

SERRANIDAE

1. BARRED SOAPFISH
Diploprion bifasciatum Cuvier, 1828
Inhabits coral reefs; distinguished by bar through eye and broad dark bar across middle of body; also known as Two-banded Soapfish; found throughout the region; N. Indian Ocean and W. Pacific; to 38 cm.

2. LILAC-TIP BASSLET
Pseudanthias rubrizonatus (Randall, 1983)
Inhabits offshore reefs, usually below 25 m depth; distinguished by dark saddle below dorsal spines and pale diagonal stripe across lower part of head; N.W. Australia, Great Barrier Reef and throughout S.E. Asia; Indo-Australian Archipelago; to 12 cm.

3. LITTLE FAIRY BASSLET
Sacura parva Heemstra & Randall, 1979
Inhabits offshore reefs, usually below 50 m depth; distinguished by elongate third dorsal spine and filament at front of soft dorsal fin; N.W. Australia only; to 12 cm.

4. RAINFORDIA
Rainfordia opercularis McCulloch, 1923
Inhabits coral reefs, usually in caves; distinguished by elongate body, flattened head and stripe pattern; N.W. Australia and Great Barrier Reef; N. Australia only; to 15 cm.

5. LINED SOAPFISH
Grammistes sexlineatus (Thunberg, 1792)
Inhabits coral reefs, usually in caves or crevices; distinguished by narrow yellow stripes on side; has mucus that is toxic to other fishes; found throughout the region; Indo-C. Pacific; to 27 cm.

PSEUDOGRAMMATIDAE

6. HONEYCOMB PODGE
Pseudogramma polyacanthum (Bleeker, 1856)
Inhabits coral reefs, in caves and crevices; distinguished by small size and dusky brown pattern with faint blotches; found throughout the region; Indo-C. Pacific; to 7 cm.

PLESIOPIDAE

7. BARRED SPINY BASSLET
Belonepterygion fasciolatum (Ogilby, 1889)
Inhabits coral reefs, in caves and crevices; distinguished by dark stripe through eye, narrow dark bars on side and long thread-like pelvic fins; N.W. Australia and Great Barrier Reef; N. Australia only; to 5 cm.

8. COMET
Calloplesiops altivelis (Steindachner, 1903)
Inhabits coral reefs, in caves and crevices; distinguished by white spots on head, body and fins and pale-edged black spot at rear of dorsal fin; N.W. Australia, Great Barrier Reef and throughout S.E. Asia; Indo-W. Pacific; to 16 cm.

9. REDTIP LONGFIN
Plesiops verecundus Mooi, 1995
Inhabits coral reefs, in caves and crevices; distinguished by deeply incised dorsal fin profile and red margin on dorsal fin; N.W. Australia, Great Barrier Reef and throughout S.E. Asia; Indo-W. Pacific; to 8 cm.

PSEUDOCHROMIDAE

10. LINED DOTTYBACK
Labracinus lineatus (Castelnau, 1875)
Inhabits coral reefs and rocky areas usually in crevices; distinguished by relatively large size and numerous narrow stripes on body and fins; also known as Lined Cichlops; W. Australia only, between Jurien Bay and Broome; to 25 cm.

11. DUSKY DOTTYBACK
Pseudochromis fuscus Müller & Troschel, 1849
Inhabits the vicinity of coral reefs; has two distinct colour phases, one entirely yellow and the other dusky brown or purplish; found throughout the region; E. Indian Ocean and W. Pacific; to 8 cm.

12. MARSHALL DOTTYBACK
Pseudochromis marshallensis Schultz, 1953
Inhabits coral reefs; distinguished by scales on sides having orange centres; N.W. Australia and throughout S.E. Asia; mainly W. Pacific; to 8 cm.

13. BLUESPOTTED DOTTYBACK
Assiculus punctatus Richardson, 1846
Inhabits sandy areas with occasional coral or rocky outcrops; distinguished by dark bluish-brown colour and relatively tall dorsal and anal fins; also the dorsal fin begins farther forward than in similar species; N. Australia only, between Shark Bay, W. Australia and Gulf of Carpentaria; to 7.5 cm.

14. SPOTTED DOTTYBACK
Pseudochromis quinquedentatus McCulloch, 1926
Inhabits sand or rubble areas with occasional outcrops that serve as shelter; distinguished by small dark spots arranged in longitudinal rows on side; N. Australia only, between Marion Islands and Capricorn Group, Queensland; to 9 cm.

15. YELLOWHEAD DOTTYBACK
Pseudochromis cyanotaenia Bleeker, 1857
Inhabits coral reef crevices; male distinguished by yellowish area on head and breast with broad pale margin on tail and dorsal fin, females by yellow-edged red tail; often misidentified as *P. tapeinosoma* (not shown); N.W. Australia, Great Barrier Reef and throughout S.E. Asia; E. Indian Ocean and W. Pacific; to 6 cm.

16. YELLOWFIN DOTTYBACK
Pseudochromis wilsoni (Whitley, 1929)
Inhabits coral reef crevices and rubble areas; males distinguished by plain purplish colour and yellow-orange iris, females by yellowish dorsal fin and yellow edges on tail; N. Australia only, between Port Denison, W. Australia and Bargara, Queensland; to 8 cm.

17. ROSE DOTTYBACK
Pseudoplesiops rosae Schultz, 1943
Inhabits coral reef crevices; distinguished by small size, yellow-brown colour, large eye and thread-like pelvic fins; N.W. Australia, Great Barrier Reef and throughout S.E. Asia; Indo-C Pacific; to 4 cm.

SLIMY SOAPFISHES

Most of the species illustrated on this plate live in caves and crevices. The Lined Soapfish *Grammistes sexlineatus* (5) and its relatives (Plate 29.2–3) are called soapfishes because of their slimy mucus coat. It is extremely bitter to the taste and probably offers some measure of protection from larger predatory species. Aquarium observations reveal it is an unpalatable mouthful when offered to a hungry Common Lionfish *Pterois volitans* (Plate 19.6) — once tasted it is quickly spat out.

PLATE 29: ROCKCODS AND DOTTYBACKS

SERRANIDAE

1. SWALLOWTAIL BASSLET
Serranocirrhitus latus Watanabe, 1949
Inhabits coral reefs, usually in caves or beneath ledges on outer reef slopes; distinguished by deep pink colour with yellow bands on head and yellow scale edges; N. Great Barrier Reef, Indonesia and New Guinea; W. Pacific; to 13 cm.

2. ARROWHEAD SOAPFISH
Belonoperca chabanaudi Fowler & Bean, 1930
Inhabits outer reef slopes, usually seen in shadows of caves and ledges; distinguished by slender shape, dark spot on first dorsal fin and bright yellow saddle on tail base; Great Barrier Reef and throughout S.E. Asia; Indo-C. Pacific; to 15 cm.

3. SPOTTED SOAPFISH
Pogonoperca punctata (Valenciennes, 1830)
Inhabits coral reefs, on outer slopes between 25–150 m; distinguished by skin flap on chin, numerous white spots and black saddles on back; throughout S.E. Asia; Indo-W. Pacific; to 33 cm.

PLESIOPIDAE

4. BLUE SCISSORTAIL
Assessor macneilli Whitley, 1935
Inhabits caves and ledges, often swims upside down; distinguished by slender shape, dark blue colour and forked tail; Great Barrier Reef and New Caledonia; to 6 cm.

5. YELLOW SCISSORTAIL
Assessor flavissimus Allen & Kuiter, 1976
Inhabits caves and ledges, often swims upside down; distinguished by slender shape, yellow colour and forked tail; N. Great Barrier Reef; to 5.5 cm.

PSEUDOCHROMIDAE

6. FIRETAIL DOTTYBACK
Labracinus cyclophthalmus (Müller & Troschel, 1849)
Inhabits coral reefs in 1–15 m depth; colour varies from bright red to grey-green or with isolated red patch on side; N.W. Australia (Kimberley district and Ashmore Reef) and throughout S.E. Asia; W. Pacific; to 20 cm.

7. ROYAL DOTTYBACK
Pictichromis paccagnellae (Axelrod, 1973)
Inhabits coral reef drop-offs, usually below 15 m depth; distinguished by brilliant bicolour pattern; Great Barrier Reef, offshore reefs of N.W. Australia and Indonesia to New Guinea; W. Pacific; to 7 cm.

8. MAGENTA DOTTYBACK
Pictichromis porphyrea (Lubbock & Goldman, 1974)
Inhabits coral reef drop-offs, usually below 10 m depth; distinguished by brilliant magenta colour; E. Indonesia and Philippines; W. Pacific; to 6 cm.

9. PURPLETOP DOTTYBACK
Pictichromis diadema (Lubbock & Randall, 1978)
Inhabits coral reef drop-offs, usually below 10 m depth; distinguished by yellow colour with bright magenta area on back; Malaysia, Borneo and Philippines; to 6 cm.

10. SPLENDID DOTTYBACK
Manonichthys splendens (Fowler, 1931)
Inhabits coral reefs in 3–30 m depth, usually seen with sponges; distinguished by close-set rows of yellow-orange spots, white snout and dark bar through eye; Indonesia (Lesser Sunda Islands and Banda Sea); to 10 cm.

11. STEENE'S DOTTYBACK
Pseudochromis steenei (Gill & Randall, 1992)
Inhabits sand-rubble slopes, around small rocky outcrops with crinoids; has narrow white bar behind eye; orange head of male is lacking in female, which is mainly dark with yellow tail; Indonesia (Bali to Flores); to 12 cm.

12. LONGFIN DOTTYBACK
Pseudochromis polynemus Fowler, 1931
Inhabits coral reef slope with abundant crevices and sponges; distinguished by light brown colour with yellow dot on each scale and long pelvic fins with orange spot at base; N. Indonesia and Philippines; to 12 cm.

13. HOWSON'S DOTTYBACK
Pseudochromis howsoni Allen, 1995
Inhabits sand-rubble bottoms around low rocky outcrops; found in pairs; similar to *P. steenei* (**11**), but lacks narrow white bar behind eye and female is entirely dark brown; Timor Sea (Ashmore Reef); to 10 cm.

14. MOORE'S DOTTYBACK
Pseudochromis moorei Fowler, 1931
Inhabits sand-rubble bottoms around low rocky outcrops; found in pairs; female entirely dark brown and male orange with dark spot on each scale of upper half of body and dark 'ear-spot'; Philippines; to 10 cm.

15. SABAH DOTTYBACK
Manonichthys alleni Gill, 2004
Inhabits steep outer reef slopes; distinguished by blue and yellow colour scheme and red spot on pelvic fins; (Malaysia and Borneo); to 8 cm.

16. SLENDER DOTTYBACK
Pseudochromis bitaeniatus (Fowler, 1931)
Inhabits coral reef drop-offs in 5–30 m depth; distinguished by pair of broad, dark brown stripes separated by white; Great Barrier Reef, offshore reefs of N.W. Australia and throughout S.E. Asia; to 8 cm.

17. LAVENDER DOTTYBACK
Cypho purpurescens (De Vis, 1884)
Inhabits coral reef crevices; distinguished by reddish colour with blue scale edges, also 'eye-spot' on dorsal fin; Great Barrier Reef; S.W. Pacific; to 7.5 cm.

18. MULTICOLOUR DOTTYBACK
Ogilbyina novaehollandiae (Steindachner, 1879)
Inhabits coral reefs; female is mainly reddish and male is reddish on head and front of body, but purplish on rear half; S. Great Barrier Reef; to 10 cm.

19. QUEENSLAND DOTTYBACK
Ogilbyina queenslandiae (Saville-Kent, 1893)
Inhabits coral reefs; similar to *O. novaehollandiae* (**18**), but female has brown bars on back; Great Barrier Reef; to 15 cm.

20. LONGTAIL DOTTYBACK
Oxycercichthys veliferus (Lubbock, 1980)
Inhabits coral reefs; distinguished by overall pale grey colour and lanceolate tail, adult has bluish forehead compared to yellowish of juvenile; Great Barrier Reef; to 12 cm.

21. BLACKSTRIPE DOTTYBACK
Pseudochromis perspicillatus Günther, 1862
Inhabits sand-rubble bottoms around low rocky outcrops; found in pairs; distinguished by white to yellow-brown colour with oblique black stripe; Indonesia and Philippines: to 12 cm.

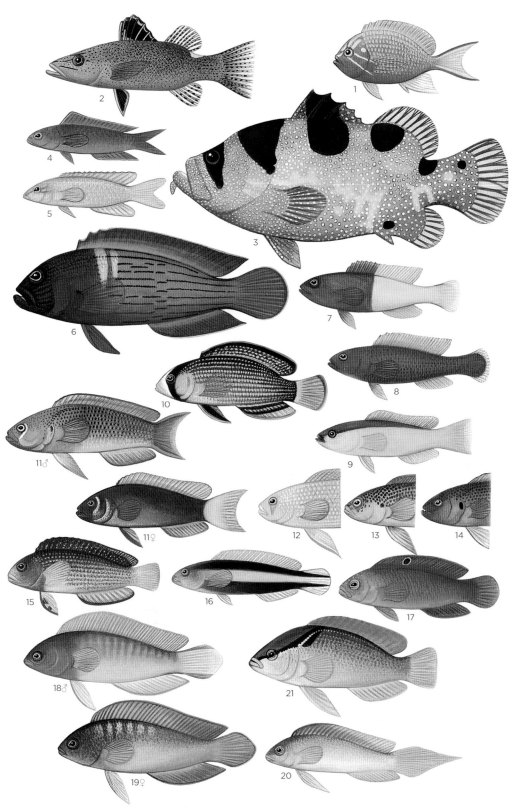

PLATE 30: GLASSFISHES, GRUNTERS AND WHITINGS

LATIDAE

1. BARRAMUNDI ☆☆☆☆
Lates calcarifer (Bloch, 1790)
Inhabits coastal waters, entering estuaries and freshwater; highly esteemed as a food fish and for its angling qualities; distinguished by silvery appearance, deeply notched dorsal fin, 'humped' back and glassy eye; found at localities throughout the region which have extensive mangrove coasts, for example N. Australia and S. New Guinea; N. Indian Ocean and W. Pacific, to 150 cm and at least 20 kg.

2. SAND BASS ☆☆
Psammoperca waigiensis (Cuvier, 1828)
Inhabits rocky or coral reefs, frequently in weedy areas; distinguished by barramundi-like appearance and glassy eyes; colour ranges from light silvery-grey to very dark brown; found throughout the region; N. Indian Ocean and W. Pacific; to 47 cm.

3. SPIKY BASS
Hypopterus macropterus (Günther, 1859)
Inhabits sand-weed areas; has similar shape to *Psammoperca waigiensis* (2), although a much smaller fish and deeper-bodied; colour is strongly mottled; W. Australia only, between Jurien Bay and Onslow; to 14 cm.

AMBASSIDAE

4. LONGSPINE GLASSFISH
Ambassis interrupta Bleeker, 1852
Inhabits brackish bays and estuaries, also mangrove-lined tidal creeks; distinguished by semi-transparent appearance, tall dorsal fin and white tips on pelvic fins and front of anal fin; found throughout the region; Andaman Islands and Indo-Australian Archipelago; to 10 cm.

5. SCALLOPED GLASSFISH
Ambassis nalua (Hamilton, 1822)
Inhabits brackish bays and estuaries, similar to *A. interrupta* (4), but has slight hump on snout, dorsal fin is slightly shorter and lacks white tip on pelvic and anal fins; found throughout the region; E. Indian Ocean and Indo-Australian Archipelago; to 12 cm.

6. VACHELL'S GLASSFISH
Ambassis vachelli Richardson, 1846
Inhabits brackish bays, estuaries and tidal creeks similar to *A. interrupta* (4) and *A. nalua* (5), but has a more slender body and lower dorsal fin; frequently misidentified as *A. dussumieri* (not shown); found throughout the region; E. Indian Ocean and Indo-Australian Archipelago; to 7 cm.

GLAUCOSOMATIDAE

7. NORTHERN PEARL PERCH ☆☆☆
Glaucosoma buergeri Richardson, 1845
Inhabits trawling grounds; distinguished by silvery appearance, large eye and single dorsal fin that is elevated on rear portion, frequently with narrow stripes which may disappear in larger fish; closely related to the jewfish (*G. hebraicum*) of S.W. Australia; N.W. Australia and scattered localities in S.E. Asia; mainly W. Pacific; to 45 cm.

8. THREADFIN PEARL PERCH ☆☆☆
Glaucosoma magnificum (Ogilby, 1915)
Inhabits trawling grounds, similar to *G. buergeri* (7) above, but has elongate dorsal fin filaments and brown bars on head; N. Australia and S. New Guinea only; to 32 cm.

TERAPONTIDAE

9. YELLOWTAIL GRUNTER ☆☆
Amniataba caudovittata (Richardson, 1845)
Inhabits estuaries over sand-weed bottoms; distinguished by yellow fins and conspicuous stripes and spots on tail; also known as Yellowtail Trumpeter and Yellowtailed Perch; W. and N. Australia and S. New Guinea; to 28 cm.

10. FOURLINE STRIPED GRUNTER ☆
Pelates quadrilineatus (Bloch, 1790)
Inhabits coastal waters, entering estuaries; distinguished by 6–8 straight dark stripes on side and none on tail; found throughout the region; Indo-W. Pacific; to 20 cm.

11. CRESCENT GRUNTER ☆
Terapon jarbua (Forsskål, 1775)
Inhabits coastal waters, entering estuaries and lower reaches of freshwater streams; distinguished by 3 or 4 curved dark stripes on side; found throughout the region; Indo-W. Pacific; to 32 cm.

12. SPINYCHEEK GRUNTER ☆
Terapon puta Cuvier, 1829
Inhabits coastal waters, entering brackish estuaries; distinguished by 3 or 4 straight dark stripes on side; also known as Three-lined Grunter; found throughout the region; N. Indian Ocean and Indo-Australian Archipelago; to 16 cm.

13. LARGESCALE GRUNTER ☆
Terapon theraps Cuvier, 1829
Inhabits coastal waters; similar to *T. puta* (12), but has wider stripes and scales much larger (46–56 in lateral line versus 70–85), also is deeper bodied; found throughout the region; Indo-W. Pacific; to 28 cm.

SILLAGINIDAE

14. GOLDENLINE WHITING ☆☆☆
Sillago analis Whitley, 1943
Inhabits sandy bottoms near shore; distinguished by golden-silver to golden-yellow stripe along middle of side; also known as Roughscale Whiting; found throughout the region; N. Australia and S. New Guinea; to 45 cm.

15. STOUT WHITING ☆☆☆
Sillago robusta Stead, 1908
Inhabits sandy bottoms near shore; distinguished by yellow blotch on cheek and silvery stripe on middle of side; most of Australia except southern coast; to 30 cm.

16. WESTERN TRUMPETER WHITING ☆☆☆
Sillago burrus Richardson, 1842
Inhabits sandy bottoms near shore, distinguished by irregular dark blotches on side; N.W. Australia, New Guinea and Indonesia; to 30 cm.

17. NORTHERN WHITING ☆☆☆
Sillago sihama (Forsskål, 1775)
Inhabits sandy bottoms near shore, a plain uniform-coloured whiting without distinguishing marks; also known as Sand Smelt; found throughout the region; Indo-W. Pacific; to 31 cm.

18. WESTERN SCHOOL WHITING ☆☆☆
Sillago vittata McKay, 1985
Inhabits sandy bottoms near shore; distinguished by dark diagonal lines on back; W. Australia only, between Rottnest Island and Pt. Maud; to 30 cm.

BARRA FACTS

The Barramundi *Lates calcarifer* (1) spawns in estuaries and coastal shallows between September and March. Growth of the young is rapid and sexual maturity is reached in 3–4 years at a length of 55–70 cm.

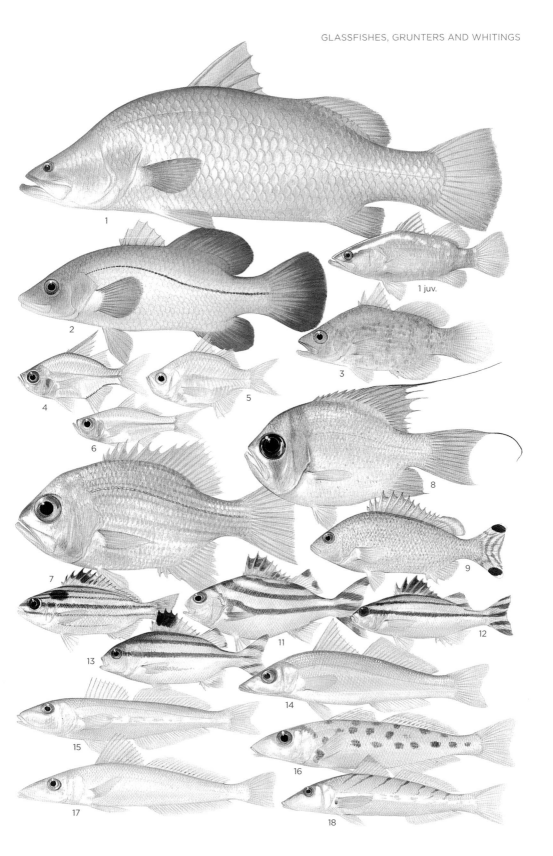

PLATE 31: BIGEYES AND CARDINALFISHES

PRIACANTHIDAE

1. WHITEBAND BIGEYE ☆☆☆
Pristigenys niphonia (Cuvier, 1829)
Inhabits deeper offshore reefs and trawling grounds;
distinguished by white bars on sides; found throughout
the region; Indo-W. Pacific; to 26 cm.

2. BLOTCHED BIGEYE ☆☆☆
Heteropriacanthus cruentatus (Lacepède, 1801)
Inhabits coral reefs, usually in caves except at night when
seen in the open; similar to *Priacanthus hamrur* (**4**), but has
lighter pelvic fin, spots (sometimes faint) on dorsal, anal and
tail fins, and tail not crescentic; spot pattern shown is not
always evident; also known as Glass Bigeye; N.W. Australia,
Great Barrier Reef and throughout S.E. Asia; Indo-C.
Pacific; to 30 cm.

3. SPOTTED BIGEYE ☆☆☆
Priacanthus macracanthus Cuvier, 1829
Inhabits inshore and offshore reefs; distinguished by
relatively short dorsal and anal fins which are distinctly
spotted; similar to *P. fitchi* (**7**), which lacks distinct spotting;
also known as Large-spined Bigeye; N.W. Australia, Great
Barrier Reef and throughout S.E. Asia; mainly W. edge of
Pacific; to 35 cm.

4. LUNARTAIL BIGEYE ☆☆☆
Priacanthus hamrur (Forsskål, 1775)
Inhabits coral reefs and rocky bottoms; similar to
Heteropriacanthus cruentatus (**2**), but has darker pelvic fins,
crescentic tail and lacks spotting on fins except a dark spot
present at base of pelvic fins; N.W. Australia, Great Barrier
Reef and throughout S.E. Asia; Indo-C. Pacific: to 40 cm.

5. PURPLESPOTTED BIGEYE ☆☆☆
Priacanthus tayenus Richardson, 1846
Inhabits coral reefs and rocky bottoms to at least 200 m
depth; distinguished by relatively tall dorsal and anal fins
and filamentous tips on tail; N.W. Australia, Great Barrier
Reef and throughout S.E. Asia; N. Indian Ocean and W.
edge of Pacific; to 35 cm.

6. ARROWFIN BIGEYE ☆☆☆
Priacanthus sagittarius Starnes, 1988
Inhabits rocky bottoms in 60–100 m depth; distinguished by
tall dorsal and anal fins, large pelvic fins and dark membrane
between first and second dorsal spines; N.W. Australia, S.E.
Asia and S. New Guinea; to 40 cm.

7. DEEPSEA BIGEYE ☆☆☆
Priacanthus fitchi Starnes, 1988
Inhabits offshore waters between 150–400 m depth; similar
to *P. macracanthus* (**3**), but lacks distinct spotting on fins;
N.W. Australia, W. Indonesia and Philippines; E. Indian
Ocean and W. Pacific; to 25 cm.

8. LONGFIN BIGEYE ☆☆☆
Cookeolus japonicus (Cuvier, 1829)
Inhabits trawl grounds and rocky bottoms; distinguished by
very large pelvic fins and tall dorsal and anal fins; found
throughout the region; Indo-C. Pacific; to 60 cm.

APOGONIDAE

9. WOLF CARDINALFISH
Cheilodipterus artus Smith, 1961
Inhabits coral reefs, in caves and crevices; distinguished by
8–10 stripes, yellow area with black spot at tail base (which
can be 'switched' off) and large canine teeth; N.W. Australia,
Great Barrier Reef and throughout S.E. Asia; Indo-C.
Pacific; to 12 cm.

10. TIGER CARDINALFISH
Cheilodipterus macrodon (Lacepède, 1802)
Inhabits coral reefs, in caves and crevices; distinguished by
striped pattern, lack of yellow on tail base and large canine
teeth; N.W. Australia, Great Barrier Reef and throughout
S.E. Asia; Indo-C. Pacific; to 22 cm.

11. FIVELINE CARDINALFISH
Cheilodipterus quinquelineatus Cuvier, 1828
Inhabits coral reefs, in caves and crevices; distinguished by 5
stripes on side, spot at tail base and large canine teeth; found
throughout the region; Indo-C. Pacific; to 12 cm.

12. SAILFIN CARDINALFISH
Quinca mirifica Mees, 1966
Inhabits coral reef caves and ledges; distinguished by
blackish colour, white tail and enlarged fins; W. Australia
only, between Ningaloo Reef and Kimberley coast; to 14 cm.

13. HARBOUR CARDINALFISH
Foa fo (Jordan & Seale, 1905)
Inhabits sand-weed areas, usually under dead coral slabs;
distinguished by mottled pattern, incomplete lateral line and
presence of teeth on palate; N.W. Australia, Great Barrier
Reef and throughout S.E. Asia; Indo-C. Pacific; to 6 cm.

14. VARIEGATED CARDINALFISH
Fowleria variegata (Valenciennes, 1832)
Inhabits coral reef crevices; distinguished by spot on gill
cover and irregular spotting on body and fins; found
throughout the region; Indo-C. Pacific; to 8 cm.

15. CROSSEYE CARDINALFISH
Fowleria aurita (Valenciennes, 1831)
Inhabits coral reef crevices; distinguished by spot on gill
cover and lack of markings on body and fins; found
throughout the region; Indo-C. Pacific; to 8 cm.

16. STRIPED SIPHONFISH
Siphamia majimai Matsubara & Iwai, 1958
Inhabits coral reefs, usually found among the spines of sea
urchins; distinguished by silver stripe on belly and
alternating black and white stripes on side, or may be entirely
blackish; found throughout the region; mainly W. Pacific;
to 5 cm.

17. PINKBREAST SIPHONFISH
Siphamia roseigaster (Ramsay & Ogilby, 1887)
Inhabits coastal reefs; distinguished by silver stripe on belly,
plain pale colouration and rosy fins; N. Australia only;
to 7 cm.

BIGEYES

Bigeyes are similar in appearance to the squirrelfishes
and soldierfishes (Plates 14–15), but are distinguished
by smaller scales, a larger, upturned mouth and
lack of spines on the head. They also exhibit
similar behaviour, being essentially nocturnal and
spending the daylight hours in caves. At night
they emerge to feed on cephalopods, crustaceans
and fishes. The approximately 20 known species
are mainly found in the Indo-Pacific region.

PLATE 32: CARDINALFISHES

APOGONIDAE

1. BROADSTRIPE CARDINALFISH
Ostorhinchus angustatus (Smith & Radcliffe, 1911)
Inhabits coral reef crevices, usually below 10–15 m depth;
distinguished by relatively thin black stripes and distinct spot
at base of tail; similar to *A. taeniophorus* (**2**), but found in
deeper water; N.W. Australia, Great Barrier Reef and
throughout S.E. Asia; mainly Indo-C. Pacific; to 9 cm.

2. PEARLY-LINE CARDINALFISH
Ostorhinchus taeniophorus (Regan, 1908)
Inhabits shallow reef flats exposed to wave action, often
found under boulders; similar to *O. angustatus* (**1**), but no
black spot at tail base; found throughout the region;
Indo-W. Pacific; to 10 cm.

3. FOURLINE CARDINALFISH
Ostorhinchus doederleini (Jordan & Snyder, 1901)
Inhabits coral reef crevices and southern rocky reefs;
distinguished by thin red to black stripes on side and spot at
tail base; N.W. Australia, Great Barrier Reef and throughout
S.E. Asia; mainly W. Pacific; to 9 cm.

4. CANDYSTRIPE CARDINALFISH
Ostorhinchus endekataenia (Bleeker, 1852)
Inhabits coral reef crevices; similar to *O. cookii* (**5**), but
stripes are thinner and lacks short (incomplete) stripe behind
upper corner of eye; N.W. Australia and S.E. Asia; mainly
W. Pacific; to 10 cm.

5. COOK'S CARDINALFISH
Ostorhinchus cookii (Macleay, 1881)
Inhabits shallow reefs; frequently in rocky crevices in weedy
areas; distinguished from other striped species by incomplete
stripe behind upper corner of eye; found throughout the
region; Indo-W. Pacific; to 10 cm.

6. BLACKTIP CARDINALFISH
Ostorhinchus semilineatus (Temminck & Schlegel, 1842)
Inhabits offshore trawling grounds; distinguished by black
tip on dorsal fin and pair of narrow stripes along back; N.W.
Australia and S.E. Asia; mainly W. Pacific; to 10 cm.

7. PALESTRIPED CARDINALFISH
Ostorhinchus pallidofasciatus (Allen, 1987)
Inhabits shallow inshore reefs, in crevices often located in
weedy areas; distinguished by dusky brown colour with faint
stripes on side; N. Australia only; to 13 cm.

8. BAR-STRIPED CARDINALFISH
Ostorhinchus quadrifasciatus (Cuvier, 1828)
Inhabits flat-sand bottoms with rocky outcrops,
distinguished by dark mid-lateral stripe and 1–2 thinner
stripes above; *O. kiensis* (Plate **36.15**) is a similar species,
but has 6 instead of 7 spines in the first dorsal fin; found
throughout the region; Indo-W. Pacific; to 10 cm

9. CAVE CARDINALFISH
Zapogon evermanni (Jordan & Snyder, 1904)
Inhabits caves, frequently on steep outer reef slopes;
distinguished by red colouration, dark stripe behind eye and
small white spot behind second dorsal fin; N.W. Australia
and throughout S.E. Asia; worldwide circumtropical; to 9 cm.

10. THREE-SADDLE CARDINALFISH
Nectamia bandanensis (Bleeker, 1854)
Inhabits coral reefs, frequently among branching corals;
similar to *N. fusca* (**11**), but dark bar completely encircles tail
base; found throughout the region; mainly W. and C. Pacific;
to 10 cm.

11. GHOST CARDINALFISH
Nectamia fusca (Quoy & Gaimard, 1825)
Inhabits coral reefs, similar to *N. bandanensis* (**10**), but bar
at tail base not complete; *A. savayensis* is a synonym; found
throughout the region; Indo-C. Pacific; to 10 cm.

12. SEVENBAND CARDINALFISH
Ostorhinchus septemstriatus (Günther, 1880)
Inhabits flat-sand bottoms and offshore trawling grounds;
similar to *O. quadrifasciatus* (**8**), but has extra stripe on
midline of forehead from snout to dorsal fin; found throughout
the region; W. Pacific and E. Indian Ocean; to 9 cm.

13. SPINYEYE CARDINALFISH
Pristiapogon fraenatus (Valenciennes, 1832)
Inhabits coral reef crevices; distinguished by black stripe
along middle of side and spot at tail base; N.W. Australia,
Great Barrier Reef and throughout S.E. Asia; Indo-C.
Pacific; to 10 cm.

14. ORANGELINED CARDINALFISH
Ostorhinchus cyanosoma (Bleeker, 1853)
Inhabits shallow reef crevices, distinguished by yellow-
orange stripes; N.W. Australia, Great Barrier Reef and
throughout S.E. Asia; Indo-W. Pacific; to 8 cm.

15. SPINYHEAD CARDINALFISH
Pristiapogon kallopterus (Bleeker, 1856)
Inhabits caves and coral reef crevices; distinguished by broad
dark stripe along middle of side, dusky colour on back and
spot at base of tail; N.W. Australia, Great Barrier Reef and
throughout S.E. Asia; Indo-C. Pacific; to 15 cm.

16. YELLOWLINED CARDINALFISH
Ostorhinchus chrysotaenia (Bleeker, 1851)
Inhabits coral reef crevices; distinguished by blue stripes on
head, faint pale stripes on side and spot on tail base; N.W.
Australia and S.E. Asia; mainly Indo-Australian Archipelago;
to 10 cm.

17. WESTERN GOBBLEGUTS
Ostorhinchus rueppellii (Günther, 1859)
Inhabits inshore reefs and weedy areas, also in estuaries;
distinguished by row of small black spots on upper side;
W. and N. Australia and S. New Guinea only; to 12 cm.

18. TIMOR CARDINALFISH
Apogonichthyoides timorensis (Bleeker, 1854)
Inhabits inshore reef flats with weed and sand, found under
rocks; distinguished by overall dusky colour, sometimes with
faint dark bars and a narrow stripe below eye; found
throughout the region; Indo-W. Pacific; to 8 cm.

CARDINALFISHES

Cardinalfishes (family Apogonidae) are shown on
Plates 31–36. They are small, reef dwelling fishes
inhabiting tropical and temperate seas. Some species
also frequent estuaries and freshwater streams.
The majority of the estimated 250 species are found
on Indo-Pacific coral reefs. Most are nocturnally
active and spend daylight hours in the dark recesses
of caves and ledges. They mainly feed on fishes and
crustaceans. A few species, for example members
of the genus *Rhabdamia*, form dense open-water
shoals that literally envelope entire coral formations.
Male cardinalfishes incubate a fertilised egg mass
in their mouth for several days until hatching.

PLATE 33: CARDINALFISHES

APOGONIDAE

1. MOLUCCAN CARDINALFISH
Ostorhinchus monospilus (Fraser, Randall & Allen, 2002)
Inhabits coral reef crevices; distinguished by broad, faint stripe on side and pearly spot just behind dorsal fin (not shown); N.W. Australia and throughout S.E. Asia; mainly Indo-Australian Archipelago; to 9 cm.

2. WHITELINE CARDINALFISH
Ostorhinchus cavitensis (Jordan & Seale, 1907)
Inhabits silty or sandy areas around rocky outcrops; distinguished by yellow-orange stripes on side and black spot on tail base; *A. virgulatus* is a synonym; found at scattered sites throughout the region; Indo-Australian Archipelago; to 8 cm.

3. HALFBAND CARDINALFISH
Apogon semiornatus Peters, 1876
Inhabits coral reef caves and crevices; distinguished by semi-transparent appearance and oblique dark bands; N.W. Australia, Great Barrier Reef and throughout S.E. Asia; Indo-C. Pacific; to 7 cm.

4. TWO-EYE CARDINALFISH
Apogonichthyoides nigripinnis (Cuvier, 1828)
Inhabits trawling grounds and inshore reefs; distinguished by dark colour and pale-edged black spot on middle of side; found throughout the region; Indo-W. Pacific; to 8 cm.

5. RUBY CARDINALFISH
Apogon crassiceps Garman, 1903
Inhabits coral reef crevices; distinguished by semi-transparent appearance and overall red colour; similar to *A. talboti* (6), but tail base is shorter; found throughout the region; Indo-C. Pacific; to 5 cm.

6. FLAME CARDINALFISH
Apogon talboti Smith, 1961
Inhabits coral reef crevices; similar to *A. crassiceps* (5), but grows much larger and has longer tail base; found throughout the region; Indo-C. Pacific; to 12 cm.

7. MANYBAND CARDINALFISH
Apogonichthyoides brevicaudatus (Weber, 1909)
Inhabits trawling grounds and inshore reefs; distinguished by 8–9 narrow stripes on side and black spot at base of second dorsal fin; N. Australia and S. New Guinea only; to 9 cm.

8. TWOBAR CARDINALFISH
Pristicon rhodopterus (Bleeker, 1852)
Inhabits coral reef crevices; very similar to *P. trimaculatus* (Plate 35.12), but lacks dark spot on gill cover and dark bar or saddle on back below junction of first and second dorsal fins; offshore reefs of N.W. Australia and Indo-Malay Archipelago to New Guinea; mainly W. Pacific; to 15 cm.

9. FLAGFINNED CARDINALFISH
Jaydia truncata (Bleeker, 1855)
Inhabits trawling grounds; distinguished by black outer half of first dorsal fin and stripe across middle of anal and second dorsal fins; found throughout the region; Indo-W. Pacific; to 12 cm.

10. PEARLYFIN CARDINALFISH
Jaydia poeciloptera (Cuvier, 1828)
Inhabits trawling grounds; similar to *Jaydia carinata* (11), but lacks dark spot at rear base of second dorsal fin; found throughout the region; mainly W. Pacific; to 12 cm.

11. OCELLATE CARDINALFISH
Jaydia carinata (Cuvier, 1828)
Inhabits trawling grounds; distinguished by dark spot at rear base of second dorsal fin; N.W. Australia and S.E. Asia; mainly W. Pacific, to 12 cm.

12. RINGTAIL CARDINALFISH
Ostorhinchus aureus (Lacepède, 1802)
Inhabits coral reef caves and crevices; distinguished by golden-orange colour and black ring around tail base; N.W. Australia, Great Barrier Reef and throughout S.E. Asia; Indo-C. Pacific; to 15 cm.

13. MONSTER CARDINALFISH
Jaydia melanopus (Weber, 1911)
Inhabits trawling grounds and inshore reefs; distinguished by dark bar below dorsal fin and one or more rows of spots on rear half of body, these markings are often faint; this fish has a very unusual spindle-shaped egg; *A. fusovatus* is a synonym; N.W. Australia and Arafura Sea only; to 12 cm.

14. CREAMSPOTTED CARDINALFISH
Ozichthys albimaculosus (Kailola, 1976)
Inhabits trawling grounds; distinguished by cluster of large white spots on side and dark spotting on fins; N. Australia and S. New Guinea only; to 10 cm.

15. SCHOOLING CARDINALFISH
Verulux cypselurus (Weber, 1909)
Inhabits coral reefs, forming large aggregations; distinguished by transparent appearance; similar to *R. gracilis* (16), but has black stripe on side of snout and dark margins on tail; N.W. Australia, Great Barrier Reef and throughout S.E. Asia; Indo-C. Pacific; to 6 cm.

16. SLENDER CARDINALFISH
Rhabdamia gracilis (Bleeker, 1856)
Inhabits coral reefs, forming large aggregations; similar to *V. cypselura* (15), but lacks stripe on snout and dark margins on tail (sometimes has black spot at tips of lobes); N.W. Australia, Great Barrier Reef and throughout S.E. Asia; Indo-C. Pacific; to 6 cm.

17. PAINTED CARDINALFISH
Taeniamia fucata (Cantor, 1849)
Inhabits coral reefs and inshore rocky areas; similar to *T. melasma* (18), but has spot on tail base and lacks dark blotch above upper edge of gill cover; found throughout the region; Indo-C. Pacific; to 9 cm.

18. ACROPORA CARDINALFISH
Taeniamia melasma (Lachner, 1951)
Inhabits coral reefs and inshore rocky areas; similar to *T. fucata* (17), but has dark blotch above upper edge of gill cover and lacks spot on tail base; N. Australia and S. New Guinea only; to 9 cm.

NEW DISCOVERIES

One of the exciting aspects of the region's fish fauna is that many new species have been discovered in recent years. More efficient methods of collecting, including the widespread application of SCUBA techniques and increased ease of access to remote areas, are contributing factors in these discoveries. Several of the cardinalfishes on Plates 32–36 were discovered and subsequently described for the first time during the past 25 years (refer to year of description after author names for each species).

PLATE 34: CARDINALFISHES

APOGONIDAE

1. INTERMEDIATE CARDINALFISH
Cheilodipterus intermedius Gon, 1993
Inhabits coral reefs; similar in appearance to *C. artus*
(Plate **31.9**), but differs in having 7–9 developed gill rakers
instead of 10–17; Great Barrier Reef and New Guinea;
W. Pacific; to 11 cm.

2. BLACKSTRIPE MIMIC CARDINALFISH
Cheilodipterus nigrotaeniatus Smith & Radcliffe, 1912
Inhabits coral reefs; active during daylight, mimics the
poison-fanged blenny *Meiacanthus grammistes* (Plate **86.10**);
Philippines and Sulu Sea; to 8 cm.

3. SINGAPORE CARDINALFISH
Cheilodipterus singapurensis Bleeker, 1859–60
Inhabits reef caves and crevices; nocturnal; distinguished by
large, fang-like teeth, relatively large size and fewer stripes
than other large *Cheilodipterus* (stripes sometimes obscure
and fish appears entirely dusky); offshore reefs of N.W.
Australia and throughout S.E. Asia; W. Pacific; to 20 cm.

4. ALLEN'S CARDINALFISH
Cheilodipterus alleni Gon, 1993
Inhabits reef caves and crevices; nocturnal; distinguished
by pattern of narrow dark stripes and black blotch covering
outer half of first dorsal fin; Indo-Malay Archipelago to
New Guinea; to 12 cm.

5. MIMIC CARDINALFISH
Cheilodipterus parazonatus Gon, 1993
Inhabits coral reefs; active during daylight, mimics the
poison-fanged blenny *Meiacanthus vittatus* (not shown);
distinguished by broad, black stripe on side; Great Barrier
Reef, New Guinea and Solomon Islands; to 7 cm.

6. YELLOWBELLY CARDINALFISH
Cheilodipterus zonatus Smith & Radcliffe, 1912
Inhabits coral reefs; active during daylight, mimics the
poison-fanged blenny *Meiacanthus geminatus* (not shown);
distinguished by black stripe on side with broad white stripe
above and yellow below; Malaysia, Philippines and Solomon
Islands; to 7 cm.

7. BANGGAII CARDINALFISH
Pterapogon kauderni (Koumans, 1933)
Inhabits seagrass areas near shore in less than 3 m depth;
associated with *Diadema* sea urchins; male broods eggs and
young in mouth; Banggai Islands, off central-eastern
Sulawesi; to 6.5 cm.

8. WHITE-JAW CARDINALFISH
Pseudamia amblyuroptera (Bleeker, 1856)
Inhabits estuaries and mangrove shores, but occasionally
found in clear water on coral reefs; nocturnal; distinguished
by pattern of fine, broken lines on side, blackish blotch on
tail base and pearly-white area on rear half of lower jaw;
Indo-Malay Archipelago and W. Melanesia; W. Pacific;
to 9 cm.

9. GELATINOUS CARDINALFISH
Pseudamia gelatinosa Smith, 1956
Inhabits reef caves and crevices usually in relatively clear
water; nocturnal; similar appearance to *P. amblyuroptera* (**8**),
but rear half of lower jaw generally brownish instead of
white, also developed gill rakers usually 8 instead of 11;
Great Barrier Reef, N.W. Australia and throughout S.E. Asia;
Indo-C. Pacific; to 8 cm.

10. PADDLEFIN CARDINALFISH
Pseudamia zonata Randall, Lachner & Fraser, 1985
Inhabits reef caves and crevices usually in clear water of outer
slopes below 10 m depth; nocturnal; distinguished by broad
black bars and fan-shaped tail; Philippines and New Guinea;
W. Pacific; to 9 cm.

11. ESTUARY CARDINALFISH
Pseudamia nigra Allen, 1992
Inhabits mangrove-lined shores and estuaries; nocturnal;
distinguished by overall blackish appearance, but may have
numerous fine, black longitudinal lines on side; N. Australia
only; to 6 cm.

12. DWARF CARDINALFISH
Fowleria vaiulae (Jordan & Seale, 1906)
Inhabits coral reef crevices, often found under dead
coral slabs or rocks; distinguished from other *Fowleria*
cardinalfishes by the lack of a pale-rimmed dark spot on the
gill cover; *F. abocellata* is a synonym; Great Barrier Reef,
offshore reefs of W. Australia and throughout S.E. Asia;
Indo-W. Pacific; to 5 cm.

13. EAR CARDINALFISH
Fowleria marmorata (Alleyne & Macleay, 1877)
Inhabits coral reef crevices; distinguished by about 10 brown
bars on side and pale-rimmed dark spot on gill cover; Great
Barrier Reef, offshore reefs of W. Australia and throughout
S.E. Asia; Indo-C. Pacific; to 6 cm.

14. DOTTED CARDINALFISH
Fowleria isostigma (Jordan & Seale, 1906)
Inhabits coral reef crevices; distinguished by small black
spots arranged in horizontal rows and pale-rimmed dark
spot on gill cover; Great Barrier Reef, offshore reefs of W.
Australia and throughout S.E. Asia; W.-C. Pacific; to 6 cm.

15. EIGHTSPINE CARDINALFISH
Neamia octospina Smith & Radcliffe, 1912
Inhabits coral reef crevices; distinguished by overall pale
colouration and trio of brown bands around rear half of eye;
Great Barrier Reef, offshore reefs of W. Australia and
throughout S.E. Asia; Indo-W. Pacific; to 5 cm.

16. GLASSY CARDINALFISH
Rhabdamia spilota (Allen & Kuiter, 1994)
Inhabits coral reefs, usually on outer slopes between
20–55 m depth; forms aggregations around coral outcrops
and gorgonian fans; distinguished by semi-transparent body
with several darks spots on middle of side just behind head;
Indonesia (Bali and Sulawesi); to 5 cm.

17. GIRDLED CARDINALFISH
Taeniamia zosterophora (Bleeker, 1856)
Inhabits coral reefs, often seen in aggregations among
branching corals; distinguished by broad dark bar across
middle of body; Great Barrier Reef, offshore reefs of
W. Australia and throughout S.E. Asia; mainly
W. Pacific; to 8 cm.

18. DUSKY-TAILED CARDINALFISH
Taeniamia macroptera (Cuvier, 1828)
Inhabits coral reefs, often seen in aggregations among
branching corals; similar to *T. fucata* (Plate **33.17**), but has
entire tail base dusky rather than a distinct spot; Indo-Malay
and Melanesian archipelagos; W. Pacific; to 9 cm.

19. BLACKSPOT CARDINALFISH
Taeniamia biguttata (Lachner, 1951)
Inhabits coral reef crevices, usually in aggregations;
distinguished by large dark blotch behind head and small
dark spot on tail base; Indo-Malay and Melanesian
archipelagos; W. Pacific; to 9 cm.

PLATE 35: CARDINALFISHES

APOGONIDAE

1. PLAIN CARDINALFISH
Ostorhinchus apogonides (Bleeker, 1856)
Inhabits coral crevices or forms small schools around coral formations, usually below 15–20 m depth; distinguished by strong yellow hue on lower half of body, pair of blue lines through eye and scattered blue spots on side; Great Barrier Reef and throughout S.E. Asia; Indo-W. Pacific; to 10 cm.

2. CORAL CARDINALFISH
Ostorhinchus properuptus (Whitley, 1964)
Inhabits coral reefs, usually in silty coastal areas; often confused with *O. cyanosoma*, which has narrower yellow stripes; Great Barrier Reef, N.W. Australia and throughout S.E. Asia; W. Pacific; to 6 cm.

3. BLUE-EYE CARDINALFISH
Ostorhinchus compressus (Smith & Radcliffe, 1911)
Inhabits branching *Acropora* corals, forming aggregations; distinguished by bold stripe pattern and neon-blue iris; young have black stripes and yellow tail base with isolated black spot; Great Barrier Reef, offshore reefs of N.W. Australia and throughout S.E. Asia; W. Pacific; to 10 cm.

4. ONELINE CARDINALFISH
Pristiapogon exostigma (Jordan & Starks, 1906)
Inhabits coral crevices; similar to *P. fraenatus* (Plate **32.13**), but small black spot on tail base is above level of mid-lateral black stripe; Great Barrier Reef, offshore reefs of N.W. Australia and throughout S.E. Asia; Indo-C. Pacific; to 11 cm.

5. SINGLESTRIPE CARDINALFISH
Ostorhinchus unitaeniatus (Allen, 1995)
Inhabits shallow bays and trawling grounds between 2–18 m depth; distinguished by thin, black, mid-lateral stripe; N.W. Australia only, between Kimberley district and vicinity of Darwin; to 6 cm.

6. MULTI-STRIPED CARDINALFISH
Ostorhinchus multilineatus (Bleeker, 1874)
Inhabits coral reef crevices; distinguished by numerous narrow stripes on side, also body and fins frequently with yellow hue; Indo-Malay Archipelago to New Guinea; W. Pacific; to 10 cm.

7. FRAGILE CARDINALFISH
Zoramia virdiventer Greenfield, Langston & Randall, 2005
Inhabits coral reefs, usually in aggregations among branching corals; distinguished by semi-transparent body and small black spot on tail base; Great Barrier Reef, offshore reefs of N.W. Australia and throughout S.E. Asia; W. Pacific; to 6 cm.

8. LONGSPINE CARDINALFISH
Zoramia leptacanthus (Bleeker, 1856–57)
Inhabits coral reefs, usually in aggregations among branching corals; distinguished by blue streaks on head and elongate dorsal fin; Great Barrier Reef, offshore reefs of N.W. Australia and throughout S.E. Asia; Indo-W. Pacific; to 6 cm.

9. BLACKSTRIPED CARDINALFISH
Ostorhinchus nigrofasciatus (Lachner, 1953)
Inhabits coral reef crevices; similar to *A. novemfasciatus* (**10**), but stripes do not converge on tail; Great Barrier Reef, offshore reefs of N.W. Australia and throughout S.E. Asia; Indo-C. Pacific; to 8 cm.

10. NINELINE CARDINALFISH
Ostorhinchus novemfasciatus (Cuvier, 1828)
Inhabits coral reefs, usually in lagoon shallows; similar to *O. nigrofasciatus* (**9**), which is found in deeper water, but has dark stripes converging on tail base; Great Barrier Reef, offshore reefs of N.W. Australia and throughout S.E. Asia; mainly W. and C. Pacific; to 9 cm.

11. THERMAL CARDINALFISH
Fibramia thermalis (Cuvier, 1829)
Inhabits silty shores around mangrove edges and branching corals; distinguished by dark band through eye and dark mark at front of first dorsal fin; Great Barrier Reef and throughout S.E. Asia; W. Pacific; to 8 cm.

12. THREESPOT CARDINALFISH
Pristicon trimaculatus (Cuvier, 1828)
Inhabits coral reef crevices; very similar to *P. rhodopterus* (Plate **33.8**), but has dark spot on gill cover and dark bar or saddle on back below junction of first and second dorsal fins; N.W. Australia, Great Barrier Reef and throughout S.E. Asia; mainly W. Pacific; to 15 cm.

13. FROSTFIN CARDINALFISH
Ostorhinchus hoevenii (Bleeker, 1854)
Inhabits coral reefs, usually associated with sponges, crinoids or *Diadema* sea urchins in weedy areas; distinguished by brilliant white posterior edge on first dorsal fin; Great Barrier Reef and throughout S.E. Asia; Indo Australian Archipelago; to 5 cm.

14. BELLY-BARRED CARDINALFISH
Ostorhinchus moluccensis (Valenciennes, 1832)
Inhabits coral reef crevices in 3–30 m depth; usually seen in pairs or aggregations; distinguished by faint brown bars on lower sides, white lines through eye and small white spot below base of last dorsal rays; Indo-Malay Archipelago to Solomon Islands; to 6 cm.

15. HOOKFIN CARDINALFISH
Ostorhinchus griffini (Seale, 1910)
Inhabits coral reefs, usually in sheltered areas near shore; distinguished by peach-coloured fins and distinct hooked shape of second dorsal fin, due to elongate anterior rays; *Apogon sabahensis* is a synonym; Borneo and Philippines; to 12 cm.

16. YELLOW CARDINALFISH
Ostorhinchus flavus (Allen & Randall, 1993)
Inhabits coral and rocky reefs in 2–25 m depth; often seen in large aggregations; similar to *A. capricornis* (**17**), but lacks blue stripes on head and dusky wavy bars on back; S. Great Barrier Reef and S.W. Coral Sea; to 12 cm.

17. CAPRICORN CARDINALFISH
Ostorhinchus capricornis (Allen & Randall, 1993)
Inhabits coral and rocky reefs in 2–15 m depth; similar to *O. flavus* (**16**), but has blue stripes on each side of eye and narrow dusky bars on back; S. Great Barrier Reef and S. Coral Sea south to Sydney; to 8 cm.

18. MINI CARDINALFISH
Ostorhinchus neotes (Allen, Kuiter & Randall, 1994)
Inhabits coral reefs of lagoons and outer slopes in 15–25 m depth; forms aggregations among soft corals and gorgonian fans; distinguished by small size and larval-like appearance with semi-transparent body; Indo-Malay Archipelago to New Guinea and Palau; to 3 cm.

19. YELLOWBAND CARDINALFISH
Ostorhinchus nanus (Allen, Kuiter & Randall, 1994)
Inhabits coral reefs of inshore silty areas; occurs in aggregations between 5–16 m depth; distinguished by small size and semi-transparent body with dusky orange mid-lateral stripe; Indo-Malay Archipelago to New Guinea; to 3.5 cm.

PLATE 36: CARDINALFISHES

APOGONIDAE

1. TAIL-EYE CARDINALFISH
Ostorhinchus ocellicaudus (Allen, Kuiter & Randall, 1994)
Inhabits coral reefs under ledges at base of coral formations; distinguished by pale-edged dark spot at base of tail and absence of stripes on body; Indonesia (Flores) and Ashmore Reef, Timor Sea; to 6 cm.

2. FRANS' CARDINALFISH
Ostorhinchus franssedai (Allen, Kuiter & Randall, 1994)
Inhabits steep outer slopes between 13–40 m depth; brownish stripes on side and large black spot on tail base; Indonesia, Philippines and Palau; to 6.5 cm.

3. RED-SPOT CARDINALFISH
Ostorhinchus parvulus (Smith & Radcliffe, 1912)
Inhabits coral reefs; distinguished by semi-transparent body and bright red spot on tail base; Indo-Malay Archipelago; W. Pacific; to 4.5 cm.

4. WHITESPOT CARDINALFISH
Ostorhinchus dispar (Fraser & Randall, 1976)
Inhabits coral reefs, usually on steep drop-offs below 20 m; distinguished by semi-transparent body, red mid-lateral stripe, small reddish spot at middle of tail base with prominent white spot just above; Indo-Malay Archipelago to New Guinea and Solomon Islands; to 5.5 cm.

5. BROWNSPOTTED CARDINALFISH
Jaydia argyrogaster (Weber, 1909)
Inhabits trawling grounds; distinguished by large dusky spots on pale background; N.W. Australia and S. Indonesia; to 6 cm.

6. BLACK CARDINALFISH
Apogonichthyoides melas (Bleeker, 1848)
Inhabits coral reef crevices; distinguished by overall dark colour and pale-edged black spot on basal half of second dorsal fin; Indo-Malay Archipelago to New Guinea; W. Pacific; to 13 cm.

7. CHEEKBAR CARDINALFISH
Ostorhinchus sealei (Fowler, 1918)
Inhabits coral reefs; see *O. chrysopomus* (**8**), also juveniles with trio of bold black stripes on side (2 stripes in **8**); Timor Sea (Cartier-Ashmore Reefs) and Indo-Malay Archipelago; to 9 cm.

8. SPOTTED-GILL CARDINALFISH
Ostorhinchus chrysopomus Bleeker, 1854
Inhabits coral reefs, often in aggregations among branching corals; very similar to *O. sealei* (**7**), but has spots on gill cover rather than vertical bands; Indo-Malay Archipelago to New Guinea and Solomon Islands; to 9 cm.

9. SILVERLINED CARDINALFISH
Ostorhinchus hartzfeldii (Bleeker, 1852)
Inhabits coral reefs, usually in sheltered bays and lagoons; often among spines of *Diadema* sea urchins; distinguished by purple-brown colour with silvery-white stripes on each side of eye and along back; juveniles have several similar stripes on sides; Indo-Malay Archipelago; to 12 cm.

10. GILBERT'S CARDINALFISH
Zoramia gilberti (Jordan & Seale, 1905)
Inhabits coral reefs; similar to *Z. virdiventer* (Plate **35.7**) and *Z. perlitus* (**11**), but entire tail base is dusky brown and dark brown 'ear-spot' often present; offshore reefs of N.W. Australia, Indonesia, Philippines and E. Caroline Islands; to 5.5 cm.

11. PEARLY CARDINALFISH
Zoramia perlitus (Fraser & Lachner, 1985)
Inhabits branching corals; similar to *Z. virdiventer* (Plate **35.7**), but has blackish strip along base of anal fin; offshore reefs of N.W. Australia, Indonesia, Philippines and E. Caroline Islands; to 5.5 cm.

12. RED-STRIPED CARDINALFISH
Ostorhinchus margaritophorus (Bleeker, 1854)
Inhabits shallow coral reefs in lagoons and sheltered bays; distinguished by broad white mid-lateral stripe with narrower stripes of red and white, forming 'window' pattern on lower side; Indo-Malay Archipelago to Solomon Islands; to 5.5 cm.

13. MANGROVE CARDINALFISH
Yarica hyalosoma (Bleeker, 1852)
Inhabits mangrove shores, estuaries and lower reaches of freshwater streams; distinguished by hump-backed appearance of adults and large dark spot at base of tail; N. Australia and throughout S.E. Asia; Indo-W. Pacific; to 20 cm.

14. PINSTRIPE CARDINALFISH
Fibramia lateralis (Valenciennes, 1832)
Inhabits mangrove shores and weed beds; distinguished by thin black mid-lateral stripe and small dark spot on tail base; N.W. Australia and Indo-Malay Archipelago to New Guinea; E. Indian Ocean and W. Pacific; to 9 cm.

15. RIFLE CARDINALFISH
Ostorhinchus kiensis (Jordan & Snyder 1901)
Inhabits sandy bottoms near coral reefs; similar to *O. quadrifasciatus* (Plate **32.8**), but has 6 instead of 7 spines in the first dorsal fin; Great Barrier Reef and throughout S.E. Asia; Indo-W. Pacific; to 9 cm.

16. SPOTNAPE CARDINALFISH
Ostorhinchus jenkinsi (Evermann & Seale, 1907)
Inhabits coral reefs; distinguished by small pale-rimmed black spot on each side of forehead; Great Barrier Reef, Timor Sea (Ashmore Reef) and Indonesia (Komodo and nearby islands); W. Pacific; to 10 cm.

17. METEOR CARDINALFISH
Ostorhinchus selas (Randall & Hayashi, 1990)
Inhabits coral reefs, usually in sheltered lagoons between 15–35 m depth; distinguished by yellow upper iris, broad dusky stripe on side and large rounded spot on tail base; Philippines, New Guinea and Solomon Islands; W. Pacific; to 5.5 cm.

18. LINESPOT CARDINALFISH
Ostorhinchus lineomaculatus (Allen & Randall, 2002)
Inhabits sandy areas with occasional coral outcrops in 15–40 m depth; distinguished by thin, dark mid-lateral stripe, dark spot on tail base and narrow bars on lower half of side; S. Indonesia only; to 7 cm.

19. PAJAMA CARDINALFISH
Sphaeramia nematoptera (Bleeker, 1856)
Inhabits rich coral areas in protected bays and lagoons; distinguished by broad dark bar across middle of side, large spots on rear half of body and filament at beginning of second dorsal fin; Great Barrier Reef and Indo-Malay Archipelago to New Guinea and Solomon Islands; W. Pacific; to 8 cm.

20. ORBICULAR CARDINALFISH
Sphaeramia orbicularis (Cuvier, 1828)
Inhabits coastal reefs and mangrove shores, frequently seen around wharves; similar to *S. nematoptera* (**19**), but pattern is duller; found throughout S.E. Asia to New Guinea and Solomon Islands; Indo-W. Pacific; to 11.5 cm.

PLATE 37: TREVALLIES

CARANGIDAE

1. PENNANTFISH ☆☆
Alectis ciliaris (Bloch, 1787)
Inhabits coastal reefs; juvenile has long filamentous fin-rays, both juvenile and adult distinguished from *A. indica* (**2**) by more rounded head profile and eye closer to mouth; found throughout the region; worldwide tropical seas; to 130 cm and 13 kg.

2. DIAMOND TREVALLY ☆☆
Alectis indica (Rüppell, 1830)
Inhabits coastal reefs; similar to *A. ciliaris* (**1**), but has more angular head profile and wider space between eye and mouth; both species differ from other trevallies by their scaleless skin; found throughout the region; Indo-W. Pacific; to 150 cm.

3. FRINGEFIN TREVALLY ☆☆
Pantolabus radiatus (Macleay, 1881)
Inhabits coastal waters, sometimes in estuaries or river mouths; distinguished by yellow tail with black upper tip; male has long filamentous rays on the dorsal and anal fins; found throughout the region; Indo-Australian Archipelago; to 40 cm.

4. SMALLMOUTH SCAD
Alepes apercna Grant, 1987
Inhabits coastal waters; distinguished by clear, fleshy eyelid covering rear half of eye and often has dark tips on lobes of tail; found throughout the region; Indo-Australian Archipelago; to 35 cm.

5. BARRED YELLOWTAIL SCAD ☆☆
Atule mate (Cuvier, 1833)
Inhabits coastal waters, forming large schools; distinguished by clear fleshy eyelid covering most of eye except narrow slit in centre; found throughout the region; Indo-C. Pacific; to 30 cm.

6. LONGNOSE TREVALLY ☆☆
Carangoides chrysophrys (Cuvier, 1833)
Inhabits coastal waters; distinguished by gently sloping head profile except abruptly vertical at tip of snout and has scaleless area on breast extending on to pectoral fin base; found throughout the region; Indo-W. Pacific; to 44 cm.

7. ONION TREVALLY ☆☆
Carangoides coeruleopinnatus (Rüppell, 1830)
Inhabits coastal waters; distinguished by relatively deep body, short dorsal and anal fin lobes, small black blotch on upper margin of gill cover and small yellow spots on body; found throughout the region; Indo-C. Pacific; to 40 cm.

8. BLUE TREVALLY ☆☆
Carangoides ferdau (Forsskål, 1775)
Inhabits coastal waters and offshore reefs; distinguished by separate scaleless areas on breast and base of pectoral fin, a bluntly rounded snout and frequently has 5–6 dusky bars on sides; found throughout the region; Indo-C. Pacific; to 70 cm.

9. TURRUM ☆☆☆
Carangoides fulvoguttatus (Forsskål, 1775)
Inhabits coastal waters; distinguished by relatively elongate shape and many gold or brassy spots on side (mainly on back), similar to *C. gymnostethus* (**15**), but has eye higher above mouth, more tapered snout and fewer yellow spots; also known as Goldspotted Trevally and Yellowspotted Trevally; found throughout the region; Indo-W. Pacific; to 130 cm and 12 kg.

10. WHITEFIN TREVALLY ☆☆
Carangoides equula (Temminck & Schlegel, 1844)
Inhabits coastal waters; distinguished by blackish or dusky submarginal band on second dorsal fin and sometimes on anal fin, by very short lobes at front of dorsal and anal fins, and a fully scaled breast; found throughout the region; Indo-W. Pacific; to 37 cm.

11. EPAULET TREVALLY ☆☆
Carangoides humerosus (McCulloch, 1915)
Inhabits coastal waters; distinguished by large eye (about equal to distance from eye to snout tip); blackish first dorsal fin and moderately long dorsal and anal lobes; found throughout the region; Indo-Australian Archipelago; to 25 cm.

12. BUMPNOSE TREVALLY ☆☆
Carangoides hedlandensis (Whitley, 1934)
Inhabits coastal waters; distinguished by long filamentous extensions on dorsal and anal fin-rays, this feature also present in adult males of *Pantolabus radiatus* (**3**), but that species much more slender and has black tip on upper lobe of tail, also known as Port Hedland Trevally; found throughout the region; Indo-C. Pacific; to 32 cm.

13. WHITETONGUE TREVALLY ☆☆
Carangoides talamparoides Bleeker, 1852
Inhabits coastal waters; distinguished by a white or pale grey tongue, relatively deep body, steep head profile and extensive scaleless area encompassing breast, pectoral fin base and small area above pectoral fin; found throughout the region; N. Indian Ocean and Indo-Australian Archipelago; to 32 cm.

14. THICKLIP TREVALLY ☆☆
Carangoides orthogrammus (Jordan & Gilbert, 1882)
Inhabits coastal areas; distinguished by several ovate yellow spots on middle of side and well-separated scaleless areas on breast and base of pectoral fin; also known as False Bluefin Trevally; found throughout the region; Indo-C. Pacific; to 70 cm.

15. BLUDGER TREVALLY ☆☆
Carangoides gymnostethus (Cuvier, 1833)
Inhabits coastal areas in the vicinity of coral or rocky reefs; distinguished by relatively elongate body and a few brown or golden spots often present on side; similar to *C. fulvoguttatus* (**9**), but has eye closer to level of mouth, fewer yellow spots and a steeper snout profile; found throughout the region; Indo-W. Pacific; to 90 cm and at least 11 kg.

16. MALABAR TREVALLY ☆☆
Carangoides malabaricus (Bloch & Schnelder, 1801)
Inhabits coastal waters; similar to *C. talamparoides* (**13**), but tongue grey-brown to brown instead of whitish; found throughout the region; Indo-W. Pacific; to 28 cm.

17. COASTAL TREVALLY ☆☆
Carangoides uii Wakiya, 1924
Inhabits coastal waters; distinguished by relatively deep body and thread-like filament at front of second dorsal (and often anal) fin; found throughout the region; Indo-W. Pacific; to 25 cm.

1

3♀

1 juv.

3♂

4

2

2 juv.

5

6

7

9

8

11

12

10

13

14

15

16

17

PLATE 38: TREVALLIES

CARANGIDAE

1. GIANT TREVALLEY ☆☆
Caranx ignobilis (Forsskål, 1775).
Inhabits coastal and offshore waters in the vicinity of reefs; the largest of the trevallies, distinguished by steep forehead profile and silvery to dusky colouration; also known as Lowly Trevally; found throughout the region; Indo-C. Pacific; to 170 cm and at least 35 kg.

2. BLACK TREVALLY ☆☆
Caranx lugubris Poey, 1860
Inhabits mainly offshore waters in the vicinity of coral reefs; distinguished by dark colouration ranging from brown to nearly black; found throughout the region; worldwide tropical seas; to 80 cm.

3. BLUEFIN TREVALLY ☆☆☆
Caranx melampygus Cuvier, 1833
Inhabits coastal and offshore waters in the vicinity of reefs; distinguished by blue fins and dark speckling on upper half of body; found throughout the region; Indo-E. Pacific; to 100 cm.

4. BRASSY TREVALLY ☆☆
Caranx papuensis Alleyne & Macleay, 1877
Inhabits coastal and offshore waters in the vicinity of reefs; similar to *C. ignobilis* (**1**), but forehead not as steep and has white margin on lower lobe of tail, also usually with scattered dark spots on upper side; also known as Papuan Trevally; found throughout the region; E. Indian Ocean and W. Pacific; to 75 cm.

5. TILLE TREVALLY ☆☆
Caranx tille Cuvier, 1833
Inhabits coastal and offshore waters in the vicinity of reefs; distinguished by relatively slender shape, well-developed gelatinous membrane covering much of eye and blackish spot on upper corner of gill cover; found throughout the region; Indo-W. Pacific; to 70 cm.

6. RAZORBELLY SCAD ☆☆
Alepes kleinii (Bloch, 1793)
Inhabits coastal waters; distinguished by small size, exaggerated profile of belly (i.e. ventral profile more convex than dorsal profile) and black spot on upper corner of gill cover; found throughout the region; Indo-W. Pacific; to 18 cm.

7. BLUESPOTTED TREVALLY ☆☆
Caranx bucculentus Alleyne & Macleay, 1877
Inhabits coastal waters; distinguished by steep forehead profile, large eye, dark spot at upper pectoral fin base and blue spots on upper side; juveniles with 6 dark bars which develop into 3 horizontal rows of square blotches; N. Australia and New Guinea only; to 66 cm.

8. BIGEYE TREVALLY ☆☆
Caranx sexfasciatus Quoy & Gaimard, 1825
Inhabits coastal and offshore waters in the vicinity of reefs; distinguished by relatively large eye with well-developed gelatinous membrane and white tip on dorsal fin lobe; juveniles have 5–6 dark bars on body and sometimes occur in freshwater and estuaries; found throughout the region; Indo-E. Pacific; to 78 cm and at least 4 kg.

9. ROUGH-EAR SCAD ☆☆
Decapterus tabl Berry, 1968
Inhabits coastal waters, occurring in schools; a slender, silvery fish distinguished from other mackerel scad by a red tail and 4–10 scales in straight part of lateral line immediately preceding expanded bony scutes on rear part of body; found throughout the region; Atlantic and Indo-C. Pacific; to 50 cm.

10. REDTAIL SCAD ☆☆
Decapterus kurroides Bleeker, 1855
Inhabits coastal waters, occurring in schools; similar to *D. tabl* (**9**), including red tail, but lacks a straight section in the lateral line (i.e. between curved anterior part and expanded bony scales on rear portion); found throughout the region; Indo-W. Pacific; to 50 cm.

11. MACKEREL SCAD ☆☆
Decapterus macarellus (Cuvier, 1833)
Inhabits coastal waters, occurring in schools; distinguished by yellow-green tail and 18–32 scales in straight part of lateral line in front of bony scutes; found throughout the region; worldwide tropical seas; to 32 cm and 1.65 kg.

12. INDIAN SCAD ☆☆☆
Decapterus russelli (Rüppell, 1830)
Inhabits coastal waters, occurring in schools; distinguished by clear to dusky tail and 0–4 scales in straight part of lateral line in front of bony scales; also known as Russell's Mackeral Scad; found throughout the region; Indo-W. Pacific; to 38 cm and 1.8 kg.

13. SLENDER SCAD ☆☆
Decapterus macrosoma Bleeker, 1851
Inhabits coastal waters, occurring in schools; distinguished by clear to dusky tail and 14–29 scales in straight part of lateral line in front of bony scutes; found throughout the region; Indo-E. Pacific; to 32 cm.

14. GOLDEN TREVALLY ☆☆☆
Gnathanodon speciosus (Forsskål, 1775)
Inhabits coastal and offshore waters, usually near reefs, sometimes occurring in schools; distinguished by large fleshy lips, lack of discernible teeth (unlike other trevallies) and golden belly; juvenile (not shown) is bright yellow with dark bars and dark tips on tail; found throughout the region; Indo-E. Pacific; to 111 cm and 15 kg.

15. FINNY SCAD ☆☆
Megalaspis cordyla (Linnaeus, 1758)
Inhabits coastal waters; distinguished by series of separate finlets behind dorsal and anal fins and greatly expanded bony scutes along middle of side; found throughout the region; Indo-C. Pacific; to 80 cm.

16. PILOTFISH ☆☆
Naucrates ductor (Linnaeus, 1758)
Inhabits oceanic waters, usually in company with sharks, rays, turtles, or large fishes; juveniles may occur in floating weed or with sea jellies; distinguished by prominent dark bars; found throughout the region; worldwide tropical seas; to 70 cm.

17. BLACK POMFRET
Parastromateus niger (Bloch, 1795)
Inhabits offshore waters of continental shelf, frequently in schools; distinguished by equal-shaped dorsal and anal fin with triangular anterior lobe; colour ranges from silvery-grey to bluish-brown; found throughout the region; Indo-W. Pacific; to 55 cm and 2.55 kg.

18. SILVER TREVALLY ☆☆
Pseudocaranx dentex (Bloch & Schneider, 1801)
Inhabits coastal waters, including estuaries, usually in schools; silvery white to pale bluish with or without diffuse dark bars on side, back greenish or bronzy, a dark spot on upper corner of gill cover and sometimes a yellow stripe on middle of sides; mainly southern half of Australia; largely anti-tropical distribution in Atlantic and Indo-C. Pacific; to 94 cm and 10 kg.

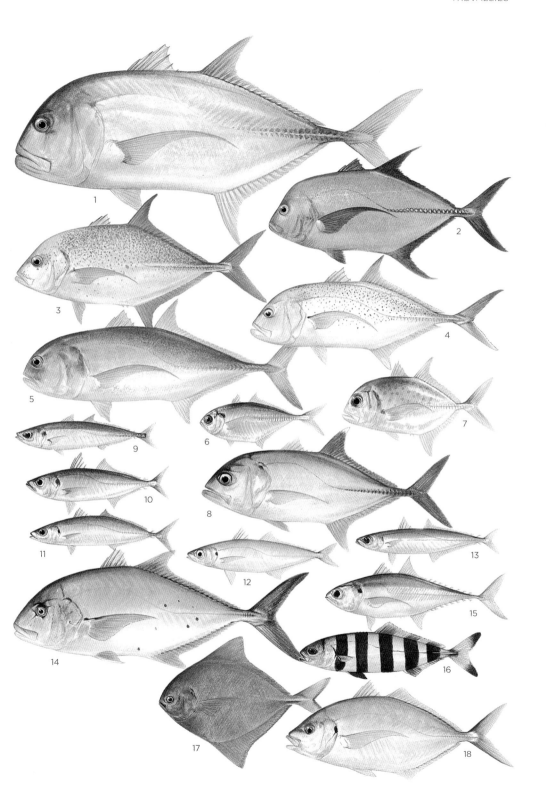

PLATE 39: DOLPHINFISHES AND TREVALLIES

CORYPHAENIDAE

1. MAHI MAHI ☆☆☆
Coryphaena hippurus Linnaeus, 1758
Inhabits mainly oceanic waters well offshore; distinguished by elongate, compressed body, long-based dorsal and anal fins and steep forehead profile; female (not shown) is less colourful and lacks a distinct hump on the forehead; also known as Common Dolphinfish and Dorado; found throughout the region; worldwide tropical and subtropical seas; to 200 cm and 22.4 kg.

CARANGIDAE

2. RAINBOW RUNNER ☆☆☆
Elagatis bipunnulata (Quoy & Gaimard, 1825)
Inhabits coastal waters and offshore reefs, usually in schools; distinguished by slender shape, yellow and blue stripes and isolated finlets on tail base; found throughout the region; worldwide tropical and subtropical seas; to 120 cm and at least 5 kg.

3. NEEDLESKIN QUEENFISH ☆☆
Scomberoides tol (Cuvier, 1832)
Inhabits coastal waters, often in small schools; distinguished by 5–8 round spots, the first 4–5 making contact with lateral line; also known as Slender Leatherskin; found throughout the region; Indo-W. Pacific; to 60 cm.

4. BARRED QUEENFISH ☆☆
Scomberoides tala (Cuvier, 1832)
Inhabits coastal waters; distinguished by 4–8 vertically elongate blotches, most of which make contact with lateral line; also known as Deep Leatherskin; found throughout the region; Indian Ocean and W. edge of Pacific; to 75 cm.

5. GIANT QUEENFISH ☆☆
Scomberoides commersonnianus Lacepède, 1801
Inhabits coastal waters, usually near reefs but occasionally in estuaries; distinguished by 5–8 blotches that are mainly above lateral line (first two may contact lateral line); also known as Leatherskin; found throughout the region; Indo-W. Pacific; to 120 cm and at least 11.4 kg.

6. LESSER QUEENFISH ☆☆
Scomberoides lysan (Forsskål, 1775)
Inhabits coastal waters, often in schools; distinguished by double row of 6–8 dark spots on side; found throughout the region; Indo-C. Pacific; to 70 cm.

7. OXEYE SCAD ☆☆
Selar boops (Cuvier, 1833)
Inhabits coastal waters in large schools; distinguished by large eye covered over by clear fleshy eyelid except for central portion, and by yellow or bronze hue on back; found throughout the region; W. Pacific and E. Indian Ocean; to 25 cm.

8. BIGEYE SCAD ☆☆
Selar crumenophthalmus (Bloch, 1793)
Inhabits coastal waters in large schools; similar to *S. boops* (**7**), but lacks bronze or yellow hue, instead usually has broad yellowish mid-lateral stripe; found throughout the region; worldwide tropical seas; to 30 cm.

9. YELLOWSTRIPE SCAD ☆☆
Selaroides leptolepis (Cuvier, 1833)
Inhabits coastal waters forming large schools over soft sand or mud bottoms; similar to *Selar boops* (**7**) and *Selar crumenophthalmus* (**8**), but has smaller plate-like scales (scutes) along rear part of lateral line, lacks teeth in upper jaw and has clear fleshy eyelid covering rear half of eye only; found throughout the region; N. Indian Ocean and W. edge of Pacific; to 20 cm.

10. BLACKSPOTTED DART ☆☆
Trachinotus baillonii (Lacepède, 1801)
Inhabits coastal waters, frequently in surge off sandy beaches; distinguished by strongly forked tail and 1–5 small black spots along middle of sides; found throughout the region; Indo-C. Pacific; to 54 cm.

11. SNUBNOSED DART ☆☆
Trachinotus blochii (Lacepède, 1801)
Inhabits coastal waters, frequently in surge off sandy beaches; distinguished by strongly forked tail, broadly rounded snout profile and lack of spots on side; found throughout the region; Indo-C. Pacific; to 65 cm and at least 9 kg.

12. COMMON DART ☆☆
Trachinotus botla (Shaw, 1803)
Inhabits coastal waters, frequently in surge off sandy beaches; distinguished by strongly forked tail and 1–5 large spots along middle of side; found throughout the region; northern W. Australia, widespread Indian Ocean; to 61 cm and at least 3.5 kg.

13. BLACKBANDED AMBERJACK ☆☆
Seriolina nigrofasciata (Rüppell, 1829)
Inhabits oceanic waters usually well offshore; distinguished by forward-slanting dark bars or large blotches arranged in ventral rows; found throughout the region; Indo-W. Pacific; to 70 cm.

14. HIGHFIN AMBERJACK ☆☆
Seriola rivoliana Valenciennes, 1833
Inhabits oceanic waters usually well offshore, occasionally visiting coastal areas; distinguished by diagonal dark band above eye and has deeper body than other *Seriola*; found throughout the region; worldwide tropical and temperate seas; to 70 cm.

15. YELLOWTAIL KINGFISH ☆☆
Seriola lalandi Valenciennes, 1833
Inhabits coastal and offshore waters, sometimes in schools; similar to *S. dumerili* (**16**), but has narrower upper jaw and yellow tail; found throughout the region; worldwide temperate and tropical seas; to 180 cm and at least 47 kg.

16. AMBERJACK ☆☆
Seriola dumerili (Risso, 1810)
Inhabits mainly offshore waters in the vicinity of reefs, sometimes adjacent to drop-offs; similar to *S. lalandi* (**15**), but lacks yellow tail and rear part of jaw broadly expanded; found throughout the region; also known as the Allied Kingfish; Atlantic and Indo-C. Pacific; to 188 cm and at least 39.5 kg.

PLATE 40: TREVALLIES, PONYFISHES AND MISCELLANEOUS FAMILIES

CARANGIDAE

1. SILVERMOUTH TREVALLY ☆☆
Ulua aurochs (Ogilby, 1915)
Inhabits coastal waters; distinguished by extremely long gill rakers that project into mouth along side of tongue, and prominent chin which protrudes well ahead of upper jaw in older specimens (not shown), similar to *U. mentalis* (**2**), but has longer dorsal fin filament, diffuse dark bars on side and deeper body; N. Australia and New Guinea; to 50 cm.

2. LONGRAKER TREVALLY ☆☆
Ulua mentalis (Cuvier, 1833)
Inhabits coastal waters; similar to *U. aurochs* (**1**), but has shorter dorsal fin filament, lacks broad diffuse bars on side (may have narrower chevron-shaped ones) and body shape is slightly more slender; found throughout the region; Indo-W. Pacific; to 90 cm.

3. WHITEMOUTH TREVALLY ☆☆
Uraspis uraspis (Günther, 1860)
Inhabits coastal waters; distinguished by white tongue and floor of mouth vividly contrasted against rest of mouth, which is blue-black, also general colouration of body and fins dusky to black shading to grey on lower part of body; found throughout the region; Indo-W. Pacific; to 30 cm.

MALACANTHIDAE

4. FLAGTAIL BLANQUILLO
Malacanthus brevirostris Guichenot, 1848
Inhabits sand and rubble areas in the vicinity of coral reefs, often occurs in pairs; distinguished by elongate shape with long-based dorsal and anal fins and pair of dark stripes on tail; N.W. Australia, Great Barrier Reef and throughout S.E. Asia; Indo-C. Pacific; to 30 cm.

POMATOMIDAE

5. TAILOR ☆☆☆
Pomatomus saltatrix (Linnaeus, 1766)
Inhabits estuaries and inshore waters; related to trevallies and amberjacks, but has larger, more obvious scales and very sharp teeth; colour silvery with green or bluish tinge; southern half of Australia, barely penetrating tropical latitudes; temperate and subtropical Atlantic and Indo-W. Pacific; to 120 cm and at least 12 kg.

RACHYCENTRIDAE

6. COBIA ☆☆☆
Rachycentron canadum (Linnaeus, 1766)
Inhabits coastal waters; distinguished by white stripe on side (may fade after death) and very small dorsal spines; also known as Black Kingfish and Sergeant Fish; found throughout the region; Atlantic and Indo-C. Pacific; to 202 cm and 61.5 kg.

ECHENEIDAE

7. SHARKSUCKER ☆☆☆
Echeneis naucrates Linnaeus, 1758
Inhabits inshore reefs and offshore oceanic waters; distinguished by striped pattern and flattened head with sucking-disk structure on top; disc is used for attaching itself to larger fishes such as sharks, rays and mackerels; found throughout the region; worldwide temperate and tropical seas; to 100 cm.

8. REMORA
Remora remora (Linnaeus, 1758)
Inhabits coastal and oceanic waters; similar in shape and with same sucking-disk apparatus as *Echeneis naucrates* (**7**), but lacks stripes and is overall brownish-black to grey in colour; found throughout the region; worldwide temperate and tropical seas; to 45 cm.

MENIDAE

9. RAZOR MOONFISH ☆☆
Mene maculata (Bloch & Schneider, 1801)
Inhabits deeper coastal waters, sometimes enters estuaries; distinguished by oval shape, protrusible jaws, very low dorsal and anal fins and silvery colour; found throughout the region; Indo-W. Pacific; to 24 cm.

LEIOGNATHIDAE

10. TOOTHED PONYFISH
Gazza minuta (Bloch, 1795)
Inhabits coastal waters to 40 m depth; distinguished from other ponyfishes on this page by canine-like teeth in jaws; found throughout the region; Indo-W. Pacific; to 14 cm.

11. ORANGEFIN PONYFISH
Photopectoralis bindus (Valenciennes, 1835)
Inhabits coastal waters to 40 m depth, occurs in schools; distinguished by protrusible jaws and black-edged orange tip of spiny dorsal fin; found throughout the region; Indo-W. Pacific; to 11 cm.

12. COMMON PONYFISH
Leiognathus equulus (Forsskål, 1775)
Inhabits coastal waters, sometimes enters estuaries, occurs in schools; distinguished by protrusible jaws and thin vertical lines on back; *L. splendens* (not shown) is similar, but has a black tip on the spiny dorsal fin; found throughout the region; Indo-W. Pacific; to 24 cm.

13. ELONGATE PONYFISH
Equulites elongatus (Günther, 1874)
Inhabits coastal waters to 40 m depth, occurs in schools; distinguished by protrusible jaws and very elongate shape; found throughout the region; Indo-W. Pacific; to 12 cm.

14. WHIPFIN PONYFISH
Equulites leuciscus (Günther, 1860)
Inhabits coastal waters, occurs in schools; distinguished by protrusible jaws, elongate filament on spiny dorsal fin and dark vermiculations on back; *L. moretoniensis* (not shown) has similar shape and markings, but has small scales on the cheek (versus no scales); *L. fasciatus* (not shown) is also similar, but has dark vertical lines on back and is deeper-bodied; found throughout the region; Indo-W. Pacific; to 12 cm.

15. LONGSPINE PONYFISH
Aurigequula longispinis (Valenciennes, 1835)
Inhabits coastal waters to 40 m depth, occurs in schools; distinguished by protrusible jaws and elongate filaments at front of both dorsal and anal fins; found throughout the region; Indo-W. Pacific; to 16 cm.

16. PUGNOSE PONYFISH
Secutor ruconius (Hamilton, 1822)
Inhabits coastal waters, sometimes entering estuaries and rivers, occurs in schools; distinguished by jaw that when protruded point upwards (those of other ponyfishes on this page point either slightly downwards or straight ahead); found throughout the region; Indo-W. Pacific; to 8 cm.

LOBOTIDAE

17. TRIPLETAIL ☆☆☆☆
Lobotes surinamensis (Bloch, 1790)
Inhabits mangrove estuaries and lower reaches of freshwater streams; distinguished by steep, sloping, humped forehead and large, rounded posterior lobes of dorsal and anal fins that are about equal to the tail in size; found throughout the region; worldwide in tropical and subtropical seas; to 100 cm and at least 7 kg.

PLATE 41: TROPICAL SNAPPERS

LUTJANIDAE

1. SMALLTOOTH JOBFISH   ☆☆☆
Aphareus furca (Lacepède, 1801)
Inhabits reefs and rocky bottoms to at least 100 m depth; distinguished by elongate body shape and deeply forked tail; similar to *A. rutilans* (Plate **43.1**), but has dark margin on edge of cheek and gill cover and body lacks yellow hue; N.W. Australia, Great Barrier Reef and throughout S.E. Asia; Indo-C. Pacific: to 80 cm and at least 4 kg.

2. GREEN JOBFISH   ☆☆☆
Aprion virescens Valenciennes, 1830
Inhabits reef areas to at least 100 m depth; distinguished by dark green to blue-grey colour and dark patches along base of dorsal fin, snout blunter, tail less forked than *A. furca* (**1**); found throughout the region; Indo-C. Pacific; to 100 cm and at least 12 kg.

3. RUBY SNAPPER
Etelis carbunculus Cuvier, 1828   ☆☆☆
Inhabits offshore reefs usually between 90–300 m depth; distinguished from *E. radiosus* (**4**) by brighter red colouration and less forked tail; N.W. Australia, N. Queensland and throughout S.E. Asia; Indo-C. Pacific; to 80 cm.

4. PALE RUBY SNAPPER   ☆☆☆
Etelis radiosus Anderson, 1981
Inhabits rocky offshore reefs, usually between 90–200 m depth; distinguished from *E. carbunculus* (**3**) by pale (pinkish) colour and more forked tail; N.W. Australia, N. Queensland and throughout S.E. Asia; W. Pacific and Indian Ocean; to 60 cm.

5. TANG'S SNAPPER   ☆☆☆
Lipocheilus carnolabrum (Chan, 1970)
Inhabits rocky bottoms of continental shelves between 90–300 m depth; distinguished by thick fleshy protrusion at the front of the upper lip; N.W. Australia, N. Queensland and throughout S.E. Asia; Indo-W. Pacific; to 60 cm.

6. ROSY SNAPPER   ☆☆☆☆
Pristipomoides filamentosus (Valenciennes, 1830)
Inhabits rocky bottoms, mainly between 90–360 m depth; distinguished by rosy colour and elongate tips at rear of dorsal and anal fins; N.W. Australia, N. Queensland and throughout S.E. Asia; Indo-W. Pacific; to 80 cm and at least 6 kg.

7. SHARPTOOTH SNAPPER   ☆☆☆
Pristipomoides typus Bleeker, 1852
Inhabits rocky bottoms between about 40–100 m depth; similar to *P. multidens* (**8**), but lacks orange stripes below eye; N.W. Australia, N. Queensland and throughout S.E. Asia; mainly western Pacific; to 70 cm.

8. GOLDBAND JOBFISH   ☆☆☆
Pristipomoides multidens (Day, 1871)
Inhabits rocky bottoms between 40–200 m depth; similar to *P. typus* (**7**), but has pair of orange stripes below eye; N.W. Australia, N. Queensland and throughout S.E. Asia; Indo-W. Pacific; to 90 cm and at least 6 kg.

9. CHINAMANFISH
Symphorus nematophorus (Bleeker, 1860)
Inhabits inshore coral reefs and deeper offshore areas to at least 50 m; recognised by distinctive shape and olive grey-brown to reddish (when freshly caught) colour of adults, young have elongate filaments on the rear part of the dorsal fin; considered dangerous to eat due to its susceptibility to ciguatera; found throughout the region; mainly western Pacific; to 80 cm and at least 18 kg.

10. MANGROVE JACK   ☆☆☆
Lutjanus argentimaculatus (Forsskål, 1775)
Inhabits estuaries and inshore and offshore reefs to 100 m depth; young and sub-adults found in mangrove estuaries; distinguished from *L. bohar* (**12**) by taller dorsal fin, lack of stripes on side and absence of black on fins, young have pronounced bars; found throughout the region; Indo-W. Pacific; to 120 cm and at least 12 kg.

11. INDONESIAN SNAPPER   ☆☆☆
Lutjanus bitaeniatus (Valenciennes, 1830)
Inhabits deeper offshore reefs between about 40–70 m; distinguished by reddish colouration and absence of stripes, although juvenile has a black stripe along middle of side; N.W. Australia and Indonesia; to 30 cm.

12. RED BASS
Lutjanus bohar (Forsskål, 1775)
Inhabits coral reefs to at least 70 m depth; distinguished by reddish hue, faint stripes on lower side and blackish colour on dorsal and anal fins (also tip of pelvic fins and upper edge of pectoral fins), juveniles and sub-adults with white spot below rear part of dorsal fin; reported to be good eating, but best avoided due to the possibility of ciguatera poisoning; found throughout the region; Indo-C. Pacific; to 75 cm and at least 11 kg.

FISH POISONING

Although relatively few cases of a form of fish poisoning known as ciguatera have been reported from the region, those of us, particularly anglers, who are regular consumers of fresh seafood should be aware of its dangers. This topic is included here because two of the snappers shown on this plate, the Chinamanfish *Symphorus nematophorus* (**9**) and Red Bass *Lutjanus bohar* (**12**), have frequently been implicated in various regions of the Indo-Pacific. The incidence of poisonous fishes is alarmingly high in some areas, particularly around some Polynesian islands. The exact nature of the causative agent has long puzzled scientists. The same species of fish can be poisonous at one locality, but safe to eat from a nearby reef. Apparently the poisonous properties are caused by a toxic dinoflagellate (*Gambierdiscus toxicus*), that lives on dead coral or among benthic algae, and is first consumed by herbivorous fishes, which are eventually eaten by larger predatory fishes. The toxin is apparently accumulative and the largest fishes are potentially the most dangerous. Young and small adults of a particular species may be eaten with impunity while large adults may be toxic.

The symptoms from eating ciguatoxic fish appear from 1 to 10 hours later and range from mild dizziness, diarrhoea and a numb sensation of the lips, hands and fingers to extreme nausea, coma and total respiratory failure causing death. The degree of poisoning depends onthe amount of fish consumed and the concentration of toxin it contains.

1

2

3

4

5

6

7

8

9

9 juv.

10

10 juv.

11 juv.

11

12

12 juv.

PLATE 42: TROPICAL SNAPPERS

LUTJANIDAE

1. CRIMSON SNAPPER ☆☆☆
Lutjanus erythropterus Bloch, 1790
Inhabits trawling grounds and reefs to depths of at least 100 m; similar to *L. malabaricus* (**4**), but head and mouth much smaller; also known as Saddle-tailed Sea Perch; found throughout the region; Indo-W. Pacific; to 100 cm.

2. STRIPEY SNAPPER ☆☆☆
Lutjanus carponotatus (Richardson, 1842)
Inhabits coral reefs in sheltered lagoons and outer reef areas; distinguished by striped pattern; found throughout the region; mainly Indo-Australian Archipelago; to 40 cm.

3. CHECKERED SNAPPER
Lutjanus decussatus (Cuvier, 1828)
Inhabits coral reefs to at least 30 m depth; distinguished by chequered pattern on the upper sides and black spot at the base of the tail; N.W. Australia, Great Barrier Reef and throughout S.E. Asia; mainly Indo-Australian Archipelago; to 30 cm.

4. SADDLETAIL SNAPPER ☆☆☆
Lutjanus malabaricus (Bloch & Schneider, 1801)
Inhabits coastal and offshore reefs, also flat-bottom trawling grounds; similar to *L. erythropterus* (**1**), but head and mouth much larger; also known as Scarlet Sea Perch; found throughout the region; Indo-W. Pacific; to 100 cm and at least 7 kg.

5. YELLOWLINED SNAPPER ☆☆☆
Lutjanus rufolineatus (Valenciennes, 1830)
Inhabits offshore coral reefs to depths of 50 m; distinguished by series of faint yellow stripes on the sides and a deep notch in the rear margin of the cheek, often has dark spot on back; previously confused with *L. boutton* (Plate **43.5**); N.W. Australia, Great Barrier Reef and throughout S.E. Asia; mainly W. Pacific; to 30 cm.

6. BLUESTRIPED SNAPPER ☆☆☆
Lutjanus kasmira (Forsskål, 1775)
Inhabits inshore coral reefs; distinguished from *L. quinquelineatus* (**7**) by its white belly and lack of a fifth blue stripe; found throughout the region; Indo-C. Pacific; to 35 cm.

7. FIVELINE SNAPPER
Lutjanus quinquelineatus (Bloch, 1790)
Inhabits sheltered lagoon reefs and outer reef areas; similar to *L. kasmira* (**6**), but has extra blue stripe on body; also known as Blue-banded Sea Perch; found throughout the region; Indo-W. Pacific; to 38 cm.

8. BLACKSPOT SNAPPER ☆☆☆
Lutjamus fulviflamma (Forsskål, 1775)
Inhabits coral reefs to at least 35 depth; distinguished by yellow stripes on sides and elongate black spot on back, snout blunter than *L. russellii* (**12**); found throughout the region; Indo-C. Pacific; to 35 cm.

9. MAORI SNAPPER ☆☆☆
Lutjanus rivulatus (Cuvier, 1828)
Inhabits inshore coral reefs and also deeper offshore waters; distinguished by 'blubbery' lips and wavy lines on head; found throughout the region; Indo-C. Pacific; to 65 cm.

10. RED EMPEROR ☆☆☆
Lutjartus sebae (Cuvier, 1816)
Inhabits the vicinity of coral reefs, often over adjacent sand and rubble flats; distinguished by shape and overall red-pink colour, juveniles and sub-adults have distinctive pattern of dark bars; juveniles sometimes found among spines of sea urchins; found throughout the region; Indo-W. Pacific; to 100 cm and at least 16 kg.

11. BROWNSTRIPE SNAPPER ☆☆☆
Lutjanus vitta (Quoy & Gaimard, 1824)
Inhabits the vicinity of coral reefs, also flat bottoms with coral outcrops, sponge and sea whips; distinguished by brown or blackish stripe along middle of sides; found throughout the region; Indo-W. Pacific; to 40 cm.

12. MOSES' SNAPPER ☆☆☆
Lutjanus russellii (Bleeker, 1849)
Inhabits inshore rock or coral reefs, also deeper offshore reefs to at least 80 m depth; distinguished by reddish colouration and black spot (sometimes faint) on back, has more pointed snout than *L. fulviflamma* (**8**); found throughout the region; W. Pacific; to 45 cm.

13. BIGEYE SNAPPER ☆☆☆
Lutjanus lutjanus Bloch, 1790
Inhabits offshore coral reefs and trawling grounds to at least 90 m depth; distinguished from *L. vitta* (**11**) by lighter mid-lateral stripe and much narrower space between eye and upper jaw; formerly known as *L. lineolatus*; found throughout the region; Indo-W. Pacific; to 30 cm.

14. DARKTAIL SNAPPER ☆☆☆
Lutjanus lemniscatus (Valenciennes, 1828)
Inhabits inshore coral reefs and deeper offshore reefs; distinguished by blackish tail; found throughout the region; mainly Indo-Australian Archipelago; to 65 cm.

TROPICAL SNAPPERS

The members of the family Lutjanidae are generally known worldwide as snappers. However, this name sometimes causes confusion in Australia, because it is also used for at least two other common fishes belonging to two different families. The common snapper of Australia's southern half belongs to the family Sparidae and is perhaps the best known of the two. The other fish is a member of the emperor family Lethrinidae (Plates 47–48). Although it is officially known as the Spangled Emperor (Plate **47.8**), it is often referred to as North-west Snapper by anglers in Western Australia.

Snappers featured on Plates 41–44 are primarily inhabitants of tropical reefs. Most species are distributed in the Indo-Pacific region, although they also occur in the Atlantic Ocean. *Lutjanus* is by far the largest genus, containing over 70 species, many of which are brightly coloured. They are active predators that feed mainly on fishes, but crabs, shrimps, gastropods, cephalopods and planktonic organisms are also eaten. The larger, deep-bodied snappers (*Lutjamus* for example) usually have well-developed canine teeth, adapted for seizing and holding larger prey items. More slender snappers such as *Pristipomoides* and *Etelis* have weaker dentition and consume a significant amount of plankton. The larger species of *Lutjanus*, particularly the 'red snappers' are favourite angling fishes and also commercially important.

PLATE 43: TROPICAL SNAPPERS

LUTJANIDAE

1. RUSTY JOBFISH ☆☆☆
Aphareus rutilans Cuvier, 1830
Inhabits reefs and rocky bottoms to at least 100 m depth; similar to *A. furca* (Plate **41.1**), but lacks distinct black outline on edge of cheek and gill cover, also has strong yellow hue on body; N.W. Australia, Great Barrier Reef and throughout S.E. Asia; to 80 cm.

2. HUSSAR
Lutjanus adetii (Castelnau, 1873)
Inhabits coral reefs, sometimes forming large daytime aggregations; distinguished by yellow iris, faint oblique lines on back, and yellow mid-lateral stripe; E. Australia, Coral Sea and New Caledonia; to 50 cm.

3. BENGAL SNAPPER
Lutjanus bengalensis (Bloch, 1790)
Inhabits coral reefs between about 10–25 m depth; similar to *L. kasmira* (Plate **42.6**), but lacks faint horizontal lines on belly; W. Indonesia; mainly N. Indian Ocean; to 30 cm.

4. TWOSPOT SNAPPER ☆☆
Lutjanus biguttatus (Valenciennes, 1930)
Inhabits coral reefs between 5–25 m depth, usually seen in rich coral areas of protected lagoons; distinguished by slender shape, mid-lateral white stripe and pair of white spots below dorsal fin; offshore reefs of N. Great Barrier Reef and throughout S.E. Asia; E. Indian and W. Pacific oceans; to 20 cm.

5. MOLUCCAN SNAPPER ☆☆☆
Lutjanus boutton (Lacepède, 1802)
Inhabits coral reefs to at least 20 m depth; found alone or in groups; distinguished by overall pink or reddish hue with yellow lower parts, also has deep notch on rear margin of cheek; E. Indonesia, New Guinea and New Britain; mainly W. Pacific; to 30 cm.

6. EHRENBERG'S SNAPPER ☆☆☆
Lutjanus ehrenbergii (Peters, 1869)
Inhabits coral reefs and inshore areas, sometimes forms aggregations under wharves; similar to *L. fulviflamma* (Plate **42.8**), but has much narrower space between eye and upper jaw and scale rows on the back are parallel to the lateral line instead of rising obliquely; N. Great Barrier Reef and throughout S.E. Asia; Indo-W. Pacific; to 35 cm.

7. BLACKTAIL SNAPPER ☆☆☆
Lutjanus fulvus (Forster, 1801)
Inhabits coral reefs; distinguished by dark tail and soft dorsal fin both of which have a narrow white margin and yellow anal, pelvic and pectoral fins; offshore reefs of N.W. Australia, Great Barrier Reef and throughout S.E. Asia; Indo-C. Pacific; to 40 cm.

8. PADDLETAIL
Lutjanus gibbus (Forsskål, 1775)
Inhabits coral reefs; distinguished by forked caudal fin with rounded lobes, a deep notch in rear margin of cheek and obliquely oriented scale rows both above and below the lateral line; frequently implicated in ciguatera fish poisoning and therefore not recommended for eating; offshore reefs of N.W. Australia, Great Barrier Reef and throughout S.E. Asia; Indo-C. Pacific; to 50 cm.

9. GOLDEN SNAPPER ☆☆☆
Lutjanus johnii (Bloch, 1792)
Inhabits coastal areas, especially where mangroves are prevalent in estuaries and tidal rivers; distinguished by metallic pale yellow to silvery colour with dusky scale edges; smaller fish usually have a round, dark smudge on back below rear half of dorsal fin; also known as Fingermark Sea Perch; found throughout the region; Indo-W. Pacific; to 70 cm.

10. LUNARTAIL SNAPPER ☆☆☆
Lutjanus lunulatus (Park, 1797)
Inhabits coral reefs between about 10–30 m depth; distinguished by black lunar-shaped marking on tail; S.E. Asia, New Guinea, Solomon Islands and Vanuatu; N. Indian Ocean and Indo-Malay and Melanesian archipelagos; to 35 cm.

11. YELLOWFIN SNAPPER ☆☆☆
Lutjanus xanthopinnis Iwatsuki, Tanaka & Allen, 2015
Inhabits coral and rocky reefs between 5–90 m depth; similar to *L. lutjanus* (Plate **42.7**), but space between eye and upper jaw is much wider; fins usually yellow; Indo-Malay Archipelago; W. Pacific; to 30 cm.

12. ONESPOT SNAPPER ☆☆☆
Lutjanus monostigma (Cuvier, 1828)
Inhabits coral reefs; distinguished by overall light grey to yellowish colouration, pinkish head and upper back, no longitudinal stripes — black spot on upper side may be faint or absent in adults; sale of this species is forbidden in Tahiti because of frequent ciguatera poisoning, but usually safe to eat in our region; N.W. Australia, Great Barrier Reef and throughout S.E. Asia; Indo-C. Pacific; to 50 cm.

13. BLACKBANDED SNAPPER ☆☆☆
Lutjanus semicinctus Quoy & Gaimard, 1824
Inhabits coral reefs, usually between 10–30 m depth; distinguished by series of dark bars on side and large dark spot at tail base; N. Great Barrier Reef, Philippines, E. Indonesia and Melanesian archipelago to Tahiti; to 35 cm.

14. TIMOR SNAPPER ☆☆☆
Lutjanus timoriensis (Quoy & Gaimard, 1824)
Inhabits coral reefs, usually below 15 m depth; distinguished by pearl-coloured spot just behind dorsal fin and black axil 'armpit' of pectoral fin; Indo-Malay Archipelago to Samoa; to 50 cm.

15. BLACK-AND-WHITE SNAPPER ☆☆☆
Macolor niger (Forsskål, 1775)
Inhabits coral reefs, most commonly encountered on outer reef slopes to at least 90 m depth; feeds on plankton; distinguished from *M. macularis* (**16**) by juvenile and adult colour pattern differences shown here; N.W. Australia, Great Barrier Reef and throughout S.E. Asia; Indo-C. Pacific; to 60 cm.

16. MIDNIGHT SNAPPER ☆☆☆
Macolor macularis Fowler, 1931
Inhabits coral reefs, usually on outer reef slopes; small juveniles of this species and *M. niger* (**15**) often seen in the vicinity of feather stars (crinoids); feeds on plankton; similar to *M. niger*, but has more spots on back in juveniles and sub-adults, yellow eye and network of bluish lines and spots on head; N.W. Australia, Great Barrier Reef and throughout S.E. Asia; W. Pacific; to 60 cm.

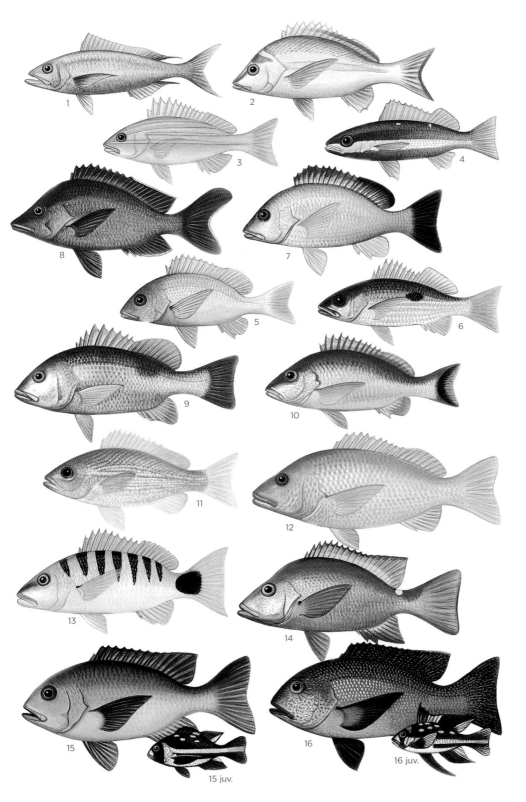

PLATE 44: TROPICAL SNAPPERS AND SWEETLIPS

LUTJANIDAE

1. PINJALO SNAPPER ☆☆☆
Pinjalo pinjalo (Bleeker, 1850)
Inhabits reefs and rocky bottoms to depths of 60 m; similar to *P. lewisi* (not shown), but lacks pearly bar on caudal peduncle and has yellowish hue on pelvic and anal fins; S.E. Asia and New Guinea; Indo-W. Pacific; to 50 cm.

2. SAILFIN SNAPPER ☆☆☆
Symphorichthys spilurus (Günther, 1874)
Inhabits sand bottoms in the vicinity of coral reefs; distinguished by unusual shape, elevated dorsal fin and black saddle on upper tail base; juvenile has white-edged black stripe on middle of side; offshore reefs of W. Australia, Great Barrier Reef and throughout S.E. Asia; mainly W. Pacific; to 60 cm.

3. SORDID SNAPPER ☆☆☆
Paracaesio sordida Abe & Shinohara, 1962
Inhabits rocky bottoms and steep outer reef slopes between 30–200 m; distinguished by blue colouration and reddish (appears brown underwater) lower caudal fin lobe; S.E. Asia to Melanesian Archipelago; E. Indian Ocean and W. Pacific; to 40 cm.

4. FALSE FUSILIER ☆☆☆
Paracaesio xanthura (Bleeker, 1869)
Inhabits rocky bottoms and outer reef slopes between about 20–150 m; distinguished by brilliant yellow back and tail; similar to some species of fusiliers (Plates 45–46), but has 10–11 soft dorsal rays and 8–9 soft anal rays (versus 14–16 and 11–12 respectively for fusiliers); N.W. Australia, Great Barrier Reef and throughout S.E. Asia; Indo-W. Pacific; to 40 cm.

5. GOLDFLAG SNAPPER ☆☆☆
Pristipomoides auricilla (Jordan, Evermann, & Tanaka, 1927)
Inhabits rocky bottoms in about 90–360 m depth; distinguished by narrow yellow bars on body and yellow upper lobe on tail; S.E. Asia and Melanesian Archipelago; mainly W. Pacific; to 45 cm.

6. GOLDENEYE SNAPPER ☆☆☆
Pristipomoides flavipinnis Shinohara, 1963
Inhabits rocky bottoms in about 90–360 m depth; distinguished by yellowish dorsal fin, yellow edge on tail and yellow iris; N. Queensland and Indo-Malay Archipelago to Samoa; mainly W. Pacific; to 60 cm.

7. OBLIQUE-BANDED SNAPPER ☆☆☆
Pristipomoides zonatus (Valenciennes, 1830)
Inhabits rocky bottoms in about 70–300 m depth; distinguished by broad yellow bands on red background colour; N. Queensland and Indo-Malay Archipelago to Tahiti; Indo-W. Pacific; to 50 cm.

HAEMULIDAE

8. STRIPED SWEETLIPS ☆☆
Plectorhinchus lessonii (Cuvier, 1830)
Inhabits coral reefs; distinguished by combination of dark stripes on upper side and spots on fins, also has prominent dark spot on upper pectoral fin base; *P. diagrammus* is a synonym; Great Barrier Reef and throughout S.E. Asia to Melanesian Archipelago; W. Pacific; to 40 cm.

9. SILVER SWEETLIPS ☆☆
Diagramma picta (Thunberg, 1792)
Inhabits sandy areas in the vicinity of coral reefs; undergoes remarkable transformation in shape and colour with increased growth, which is true of other sweetlips; Indo-Malay Archipelago; mainly W. Pacific; to 90 cm.

10. ORIENTAL SWEETLIPS ☆☆
Plectorhinchus vittatus (Linnaeus, 1758)
Inhabits coral reefs; similar to *P. lineatus* (**13**), but black stripes are horizontal rather than oblique; throughout S.E. Asia to New Guinea; Indo-W. Pacific; to 50 cm.

11. GIANT SWEETLIPS ☆☆
Plectorhinchus obscurus (Günther, 1872)
Inhabits coral reefs; usually recognised by its large size, blubbery lips and black markings on fins; *P. harrawayi* is a synonym; Great Barrier Reef and throughout S.E. Asia to Melanesian Archipelago; Indo-W. Pacific; to at least 100 cm.

12. DOTTED SWEETLIPS ☆☆
Plectorhinchus picus (Cuvier, 1828)
Inhabits coral reefs; distinguished by pattern of small dark spots on head, body and fins, also dark upper lip; juvenile has distinctive black and white pattern; Great Barrier Reef and throughout S.E. Asia to Melanesian Archipelago; Indo-W. Pacific; to 50 cm.

13. OBLIQUE-BANDED SWEETLIPS ☆☆
Plectorhinchus lineatus (Linnaeus, 1758)
Inhabits coral reefs; distinguished by combination of oblique black bands, blackspotted yellow fins and yellow lips; *P. goldmanni* is a synonym; Great Barrier Reef and throughout S.E. Asia to Melanesian Archipelago; W. Pacific; to 50 cm.

DEEPWATER SNAPPERS

Some of the best eating fishes live well below the depths penetrated by most recreational anglers, but their existence is no secret to villagers in South-East Asia, who have utilised this food source for centuries. Volcanic island shores drop quickly into deep water throughout the Malay-Indonesian-Melanesian Archipelago. In many cases it requires only a few hundred metres of paddling in a small boat to reach this habitat. But getting there is only half the battle. Fishers utilise extraordinary lengths of monofilament handline, weighted with rocks. Depths between 50–100 m are routinely fished, but in some cases much deeper water is penetrated. However, as the depth increases, so does the risk of sharks. If the exposure time after hooking a fish is lengthy, say 5 or 10 minutes, the catch will certainly be devoured by sharks on the way up.

Snappers (also called jobfishes) in the genera *Paracaesio* and *Pristipomoides* are prime targets of handline anglers. Their mild-tasting flesh has a delicate consistency and is highly prized. At Hawaii and other Pacific islands the Rosy Snapper *Pristipomoides filamentosus* (Plate **41.6**) is captured commercially in 100–300 m depth with handlines and bottom longlines that are hauled with motorised winches. This fish, locally known as Opakapaka, retails for more than US$25 per kilogram in Hawaii. In Australia, stocks of this fish and several other deep-dwelling snappers have only recently been discovered on the edge of the continental shelf.

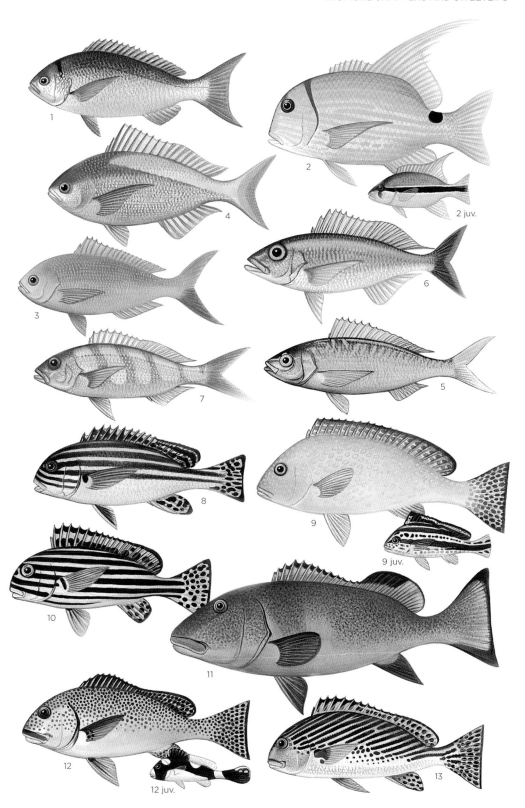

1

2

2 juv.

4

6

3

7

5

8

9

9 juv.

10

11

12

12 juv.

13

PLATE 45: SWEETLIPS, FUSILIERS AND BANJOFISHES

HAEMULIDAE ☆☆

1. BLUE BASTARD SWEETLIPS
Plectorhinchus caeruleonothus Johnson & Wilmer, 2015
Inhabits caves and crevices of coral reefs; similar to
P. gibbosus (**5**), but distinguished by 11 or 12 dorsal spines
(versus 13 or 14); N.W. Australia to Great Barrier Reef;
to 60 cm.

2. SPOTTED SWEETLIPS ☆☆
Plectorhinchus chaetodontoides Lacepède, 1801
Inhabits caves and crevices of coral reefs; distinguished by
spotted pattern; juvenile has peculiar undulating motion;
N.W. Australia, Great Barrier Reef and throughout S.E. Asia;
Indo-W. Pacific; to 60 cm and at least 7 kg.

3. MANYLINE SWEETLIPS ☆☆
Plectorhinchus multivittatus (Macleay, 1878)
Inhabits coral reefs; distinguished by yellow spots arranged
in horizontal rows and yellow fins; N.W. Australia and
throughout S.E. Asia; Indo-W. Pacific; to 50 cm.

4. GOLDLINED SWEETLIPS ☆☆
Plectorhinchus chrysotaenia (Bleeker, 1855)
Inhabits coral reefs; distinguished by yellow stripes on head
and sides; *P. celebicus* is a synonym; N.W. Australia, Great
Barrier Reef and throughout S.E. Asia; W. Pacific; to 40 cm.

5. BROWN SWEETLIPS ☆☆
Plectorhinchus gibbosus (Lacepède, 1802)
Inhabits coral reefs; similar to *P. caeruleonothus* (**1**), but
distinguished by 13 or 14 dorsal spines (versus 11 or 12);
formerly known as *P. nigrus*; found throughout the region;
Indo-W. Pacific: to 60 cm and at least 6 kg.

6. PAINTED SWEETLIPS ☆☆
Diagramma labiosum Macleay, 1883
Inhabits coral reefs; sometimes seen in schools, adults
distinguished by silvery body colour, smaller specimens have
spots or stripes, but differs from *Plectorhinchus chaetodontoides*
(**2**) in having 9 or 10 dorsal spines (versus 12) and lacks notch
in dorsal fin profile; found throughout the region; Indo-W.
Pacific; to 90 cm and at least 6 kg.

7. RIBBON SWEETLIPS ☆☆
Plectorhinchus polytaenia (Bleeker, 1852)
Inhabits coral reefs; distinguished by vivid pattern of
dark-edged orange and white stripes; N.W. Australia and
throughout S.E. Asia; Indo-Australian Archipelago;
to 40 cm.

8. SPOTTED JAVELINFISH ☆☆☆
Pomadasys kaakan (Cuvier, 1830)
Inhabits estuaries and coastal waters usually over sand or
mud bottoms; distinguished by series of spots arranged in
vertical rows on upper side and spots on dorsal fin; formerly
known as *P. hasta*; found throughout the region; Indo-W.
Pacific; to 38 cm and 6 kg.

9. BLOTCHED JAVELINFISH ☆☆☆
Pomadasys maculatus (Bloch, 1793)
Inhabits estuaries and coastal waters usually over sand or
mud bottoms, distinguished by large dark blotches mainly
on upper sides; found throughout the region; Indo-W.
Pacific; to 45 cm.

10. GOLDSPOTTED SWEETLIPS ☆☆
Plectorhinchus flavomaculatus (Cuvier, 1830)
Inhabits coral reefs and subtropical rocky reefs; similar to
P. multivittatus (**3**), but lacks yellow on fins and has small
dark spots on dorsal fin and tail; found throughout the
region; Indo-W. Pacific; to 50 cm and 3 kg.

HAPALOGENYIDAE

11. LINED JAVELINFISH ☆☆☆
Hapalogenys kishinouyei Smith & Pope, 1906
Inhabits coastal waters, usually over mud or sand bottoms;
distinguished by brown stripes on upper part of back; N.W.
Australia, Indonesia and Philippines; W. Pacific; to 30 cm.

CAESIONIDAE

12. YELLOWTAIL FUSILIER ☆☆☆
Caesio cuning (Bloch, 1791)
Inhabits coral reefs, forming midwater schools; distinguished
by yellow tail, similar to *C. lunaris* (**13**), but lacks black tips of
tail; found throughout the region; Indo-W. Pacific; to 43 cm.

13. LUNAR FUSILIER ☆☆☆
Caesio lunaris Cuvier, 1830
Inhabits coral reefs, forming midwinter schools; similar to
C. cuning (**12**), but has blue tail with black tips; N.W.
Australia, Great Barrier Reef and throughout S.E. Asia;
Indo-W. Pacific; to 38 cm.

14. DOUBLELINE FUSILIER ☆☆
Pterocaesio digramma (Bleeker, 1864)
Inhabits coral reefs, forming mid-water schools;
distinguished from *C. cuning* (**12**) and *C. lunaris* (**13**)
by more slender shape and pair of yellow stripes on upper
side; found throughout the region; to 28 cm.

BANJOSIDAE

15. BANJOFISH
Banjos banjos (Richardson, 1846)
Inhabits coastal waters usually over sand bottoms;
distinguished by stout dorsal and anal spines, angular
forehead and black margin on soft dorsal and caudal fins;
found throughout the region; Indo-W. Pacific; to 30 cm.

SWEETLIPS AND RELATIVES

Most of the fishes on Plate 45 belong to the family
Haemulidae, commonly known as Grunts. Most
members of this family found in reef habitats
in the region belong to the genus *Plectorhinchus*
and are referred to as Sweetlips. Perhaps the
most notable aspect of these fishes, besides
their use as food, is the dramatic changes which
many of the species undergo. Juveniles often
exhibit striking patterns that gradually change
with advancing age. Two examples (**2** and **6**)
of these transformations are shown. The young
of *Plectorhinchus chaetodontoides* is thought to
mimic unpalatable soft-bodied invertebrates such
as nudibranchs or turbellarians and thus enjoy
some measure of freedom from predation. Young
grunts feed on zooplankton, whereas adults eat a
variety of benthic invertebrates. Maximum size is
about 1 m total length, but many species are under
40–50 cm. Worldwide the family contains about
175 species and is represented in all tropical seas.

Fusilers in the family Caesionidae are closely
related to snappers (Plates 41–44). The family
contains 20 species which are distributed across the
Indo-Pacific region. They frequently form schools
containing up to several hundred individuals that
feed in mid water on plankton above coral reefs.

1

2

2 juv.

3

4

5

6

7

6 subadult

6 juv.

8

9

11

12

13

14

15

10

PLATE 46: FUSILIERS AND TILEFISHES

CAESIONIDAE

1. BLUE FUSILIER ☆☆
Caesio teres Seale, 1906
Inhabits coral reefs, forming mid-water schools; distinguished by yellow area encompassing dorsal fin, upper back and tail; offshore reefs of N.W. Australia; Great Barrier Reef and throughout S.E. Asia; Indo-C. Pacific; to 40 cm.

2. YELLOWBACK FUSILIER ☆☆
Caesio xanthonota Bleeker, 1853
Inhabits coral reefs, forming mid-water schools; similar to *C. teres* (1), but yellow area on back more extensive, extending forward onto head; S. Indonesia; mainly Indian Ocean; to 40 cm.

3. GOLDBAND FUSILIER ☆☆
Caesio caerulaurea Lacepède, 1801
Inhabits coral reefs, forming mid-water schools; distinguished by yellow stripe above lateral line and dark streak along edge of upper and lower lobe of tail; N.W. Australia, Great Barrier Reef and throughout S.E. Asia; Indo-W. Pacific; to 35 cm.

4. THREESTRIPE FUSILIER ☆☆
Pterocaesio trilineata Carpenter, 1987
Inhabits coral reefs, forming mid-water schools; distinguished by trio of alternating dark and light stripes on upper back; offshore reefs of N.W. Australia, Great Barrier Reef, Philippines and E. Indonesia; W. Pacific; to 20 cm.

5. BIGTAIL FUSILIER ☆☆
Pterocaesio marri Schultz, 1953
Inhabits coral reefs, forming mid-water schools; distinguished by pair of thin yellow stripes on side, the lower covering lateral line for most of its length; Great Barrier Reef and throughout S.E. Asia; Indo-C. Pacific; to 25 cm.

6. NEON FUSILIER ☆☆
Pterocaesio tile (Cuvier, 1830)
Inhabits outer reef slopes, forming mid-water schools; distinguished by dark stripe on upper side and neon-blue band on middle of sides, also has dark streak on each lobe of tail; offshore reefs of N.W. Australia, Great Barrier Reef and throughout S.E. Asia; Indo-C. Pacific; to 30 cm.

7. WIDE-BAND FUSILIER ☆☆
Pterocaesio lativittata Carpenter, 1987
Inhabits coral reefs, forming mid-water schools; distinguished by broad yellow stripe on middle of side and dark tips on tail; Indo-Malay Archipelago to New Guinea; C. and E. Indian Ocean and W. Pacific; to 20 cm.

8. RANDALL'S FUSILIER ☆☆
Pterocaesio randalli Carpenter, 1987
Inhabits coral reefs, forming mid-water schools; distinguished by elongate blotch of golden yellow on anterior part of body; Indo-Malay Archipelago; to 25 cm.

9. ONE-STRIPE FUSILIER ☆☆
Pterocaesio tessellata Carpenter, 1987
Inhabits coral reefs, forming mid-water schools; distinguished by narrow yellow stripe along lateral line, dusky scale edges giving appearance of wavy stripes on side and dark tips on tail; Indo-Malay and Melanesian archipelagos; E. Indian Ocean and W. Pacific; to 25 cm.

10. YELLOWBAND FUSILIER ☆☆
Pterocaesio chrysozona (Cuvier, 1830)
Inhabits coral reefs, forming mid-water schools; similar to *P. lativittata* (7), but has narrower yellow stripe that is mainly below lateral line (except on tail base); found throughout the region; Indo-W. Pacific; to 21 cm.

11. BANANA FUSILIER ☆☆
Pterocaesio pisang (Bleeker, 1853)
Inhabits coral reefs, forming mid-water schools; distinguished by lack of yellow stripe on side and dark (often red) tips on tail, overall colouration is sometimes reddish; Indo-Malay and Melanesian archipelagos; Indo-W. Pacific; to 21 cm.

12. MOTTLED FUSILIER ☆☆
Dipterygonatus balteatus (Valenciennes, 1830)
Inhabits coral reefs, forming mid-water schools; distinguished by small size, very slender shape and narrow, tan-coloured stripe just above lateral line of light, wavy lines immediately above, also lack of dark tips on tail; found throughout the region; Indo-W. Pacific; to 14 cm.

13. SLENDER FUSILIER ☆
Gymnocaesio gymnoptera (Bleeker, 1856)
Inhabits coral reefs, forming mid-water schools; similar in appearance to some species of *Pterocaesio*, but lacks scales on dorsal and anal fins; Indo-Malay and Melanesian archipelagos; Indo-W. Pacific; to 18 cm.

MALACANTHIDAE

14. BLUE BLANQUILLO ☆☆
Malacanthus latovittatus (Lacepède, 1801)
Inhabits sand-rubble bottoms, usually near edge of coral reefs; distinguished by elongate shape, bluish colouration and broad black stripe which extends onto tail; offshore reefs of W. Australia, Great Barrier Reef and throughout S.E. Asia; Indo-C. Pacific; to 35 cm.

15. YELLOWSPOTTED TILEFISH
Hoplolatilus fourmanoiri Smith, 1963
Inhabits silt-sand bottoms in 40–60 m depth; like other members of the genus it is frequently found in pairs that share a burrow; distinguished by light grey body with scattered yellow patches on head and body, a large dark 'ear-spot' and longitudinal nearly triangular black spot on middle of tail; also yellow variety formerly considered as separate species, *H. luteus*; South China Sea to Solomon Islands; to 14 cm.

16. GREY TILEFISH
Hoplolatilus cuniculus Randall & Dooley, 1974
Inhabits sand-rubble bottoms, usually between 25–100 m depth; retreats to sandy burrow if disturbed; colour entirely grey; Great Barrier Reef and throughout S.E. Asia; Indo-W. Pacific; to 15 cm.

17. BLUEHEAD TILEEFISH
Hoplolatilus starcki Randall & Dooley, 1974
Inhabits steep outer reef slopes below about 20 m depth, often found in pairs; retreats to sandy burrow if disturbed; distinguished by slender shape, blue head and forked yellow tail; young fish entirely blue; offshore reefs of W. Australia, Great Barrier Reef and throughout S.E. Asia; W. and C. Pacific; to 15 cm.

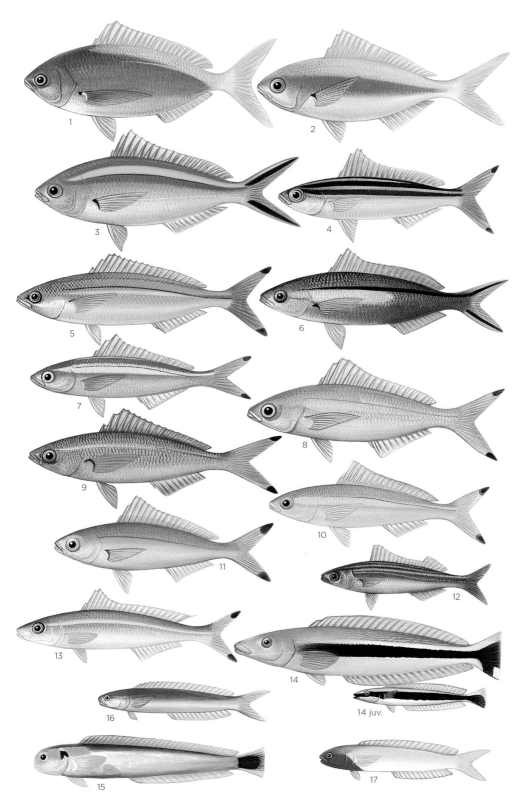

PLATE 47: EMPERORS AND BREAMS

LETHRINIDAE

1. BIGEYE SEABREAM ☆☆☆
Monotaxis grandoculis (Forsskål, 1775)
Inhabits coral reefs, frequently over adjacent sand or rubble areas; distinguished by large eye and bluntly rounded snout, juvenile with dark bars that are reduced to saddles on back of adults; found throughout the region; Indo-C. Pacific; to 60 cm.

2. SWALLOWTAIL SEABREAM ☆☆
Gymnocranius elongatus Senta, 1973
Inhabits sand bottoms and trawling grounds; distinguished by 5 narrow bars on side and strongly forked tail; found throughout the region; E. Indian Ocean and W. Pacific; to 18 cm.

3. GREY SEABREAM ☆☆
Gymnocranius griseus (Schlegel, 1844)
Inhabits sand bottoms and trawling grounds; similar to *G. elongatus* (2), but bars generally wider and more diffuse and tail not as forked; N.W. Australia and throughout S.E. Asia; mainly W. Pacific; to 35 cm.

4. ROBINSON'S SEABREAM ☆☆☆
Gymnocranius grandoculis (Valenciennes, 1830)
Inhabits sand bottoms and trawling grounds; distinguished by wavy blue lines on cheek and snout; also known as Bluelined Seabream; found throughout the region; Indo-W. Pacific; to 80 cm and at least 5 kg.

5. LONGNOSE EMPEROR ☆☆☆
Lethrinus olivaceus Valenciennes, 1830
Inhabits coral reefs; distinguished by long painted snout and overall greyish colour; found throughout the region; Indo-C. Pacific; to 100 cm and 10 kg.

6. REDTHROAT EMPEROR ☆☆☆☆
Lethrinus miniatus (Forster, 1801)
Inhabits coral reefs; distinguished by orange area around eyes, bright red dorsal fin and red patch at base of pectoral fin; sometimes a series of dark bars on side; formerly known as *L. chrysostomus*; N. Australia, Coral Sea, New Caledonia and Ryukyu Is. to Taiwan; to 90 cm and at least 7 kg.

7. GRASS EMPEROR ☆☆☆☆
Lethrinus laticaudis Alleyne & Macleay, 1877
Inhabits coral reefs and adjacent sand-rubble areas; similar to *L. nebulosus* (8), but has blue spots (versus blue bars) on cheek, whitish oblique bar behind eye and brownish band from eye to mouth; often assumes barred pattern when under stress; S. Indonesia, N. Australia, New Guinea and Solomon Islands; to 80 cm.

8. SPANGLED EMPEROR ☆☆☆☆
Lethrinus nebulosus (Forsskål, 1775)
Inhabits coral reefs, usually over adjacent sandy areas; distinguished by blue spots on scales, similar to *L. laticaudis* (7), but has blue bars (versus spots) on cheek and lacks other marks on head as described above; also known as Northwest Snapper; found throughout the region; Indo-W. Pacific; to 86 cm and 6.5 kg.

9. BLUELINED EMPEROR ☆☆☆☆
Lethrinus sp.
Inhabits coastal reefs, usually over adjacent sand or rubble areas; similar to *L. laticaudis* (7) and *L. nebulosus* (8), but has dark streak on each scale instead of blue spots and has short blue lines radiating from eye of which several cross forehead and connect with opposite eye; an undescribed species; N. Australia; to 60 cm.

10. THREADFIN EMPEROR ☆☆
Lethrinus genivittatus Valenciennes, 1830
Inhabits sand-weed areas, sometimes in estuaries; distinguished by dark blotch above pectoral fin and elongate filament near front of dorsal fin, also known as Longspine Emperor and Lancer; found throughout the region; E. Indian Ocean and W. Pacific; to 25 cm.

11. REDSPOT EMPEROR ☆☆☆
Lethrinus lentjan (Lacepède, 1802)
Inhabits sandy areas next to coral reefs; distinguished by pale spots on scales, red margin on gill cover and red spot at base of pectoral fin; head of fresh-caught specimens usually turns to purple colour; also known as Pink-eared Emperor; found throughout the region; Indo-W. Pacific; to 50 cm.

12. SPOTCHEEK EMPEROR ☆☆☆
Lethrinus rubrioperculatus Sato, 1978
Inhabits coral reefs and trawling grounds; distinguished by elongate shape, and red or brown blotch on upper margin of gill cover; colour varies from uniform greyish to blotchy pattern as shown (most emperors can quickly assume a similar pattern); found throughout the region; Indo-C. Pacific; to 50 cm.

13. VARIEGATED EMPEROR ☆☆
Lethrinus variegatus Valenciennes, 1830
Inhabits sand-weed areas near coral reefs; distinguished by elongate shape and blotchy pattern with faint crossbands on tail, similar to *L. rubrioperculatus* (12), but lacks blotch on upper gill cover; found throughout the region; Indo-W. Pacific; to 20 cm.

SPARIDAE

14. NORTHWEST BLACK BREAM ☆☆☆
Acanthopagrus palmaris (Whitley, 1935)
Inhabits coastal reefs, sometimes in estuaries; similar to *A. latus* (15), but is generally darker and lacks yellow on fins; N.W. Australia only; to 40 cm.

15. WESTERN YELLOWFIN BREAM ☆☆☆
Acanthopagrus latus (Houttuyn, 1782)
Inhabits coastal reefs, frequently in schools; similar to *A. palmaris* (14), but lighter in colour and with yellow fins; found throughout the region; N.W. Australia and S.E. Asia; N. Indian Ocean and W. Pacific; to 45 cm.

16. FRYPAN BREAM ☆☆
Argyrops spinifer (Forsskål, 1775)
Inhabits coastal waters and deeper trawling grounds; distinguished by filamentous dorsal spines and angular forehead profile; found throughout the region; Indo-W. Pacific; to 65 cm and at least 2 kg.

17. YELLOWBACK BREAM ☆☆☆
Evynnis tumifrons (Temminck & Schlegel, 1843)
Inhabits trawling grounds; similar to *Argyrops spinifer* (16), but lacks filamentous dorsal spines and forehead is more rounded; N.W. Australia and S. Indonesia; mainly W. Pacific; to 35 cm.

PLATE 48: EMPERORS

LETHRINIDAE

1. GOLDSPOT SEABREAM
Gnathodentex aureolineatus (Lacepède, 1802)
Inhabits coral reefs, sometimes seen in groups; distinguished by orange-brown stripes on side and yellow patch below rear part of dorsal fin; Great Barrier Reef, offshore reefs of W. Australia and throughout S.E. Asia; Indo-C. Pacific; to 30 cm.

2. COLLAR SEABREAM
Gymnocranius audleyi Ogilby, 1916
Inhabits sand-rubble fringe of coral reefs; distinguished by pale-edged dark mark above and behind eye; S. Great Barrier Reef; S. Queensland only; to 40 cm.

3. PADDLETAIL SEABREAM
Gymnocranius euanus Günther, 1879
Inhabits sand-rubble fringe of coral reefs; distinguished by dark flecks on otherwise pale (often silvery) body; Great Barrier Reef, New Guinea, Philippines and S. China Sea; W. Pacific; to 45 cm.

4. BLACKNAPE LARGE-EYE BREAM
Gymnocranius satoi Borsa, Béarez, Paijo & Chen 2013
Inhabits sand-rubble fringe of coral reefs; distinguished by dusky back, dark mark immediately above eye and faint dark bar below eye; Great Barrier Reef, Coral Sea, New Caledonia and Japan; to 45 cm.

5. BLUESPOTTED SEABREAM
Gymnocranius microdon (Bleeker, 1851)
Inhabits sand-rubble fringe of coral reefs; distinguished by blue spots on head; Indo-Malay Archipelago; W. Pacific; to 45 cm.

6. YELLOWSNOUT LARGE-EYE BREAM
Gymnocranius frenatus Bleeker, 1873
Inhabits sand and mud bottoms between 20–80 m depth; distinguished by yellow snout and diagonal blue bands on head; Indo-Malay Archipelago and S. China Sea; to 35 cm.

7. ORANGESTRIPED EMPEROR
Lethrinus obsoletus (Forsskål, 1775)
Inhabits coral reefs; distinguished by yellow stripe on lower side, can also assume mottled pattern; Great Barrier Reef, offshore reefs of W. Australia and throughout S.E. Asia; Indo-W. Pacific; to 40 cm.

8. SMALLTOOTH EMPEROR
Lethrinus microdon Valenciennes, 1830
Inhabits coral reefs; similar to *L. olivaceus* (Plate **47.5**), but snout slightly shorter and 4.5 scales between lateral line and base of middle dorsal spine instead of 5.5 scales; N.W. Australia and Indo-Malay Archipelago to New Guinea; Indo-W. Pacific; to 50 cm.

9. ORNATE EMPEROR
Lethrinus ornatus Valenciennes, 1830
Inhabits coral reefs; distinguished by yellow stripes on side and red margin on cheek and gill cover; Great Barrier Reef and Indo-Malay Archipelago to New Guinea; E. Indian Ocean and W. Pacific; to 40 cm.

10. YELLOWLIP EMPEROR
Lethrinus xanthochilu Klunzinger, 1870
Inhabits coral reefs; distinguished by relatively large size, elongate shape and yellowish lips; N. Great Barrier Reef and throughout S.E. Asia; Indo-C. Pacific; to 60 cm.

11. ORANGESPOTTED EMPEROR
Lethrinus erythracanthus Valenciennes, 1830
Inhabits coral reefs, usually seen on outer slopes; distinguished by overall dusky-grey colour (often with scattered white spots), yellowish fins and large fleshy lips; juvenile yellowish with narrow blue lines or horizontal rows of blue spots; N. Great Barrier Reef and throughout S.E. Asia; Indo-W. Pacific; to 60 cm.

12. LONGFIN EMPEROR
Lethrinus erythropterus Valenciennes, 1830
Inhabits coral reefs; distinguished by dark band from eye to snout and light bars usually on rear half of body; Indo-Malay Archipelago to New Guinea; Indo-W. Pacific; to 45 cm.

13. AMBON EMPEROR
Lethrinus amboinensis Bleeker, 1854
Inhabits sand-rubble fringe of coral reefs; distinguished by elongate shape and yellow pectoral fins; N.W. Australia and throughout S.E. Asia; W. and C. Pacific; to 60 cm.

14. RED SNOUT EMPEROR
Lethrinus reticulatus Valenciennes, 1830
Inhabits sand-mud bottoms, often caught by trawlers; a nondescript emperor with dark head and tail, and yellowish pectoral fins; Indonesia and Philippines; Indo-W. Pacific; to 40 cm.

15. THUMBPRINT EMPEROR
Lethrinus harak (Forsskål, 1775)
Inhabits sand-rubble bottoms, weedy areas and mangroves near coral reefs; distinguished by dark blotch on middle of side; N. Queensland and throughout S.E. Asia; Indo-W. Pacific; to 50 cm.

16. BLACKBLOTCH EMPEROR
Lethrinus semicinctus Valenciennes, 1830
Inhabits sand-rubble bottoms near coral reefs; distinguished by irregular dark bars on side, including enlarged dark blotch below rear part of dorsal fin; found throughout the region; E. Indian Ocean and W. Pacific; to 35 cm.

17. YELLOWTAIL EMPEROR ☆☆☆☆
Lethrinus atkinsoni Seale, 1910
Inhabits coral reefs; distinguished by steep forehead and yellow area along middle of sides extending to tail; formerly confused with *L. mahsena* from the W. Indian Ocean; found throughout the region; E. Indian Ocean and W. and C. Pacific; to 43 cm and 2 kg.

EMPERORS

The members of the family Lethrinidae, commonly known as emperors and seabreams, are mainly reef fishes that prefer sand and rubble bottoms. Most species occur in relatively shallow water (5–30 m), but a few range to the edge of continental shelves to depths of 100 m or more. Their diet consists of small fishes and a variety of invertebrates including polychaete worms, crabs, shrimps, squid, octopus and seastars. Some species have well-developed molar-like teeth adapted for crushing hard-shelled prey such as molluscs, crustaceans and sea urchins.

Mature adults are initially female, but change to the male sex later in life. There is little information about spawning other than a few observations by fishermen. Most species are believed to spawn after dark, following a local migration to particular areas near a reef, either in sheltered lagoons or on the edge of exposed oceanic reefs. Spawning apparently occurs in large aggregations, which mill about near the surface, or near the bottom of reef slopes. Reproductive activity generally peaks around the time of the new moon. The tiny (0.6–0.8 mm) fertilised eggs rise to the surface and float with the currents until hatching about 20 to 40 hours later. The larvae measure 1.3–1.7 mm in length and lead a pelagic existence for several weeks. Growth rings on scales and ear bones (otoliths) have been used to determine the age of emperors. Most species appear to live at least 15 years and some may reach twice this age.

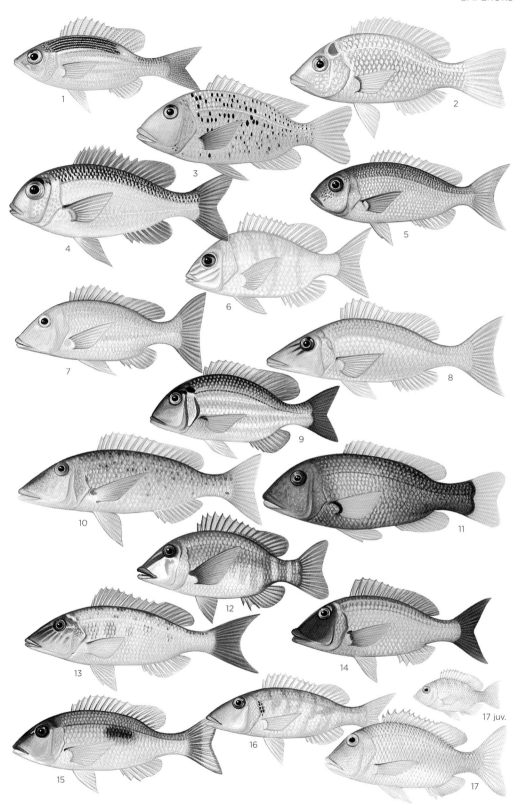

PLATE 49: THREADFIN-BREAMS

NEMIPTERIDAE

1. BALI THREADFIN-BREAM ☆☆
Nemipterus balinensis (Bleeker, 1859)
Inhabits trawling grounds; distinguished by single yellow band on side and slender shape; Indo-Malay Archipelago; to 24 cm.

2. YELLOWBELLY THREADFIN-BREAM ☆☆
Nemipterus bathybius Snyder, 1911
Inhabits trawling grounds; distinguished by 2 yellow bands on side and pair of yellow stripes along ventral profile of head and body; N.W. Australia and throughout S.E. Asia; W. Pacific and E. Indian Ocean; to 20 cm.

3. CELEBES THREADFIN-BREAM ☆☆
Nemipterus celebicus (Bleeker, 1854)
Inhabits trawling grounds; distinguished by 4–5 silvery yellow stripes on side, equal-sized tail lobes and reddish tip on upper lobe of tail; N. Australia, S. Indonesia and S. New Guinea; to 22 cm.

4. ROSY THREADFIN-BREAM ☆☆
Nemipterus furcosus (Valenciennes, 1830)
Inhabits trawling grounds; distinguished by series of faint dark blotches on upper back, and uniform fins without stripes or spots; found throughout the region; W. Pacific and E. Indian Ocean; to 35 cm.

5. ORNATE THREADFIN-BREAM ☆☆
Nemipterus hexodon (Quoy & Gaimard, 1824)
Inhabits trawling grounds; distinguished by broad yellow stripe on upper side (with narrower stripes below), oblique yellow stripe on dorsal fin and, yellow tip on upper lobe of tail; found throughout the region; W. Pacific and E. Indian Ocean; to 30 cm.

6. TEARDROP THREADFIN-BREAM ☆☆
Nemipterus isacanthus (Bleeker, 1873)
Inhabits trawling grounds; distinguished by 2 broad yellow stripes along side, bright yellow band along ventral profile and yellow patch below eye; N.W. Australia and throughout S.E. Asia; Indo-Australian Archipelago; to 24 cm.

7. ORIENTAL THREADFIN-BREAM ☆☆
Nemipterus japonicus (Bloch, 1791)
Inhabits trawling grounds; distinguished by broad yellow band along base of dorsal fin, bright pink-red 'shoulder' spot, yellow stripe along ventral profile and elongate yellow filament on upper lobe of tail; colour generally more pink (less blue than shown); N.W. Australia and throughout S.E. Asia; W. Pacific and E. Indian Ocean; to 32 cm.

8. MAUVELIP THREADFIN-BREAM ☆☆
Nemipterus mesoprion (Bleeker, 1853)
Inhabits trawling grounds, similar to *N. isacanthus* (**6**), but lacks yellow patch below eye; S. Indonesia and Gulf of Thailand; to 20 cm.

9. SLENDER THREADFIN-BREAM ☆☆
Nemipterus zysron (Bleeker, 1857)
Inhabits trawling grounds; distinguished by broad yellow stripe below eye and elongate yellow filament on upper lobe of tail; N.W. Australia and throughout S.E. Asia; Indo-W. Pacific; to 28 cm.

10. DOUBLEWHIP THREADFIN-BREAM ☆☆☆
Nemipterus nematophorus (Bleeker, 1853)
Inhabits trawling grounds; distinguished by elongate filaments at front of dorsal fin and on upper lobe of tail (these features not shown, but usually present); found throughout most of S.E. Asia; E. Indian Ocean and Indo-Malay Archipelago; to 25 cm.

11. NOTCHED THREADFIN-BREAM ☆☆
Nemipterus peronii (Valenciennes, 1830)
Inhabits trawling grounds; distinguished by deep notches along margin of dorsal fin between spines; found throughout the region; Indo-W. Pacific; to 30 cm.

12. PINKFIN THREADFIN-BREAM ☆☆
Nemipterus sugillatus Russell & Ho, 2017
Inhabits trawling grounds; distinguished 6–7 yellow stripes on side, a yellow margin on dorsal fin and single yellow stripe on anal fin; Indo-Malay Archipelago, to 30 cm.

13. GOLDEN THREADFIN-BREAM ☆☆
Nemipterus virgatus (Houttuyn, 1782)
Inhabits trawling grounds; distinguished by bright yellow lips (not shown), thin yellow stripes on sides; pair of thin stripes on dorsal and anal fins; N.W. Australia and Philippines; W. Pacific and E. Indian Ocean; to 40 cm.

14. YELLOWTIP THREADFIN-BREAM ☆☆
Nemipterus nematopus (Bleeker, 1851)
Inhabits trawling grounds; distinguished by pair of yellow stripes on side, lowermost wider and curved slightly upwards above base of pectoral fin, also has vivid yellow spot on tip of upper tail lobe and frequently has pair of yellow stripes along ventral surface of head and body; N Australia, Indonesia and Philippines; W. Pacific and E. Indian Ocean; to 40 cm.

THREADFIN AND MONOCLE-BREAMS

The seabreams of the family Nemipteridae (Plates 48–49) are confined to the Indo-West Pacific region, primarily in tropical and subtropical latitudes. The family contains about 70 species, several of which are still undescribed. The largest genera are *Nemipterus* and *Scolopsis*, each having about 20 species. Both are commonly offered in South-East Asian fish markets, although they are relatively small in size (usually less than 40 cm total length). *Scolopsis* and *Pentapodus* are closely associated with coral or rubble reefs, being particularly abundant in sandy areas between reefs. *Nemipterus* and *Parascolopsis* generally occur in deeper water, frequently between 30–100 m depth. They form a significant portion of trawl catches on continental shelves. Breams forage for worms, crustaceans, molluscs and other invertebrates; small fishes are also sometimes eaten.

PLATE 50: MONOCLE-BREAMS AND SILVER BIDDIES

NEMIPTERIDAE

1. ROSY SEA PERCH ☆☆
Parascolopsis eriomma (Jordan & Richardson, 1909)
Inhabits offshore trawling grounds; distinguished by rosy colour on back with diffuse, yellow longitudinal band along middle of side; N.W. Australia and throughout S.E. Asia; Indo-W. Pacific; to 30 cm.

2. LONGRAY MONOCLE-BREAM ☆☆
Parascolopsis tanyactis Russell, 1986
Inhabits offshore trawling grounds in 45–80 m depth; distinguished by 2 dark bars on back, becoming diffused on lower side and additional bar across tail base, also 4th and 5th soft dorsal rays elongated (not shown); *P. rufomaculatus* (not shown) is similar but soft dorsal rays not elongated and has broad golden stripe along middle of side; N.W. Australia, Indonesia and Philippines; Indo-Australian Archipelago and W. Pacific; to 20 cm.

3. PURPLE THREADFIN-BREAM ☆☆
Pentapodus emeryii (Richardson, 1843)
Inhabits coastal reefs; distinguished by bright yellow stripe from eye to tail, adults more bluish than shown and have long filaments at the tip of each caudal lobe; N.W. Australia, Indonesia and Philippines; to 25 cm.

4. JAPANESE THREADFIN-BREAM ☆☆
Pentapodus nagasakiensis (Tanaka, 1915)
Inhabits sand-rubble areas adjacent to deeper offshore reefs; distinguished by orange stripe from eye to tail base, with pearly stripe just below it and often a narrower pale stripe along base of dorsal fin; N.W. Australia, Indonesia and Philippines; mainly W. Pacific; to 20 cm.

5. NORTHWEST THREADFIN-BREAM ☆☆
Pentapodus porosus (Valenciennes, 1830)
Inhabits sand and rubble bottoms frequently near coastal reefs; distinguished by broad, longitudinal brown band on middle of sides, <-shaped blue mark and small black spot at tail base; N.W. Australia and S. New Guinea only; to 25 cm.

6. WESTERN BUTTERFISH ☆☆
Pentapodus vitta Quoy & Gaimard, 1824
Inhabits sand-weed areas or rocky bottoms close to shore, often in schools; distinguished by dark stripe bordered by blue from snout to tail base; W. Australia only, between Geographe Bay and Dampier Archipelago; to 31 cm.

7. RAINBOW MONOCLE-BREAM ☆☆
Scolopsis monogramma (Cuvier, 1830)
Inhabits sandy areas in the vicinity of coral reefs; distinguished by 3 blue stripes on snout (often with orange between them), generally pale body except may have series of slanting dotted lines on middle of side which sometimes form a solid broad stripe when viewed underwater and blue edged tail with prolonged filament on upper lobe; often misidentified as *S. temporalis*, a similar species from New Guinea and other Melanesian islands; also known as Barred-face Spinecheek; found throughout the region; mainly W. Pacific; to 30 cm.

8. TWO-LINE MONOCLE-BREAM ☆☆
Scolopsis bilineata (Bloch, 1793)
Inhabits coral reefs; distinguished by curved, black-edged white stripe from below eye to midbase of dorsal fin; also known as Bridled Spinecheek and Double-lined Coral Bream; found throughout the region; E. Indian Ocean and W. Pacific; to 23 cm.

9. WHITECHEEK MONOCLE-BREAM ☆☆
Scolopsis japonicus (Bloch, 1793)
Inhabits coastal reefs; distinguished by relatively deep body and white bar behind eye; N.W. Australia and throughout S.E. Asia to Japan; W. Pacific; to 25 cm.

10. REDSPOT MONOCLE-BREAM ☆☆
Scolopsis taenioptera (Cuvier, 1830)
Inhabits sandy areas in the vicinity of coral reefs; similar to *S. monogramma* (**7**), but has small red spot in axil 'armpit' of pectoral fin, lacks distinct blue stripes on snout, but has blue bands between eyes and lacks dark spots or stripes on side; found throughout the region; mainly Indo-Australian Archipelago; to 23 cm.

11. OBLIQUE-BAR MONOCLE-BREAM ☆☆
Scolopsis xenochrous Günther, 1872
Inhabits sand or rubble areas near coral reefs; distinguished by diagonal pearl-blue streak bordered with black spots above pectoral fin, and series of slanted rows of dots on middle of side followed by broad white streak; found throughout the region; E. Indian Ocean and Indo-Australian Archipelago; to 18 cm.

12. CORAL MONOCLE-BREAM ☆☆
Scaevius milii (Bory de Saint-Vincent, 1823)
Inhabits coastal waters, frequently on sand or rubble bottoms; distinguished by 2 blue stripes on upper side ending on top of tail base, and wider orange stripe below along middle of side with small pale-edged black spot on upper tail base; also known as Jurgen; Australia only from Abrolhos Islands, W. Australia to Gulf of Carpentaria; to 25 cm.

GERREIDAE

13. LONGFIN SILVERBIDDY ☆
Pentaprion longimanus (Cantor, 1849)
Inhabits coastal waters over sand bottoms; similar to *Gerres filamentosus* (**14**), *G. oyena* (**15**), and *G. subfasciatus* (**16**), but has much larger anal fin base (anal fin contains 12–14 soft rays versus 7–8 in others); found throughout the region; Indo-W. Pacific; to 15 cm.

14. THREADFIN SILVERBIDDY ☆
Gerres filamentosus Cuvier, 1829
Inhabits coastal waters including estuaries, usually on sand or mud bottoms; distinguished by long filament at front of dorsal fin and series of spots in vertical rows on side; numerous species of similar silver-biddies found in the region, only 3 of the most common shown here; this species found throughout the region; Indo-W. Pacific; to 25 cm.

15. BLACKTIP SILVERBIDDY ☆
Gerres oyena (Forsskål, 1775)
Inhabits coastal waters including estuaries, usually on sand or mud bottoms; distinguished by relatively elongate body and lack of markings; also known as Silverbelly; found throughout the region; Indo-W. Pacific; to 25 cm.

16. COMMON SILVERBIDDY
Gerres subfasciatus Cuvier, 1830
Inhabits coastal waters entering bays and estuaries, usually on sand or mud bottoms; distinguished by narrow dark bars on side; also known as Ovate Silverbiddy; N. Australia, ranging down east and west coasts into subtropical and temperate seas; 22 cm.

PLATE 51: MONOCLE-BREAMS AND GOATFISHES

NEMIPTERIDAE

1. WHITE-SHOULDERED WHIPTAIL ☆☆
Pentapodus bifasciatus (Bleeker, 1848)
Inhabits coral reefs; distinguished by pair of pale stripes and narrow white bar between the two pale stripes, just behind head; W. Indonesia and Philippines; to 18 cm.

2. SMALL-TOOTHED WHIPTAIL ☆☆
Pentapodus caninus (Cuvier, 1830)
Inhabits sand-rubble fringe of coral reefs; distinguished by single pale stripe, similar to *P. aureofasciatus* (**5**), but stripe is angled slightly instead of horizontal; throughout S.E. Asia; W. Pacific; to 20 cm.

3. PARADISE THREADFIN-BREAM ☆☆
Pentapodus paradiseus (Günther, 1859)
Inhabits sand-rubble fringe of coral reefs; distinguished by diagonal pale stripe on side, small blue-edged dark spot at middle of tail base and long filament on upper lobe of tail; Great Barrier Reef, Gulf of Carpentaria and E. New Guinea to Solomon Islands; to 25 cm.

4. BUTTERFLY WHIPTAIL ☆☆
Pentapodus setosus (Valenciennes, 1830)
Inhabits sand-rubble fringe of coral reefs; nearly identical in appearance to *P. paradiseus* (**3**), but distributions do not overlap; Indo-Malay Archipelago; to 20 cm.

5. YELLOWSTRIPE THREADFIN-BREAM ☆☆
Pentapodus aureofasciatus Russell, 2001
Inhabits sand-rubble fringe of coral reefs; distinguished by blue colour on upper half of body, with pair of narrow yellow stripes; juvenile is brilliant blue with pair of well-contrasted yellow stripes; Great Barrier Reef, New Guinea, E. Indonesia and Philippines; W. Pacific; to 18 cm.

6. THREE-STRIPED WHIPTAIL ☆☆
Pentapodus trivittatus (Bloch, 1791)
Inhabits coral reefs, frequently seen in lagoons; distinguished by pattern of light and dark stripes, narrow, pale cross-bars on back and diagonal dark band below eye; throughout S.E. Asia; W. Pacific; to 22 cm.

7. BRIDLED MONOCLE-BREAM ☆☆
Scolopsis affinis Peters, 1877
Inhabits sand-rubble fringe of coral reefs; similar to *S. aurata* (**8**), but head scales reach forward to level of rear nostril (do not reach nostril in **8**); Great Barrier Reef, offshore reefs of N.W. Australia and throughout S.E. Asia; to 22 cm.

8. YELLOWSTRIPE MONOCLE-BREAM ☆☆
Scolopsis aurata (Park, 1797)
Inhabits sand-rubble fringe of coral reefs; distinguished by pale yellow stripe on side, similar to some species of *Pentapodus* shown on this plate, but is deeper-bodied; Indonesia (Sumatra, Java, Bali, Lombok, Sumbawa); C. and E. Indian Ocean; to 22 cm.

9. SAW-JAWED MONOCLE-BREAM ☆☆
Scolopsis ciliata (Lacepède, 1802)
Inhabits lagoon and inshore reefs, usually in sand or silt-bottom areas; distinguished by pearly streak just below dorsal fin and yellow spots on scales of side; throughout S.E. Asia; to 16 cm.

10. LINED MONOCLE-BREAM ☆☆
Scolopsis lineata Quoy & Gaimard, 1824
Inhabits sandy areas near coral reefs; distinguished by bold black stripes and square blotches on upper half of body; *S. cancellatus* is a synonym; Great Barrier Reef, offshore reefs of N.W. Australia and throughout S.E. Asia; mainly W. Pacific; to 20 cm.

11. PEARLY MONOCLE-BREAM ☆☆
Scolopsis margaritifera (Cuvier, 1830)
Inhabits inshore and lagoon reefs; distinguished by pearly colour on sides and belly, dusky back and yellowish pectoral fins; juveniles have a single black stripe on middle of side; Great Barrier Reef and throughout S.E. Asia; W. Pacific; to 20 cm.

12. BALD-SPOT MONOCLE-BREAM ☆☆
Scolopsis temporalis (Cuvier, 1830)
Inhabits sand-rubble areas near coral reefs; similar to *S. monogramma* (Plate **50.7**), but has blue-rimmed pale spot above and behind eye; E. Indonesia, New Guinea and Solomon Islands; to 35 cm.

13. THREELINE MONOCLE-BREAM ☆☆
Scolopsis trilineata Kner, 1868
Inhabits sandy or rubble fringe of coral reefs; distinguished by pale stripe from lower corner of eye that joins diagonal pale band running between eye and base of posterior part of dorsal fin; Great Barrier Reef, offshore reefs of N.W. Australia and throughout S.E. Asia; W. Pacific; to 18 cm.

MULLIDAE

14. YELLOWSTRIPE GOATFISH ☆☆☆
Mulloidichthys flavolineatus (Lacepède, 1801)
Inhabits sandy areas adjacent to coral reefs, often seen in schools; similar to *M. vanicolensis* (**15**), but lacks yellow fins and has dark spot above pectoral fin; Great Barrier Reef, offshore reefs of N.W. Australia and throughout S.E. Asia; Indo-C. Pacific; to 30 cm.

15. GOLDSTRIPE GOATFISH ☆☆☆
Mulloidichthys vanicolensis (Valcennnes, 1831)
Inhabits sandy areas adjacent to coral reefs, often seen in schools; distinguished by bright yellow fins and yellow stripe on middle of side; Great Barrier Reef, offshore reefs of N.W. Australia and throughout S.E. Asia; Indo-C. Pacific; to 33 cm.

16. DOT-AND-DASH GOATFISH ☆☆☆
Parupeneus barberinus (Lacepède, 1801)
Inhabits sand-rubble bottoms near coral reefs; distinguished by black stripe from snout through eye then continuing on upper side, and large black spot on tail base; Great Barrier Reef, offshore reefs of N.W. Australia and throughout S.E. Asia; Indo-W. Pacific; to 30 cm.

17. LONG-BARBELED GOATFISH ☆☆☆
Parupeneus macronemus (Lacepède, 1801)
Inhabits coral reefs; similar to *P. pleurostigma* (Plate **52.9**), but has broad black stripe on head and front of body, and black spot on middle of tail base; Indo-Malay Archipelago; Indo-W. Pacific; to 35 cm.

PLATE 52: GOATFISHES

MULLIDAE

1. GOLDSADDLE GOATFISH ☆☆☆
Parupeneus cyclostomus (Lacepède, 1801)
Inhabits coral reefs; has 2 colour varieties: one is entirely yellow, the other is purplish-pink or bluish with gold saddle on top of tail base; found throughout the region; Indo-C. Pacific; to 50 cm.

2. BICOLOR GOATFISH ☆☆☆
Parupeneus barberinoides (Bleeker, 1852)
Inhabits weed-sand areas near coral reefs; distinguished by dark anterior half and pale rear portion with black spot in front of tail base; found throughout the region; mainly W. Pacific; to 25 cm.

3. DOUBLEBAR GOATFISH ☆☆☆
Parupeneus crassilabris (Valenciennes, 1831)
Inhabits coral reefs; distinguished by 2 dark saddles on upper half of body; found throughout the region; E. Indo-W. Pacific; to 35 cm.

4. YELLOWSTRIPED GOATFISH ☆☆☆
Parupeneus chrysopleuron (Temminck & Schlegel, 1843)
Inhabits sandy bottoms near rocky areas and coral reefs; distinguished by reddish colour and yellow stripe on upper side, *Upeneus sundaicus* (**12**) is similar but has patches of teeth on roof of mouth; N.W. Australia and scattered localities in Indo-Malay region; W. Pacific and E. Indian Ocean; to 33 cm.

5. BLACKSADDLE GOATFISH ☆☆☆
Parupeneus spilurus (Bleeker, 1854)
Inhabits weed-sand areas adjacent to coral reefs and southern rocky reefs; distinguished by alternating light and dark stripes on head and body, and black spot on upper half of tail base; *P. signatus* is a synonym; W. Australia and S.E. Pacific; to 47 cm.

6. YELLOWSPOT GOATFISH ☆☆☆
Parupeneus indicus (Shaw, 1803)
Inhabits sand-weed areas in the vicinity of coral reefs; distinguished by elongate yellow blotch on middle of upper sides and black spot on tail base; found throughout the region; Indo-C. Pacific; to 40 cm.

7. OPALESCENT GOATFISH ☆☆☆
Parupeneus heptacanthus (Lacepède, 1802)
Inhabits sand-weed areas in the vicinity of coral or rocky reefs; distinguished by reddish-pink colour and yellow stripes on side, often has small red to brown spot on upper side above pectoral fin; found throughout the region; Indo-W. Pacific; to 30 cm.

8. BANDED GOATFISH ☆☆☆
Parupeneus multifasciatus (Quoy & Gaimard, 1825)
Inhabits weed-sand areas in the vicinity of coral reefs; distinguished by broad, dark bars on side and large spot or bar on tail base; found throughout the region; Indo-C. Pacific; to 30 cm.

9. SIDESPOT GOATFISH ☆☆☆
Parupeneus pleurostigma (Bennett, 1831)
Inhabits sand and rubble areas in the vicinity of coral reefs, distinguished by black spot on middle of upper sides followed by pearly white patch; found throughout the region; Indo-C. Pacific; to 33 cm.

10. GOLDBAND GOATFISH ☆☆☆
Upeneus moluccensis (Bleeker, 1855)
Inhabits sandy or weed-covered areas; distinguished by yellow stripe from eye to tail and narrow stripes on both dorsal fins and upper lobe of tail; N.W. Australia and throughout S.E. Asia; Indo-W. Pacific; to 20 cm.

11. SUNRISE GOATFISH ☆☆☆
Upeneus sulphureus Cuvier, 1829
Inhabits sandy or weed-covered areas; distinguished by black tip on first dorsal fin and 2–3 gold stripes on side, similar to *U. vittatus* (**13**), but lacks stripes on tail; N.W. Australia and throughout S.E. Asia; Indo-W. Pacific; to 23 cm.

12. OCHREBAND GOATFISH ☆☆☆
Upeneus sundaicus (Bleeker, 1855)
Inhabits sandy or weed-covered areas; distinguished by yellow stripe on upper sides, similar to *Parupeneus chrysopleuron* (**4**), but has patches of teeth on roof of mouth, also rear margin of lower lobe of tail usually dark; N.W. Australia and throughout S.E. Asia; N. Indian Ocean and Indo-Australian Archipelago; to 22 cm.

13. STRIPED GOATFISH ☆☆☆
Upeneus vittatus (Forsskål, 1775)
Inhabits sandy or weed-covered areas; distinguished by 4 orange-yellow stripes on side, black tip on first dorsal fin and stripes on tail; N.W. Australia and throughout S.E. Asia; Indo-C. Pacific; to 28 cm.

14. BARTAIL GOATFISH ☆☆☆
Upeneus tragula Richardson, 1846
Inhabits sandy or weed-covered areas; similar to *U. asymmetricus* (**15**), but stripe on side dark (reddish-brown to blackish), sides mottled with spots and 8 spines (versus 7) in first dorsal fin; found throughout the region; Indo-W. Pacific; to 30 cm.

15. ASYMMETRIC GOATFISH ☆☆☆
Upeneus asymmetricus Lachner, 1954
Inhabits sandy or weed-covered areas; similar to *U. tragula* (**14**), but stripe on side yellow, fewer small spots on sides and 7 spines (versus 8) in first dorsal fin; N.W. Australia and throughout S.E. Asia; Indo-W. Pacific; to 30 cm.

GOATFISHES

The goatfishes (family Mullidae) are found mainly in tropical and subtropical seas, usually in the vicinity of reefs. Worldwide about 90 species are known. They are characterised by a relatively elongate body, two widely separated dorsal fins and the presence of a pair of long chin barbels that are used for detecting food. The barbels are also used by males to attract females during courtship. When they are not being used the barbels are tucked tightly under the chin. Goatfishes feed on small fishes and a variety of mainly sand- and weed-dwelling organisms including worms, shrimps, crabs, molluscs and echinoderms. They are frequently seen in large schools and most species are considered to be good eating. The maximum size is about 60 cm, but most species are much smaller. The majority of goatfishes are distributed in the Indo-West Pacific region, but there are also a few representatives in the Atlantic and eastern Pacific Oceans.

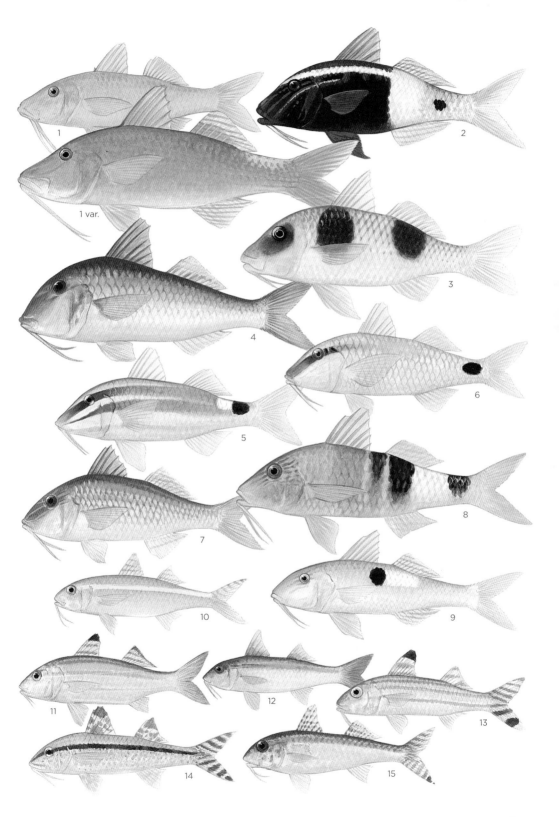

PLATE 53: CROAKERS, BULLSEYES AND DRUMMERS

SCIAENIDAE

1. BLACK JEWFISH ☆☆☆
Protonibea diacanthus (Lacepède, 1802)
Inhabits coastal waters, sometimes entering estuaries; distinguished by large size and overall grey to blackish colour, young fish have black spots on the back, dorsal fin and tail; also known as Spotted Croaker or Spotted Jewfish; found throughout the region; Indo-W. Pacific; to 150 cm and at least 16 kg.

2. ORANGE JEWFISH ☆☆
Atrobucca brevis Sasaki & Kailola, 1988
Inhabits coastal waters in 60–112 m depth; distinguished by faint orange tinge on lower third of body when fresh, otherwise without distinctive marks; N. Australia and S. New Guinea only; to 35 cm.

3. COITOR CROAKER ☆☆
Johnius coitor (Hamilton, 1822)
Inhabits coastal waters; distinguished by bulging snout with small mouth below, similar to *J. amblycephalus* (**4**), but has dark blotch on gill cover, more soft dorsal rays (30–32 versus 23–26) and more gill rakers on the lower limb of the first gill arch (11 or 12 versus 6–10); found throughout the region; Indo-W. Pacific; to 16 cm.

4. BEARDED JEWFISH ☆☆
Johnius amblycephalus (Bleeker, 1855)
Inhabits coastal waters; distinguished by bulging snout with small mouth below, similar to *J. coitor* (**3**), but distinguished by differences mentioned under that species, also has taller first dorsal fin; found throughout the region; W. Pacific and E. Indian Ocean; to 20 cm.

5. RIVER JEWFISH ☆☆
Johnius borneensis (Bleeker, 1851)
Inhabits coastal waters including estuaries; distinguished by black outer portion of first dorsal fin and diffuse dark stripe often present on basal part of second dorsal fin; found throughout the region; E. Indian Ocean and Indo-Australian Archipelago, to 22 cm.

MONODACTYLIDAE

6. DIAMONDFISH ☆
Monodactylus argenteus (Linnaeus, 1758)
Inhabits estuaries and lower reaches of freshwater streams, also in harbours around wharves and jetties; distinguished by diamond shape and silvery colour; also known as Silver Batfish; found throughout the region; Indo-W. Pacific; to 27 cm.

LEPTOBRAMIDAE

7. BEACH SALMON ☆☆
Leptobrama muelleri Steindachner, 1878
Inhabits coastal waters, frequently in schools off sandy beaches; distinguished by steel-blue colour on back and a single black-tipped dorsal fin that is set well back on the body; N. Australia and S. New Guinea only; to 43 cm.

PEMPHERIDAE

8. GOLDEN BULLSEYE
Parapriacanthus ransonneti Steindachner, 1870
Inhabits coral reefs, usually in large aggregations in caves; distinguished by semi-transparent appearance, yellowish head, silvery belly and a single dorsal fin; *P. unwini* is a synonym; found throughout the region; Indo-W. Pacific; to 7.5 cm.

9. BRONZE BULLSEYE
Pempheris analis Waite, 1910
Inhabits coral or rocky reefs, usually in caves similar to *P. schwenkii* (**11**), but has smaller scales and blackish tips on dorsal and anal fins and sometimes on lobes of tail; W. Australia, S. Great Barrier Reef, Lord Howe Island and Kermadec Islands; to 17 cm.

10. NORTHWEST BULLSEYE
Pempheris sp.
Inhabits coral or rocky reefs, usually in caves; distinguished by relatively large scales and series of dark stripes on side; N.W. Australia, possibly more widespread; to 20 cm.

11. SILVER BULLSEYE
Pempheris schwenkii Bleeker, 1855
Inhabits coral or rocky reefs, usually in caves, similar to *P. analis* (**9**), but has larger scales, a yellowish tail, blackish anal fin base and lacks dark fin tips; found throughout the region; Indo-W. Pacific; to 15 cm.

KYPHOSIDAE

12. GREY DRUMMER ☆
Kyphosus bigibbus Lacepède, 1801
Inhabits coral reefs, usually in large schools; similar to *K. vaigiensis* (**14**), but lacks well pronounced narrow stripes on side and has 12–13 soft dorsal rays (versus 14 or 15); sometimes misidentified as *K. gibsoni*; found throughout the region; Indo-C. Pacific; to 58 cm.

13. WESTERN BUFFALO BREAM ☆
Kyphosus cornelii (Whitley, 1944)
Inhabits coral and rocky reefs, occurring in large schools; distinguished by dark streak on each tail lobe with white outer margin; W. Australia only, between Cape Leeuwin and Coral Bay; to 60 cm.

14. BRASSY DRUMMER ☆
Kyphosus vaigiensis (Quoy & Gaimard, 1825)
Inhabits coral reefs, frequently in schools; similar to *K. bigibbus* (**12**), but has pronounced narrow stripes on side and 14–15 soft dorsal rays (versus 12–13); found throughout the region; Indo-C. Pacific; to 50 cm.

15. STRIPEY
Microcanthus strigatus (Cuvier, 1831)
Inhabits rocky areas and coral reefs, sometimes forms schools around jetties; distinguished by bold pattern of slanting stripes; E. and W. coasts of Australia, Taiwan, S. Japan and Hawaii; to 16 cm.

CROAKERS, DRUMMERS AND RELATIVES

Croakers of the family Sciaenidae live in a variety of marine and estuarine habitats. They can produce a 'drumming' sound with the aid of their swim bladder. The maximum size is about 2 m, but most are under 50 cm. Some species are important food fishes.

The Diamondfish (family Monodactylidae) appears to be equally at home in saltwater or freshwater. It is sometimes found in large aggregations. Young specimens make excellent aquarium pets.

Bulleyes of the Indo-Pacific family Pempheridae are cave and crevice dwellers that often occur in large aggregations. They feed mainly on crustaceans, but also consume worms and cephalopods.

Drummers of the family Kyphosidae are common inhabitants of reefs and weed beds in tropical and temperate seas. They feed mainly on plants and most are less than 50 cm total length. Although eaten in some localities, the flesh is usually not very highly regarded. Some species of *Kyphosus* are reported to produce a mild hallucinogenic effect when consumed.

PLATE 54: ARCHERFISHES, SCATS AND BATFISHES

TOXOTIDAE

1. SEVENSPOT ARCHERFISH ☆☆☆
Toxotes chatareus (Hamilton, 1822)
Inhabits mangrove estuaries and freshwater streams; has ability to knock insects from overhanging vegetation by squirting jets of water from mouth; distinguished from *T. jaculatrix* (**2**) by spotted pattern; found throughout the region; Indo-Australian Archipelago and Andaman Sea; to 30 cm.

2. BANDED ARCHERFISH ☆☆☆
Toxotes jaculatrix (Pallas, 1767)
Inhabits brackish mangrove estuaries; distinguished from *T. chatareus* (**1**) by 4 dorsal spines (versus 5) and barred pattern; found throughout the region; Indo-Australian Archipelago and Andaman Sea; to 20 cm.

SCATOPHAGIDAE

3. STRIPED SCAT ☆☆
Selenotoca multifasciata (Richardsonm 1846)
Inhabits brackish mangrove estuaries and freshwater streams; similar to *S. argus* (**4**), but has more silvery body colour and combination of bars and spots, also known as Banded Scat; N. Australia, Papua New Guinea, and E. Indonesia; to 28 cm.

4. SPOTTED SCAT ☆☆
Scatophagus argus (Linnaeus, 1766)
Inhabits brackish mangrove estuaries and freshwater streams; similar to *S. multifasciata* (**3**), but has numerous round spots on side; found throughout the region; Indo-W. Pacific; to 33 cm.

DREPANEIDAE

5. SICKLEFISH ☆☆☆
Drepane punctata (Linnaeus, 1758)
Inhabits coastal reefs; distinguished by its triangular shape and vertical rows of small spots; found throughout the region; Indo-W. Pacific; to 50 cm.

EPHIPPIDAE

6. HUMPHEAD BATFISH ☆☆
Platax batavianus Cuvier, 1831
Inhabits coastal reefs; distinguished by humped forehead and relatively elongate body of adult; found throughout the region; small juveniles (not shown) have spectacular zebra-like markings; Indo-Australian Archipelago; to 50 cm.

7. LONGFIN BATFISH ☆☆
Platax pinnatus (Linnaeus, 1758)
Inhabits coral reefs; adult distinguished by slightly protruding snout; found throughout the region; mainly Indo-Australian Archipelago; to 50 cm.

8. ROUND BATFISH ☆☆
Platax orbicularis (Forsskål, 1775)
Inhabits coral reefs and inshore areas; similar to *P. batavianus* (**6**), but spot below pectoral fin generally more intense and second spot absent, juvenile effectively mimics dead leaves; found throughout the region; Indo-C. Pacific; to 50 cm.

9. ROUNDFACE BATFISH ☆☆
Platax teira (Forsskål, 1775)
Inhabits coral reefs; distinguished by dark blotch below pectoral fin and second blotch above front of anal fin, juvenile with very long dorsal, anal and pelvic fins; found throughout the region; Indo-W. Pacific; to 60 cm.

10. SHORTFIN BATFISH ☆☆
Zabidius novemaculeatus (McCulloch, 1916)
Inhabits coastal reefs; similar to *Platax batavianus* (**6**), but has 9 dorsal spines (versus 7) and adults lack pronounced hump on forehead; N. Australia and S. New Guinea only; to 45 cm.

11. THREADFIN SCAT ☆☆
Rhinoprenes pentanemus Munro, 1964
Inhabits coastal seas; distinguished by bulbous snout, laterally compressed body and long dorsal and anal fin filaments; N.W. Australia and S. New Guinea; to 15 cm.

AMAZING ARCHERFISHES

Archerfishes of the family Toxotidae exhibit one of nature's most remarkable feeding adaptations. They are renowned for their ability to knock down insects with a squirt of water at a distance of 2 m or more. Archers produce their aqueous bullets by suddenly pulling in their gill flaps, forcing water through a tube formed by a groove on the roof of the mouth and the tongue. This clever mechanism is similar to that employed by a toy water pistol. The fish's accuracy is even more amazing, considering that it must compensate for the angle of refraction of light. In other words, due to the bending of light its target is not where it actually appears to be.

Archerfishes are common residents of South-East Asia and northern Australian. The family contains 6 species (all in the genus *Toxotes*). It is distributed in fresh and brackish waters from India eastward to Australia and the Melanesian Archipelago. The Sevenspot Archerfish *T. chatareus* (**1**) is one of the most common representatives. It inhabits rivers and creeks, usually near the coast, but may penetrate more than 200 km upstream in larger rivers. It usually occurs in schools which patrol the shoreline for insects and other prey items. A specimen from the Fly River in Papua New Guinea measured 50 cm, but Australian fish are usually about half this size. Juveniles make excellent aquarium pets.

BEAUTIFUL BATFISHES

The graceful batfishes are a favourite of underwater photographers. Five species occur in the Indo-Pacific area, all belonging to the genus *Platax*. The handsome juveniles make excellent aquarium pets. They become tame very quickly and will accept feedings by hand. The young have highly exaggerated dorsal, anal and pelvic fins. For example, an 8 cm long Roundface Batfish *P. teira* (**9**) may measure over 25 cm from dorsal fin tip to anal fin tip. As the fish grows older, the fins become proportionally smaller until the shape is approximately round. Young fish occur singly or in small groups and never stray far from shelter. They are usually seen hovering under coral heads or in the shadows of boat moorings and wharves. At least two species employ clever disguises in their youthful stage to avoid predation. The Round Batfish *P. orbicularis* (**8**) lies on its side and drifts back and forth with the waves, appearing very much like a water-logged leaf. The tiny young of the Longfin Batfish *P. pinnatus* (**7**) swims on its side with a strange undulating motion — apparently mimicking a toxic polyclad flatworm.

Scats (**3** and **4**) are related to surgeonfishes. They generally occur around wharves in harbours, mangrove estuaries and the lower reaches of streams. Juveniles are popular aquarium fishes.

1

2

3

4

5

6

6 subadult

6 juv.

7

7 subadult

8

8 subadult

8 juv.

9

9 juv.

9 subadult

10

11

PLATE 55: BUTTERFLYFISHES

CHAETODONTIDAE

1. PHILIPPINE BUTTERFLYFISH
Chaetodon adiergastos Seale, 1910
Inhabits coral reefs; distinguished by broad eye bar and narrow diagonal stripes on side; N.W. Australia and throughout Indo-Malay region; Indo-Australian Archipelago; to 15 cm.

2. WESTERN BUTTERFLYFISH
Chaetodon assarius Waite, 1905
Inhabits rocky reefs and sand-weed flats; distinguished by several rows of small dots on sides; W. Australia only, between Recherche Archipelago and Montebello Islands; to 16 cm.

3. THREADFIN BUTTERFLYFISH
Chaetodon auriga Forsskål, 1775
Inhabits coral reefs and sand-weed flats; distinguished by chevron markings and yellow posterior; N.W. Australia, Great Barrier Reef and throughout S.E. Asia; Indo-C. Pacific; to 23 cm.

4. GOLDSTRIPE BUTTERFLYFISH
Chaetodon aureofasciatus Macleay, 1878
Inhabits coral reefs, distinguished by overall yellow-orange colour and pair of orange stripes on head and anterior part of body; N. Australia and S. New Guinea; to 14 cm.

5. CITRON BUTTERFLYFISH
Chaetodon citrinellus Cuvier, 1831
Inhabits shallow coral reefs, where live coral is sparse; distinguished by small dots on yellow background; N.W. Australia, Great Barrier Reef and throughout S.E. Asia; Indo-C. Pacific; to 13 cm.

6. SADDLE BUTTERFLYFISH
Chaetodon ephippium Cuvier, 1831
Inhabits coral reefs; distinguished by large black saddle; N.W. Australia, Great Barrier Reef and throughout S.E. Asia; Indo-C. Pacific; to 23 cm.

7. LINED BUTTERFLYFISH
Chaetodon lineolatus Cuvier, 1831
Inhabits coral reefs; distinguished by narrow black stripes on sides and broad black area along dorsal fin base; N.W. Australia, Great Barrier Reef and throughout S.E. Asia; Indo-C. Pacific; to 30 cm.

8. MEYER'S BUTTERFLYFISH
Chaetodon meyeri Bloch & Schneider, 1801
Inhabits coral reefs; distinguished by black diagonal stripes; N.W. Australia, Great Barrier Reef and throughout S.E. Asia; Indo-W. Pacific; to 20 cm.

9. KLEIN'S BUTTERFLYFISH
Chaetodon kleinii Bloch, 1790
Inhabits coral reefs; distinguished by combination of bars on front of body and golden-brown area on rear half; N.W. Australia, Great Barrier Reef and throughout S.E. Asia; Indo-C. Pacific; to 13 cm.

10. BLUESPOT BUTTERFLYFISH
Chaetodon plebeius Cuvier, 1831
Inhabits coral reefs; distinguished by ovate blue spot on yellow background; N.W. Australia, Great Barrier Reef and throughout S.E. Asia; Indo-W. Pacific; to 13 cm.

11. RACOON BUTTERFLYFISH
Chaetodon lunula (Lacepède, 1802)
Inhabits coral reefs, distinguished by black 'mask' and diagonal black bar behind head, with golden colour on lower sides; N.W. Australia, Great Barrier Reef and throughout S.E. Asia; Indo-C. Pacific: to 21 cm.

12. ORNATE BUTTERFLYFISH
Chaetodon ornatissimus Cuvier, 1831
Inhabits coral reefs; distinguished by brown-orange diagonal stripes; N.W. Australia, Great Barrier Reef and throughout S.E. Asia; mainly W. and C. Pacific; to 18 cm.

COLOURFUL BUTTERFLYFISHES

Butterflyfishes of the family Chaetodontidae (Plates 55–58) are renowned for their striking colour patterns, delicate shape and graceful swimming movements. The family contains about 130 species which occur mainly in tropical seas around coral reefs. Most of the species dwell in depths of less than 20 m, but some are restricted to deeper sections of the reef, to at least 200 m. Butterflyfishes are active during daylight hours and seek shelter close to the reef's surface during the night. They often assume a drab nocturnal colour pattern. Most species are restricted to a relatively small area of the reef, perhaps an isolated patch-reef or part of a more extensive reef system. They travel extensively throughout their home range foraging for food. Many species feed on live coral polyps; others consume a mixed diet consisting of small invertebrates and algae. A few species, for example *Heniochus diphreutes* (Plate **56.13**), feed in mid water on zooplankton. Young butterflyfishes are highly prized as aquarium pets. Most species grow to a maximum length of under 30 cm.

Butterflyfishes are one of the most conspicuous inhabitants of tropical reefs and have attracted the attention of behavioural scientists. Some species are generally found solitarily or occasionally in small groups. Others form pairs, and depending on the frequency of their pairing tendencies are termed weakly or strongly paired. The weak category includes such species as *Chaetodon assarius* (**2**), *C. citrinellus* (**5**), *C. lunula* (**11**), and *C. ornatissimus* (**12**). Examples of strong pairing species are *C. ephippium* (**6**) and *C. punctatofasciatus* (Plate **56.2**), and *C. trifascialis* (Plate **56.5**) and *C. trifasciatus* (Plate **56.6**). There is strong evidence that fishes in the latter category form lifetime relationships.

PLATE 56: BUTTERFLYFISHES

CHAETODONTIDAE

1. TEARDROP BUTTERFLYFISH
Chaetodon unimaculatus Bloch, 1787
Inhabits coral reefs; distinguished by black spot on white background and yellow fins; N.W. Australia, Great Barrier Reef and throughout S.E. Asia; Indo-C. Pacific; to 23 cm.

2. SPOTBANDED BUTTERFLYFISH
Chaetodon punctatofasciatus Cuvier, 1831
Inhabits coral reefs; distinguished by bars on back and spots below; N.W. Australia, Great Barrier Reef and throughout S.E. Asia; mainly W. Pacific; to 13 cm.

3. OVALSPOT BUTTERFLYFISH
Chaetodon speculum Cuvier, 1831
Inhabits coral reefs; distinguished by round spot on yellow background; N.W. Australia, Great Barrier Reef and throughout S.E. Asia; mainly W. Pacific; to 15 cm.

4. DOUBLESADDLE BUTTERFLYFISH
Chaetodon ulietensis Cuvier, 1831
Inhabits coral reefs distinguished by two broad blackish bars and a series of narrow vertical lines on white background; N.W. Australia, Great Barrier Reef and throughout S.E. Asia; mainly W. Pacific; to 14 cm.

5. CHEVRON BUTTERFLYFISH
Chaetodon trifascialis Quoy & Gaimard, 1825
Inhabits coral reefs; distinguished by triangular-shaped body and narrow chevron markings; N.W. Australia, Great Barrier Reef and throughout S.E. Asia; Indo-C. Pacific; to 18 cm.

6. INDIAN REDFIN BUTTERFLYFISH
Chaetodon trifasciatus Park, 1797
Inhabits coral reefs; distinguished by dark stripes on orange to purple background and reddish anal fin; Indian Ocean ranging to Sumatra, Java and Bali; *C. lunulatus* (not shown) is a nearly identical species found in Australia and the W. and C. Pacific; to 15 cm.

7. ORANGEBANDED CORALFISH
Coradion chrysozonus (Cuvier, 1831)
Inhabits coral reefs and trawl grounds; distinguished by orange-brown bars and black pelvic fins; N.W. Australia, Great Barrier Reef and throughout S.E. Asia; mainly Indo-Australian Archipelago; to 13 cm.

8. MARGINED CORALFISH
Chelmon marginalis Richardson, 1842
Inhabits coral reefs, distinguished by long snout and orange bars; N. Australia from Shark Bay, W. Australia to Torres Strait, Queensland; also E. Lesser Sunda Islands, Indonesia; to 20 cm.

9. FORCEPS FISH
Forcipiger flavissimus Jordan & McGregor, 1898
Inhabits coral reefs; distinguished by long snout, black colour on upper half of head and yellow colour of body; N.W. Australia, Great Barrier Reef and throughout S.E. Asia; Indo-E. Pacific; to 17 cm.

10. PENNANT BANNERFISH
Heniochus chrysostomus Cuvier, 1831
Inhabits coral reefs; distinguished by short 'banner' and broad black band across head that is continuous with pelvic fins; N.W. Australia, Great Barrier Reef and throughout S.E. Asia; mainly W. and C. Pacific; to 17 cm.

11. SINGULAR BANNERFISH
Heniochus singularius Smith & Radcliffe, 1911
Inhabits coral reefs; distinguished by short 'banner', slight hump on forehead and yellow dorsal and caudal fins; N.W. Australia, Great Barrier Reef and throughout S.E Asia; mainly W. and C. Pacific; to 25 cm.

12. LONGFIN BANNERFISH
Heniochus acuminatus (Linnaeus, 1758)
Inhabits coral reefs, often in pairs or alone; distinguished by elongated dorsal rays, resembles *H. diphreutes* (13), but longer snout and rounded anal fin; found throughout the region; Indo-C. Pacific; to 20 cm.

13. SCHOOLING BANNERFISH
Heniochus diphreutes Jordan, 1903
Inhabits sandy areas around outcrops; usually in schools; distinguished by elongated dorsal rays, resembles *H. acuminatus* (12), but has shorter snout and angular anal fin; N.W. Australia, Great Barrier Reef and throughout S.E. Asia; Indo-C. Pacific; to 20 cm.

14. HORNED BANNERFISH
Heniochus varius (Cuvier, 1829)
Inhabits coral reefs; distinguished by lack of 'banner', and forehead bump and 'horns'; offshore reefs of N.W. Australia, Great Barrier Reef and throughout S.E. Asia; mainly W. and C. Pacific; to 18 cm.

15. OCELLATE BUTTERFLYFISH
Parachaetodon ocellatus (Cuvier, 1831)
Inhabits silty coral reefs, often seen on sand or silt bottoms near reefs; distinguished by tall, triangular dorsal fin and orange-brown bars; found throughout the region; Indo-W. Pacific; to 18 cm.

TWIN SPECIES

Many reef fishes have close relatives or 'sister' species that are very similar in overall appearance. These pairs have obviously evolved from a common ancestral population that became fragmented by such barriers as shifting ocean currents, sea temperature changes and emergent land resulting from lowered sea levels or tectonic processes. In cases where the ancestral stock is widely distributed it may become fragmented into more than two populations, evolving into 'complexes' of several closely allied species. As the barriers may be only temporary, though persisting for thousands of years (a short span in terms of geological time), members of a pair may once again occur in the same area.

The two similar species of *Heniochus* are good examples of this process. Although they now have overlapping distributions, they are more or less ecologically separated. The Schooling Bannerfish *H. diphreutes* (13) forms groups which feed on plankton high above the bottom, whereas the Longfin Bannerfish *H. acuminatus* (12) lives alone or in small groups which forage on bottom-dwelling invertebrates. Other species-pairs continue to exist more or less separately, except for a relatively small overlap zone. For example, a number of pairs have one member in the Indian Ocean and another in the Pacific.

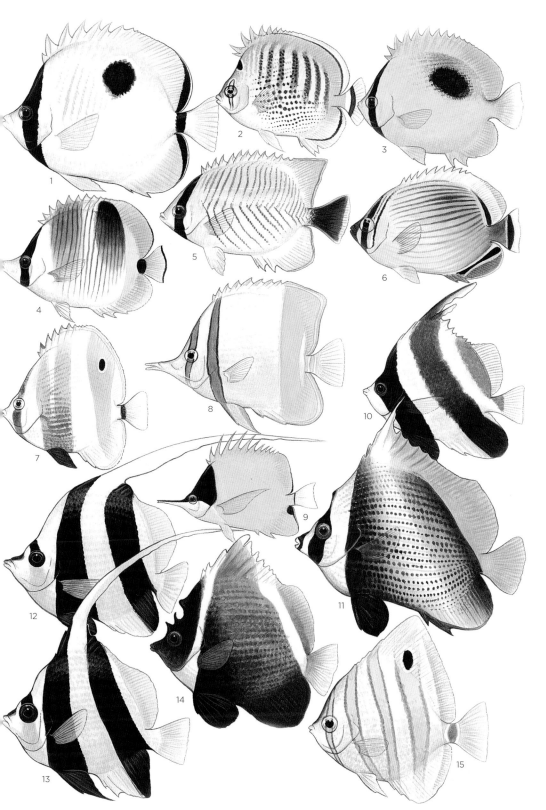

PLATE 57: BUTTERFLYFISHES

CHAETODONTIDAE

1. MERTENS' BUTTERFLYFISH
Chaetodon mertensii Cuvier, 1831
Inhabits coral reefs; distinguished by orange areas on posterior part of body and tail and dark chevron markings on side; *C. madagaskariensis* of Indian Ocean is a synonym; Great Barrier Reef, New Guinea and Philippines; Indo-C. Pacific; to 12 cm.

2. SPOTTED BUTTERFLYFISH
Chaetodon guttatissimus Bennett, 1833
Inhabits coral reefs, commonly seen on outer slopes; similar to *C. punctatofasciatus* (Plate **56**.2), but lacks vertical bars; an Indian Ocean species found in our region only at Christmas Island and off the Indian Ocean coast of Sumatra; to 11 cm.

3. LATTICE BUTTERFLYFISH
Chaetodon rafflesii Bennett, 1830
Inhabits coral reefs; distinguished by network pattern on sides, and overall yellow colouration with black band on tail and rear part of dorsal fin; Great Barrier Reef, offshore reefs of W. Australia and throughout S.E. Asia; E. Indian Ocean and W. and C. Pacific; to 15 cm.

4. DOTTED BUTTERFLYFISH
Chaetodon semeion Bleeker, 1855
Inhabits coral reefs, usually seen in pairs on outer slopes; distinguished by overall yellow colour, horizontal rows of small dark spots on side, blue area in front of eyes and on forehead, and broad black band at base of dorsal and anal fins; Great Barrier Reef, offshore reefs of W. Australia and throughout S.E. Asia; E. Indian Ocean and W. Pacific; to 23 cm.

5. YELLOWTAIL BUTTERFLYFISH
Chaetodon xanthurus Bleeker, 1857
Inhabits coral reefs, usually below 15–20 m depth; similar to *C. mertensii* (**1**), but has reticulated pattern on sides rather than dark chevrons; Indonesia and Philippines north to Japan; to 14 cm.

6. DOT-AND-DASH BUTTERFLYFISH
Chaetodon pelewensis Kner, 1868
Inhabits coral reefs, usually seen on outer reef slopes; distinguished by dark-edged orange bar through eye, diagonal rows of spots and lines on side, and yellow to orange tail base; Great Barrier Reef, offshore reefs of W. Australia and throughout S.E. Asia; S.W. and C. Pacific; to 12 cm.

7. ECLIPSE BUTTERFLYFISH
Chaetodon bennetti Cuvier, 1831
Inhabits coral reefs, usually seen on outer reef slopes; distinguished by large, pale-edged black spot on upper side and pair of pale (white to bluish) diagonal bands between gill cover and anal fin; Great Barrier Reef, offshore reefs of W. Australia and throughout S.E. Asia; Indo-C. Pacific; to 18 cm.

8. YELLOW-DOTTED BUTTERFLYFISH
Chaetodon selene Bleeker, 1853
Inhabits coral reefs, but generally rare in New Guinea; distinguished by general white colour, diagonal rows of yellow spots on the front, upper part of body; yellow dorsal and anal fins, and black rim around posterior and dorsal part of body; Indonesia and New Guinea northward to Japan; to 15 cm.

9. SPOTNAPE BUTTERFLYFISH
Chaetodon oxycephalus Bleeker, 1853
Inhabits coral reefs; feeds on coral polyps and anemones; very similar to *C. lineolatus* (Plate **55**.7), but has isolated dark patch on forehead; Great Barrier Reef and throughout S.E. Asia; E. Indian Ocean and W. Pacific; to 25 cm.

10. SPOT-TAIL BUTTERFLYFISH
Chaetodon ocellicaudus Cuvier, 1831
Inhabits coral reefs; very similar to *C. melannotus* (**11**), but has isolated spot on tail base; Great Barrier Reef, offshore reefs of W. Australia and throughout S.E. Asia; to 14 cm.

11. BLACKBACK BUTTERFLYFISH
Chaetodon melannotus Bloch & Schneider, 1801
Inhabits coral reefs; feeds mainly on coral polyps; distinguished by thin eye-bar, yellow snout and fins, narrow diagonal black stripes on side and black upper back; very similar to *C. ocellicaudus* (**10**), but lacks isolated spot on tail base; Great Barrier Reef, offshore reefs of W. Australia and throughout S.E. Asia; Indo-W. Pacific; to 15 cm.

12. VAGABOND BUTTERFLYFISH
Chaetodon vagabundus Linnaeus, 1758
Inhabits coral reefs; distinguished by pattern of narrow diagonal lines on side, blackish band across posterior part of body and dark bar on middle of tail; Great Barrier Reef, Kimberley coast and offshore reefs of W. Australia and throughout S.E. Asia; Indo-C. Pacific; to 18 cm.

13. WHITE COLLAR BUTTERFLYFISH
Chaetodon collare Bloch, 1787
Inhabits coral reefs in 3–20 m depth; distinguished by dark overall colour with pale scale centres, brilliant white bar behind eye, and red on basal half of tail; Sumatra, Java and Bali, mainly on Indian Ocean coasts; mainly Indian Ocean; to 16 cm.

14. RETICULATE BUTTERFLYFISH
Chaetodon reticulatus Cuvier, 1831
Inhabits coral reefs, usually seen in pairs on outer reefs; feeds mainly on corals; distinguished by overall blackish colour with rows of pale spots on side, broad pale band behind head and pale dorsal fin; Great Barrier Reef, New Guinea, Philippines and N. Sulawesi; W. and C. Pacific; to 16 cm.

HYBRID BUTTERFLYFISHES AND ANGELFISHES

Although hybridisation is common in freshwater fishes, very few marine hybrids are known. Therefore it is surprising that this phenomenon is relatively common among the butterflyfishes (Plates 55–58) and the related angelfishes (Plates 58–60). Approximately 15 cases have been reported for butterflyfishes and another 8 for angelfishes. It is interesting to speculate on the circumstances under which this event might occur. Behavioural research reveals that butterflyfishes can be categorised as solitary, pair-forming or aggregating according to their social disposition. Most of the butterfly and angelfish species involved in hybridisation belong to solitary or pair-forming species. It seems likely that this phenomenon results when there is a shortage of mates belonging to the same species. Therefore, individuals are forced to spawn with a closely related species. The aberrant colour patterns of hybrid individuals are usually very distinct. They generally possess a mixture of colour pattern features from each of the parent species. A few of the butterflyfish hybrids observed in our region include *Chaetodon auriga* x *C. ephippium*, *C. ephippium* x *C. semeion*, *C. kleinii* x *C. unimaculatus* and *C. meyeri* x *C. ornatissimus*.

PLATE 58: BUTTERFLYFISHES AND ANGELFISHES

CHAETODONTIDAE

1. TRIANGULAR BUTTERFLYFISH
Chaetodon baronessa Cuvier, 1829
Inhabits coral reefs, usually seen in rich areas of live coral growth, often amongst branching *Acropora*; feeds on corals; distinguished by elevated shape and dark-coloured body with narrow-pale chevron markings; Great Barrier Reef, offshore reefs of W. Australia and throughout S.E. Asia; E. Indian Ocean and W. Pacific; to 15 cm.

2. DUSKY BUTTERFLYFISH
Chaetodon flavirostris Günther, 1874
Inhabits coral reefs, often seen in pairs; distinguished by dark body colour and yellow fins; S. Pacific from Great Barrier Reef to Pitcairn Group; to 20 cm.

3. THREE-STRIPED BUTTERFLYFISH
Chaetodon tricinctus Waite, 1901
Inhabits outer reefs and lagoons in areas of rich coral growth at depths of about 3–15 m; Distinguished by three dark bands on white background; Lord Howe I., Norfolk I., and N. Tasman Sea (Elizabeth and Middleton reefs); to 15 cm.

4. TWOSPOT CORALFISH
Coradion melanopus (Cuvier, 1831)
Inhabits coastal, lagoon and seaward coral reefs; similar to *Chelmon muelleri* (**10**), but has double-bar in front of tail base and pair of ocellated spots; Indonesia, Philippines and New Guinea; to 15 cm.

5. GÜNTHER'S BUTTERFLYFISH
Chaetodon guentheri Ahl, 1913
Inhabits coral reefs and rocky areas, usually seen in aggregations at depths of 5–40 m; distinguished by spotted pattern and bright yellow dorsal and anal fins; Great Barrier Reef (rare) and scattered localities in Indonesia exposed to cool upwelling; edge of W. Pacific; to 14 cm.

6. RAINFORD'S BUTTERFLYFISH
Chaetodon rainfordi McCulloch, 1923
Inhabits coral reefs; distinguished by broad bluish-grey bars and orange margins and orange eye bar; coastal Queensland, Great Barrier Reef, Lord Howe I. and S. Papua New Guinea; to 15 cm.

7. BEAKED CORALFISH
Chelmon rostratus (Linnaeus, 1758)
Inhabits coral reefs, frequently seen in pairs; distinguished by elongate snout, and pattern of orange bars with black ocellus on basal part of dorsal fin; also known as Copperband Butterflyfish; Great Barrier Reef and throughout S.E. Asia; Andaman Sea and W. Pacific; to 20 cm.

8. EIGHTBAND BUTTERFLYFISH
Chaetodon octofasciatus Bloch, 1787
Inhabits shallow, sheltered lagoons (often turbid and silty) and inner coral reefs at depths of about 3–20 m; distinguished by eight narrow, dark bands (including tail) on either yellow or white background; Sri Lanka to New Guinea and Solomon Islands and north to S. Japan; Indo-W. Pacific; to 12 cm.

9. BURGESS' BUTTERFLYFISH
Chaetodon burgessi Allen & Stark, 1973
Inhabits coral reefs, usually adjacent to steep drop-offs below 20 m depth; distinguished by diagonal black bar behind head and diagonal demarcation between dark and light areas of body; Indonesia, Philippines and Caroline Islands; to 14 cm.

10. MULLER'S CORALFISH
Chelmon muelleri (Klunzinger, 1879)
Inhabits silty coastal reefs and estuaries; similar to *C. rostratus* (**7**), but bars are brown instead of orange; Northern Territory and Queensland; to 18 cm.

11. HIGHFIN CORALFISH
Coradion altivelis McCulloch, 1916
Inhabits coral reefs, usually in lagoons or on silty coastal reefs; similar to *C. chrysozonus* (Plate **56**.7), but the double-bars on the anterior part of the body are narrower and darker and the ocellus on the dorsal fin is usually faint or absent in adults; Great Barrier Reef, offshore reefs of W. Australia and throughout S.E. Asia; W. Pacific; to 15 cm.

12. PYRAMID BUTTERFLYFISH
Hemitaurichthys polylepis (Bleeker, 1857)
Inhabits coral reefs, seen on outer reef slopes; forms large mid-water aggregations that feed on zooplankton; distinguished by a pyramid-shaped white area surrounded by yellow, head is usually brown; Great Barrier Reef, offshore reefs of W. Australia and throughout S.E. Asia; W. and C. Pacific; to 18 cm.

13. LONGNOSE BUTTERFLYFISH
Forcipiger longirostris (Broussonet, 1782)
Inhabits coral reefs; distinguished by elongate snout and rich yellow colouration with upper part of head black; very similar to *F. flavissimus* (Plate **56**.9), but has much longer snout and rows of black dots on the chest, it also possesses a rare all-black or brown colour phase; *F. wanai* (not shown) is a similar species found at Cenderawasih Bay, West Papua; Great Barrier Reef, offshore reefs of W. Australia and throughout S.E. Asia; Indo-C. Pacific; to 22 cm.

14. MASKED BANNERFISH
Heniochus monoceros Cuvier, 1831
Inhabits coral reefs, usually seen in pairs that shelter in crevices; similar to *H. singularius* (Plate **56**.11), but dark head bar extends to base of dorsal, and pattern of banding on the body is different; Great Barrier Reef, offshore reefs of W. Australia and throughout S.E. Asia; Indo-C. Pacific; to 23 cm.

POMACANTHIDAE

15. CORAL BEAUTY
Centropyge bispinosa (Günther, 1860)
Inhabits coral reefs, common on outer reef slopes; distinguished by blue head and fins and pattern of blue bars on red-orange background, the number and width of the blue bars is quite variable; Great Barrier Reef, offshore reefs of W. Australia and throughout S.E. Asia; Indo-C. Pacific; to 10 cm.

16. FLAME ANGELFISH
Centropyge loricula (Günther, 1874)
Inhabits coral reefs in lagoons and seaward slope between 2–55 m depth; distinguished by bright red colouration and black bars; Great Barrier Reef and Coral Sea; W. and C. Pacific; to 10 cm.

17. WHITETAIL ANGELFISH
Centropyge fisheri (Snyder, 1904)
Inhabits rubble areas in the vicinity of coral reefs, usually seen below 20 m depth; distinguished by dark blue to blackish colour with contrasted pale caudal fin; Great Barrier Reef, offshore reefs of W. Australia and throughout S.E. Asia; W. and C. Pacific; to 7 cm.

LONGNOSE VERSUS LONGNOSE

Longnose Butterflyfishes are among the most conspicuous of reef fishes, but their identification is sometimes confusing. The true Longnose Butterflyfish *Forcipiger longirostris* (**13**) is one of the widest ranging of all coral-reef fishes, ranging from Africa to the Americas. The elongated snout and brilliant yellow colouration are readily diagnostic — except they offer little help when trying to differentiate it from the Forceps Fish *F. flavissimus* (Plate **56**.9). Although colour patterns of the two are nearly identical, there is a significant difference in snout length — that of the Longnose is nearly one-half to one-third longer. The Longnose is further distinguished by several rows of small black dots on the breast. It is also characterised by a relatively rare dark-brown variety, which is most often seen around volcanic islands.

PLATE 59: ANGELFISHES

POMACANTHIDAE

1. THREESPOT ANGELFISH
Apolemichthys trimaculatus (Cuvier, 1831)
Inhabits offshore coral reefs, usually below 15 m depth; distinguished by blue lips, black spot on forehead and broad black margin on anal fin; N.W. Australia, Great Barrier Reef and throughout S.E. Asia; Indo-W. Pacific; to 20 cm.

2. BICOLOR ANGELFISH
Centropyge bicolor (Bloch, 1787)
Inhabits coral reefs; distinguished by blue band through eye and yellow-blue combination on head and body; N.W. Australia (rare inshore), Great Barrier Reef and throughout S.E. Asia; mainly central and W. Pacific; to 15 cm.

3. EIBL'S ANGELFISH
Centropyge eibli Klausewitz, 1963
Inhabits coral reefs; distinguished by black tail and narrow brown or orange bars on side; W. Australia (Ningaloo and offshore reefs) and S. Indonesia (Sumatra to Flores); C. and E. Indian Ocean; to 11 cm.

4. KEYHOLE ANGELFISH
Centropyge tibicen (Cuvier, 1831)
Inhabits coral reefs; distinguished by vertically elongate white spot on middle of side and yellow margin on pelvic and anal fins; N.W. Australia, Great Barrier Reef and throughout S.E. Asia; mainly W. Pacific; to 14 cm.

5. SCRIBBLED ANGELFISH
Chaetodontoplus duboulayi (Günther, 1867)
Inhabits coastal reefs on rubble, soft bottoms, or open flat bottoms with rock, coral, sponge and seawhip outcrops; distinguished by dark bar through eye, yellow arc along back and yellow tail, female (not shown) is dark on sides or has numerous blue or yellowish spots, male has broken wavy blue lines; N. Australia and S. New Guinea, also reported from Taiwan; to 28 cm.

6. YELLOWTAIL ANGELFISH
Chaetodontoplus personifer (McCulloch, 1914)
Inhabits similar areas to *C. duboulayi* (5), usually in the vicinity of reefs; distinguished by blue 'mask' with yellow spots on cheek and above eye, juvenile is black with broad white bar behind eye and has yellow pelvic fins and tail; N. Australia only between Abrolhos Islands and Gulf of Carpentaria; *C. meredithi* (Plate **60.6**) is a nearly identical species from E. Australia; to 35 cm.

7. SIXBAND ANGELFISH
Pomacanthus sexstriatus (Cuvier, 1831)
Inhabits coral reefs; distinguished by white bar behind eye, 4–5 dark bars on side and numerous blue spots on body and fins, juvenile similar to *P. navarchus* (**8**), but white bars generally broader; N.W. Australia, Great Barrier Reef and throughout S.E. Asia; Indo-Australian Archipelago; to 45 cm.

8. BLUEGIRDLE ANGELFISH
Pomacanthus navarchus (Cuvier, 1831)
Inhabits protected lagoon coral reefs; distinguished by broad yellow-orange area on sides with small dark spots, yellow-orange dorsal and tail fins and bright blue stripe from snout to belly, also narrow blue margins on most fins; offshore reefs of N.W. Australia, Great Barrier Reef and throughout S.E. Asia; Indo-Australian Archipelago; to 28 cm.

9. EMPEROR ANGELFISH
Pomacanthus imperator (Bloch, 1787)
Inhabits coral reefs; distinguished by blue-edged black band through eye and narrow yellow stripes on side, juveniles dark with narrow white lines forming concentric circles on rear part of body; N.W. Australia, Great Barrier Reef and throughout S.E. Asia; Indo-C. Pacific; to 31 cm.

10. BLUE ANGELFISH
Pomacanthus semicirculatus (Cuvier, 1831)
Inhabits coral reefs; distinguished by brown to yellowish colour with overall bluish hue imparted by numerous blue spots on body and fins, also has blue margins on cheek, gill cover and most fins; juveniles similar to *P. sexstriatus* (**7**) and *P. navarchus* (**8**), but posterior white bars are strongly curved; N.W. Australia, Great Barrier Reef and throughout S.E. Asia; Indo-W. Pacific; to 38 cm.

11. REGAL ANGELFISH
Pygoplites diacanthus (Boddaert, 1772)
Inhabits coral reefs; distinguished by alternating dark-edged white and yellow-orange cross-bars; offshore reefs of N.W. Australia, Great Barrier Reef and throughout S.E. Asia; Indo-C. Pacific; to 25 cm.

BIOLOGY OF ANGELFISHES

Most angelfishes are greatly dependent on shelter in the form of boulders, caves and coral crevices. Aside from a few *Chaetodontoplus* species, they are seldom seen in the open. Typically, most species are territorial, spending much of the time on the bottom in search of food or dashing back and forth into shelter. Members of the genus *Genicanthus* are usually open-water swimmers, often forming aggregations that forage on plankton well above the bottom. Two other basic types of feeding are apparent among the other genera. Many of the smaller species, including those in *Centropyge*, feed mainly on algae, which is grazed from rocky surfaces. Most of the larger angels, particularly those in *Pomacanthus*, consume sponges, supplemented with algae, zooantharians, tunicates, gorgonians, hydroids and seagrasses. Spawning occurs at dusk and usually involves a single pair, although individual males may mate successively with several different females. Males set up territories by driving away other male competitors. They then swim up off the bottom and await the arrival of one or more females. When a prospective mate approaches, the male exhibits a courtship display that may include fin erection, rapid back and forth swimming and body 'quivering'. Eventually the pair spiral slowly towards the surface, suddenly shed eggs and sperm at the apex of the ascent, then swim back to the bottom. Hatching of the tiny (less than 1 mm) eggs occurs in 15–20 hours. Angelfishes offer a dazzling array of patterns — sparking a great deal of scientific controversy about their possible purpose. Many theories have been proposed, but none have been proved with any certainty. Large angelfishes are famous for their dramatically different juvenile patterns, which gradually change as the fish grows older. According to one theory, the striking juvenile livery is actually a type of camouflage, serving to break up the outline of the fish so it effectively blends with the high contrast pattern of bright sunlit patches and shadows that characterise the reef environment.

PLATE 60: ANGELFISHES

POMACANTHIDAE

1. LEMONPEEL ANGELFISH
Centropyge flavissima (Cuvier, 1831)
Inhabits coral reefs, common in lagoons of oceanic islands
and atolls; distinguished by bright yellow colour with blue
cheek spine, and blue margin on edge of gill cover followed
by thin dark bar; Great Barrier Reef (rare); *C. cocosensis* (not
shown) is a similar species from Christmas and Cocos-
Keeling Islands; W. and C. Pacific to 14 cm.

2. YELLOW ANGELFISH
Centropyge heraldi Woods & Schultz, 1953
Inhabits coral reefs in 5–20 m depth; similar to *C. flavissima*
(1), but yellow colour is duller and has dusky patch behind
eye, also lacks blue markings on head; Great Barrier Reef
north to Taiwan and eastward to Tuamotu Islands;
C. woodheadi (not shown) is a similar species with black edge
on rear dorsal fin, from Coral Sea to Fiji and Tonga; to 11 cm.

3. MULTI-BARRED ANGELFISH
Paracentropyge multifasciata (Smith & Radcliffe, 1911)
Inhabits outer reef slopes, usually seen in caves and crevices of
steep slopes below 20 m depth; distinguished by bold pattern
of black bars and yellow pelvic and anal fins; Great Barrier
Reef and throughout S.E. Asia; W. and C. Pacific; to 10 cm.

4. MIDNIGHT ANGELFISH
Centropyge nox (Bleeker, 1853)
Inhabits coral reefs, but generally rare; distinguished by all
black colouration including tail; Great Barrier Reef, offshore
reefs of W. Australia and throughout S.E. Asia; W. Pacific;
to 9 cm.

5. PEARLSCALE ANGELFISH
Centropyge vrolikii (Bleeker, 1853)
Inhabits coral reefs, common in lagoons and on outer reefs;
distinguished by grey colour on anterior part of body and
dark colouration posteriorly, also has dark streak on upper
edge of gill cover; Great Barrier Reef, offshore reefs of
W. Australia and throughout S.E. Asia; W. and C. Pacific;
to 10 cm.

6. QUEENSLAND YELLOWTAIL ANGELFISH
Chaetodontoplus meredithi Kuiter, 1990
Inhabits silty coastal and inner reefs; distinguished by black
body, blue head with yellow spots and yellow tail; similar to
C. personifer (Patete **59.6**) from N.W. Australia; Queensland;
to 25 cm.

7. BLACK VELVET ANGELFISH
Chaetodontoplus melanosoma (Bleeker, 1853)
Inhabits coral and rocky reefs in 10–40 m depth, often on
steep drop-offs; distinguished by black body with pale wash
at front and yellow margin on dorsal, anal and caudal fins;
Indonesia to New Guinea; W. Pacific; to 7 cm.

8. VERMICULATE ANGELFISH
Chaetodontoplus mesoleucus (Bloch, 1787)
Inhabits coastal coral reefs and sheltered lagoons, usually
on silty reefs; distinguished by purplish-brown colour on
posterior part of body and on dorsal and anal fins, also has
undulating, narrow pale lines on side; Indonesia and New
Guinea northward to Japan; to 17 cm.

9. ORNATE ANGELFISH
Genicanthus bellus Randall, 1975
Inhabits outer reef slopes, usually at depths of 50–100 m, but
often seen in 20–30 m at Cenderawasih Bay, W. Papua; male
with with golden, mid-lateral orange stripe and another at
dorsal-fin base; female with black dorsal fin; black band on
body, and black caudal-fin margins; also known as Bellus
Angelfish; E. Indian Ocean and W.-C. Pacific, including
Cocos-Keeling Is., West Papua, Philippines, Mariana Is.
and Society Is. to 18 cm.

10. LAMARCK'S ANGELFISH
Genicanthus lamarck (Lacepède, 1802)
Inhabits coral reefs, often seen in groups; feeds on plankton;
distinguished by pattern of black stripes, black dorsal fin and
prolonged tail filaments; female (not shown) has white pelvic
fin and prominent black upper and lower margins on tail;
throughout S.E. Asia; Indo-W. Pacific; to 20 cm.

11. SWALLOWTAIL ANGELFISH
Genicanthus melanospilos (Bleeker, 1857)
Inhabits coral reefs, usually seen on steep outer-reef slopes;
generally found in groups with one male per several females;
feeds on plankton; male distinguished by numerous narrow
dark bars on side and black spot on midline of breast, females
lack these features, but possess bold black upper and lower
margins on the caudal fin; Great Barrier Reef, offshore
reefs of W. Australia and throughout S. E. Asia; mainly
W. Pacific; to 18 cm.

12. WATANABE'S ANGELFISH
Genicanthus watanabei (Yasuda & Tominaga, 1970)
Inhabits coral reefs, usually seen on outer slopes and
drop-offs below 20 m depth; male distinguished by blue back
and dark stripes on lower side; female is plain light grey with
black margins on fins; Queensland eastward to Tuamotus
and north to Ryukyu Islands; to 18 cm.

13. BLUEFACE ANGELFISH
Pomacanthus xanthometopon (Bleeker, 1853)
Inhabits coral reefs, usually seen solitarily on outer reefs;
distinguished by blue scribble markings on head, yellow
'mask', yellow to orange breast and pectoral fins, black spot
at base of posterior part of dorsal fin and bright yellow tail;
juvenile (not shown) is similar to that of *P. sexstriatus* (Plate
59.6), but pale bars (about 15 between eye and tail); Great
Barrier Reef, offshore reefs of W. Australia and throughout
S.E. Asia; Maldive Islands to W. Pacific; to 38 cm.

14. BLUE-RINGED ANGELFISH
Pomacanthus annularis (Bloch, 1787)
Inhabits coral reefs, sometimes seen in silty bays or harbours;
distinguished by diagonal blue bands on side, blue ring above
upper rear corner of gill cover, and white tail; juveniles are
bluish-black with narrow white and blue bars; throughout
S.E. Asia; E. Indian Ocean and W. Pacific; to 30 cm.

MORE ABOUT ANGELFISHES

Angelfishes of the family Pomacanthidae are close
relatives of the butterflyfishes (Plates 55–58) and until
recently were considered to belong in the same family.
Worldwide there are about 90 known species. Most
are inhabitants of tropical seas, being found mainly in
the vicinity of coral reefs. They occur either as solitary
individuals or in aggregations. Many species inhabit
shallow water, from only 2–3 m down to 10–15 m
depth. Others are restricted to deep water (to at least
75 m depth). Angelfishes are favourite aquarium pets,
well known for their brilliant array of colour patterns.
Many species exhibit dramatic changes from
the juvenile to adult stage. Most angelfishes are
dependent on shelter in the form of boulders, caves,
or coral crevices. Typically, most species are territorial
and spend the daylight hours near the bottom in
search of food. The diet varies according to species;
some feed almost exclusively on algae, others
prefer mainly sponges supplemented by a variety
of benthic invertebrates, and a few are mid-water
zooplankton feeders. Divers are sometimes startled
by the powerful drumming or thumping sound
produced by large adults in the genus *Pomacanthus*.

PLATE 61: DAMSELFISHES

POMACENTRIDAE

1. BANDED SERGEANT
Abudefduf septemfasciatus (Cuvier, 1830)
Inhabits shallow, wave-swept reefs; distinguished by 7 grey bars; found throughout the region; Indo-C. Pacific; to 22 cm.

2. BLACKSPOT SERGEANT
Abudefduf sordidus (Forsskål, 1775)
Inhabits shallow, wave-swept reefs; similar to *A. septemfasciatus* (**1**), but has black spot on top of tail base; found throughout the region; Indo-C. Pacific; to 22 cm.

3. INDO-PACIFIC SERGEANT
Abudefduf vaigiensis (Quoy & Gaimard, 1825)
Inhabits coral, rocky and weedy reefs; distinguished by 5 dark bars; found throughout the region; Indo-C. Pacific; to 22 cm.

4. BENGAL SERGEANT
Abudefduf bengalensis (Bloch, 1787)
Inhabits coral and weedy reefs, distinguished from other *Abudefduf* by narrower bars and rounded lobes of tail; also known as Narrow-banded Sergeant Major; found throughout the region; Indo-W. Pacific; to 18 cm.

5. SCISSORTAIL SERGEANT
Abudefduf sexfasciatus (Lacepède, 1801)
Inhabits coral and weedy reefs; similar to *A. vaigiensis* (**3**), but has black streaks on tail fin; found throughout the region; Indo-C. Pacific; to 22 cm.

6. STAGHORN DAMSEL
Amblyglyphidodon curacao (Bloch, 1787)
Inhabits coral reefs, often among staghorn corals; distinguished by ovate shape and faint bars; found throughout the region; mainly W. Pacific; to 13 cm.

7. BANDED DAMSEL
Dischistodus darwiniensis (Whitley, 1928)
Inhabits coral and rocky reefs near sand; distinguished by brown bands on side and 2 dark spots on dorsal fin; N. Australia only, between Dampier, W. Australia and Gulf of Carpentaria; to 15 cm.

8. HONEYHEAD DAMSEL
Dischistodus prosopotaenia (Bleeker, 1852)
Inhabits coral reefs near sand; distinguished by pale band through middle of body; found throughout the region; mainly W. Pacific; to 20 cm.

9. REGAL DEMOISELLE
Neopomacentrus cyanomos (Bleeker, 1856)
Inhabits coral reefs, distinguished by slender shape and white or yellow on rear of dorsal, anal and tail fins; found throughout the region; Indo-W. Pacific; to 10 cm.

10. BROWN DEMOISELLE
Neopomacentrus filamentosus (Macleay, 1882)
Inhabits coral reefs; distinguished by slender shape, blue border on fins and dark margins on tail; *N. aktites* (not shown) is a similar species found in N.W. Australia; Indo-Malay Archipelago; to 9 cm.

11. YELLOWTAIL DEMOISELLE
Neopomacentrus azysron (Bleeker, 1877)
Inhabits coral reefs; distinguished by slender shape, dark 'ear-spot' and yellow tail; found throughout the region; W. Pacific; to 9 cm.

12. LAGOON DAMSEL
Hemiglyphidodon plagiometopon (Bleeker, 1852)
Inhabits coral reefs, distinguished by plain brown colouration, pointed snout and lack of spines along the margin of the cheek; found throughout the region; mainly W. Pacific; to 22 cm.

13. BLACK DAMSEL
Neoglyphidodon melas (Cuvier, 1830)
Inhabits coral reefs, often with soft corals; adults entirely black; found throughout the region; Indo-W. Pacific; to 16 cm.

14. SCARFACE DAMSEL
Neoglyphidodon nigroris (Cuvier, 1830)
Inhabits coral reefs; adults variable, mainly dark brown off N.W. Australia and some parts of W. Indonesia, bright yellow on posterior third of body at other locations; juveniles brilliant yellow with pair of black stripes; found throughout the region; mainly W. Pacific; to 14 cm.

DAMSELS OF THE SEA

The damselfishes of the family Pomacentridae (Plates 61–67) are one of the most abundant groups of coral reef fishes. Approximately 400 species occur worldwide including over 170 from Australia and S.E. Asia. Most inhabit the tropics, but a number of species live in cooler temperate waters. They display remarkable diversity with regards to habitat preference, feeding habits and behaviour. Colouration is highly variable, ranging from drab hues of brown, grey and black to brilliant combinations of orange, yellow and neon blue. A number of species have juvenile stages characterised by a yellow body with bright blue stripes crossing the upper head and back. Most damselfishes are territorial, particularly algal-feeders such as species of the genus *Stegastes* (Plate **66.12–15**). They zealously defend their small plot against all intruders regardless of size. Damsels exhibit a highly stereotypical mode of reproduction, in which one or both partners clear a nest site on the bottom and engage in courtship displays of rapid swimming and fin extension. Males generally guard the eggs which are attached to the bottom by adhesive strands. The eggs hatch within about 2–7 days and the fragile larvae rise to the surface. They are transported by ocean currents for periods which vary from 10–50 days, depending on the species. Eventually the young fish settle to the bottom and their largely transparent bodies quickly assume the juvenile colouration. The growth rate of juveniles generally ranges from about 5–15 mm per month, gradually tapering off as maturity approaches. There is little reliable data concerning their longevity, but it appears they are capable of living to at least an age of 10 years. An unusual type of sex change has been documented in the anemonefishes (Plates 63–64) in which males eventually become females. Damselfishes feed on a wide variety of plant and animal material. Generally, the drab-coloured species feed mainly on algae, whereas many of the brightly patterned species and also members of the genus *Chromis* (Plates 64–65) obtain their nourishment from current-borne plankton.

PLATE 62: DAMSELFISHES

POMACENTRIDAE

1. BLUE DEMOISELLE
Chrysiptera cyanea (Quoy & Gaimard, 1825)
Inhabits inshore and lagoon coral reefs in 3–10 m depth; feeds mainly on algae and planktonic copepods and amphipods; distinguished by brilliant blue colour with dark stripe on snout; male differs from female in having orange margin on tail (absent at some localities) and female has dark spot at base of posterior part of dorsal fin; Great Barrier Reef, offshore reefs of W. Australia and throughout S.E. Asia; W. Pacific; to 8.5 cm.

2. GREY DEMOISELLE
Chrysiptera glauca (Cuvier, 1830)
Inhabits shallow wave-swept reefs; feeds on algae and a variety of benthic and planktonic invertebrates; distinguished by overall light grey colour and black anus; juvenile is blue with neon-blue stripe above eye; Great Barrier Reef, offshore reefs of W. Australia and throughout S.E. Asia; Indo-C. Pacific; to 11 cm.

3. PINK DEMOISELLE
Chrysiptera rex (Snyder, 1909)
Inhabits upper edge of outer reef slopes in 1–6 m depth; feeds on algae, fish eggs and planktonic copepods; distinguished by overall pale yellow to orange colour with bluish tint on head and upper back; Great Barrier Reef, offshore reefs of W. Australia and throughout S.E. Asia; W. Pacific; to 7 cm.

4. TALBOT'S DEMOISELLE
Chrysiptera talboti (Allen, 1975)
Inhabits coral reefs in 6–35 m depth, usually seen on outer slopes; feeds on algae and plankton; distinguished by yellow head and pelvic fins, purplish body and black spot at base of dorsal fin; Great Barrier Reef and throughout S.E. Asia; Andaman Sea to Fiji Islands; to 6 cm.

5. BLUEHEAD DEMOISELLE
Chrysiptera rollandi (Whitley, 1961)
Inhabits both inshore and outer reefs in 2–35 m depth; feeds on algae, plankton and small benthic invertebrates; distinguished by white body with greyish head and back; also known as Rolland's Demoiselle; Great Barrier Reef and throughout S.E. Asia; Thailand to New Caledonia; to 6 cm.

6. TWOSPOT DEMOISELLE
Chrysiptera biocellata (Quoy & Gaimard, 1825)
Inhabits lagoons and coastal coral reefs, usually seen in sandy areas with scattered coral or rock outcrops; feeds on algae, plankton and benthic invertebrates; distinguished by white bar on middle of side, juvenile is yellow with ocellus at base of middle dorsal rays and small black spot behind last dorsal ray; Great Barrier Reef, offshore reefs of W. Australia and throughout S.E. Asia; Indo-C. Pacific; to 10 cm.

7. ONESPOT DEMOISELLE
Chrysiptera unimaculata (Cuvier, 1830)
Inhabits shallow, wave-swept reef flats; feeds on algae, planktonic copepods and amphipods and a wide variety of benthic invertebrates; similar to *C. biocellata* (**6**), but lacks white bar, usually has black spot at base of last few dorsal rays; juvenile mainly yellow with blue stripe on back and ocellus on middle of dorsal fin; Great Barrier Reef and throughout S.E. Asia; Indo-C. Pacific; to 8.5 cm.

8. YELLOWFIN DEMOISELLE
Chrysiptera flavipinnis (Allen & Robertson, 1974)
Inhabits coral reefs at depths between 3–38 m; distinguished by overall blue colour and yellow upper back and dorsal fin; *C. bleekeri* (not shown) from S.E. Asia is nearly identical; S.W. Pacific, including New Guinea, E. Australia and Coral Sea; to 8.5 cm.

9. SURGE DAMSELFISH
Chrysiptera leucopoma (Cuvier, 1830)
Inhabits shallow reefs exposed to surge; feeds on algae, fish eggs and small benthic invertebrates; two colour forms are commonly seen: a mainly yellow variety with brilliant blue stripe along the back (shown here) and a dark variety with white bars; Great Barrier Reef, offshore reefs of W. Australia and throughout S.E. Asia; W.-C. Pacific; to 8.5 cm.

10. YELLOWTAIL BLUE DAMSELFISH
Chrysiptera arnazae Allen, Erdmann & Barber, 2010
Inhabits sheltered lagoons in rich coral areas; feeds mainly on algae and zooplankton; distinguished by deep blue body colour and yellow tail; *C. hemicyanea* (not shown) from offshore reefs of W. Australia and parts of Indonesia is similar, belly and pelvic/anal fins are entirely yellow; known only from N. Papua New Guinea and E. Indonesia; to 5.5 cm.

11. SPRINGER'S DEMOISELLE
Chrysiptera springeri (Allen & Lubbock, 1976)
Inhabits sheltered lagoons and inshore coral reefs in depth range of 5–30 m; distinguished by deep blue colour; *C. sinclairi* (not shown) from New Guinea nearly identical; Indonesia and Philippines; to 5.5 cm.

12. RICHARDSON'S DAMSEL
Pomachromis richardsoni (Snyder, 1909)
Inhabits coral or rocky reefs, frequently in areas exposed to surge; forms aggregations; distinguished by bold black tail margins; Great Barrier Reef, offshore reefs of W. Australia and scattered localities in S.E. Asia; Indo-W. Pacific; to 8 cm.

13. WHITEPATCH DAMSEL
Dischistodus chrysopoecilus (Schlegel & Müller, 1839)
Inhabits coastal reefs and silty lagoons, sometimes in seagrass beds; feeds on algae and detritus; distinguished by white spot below middle of dorsal fin, also pale band across forehead; Indo-Malay Archipelago; Thailand to Solomon Islands; to 16 cm.

14. BANDED DAMSELFISH
Dischistodus fasciatus (Cuvier, 1830)
Inhabits lagoon and inshore reefs with silty or sandy bottoms and coral outcrops, often in seagrass areas; feeds on detritus and algae; distinguished by dark body and pale bars; small juveniles white with dark bars; *D. darwiniensis* (not shown) from N.W. Australia is similar; Indo-Malay Archipelago; to 14 cm.

15. SILVER DEMOISELLE
Neopomacentrus anabatoides (Bleeker, 1847)
Inhabits sandy or silty bottoms around coral or rock outcrops; feeds on zooplankton in huge aggregations; distinguished by overall silvery sheen and black streaks on tail; W. Indonesia and Malaysia to Ryukyu Islands; to 8 cm.

16. BLACKVENT DAMSEL
Dischistodus melanotus (Bleeker, 1858)
Inhabits lagoon and coastal reefs; feeds on algae and detritus; distinguished by brown head and upper front part of body, and large dark blotch in front of anal fin; Great Barrier Reef and throughout S.E. Asia; edge of W. Pacific; to 16 cm.

17. WHITE DAMSEL
Dischistodus perspicillatus (Cuvier, 1830)
Inhabits sandy areas near coral reefs; feeds on algae and detritus; distinguished by mainly white colour with 3 saddle-like black spots on dorsal part of head and body; Great Barrier Reef, offshore reefs of W. Australia and throughout S.E. Asia; Andaman Sea to Vanuatu; to 20 cm.

18. VIOLET DEMOISELLE
Neopomacentrus violascens (Bleeker, 1848)
Inhabits inshore reefs on soft bottoms, forming aggregations around coral and rock outcrops, wharf pilings and wreckage; distinguished by dark brown body, yellow tail and dark 'ear-spot'; Indo-Malay Archipelago; Indonesia to Fiji; to 6 cm.

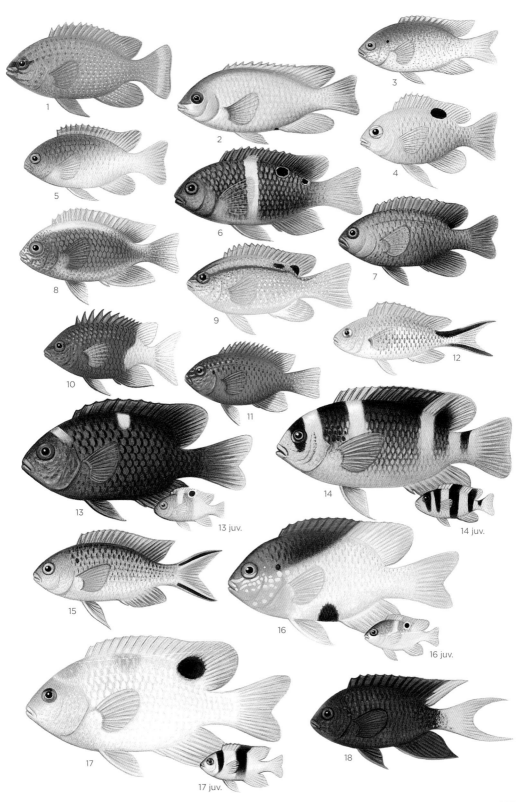

PLATE 63: DAMSELFISHES AND ANEMONEFISHES

POMACENTRIDAE

1. SPINY PULLER
Acanthochromis polyacanthus (Bleeker, 1855)
Inhabits coral reefs from the shallows to 65 m; young stay with parents after hatching, which is unlike the planktonic larval stage of all other damselfishes; feeds on plankton; distinguished by 17 dorsal spines (14 or less in other pomacentrids); colour pattern extremely variable depending on geographic locality (4 of these shown here); Great Barrier Reef, Kimberley coast of W. Australia and throughout S.E. Asia; Indo-Australian Archipelago; to 14 cm.

2. BLACKTAIL SERGEANT
Abudefduf lorenzi Hensley & Allen, 1977
Inhabits lagoons and sheltered coastal reefs to about 6 m depth, often common immediately adjacent to shore; feeds on algae; distinguished by 6 black bars and large black patch at tail base; Philippines to Solomon Islands; to 17 cm.

3. WHITLEY'S SERGEANT
Abudefduf whitleyi Allen & Robertson, 1974
Inhabits coral reefs at depths between 1–5 m; distinguished by lime-green colour, 5 narrow dark bars on side and blackish tail; Great Barrier Reef, Coral Sea and New Caledonia; to 17 cm.

4. YELLOWTAIL SERGEANT
Abudefduf notatus (Day, 1870)
Inhabits rocky inshore areas where there is usually moderate to strong wave action; distinguished by dark grey colouration, 5 narrow white bars and yellowish tail; found throughout the region, but not yet recorded from Australia; Indo-W. Pacific; to 17 cm.

5. BATUNA DAMSEL
Amblyglyphidodon batunai Allen, 1995
Inhabits sheltered, silty coastal reefs and lagoons, usually among beds of staghorn coral in 2–10 m depth; feeds mainly on zooplankton and algae; distinguished by overall pale colour becoming greenish on back, pearly lustre of scales on nape and dark, saddle-like mark on upper tail base; *A. ternatensis* (not shown) is similar and lives in the same habitat, but is overall yellowish (sometimes faintly yellow); Kimberley coast of W. Australia and Indo-Malay Archipelago; to 10 cm.

6. BLACKTAIL HUMBUG
Dascyllus melanurus Bleeker, 1854
Inhabits sheltered, silty coastal reefs and lagoons, usually associated with isolated coral heads; feeds mainly on zooplankton and algae; similar to *D. aruanus* (Plate **64.15**), but has extra black band across rear part of tail; Great Barrier Reef and throughout S.E. Asia; Indo-Malay Archipelago to W. Micronesia; to 8.5 cm.

7. BLACKBACK ANEMONEFISH
Amphiprion melanopus Bleeker, 1852
Commensal with sea anemones (usually *Entacmaea quadricolor*), in lagoons and on outer reefs; feeds mainly on planktonic copepods and benthic algae; distinguished by single white bar behind the eye, overall blackish colour and black pelvic and anal fins; young are red with 2–3 white bars; Great Barrier Reef and throughout S.E. Asia W. and C. Pacific; to 12 cm.

8. SADDLEBACK ANEMONEFISH
Amphiprion polymnus (Linnaeus, 1758)
Commensal with sea anemones (usually *Stichodactyla haddoni*), in sandy or silty lagoons and coastal embayments; feeds mainly on zooplankton; distinguished by broad white bar behind eye and large white saddle (variable in length) on back; some individuals have black pelvic and anal fins; amount of yellow colour on head and body is variable (sometimes absent); Northern Territory and throughout S.E. Asia; W. Pacific; to 13 cm.

9. BARRIER REEF ANEMONEFISH
Amphiprion akindynos Allen, 1972
Commensal with several sea anemones in lagoons and on outer reefs; feeds mainly on planktonic copepods and benthic algae; distinguished by brown to orange-brown body with pair of whitish bars; S.W. Pacific including Great Barrier Reef, N. New South Wales, Coral Sea, New Caledonia and Loyalty Islands; to 12 cm.

10. RED SADDLEBACK ANEMONEFISH
Amphiprion ephippium (Bloch, 1790)
Commensal with sea anemones (usually *Entacmaea quadricolor* or *Heteractis crispa*), on sheltered, silty inshore reefs; feeds on zooplankton and algae; distinguished by bright red-orange colour and black blotch on side, which becomes larger with increased growth; small juveniles lack black entirely and have a white bar behind the eye; also known as Fire Clownfish; Andaman Sea, Thailand, Malaysia, Sumatra and Java; to 12 cm.

11. TOMATO CLOWNFISH
Amphiprion frenatus Brevoort, 1856
Commensal with sea anemones (usually *Entacmaea quadricolor*), in lagoons and on outer reefs; feeds mainly on planktonic copepods and benthic algae; distinguished by single white bar behind the eye, overall blackish colour and red fins; young are red with 2–3 white bars; throughout S.E. Asia; western edge of Pacific to Japan; to 12 cm.

12. ORANGEFIN ANEMONEFISH
Amphiprion chrysopterus Cuvier, 1830
Commensal with several sea anemones, usually in passages or on outer reef slopes; feeds mainly on zooplankton and algae; distinguished by pair of bluish-white bars, orange dorsal fin and black pelvic and anal fins; young specimens are mainly brown with two white or blue-white bars; Great Barrier Reef (rare) and New Guinea; W. and C. Pacific; to 16 cm.

13. SPINE-CHEEK CLOWNFISH
Premnas biaculeatus (Bloch, 1790)
Commensal with sea anemones (usually *Entacmaea quadricolor*), both on sheltered inshore reefs and on outer slopes; feeds on zooplankton and algae; distinguished by overall red colour, 3 pale bars and enlarged spine below eye; found in pairs, female is usually 2–3 times size of male; female colour less brilliant; also known as Maroon Clownfish; Great Barrier Reef, offshore reefs of W. Australia and throughout S.E. Asia; to 16 cm.

1 var. (Coral Sea)

1 var. (Great Barrier Reef)

1 var. (N.W. Australia)

PLATE 64: DAMSELFISHES AND ANEMONEFISHES

POMACENTRIDAE

1. CLARK'S ANEMONEFISH
Amphiprion clarkii (Bennett, 1830)
Inhabits coral reefs, associated with large sea anemones; distinguished by 2 white bars and abruptly pale tail; found throughout the region; Indo-W. Pacific; to 13 cm.

2. WESTERN CLOWN ANEMONEFISH
Amphiprion ocellaris Cuvier, 1830
Inhabits coral reefs in protected waters; associated with large sea anemones; distinguished by 3 white bars on head and body (middle bar with expanded anterior projection) and black submarginal bands on fins; an all-black (except for white bars) variety occurs off of Northern Territory, Australia; N.W. Australia and throughout S.E. Asia; Andaman Sea and Indo-Australian Archipelago, north to Ryukyu Islands; also known as False Clown Anemonefish; *A. percula* (not shown) is a nearly identical species occurring in Queensland and New Guinea; to 7.5 cm.

3. PINK ANEMONEFISH
Amphiprion perideraion Bleeker, 1855
Inhabits coral reefs; associated with large sea anemones; distinguished by a single narrow bar on each side of head; also known as Skunk Clownfish; N.W. Australia, Great Barrier Reef and throughout S.E. Asia; mainly W. and C. Pacific; to 10 cm.

4. ORANGE ANEMONEFISH
Amphiprion sandaracinos Allen, 1972
Inhabits coral reefs; associated with large sea anemones; distinguished by a white stripe along the base of the dorsal fin; N.W. Australia, Great Barrier Reef and throughout S.E. Asia; mainly W. Pacific; to 13 cm.

5. AUSTRALIAN ANEMONEFISH
Amphiprion rubrocinctus Richardson, 1842
Inhabits coral reefs; associated with large sea anemones; distinguished by black to reddish colour and white bar on head (sometimes weakly developed or absent); N. Australia only, between Point Quobba, W. Australia and Gulf of Carpentaria; to 13 cm.

6. BIGLIP DAMSEL
Cheiloprion labiatus (Day, 1877)
Inhabits coral reefs; usually amongst beds of branching *Acropora* corals; feeds partly on live corals; distinguished by enlarged lips; juveniles are primarily blackish with a neon-blue stripe along the upper back; found throughout the region; Indo-W. Pacific; to 8 cm.

7. BLACKAXIL PULLER
Chromis atripectoralis Welander & Schultz, 1951
Inhabits coral reefs; forms large aggregations above coral bommies; distinguished from *C. viridis* (**8**) by the black 'armpit' of the pectoral fin; found throughout the region; Indo-C. Pacific; to 10 cm.

8. BLUE-GREEN PULLER
Chromis viridis (Cuvier, 1830)
Inhabits coral reefs; forms aggregations that shelter in branching coral; distinguished from *C. atripectoralis* (**7**) by smaller size and lack of black colour on inside of pectoral fin base; found throughout the region; Indo-C. Pacific; to 8 cm.

9. GREEN PULLER
Chromis cinerascens (Cuvier, 1830)
Inhabits coral reefs; distinguished by overall dusky green appearance and faint longitudinal lines along the side of the body; Dampier Archipelago northwards; W. Pacific and E. Indian Ocean; to 10 cm.

10. SMOKEY PULLER
Chromis fumea (Tanaka, 1917)
Inhabits coral reefs, usually in deeper water (below 10–15 m); distinguished by dark caudal fin margins and pearly spot behind dorsal fin; W. Australia, E. Malay Peninsula; mainly W. Pacific in subtropical and warm temperate seas; to 9 cm.

11. WHITETAIL PULLER
Chromis margaritifer Fowler, 1946
Inhabits coral reefs; distinguished by two-tone colour pattern; N.W. Australia, Great Barrier Reef and throughout S.E. Asia; mainly W. Pacific; to 7.5 cm.

12. WEBER'S PULLER
Chromis weberi Fowler & Bean, 1928
Inhabits coral reefs; distinguished by dark scale edges forming a network pattern and by the dark tips on the tail; N.W. Australia, Great Barrier Reef and throughout S.E. Asia; Indo-C. Pacific; to 12 cm.

13. THREESPOT HUMBUG
Dascyllus trimaculatus (Rüppell, 1829)
Inhabits coral reefs, juveniles sometimes associated with branching corals or large sea anemones; distinguished by white spot on forehead and similar spot on each side of body which gradually fade with increased size; found throughout the region; Indo-C. Pacific; to 13 cm.

14. HEADBAND HUMBUG
Dascyllus reticulatus (Richardson, 1846)
Inhabits coral reefs, occurs in aggregations around small coral formations; distinguished by black bar on front of body; N.W. Australia, Great Barrier Reef and throughout S.E. Asia; Indo-C. Pacific; to 9 cm.

15. BANDED HUMBUG
Dascyllus aruanus (Linneaus, 1758)
Inhabits coral reefs, usually seen in aggregations around small coral formations; distinguished by 3 black bars; N.W. Australia, Great Barrier Reef and throughout S.E. Asia; Indo-C. Pacific; to 8 cm.

SYMBIOTIC DAMSELS

'Symbiosis' is a biological term for the interaction between two dissimilar organisms living together in close association. There are many examples of this phenomenom in nature, but one of the most colourful and well documented involves damselfishes belonging to the genera *Amphiprion* and *Premnas* (Plates 63–64). Together, the genera contain over 25 species that occur throughout the tropical Indo-West Pacific region. All of the species are associated with large sea anemones that normally sting fishes which make contact with their tentacles. However, anemonefishes are never stung. There are two factors which contribute to the fishes' apparent immunity. Apparently their distinctive swimming behaviour and special chemicals in the external mucus coat of the fish prevent the anemone from firing its nematocysts (stinging cells). Anemonefishes gain security from predators because of their special association and the anemones themselves are protected from coelenterate feeders such as butterflyfishes. The fishes also keep their host free of debris. Experiments reveal that the fishes directly contribute to the anemone's wellbeing by keeping the tentacles in robust condition.

PLATE 65: DAMSELFISHES

POMACENTRIDAE

1. YELLOWSPECKLED PULLER
Chromis alpha Randall, 1988
Inhabits outer reef slopes between 18–95 m depth; distinguished by plain brown colouration with bluish belly and anal fin, sometimes with yellow scale centres on side of body; Great Barrier Reef, offshore reefs of N.W. Australia and throughout S.E. Asia; W. and C. Pacific; to 12 cm.

2. YELLOW PULLER
Chromis analis (Cuvier, 1830)
Inhabits coral reefs, usually seen on steep outer slopes between 18–70 m; colouration ranges from yellow-brown with yellow fins to entirely yellow; Great Barrier Reef, offshore reefs of W. Australia and throughout S.E. Asia; mainly W. Pacific; to 15 cm.

3. AMBON PULLER
Chromis amboinensis (Bleeker, 1871)
Inhabits coral reefs, including passages, lagoons and outer slopes to 65 m depth; distinguished by light golden-brown colour, orange bar at pectoral fin base and dark upper and lower caudal fin margins; Great Barrier Reef, offshore reefs of W. Australia and throughout S.E. Asia; W. and C. Pacific; to 8 cm.

4. DARKFIN PULLER
Chromis atripes Fowler & Bean, 1928
Inhabits reef passages and outer slopes in 2–35 m depth; distinguished by plain brown colouration, dark areas on soft dorsal and anal fins, and dark marking at base of upper pectoral fin-rays; Great Barrier Reef, offshore reefs of W. Australia and throughout S.E. Asia; mainly W. Pacific; to 7 cm.

5. TWINSPOT PULLER
Chromis elerae Fowler & Bean, 1928
Inhabits caves, ledges and thickets of black coral on steep outer slopes at depths between 12–70 m; distinguished by white spot at base of last dorsal and anal rays; Great Barrier Reef, offshore reefs of W. Australia and throughout S.E. Asia; E. Indian Ocean and W. Pacific; to 6.5 cm.

6. STOUTBODY PULLER
Chromis chrysura (Bliss, 1883)
Inhabits outer coral or rocky reefs at depths between 6–30 m; distinguished by deep-bodied shape, dusky streak on each scale and abruptly white tail; Great Barrier Reef and Coral Sea; 3 isolated populations: (1) Mauritius and Réunion, (2) S. Japan to Taiwan, and (3) E. Australia to Fiji; to 14 cm.

7. HALF-AND-HALF PULLER
Chromis iomelas Jordan & Seale, 1906
Inhabits outer coral reefs in 3–35 m depth; distinguished by bicolour pattern with abrupt demarcation in middle of body between dark and light areas; S. W. Pacific from Great Barrier Reef to Society Islands; to 5.5 cm.

8. SCALY PULLER
Chromis lepidolepis Bleeker, 1877
Inhabits coral reefs, both inshore reefs and outer slopes in 2–20 m depth; feeds on zooplankton; distinguished by black margin on dorsal fin with fine white tips on each spine and black tips on lobes of tail; Great Barrier Reef, offshore reefs of W. Australia and throughout S.E. Asia; Indo-C. Pacific; to 8 cm.

9. SCISSORS-TAIL PULLER
Chromis scotochilopterus Fowler, 1918
Inhabits coral reefs on sheltered seaward slopes in 5–20 m depth; distinguished by deep-bodied shape, black upper and lower margins on tail and black band on front of anal fin; Philippines and Indonesia; to 14 cm.

10. SWALLOWTAIL PULLER
Chromis ternatensis (Bleeker, 1856)
Inhabits lagoons and outer reef slopes in 2–15 m depth; sometimes forms large aggregations; distinguished by dusky scale margins and dark upper and lower margins on tail; Great Barrier Reef, offshore reefs of W. Australia and throughout S.E. Asia; Indo-C. Pacific; to 9 cm.

11. LINED PULLER
Chromis lineata Fowler & Bean, 1928
Inhabits upper edge of outer reef slopes in 2–10 m depth; distinguished by horizontal rows of blue spots on side; *C. vanderbilti* (not shown) is similar, but most of anal fin dark and lower lobe of caudal fin with broad black band; throughout Indo-Malay Archipelago to Solomon Islands; to 6 cm.

12. YELLOW-AXIL PULLER
Chromis xanthochira (Bleeker, 1851)
Inhabits outer reef slopes in about 10–48 m; feeds on plankton; distinguished by dark rear margin on cheek, yellow pectoral fin base, dark scale outlines and dark band on each caudal fin lobe; Indo-Malay Archipelago to Great Barrier Reef, New Guinea and Solomon Islands; to 14 cm.

13. BLACKBAR PULLER
Chromis retrofasciata Weber, 1913
Inhabits coral reef lagoons and outer slopes between depths of 5–65 m; distinguished by yellow-tan colour and prominent black bar across rear of body; Great Barrier Reef and throughout S.E. Asia; Indo-Malay Archipelago to Fiji; to 6 cm.

14. YELLOWBACK PULLER
Chromis nitida (Whitley, 1928)
Inhabits coral reefs in 5–25 m depth; distinguished by diagonal demarcation between dark upper body and white lower parts; central and southern Great Barrier Reef south to Sydney and Lord Howe Island; to 8 cm.

15. PALE-TAIL PULLER
Chromis xanthura (Bleeker, 1854)
Inhabits outer reef slopes in 10–48 m depth; feeds on zooplankton; distinguished by black edges on cheek and gill cover and white tail; Great Barrier Reef, offshore reefs of W. Australia and throughout S.E. Asia; Indo-C. Pacific; to 15 cm.

16. DUSKY PULLER
Chromis caudalis Randall, 1988
Inhabits steep outer reef slopes in 20–50 m depth; distinguished by brownish-grey to nearly blackish body with whitish tail, also has blue spot in axil 'armpit' of pectoral fin; throughout S.E. Asia; E. Indian Ocean and W. Pacific; to 9 cm.

STRENGTH IN NUMBERS

Masses of plankton-feeding *Chromis* damselfishes form an integral part of the reef community. These fishes occur in prodigious numbers on some reefs, forming an efficient live filtering device that sifts out planktonic organisms from the passing currents. The genus is by far the largest group within the family Pomacentridae, with approximately 100 species; allmost all inhabit the Indo-West and central Pacific region. Most species dwell on outer reef slopes and passages at depths between 5–40 m.

PLATE 66: DAMSELFISHES

POMACENTRIDAE

1. DICK'S DAMSEL
Plectroglyphidodon dickii (Liénard, 1839)
Inhabits coral reefs, frequently associated with *Acropora* coral heads; distinguished by intense blackish bar on rear part of body; N.W. Australia, Great Barrier Reef and throughout S.E. Asia; Indo-C. Pacific; to 10 cm.

2. JOHNSTON DAMSEL
Plectroglyphidodon johnstonianus Fowler & Ball, 1924
Inhabits coral reefs, frequently associated with *Acropora* or *Pocillopora* coral heads; similar to *P. dickii* (**1**), but posterior blackish area broader and more diffuse; N.W. Australia, Great Barrier Reef and throughout S.E. Asia; Indo-C. Pacific; to 9 cm.

3. JEWEL DAMSEL
Plectroglyphidodon lacrymatus (Quoy & Gaimard, 1825)
Inhabits coral reefs, a territorial species that consumes algae; distinguished by numerous bright blue spots on the head and body; found throughout the region; Indo-C. Pacific; to 10 cm.

4. WHITEBAND DAMSEL
Plectroglyphidodon leucozona (Bleeker, 1859)
Inhabits coral reefs exposed to wave action; distinguished by broad white bar on sides; N.W. Australia, Great Barrier Reef and throughout S.E. Asia; Indo-C. Pacific; to 12 cm.

5. ALEXANDER'S DAMSEL
Pomacentrus alexanderae Evermann & Seale, 1907
Inhabits coral reefs; distinguished by light body colour and black pectoral fin base; Indo-Malay Archipelago north to Ryukyu Islands; to 11 cm.

6. AMBON DAMSEL
Pomacentrus amboinensis Bleeker, 1868
Inhabits coral reefs, often in sandy areas; distinguished from *P. moluccensis* (**9**) by its preference for open, sandy habitats, less- brilliant yellow colour and slightly larger spot on the upper pectoral fin base; juvenile has spot at rear of dorsal fin; N.W. Australia, Great Barrier Reef and throughout S.E. Asia; W. Pacific and E. Indian Ocean; to 11 cm.

7. NEON DAMSEL
Pomacentrus coelestis Jordan & Starks, 1901
Inhabits coral reefs, frequently among dead coral rubble; distinguished by bright blue colouration; N.W. Australia, Great Barrier Reef and throughout S.E. Asia; Indo-C. Pacific; to 9 cm.

8. MILLER'S DAMSEL
Pomacentrus milleri Taylor, 1964
Inhabits coral and rocky reefs, usually near shore; distinguished by plain brownish or grey colour and 14 dorsal spines (other similar species have 12 or 13); juveniles mainly yellow with blue stripes on back; Australia only, between Rottnest Island, W. Australia and Gulf of Carpentaria; also Aru Islands, Indonesia; to 10 cm.

9. LEMON DAMSEL
Pomacentrus moluccensis Bleeker, 1853
Inhabits coral reefs, usually in the vicinity of live branching corals; distinguished from *P. amboinensis* (**6**) by brighter colouration and smaller spot on the upper pectoral fin base; N.W. Australia, Great Barrier Reef and throughout S.E. Asia; mainly W. Pacific; to 7.5 cm.

10. PRINCESS DAMSEL
Pomacentrus vaiuli Jordan & Seale, 1906
Inhabits coral reefs; distinguished by rows of spots along side of body and spot on rear part of dorsal fin; N.W. Australia, Great Barrier Reef and throughout S.E. Asia; mainly W. and C. Pacific; to 9 cm.

11. BLUE-SCRIBBLED DAMSEL
Pomacentrus nagasakiensis Tanaka, 1917
Inhabits coral reefs, usually found in sandy areas around coral or rock outcrops; distinguished by black pectoral base, pale tail and faint, wavy stripes on tail and rear part of dorsal and anal fins; juveniles are mainly bluish; N.W. Australia, Great Barrier Reef and throughout S.E. Asia; W. Pacific and E. Indian Ocean; to 10 cm.

12. PACIFIC GREGORY
Stegastes fasciolatus (Ogilby, 1889)
Inhabits coral reefs, usually in areas exposed to moderate wave action; distinguished by overall brownish colour and lavender spots on cheek and belly; N.W. Australia, Great Barrier Reef and throughout S.E. Asia; W. Pacific; to 13 cm.

13. BLUNTSNOUT GREGORY
Stegastes punctatus (Quoy & Gaimard, 1825)
Inhabits coral reefs, usually among dead staghorn coral; a very pugnacious fish that continually chases other fishes (and divers) from its territory; distinguished from the similar *S. fasciolatus* (**12**) by the blunter snout and much wider gap between the eye and mouth; colour is variable, some fish are entirely brown; N.W. Australia, Great Barrier Reef and throughout S.E. Asia; Indo-C. Pacific; to 15 cm.

14. WESTERN GREGORY
Stegastes obreptus (Whitley, 1948)
Inhabits coral and rocky reefs, sometimes in weedy areas; distinguished by overall dark brown colour; juvenile is bright yellow with a spot on the dorsal fin; *S. apicalis* (not shown) from E. Australia is similar, but has red-orange margin on upper caudal fin lobe and on edge of rear part of dorsal fin; W. and N.W. Australia, Indo-Malay Archipelago; W. Pacific and E. Indian Ocean; to 15 cm.

15. DUSKY GREGORY
Stegastes nigricans (Lacepède, 1802)
Inhabits coral reefs usually among algal-covered branches of dead coral; distinguished by blackish spots at base of upper pectoral fin and last dorsal fin-ray, nest-guarding males assume a very different pattern as shown; N.W. Australia, Great Barrier Reef and throughout S.E. Asia; Indo-C. Pacific; to 14 cm.

16. GULF DAMSEL
Pristotis obtusirostris (Günther, 1862)
Inhabits flat, sandy bottoms; often caught by trawlers; distinguished by plain colouration, slender shape, forked tail and small black spot on upper pectoral fin base; *P. jerdoni* is a synonym; found throughout the region; Indo-W. Pacific; to 14 cm.

PLATE 67: DAMSELFISHES AND HAWKFISHES

POMACENTRIDAE

1. BLUESTREAK DAMSEL
Neoglyphidodon oxyodon (Bleeker, 1858)
Inhabits sheltered reef flats of lagoons and inshore reefs; adults entirely blackish, but lighter on front portion of body; juveniles with neon-blue bands and pale bar across front of body; Indo-Malay Archipelago, including Ashmore Reef off N.W. Australia; to 14 cm.

2. BARHEAD DAMSEL
Neoglyphidodon thoracotaeniatus (Fowler & Bean, 1928)
Inhabits outer reef slopes in 15–45 m depth; distinguished by pair of brown bars on head with whitish areas between; *N. mitratus* (not shown) is similar, found at Papua New Guinea and Solomon Islands; Philippines and Indonesia; to 12 cm.

3. CROSS' DAMSEL
Neoglyphidodon crossi Allen, 1991
Inhabits rocky areas or coral reefs in sheltered bays and lagoons; feeds on algae and zooplankton; adults are plain brown, juvenile has brilliant orange and blue combination; known only from Indonesia at Sulawesi, Bali, Flores and Molucca Islands; to 13 cm.

4. GOLDBACK DAMSEL
Pomacentrus nigromanus Weber, 1913
Inhabits lagoons and outer reef slopes in 6–60 m depth; distinguished by black pectoral spot, yellow on rear part of body (absent on fish from N.W. Australia) and broad black margin on anal fin; *P. nigromarginatus* (not shown) is similar, but has fine black border on rear edge of tail; N.W. Australia, Indonesia, Philippines and New Guinea; Indo-Australian Archipelago; to 9 cm.

5. OBSCURE DAMSEL
Pomacentrus adelus Allen, 1991
Inhabits most coral reef habitats in 2–8 m depth; feeds mainly on algae; distinguished by dusky brown colour, often with ocellus on rear part of dorsal fin; northern Great Barrier Reef, offshore reefs of W. Australia and throughout S.E. Asia; W. Pacific; to 9 cm.

6. SCALY DAMSEL
Pomacentrus lepidogenys Fowler & Bean, 1928
Inhabits lagoons, passes and outer reefs in 1–12 m depth; feeds on zooplankton and algae; distinguished by pale grey colour and yellow dorsal and caudal fins; Great Barrier Reef, offshore reefs of W. Australia and throughout S.E. Asia; Philippines and Indonesia to Fiji; to 9 cm.

7. PEACOCK DAMSEL
Pomacentrus pavo (Bloch, 1787)
Inhabits sandy areas around coral outcrops or soft coral growths to 16 m depth; feeds on plankton and algae; distinguished by blue stripes on head, dark 'ear-spot' and dusky vertical marks on scales; can 'switch on' electric blue-green colour; Great Barrier Reef, offshore reefs of W. Australia and throughout S.E. Asia; Indo-C. Pacific; to 11 cm.

8. PHILIPPINE DAMSEL
Pomacentrus philippinus Evermann & Seale, 1907
Inhabits passes and outer reef slopes in 2–12 m depth, usually seen near caves and ledges; feeds on zooplankton, algae and benthic invertebrates; distinguished by black spot on pectoral fin base, dark scale margins and yellow colour of tail and posterior dorsal and anal rays; Great Barrier Reef, offshore reefs of W. Australia and throughout S.E. Asia; W. Pacific; to 11 cm.

9. CHARCOAL DAMSEL
Pomacentrus brachialis Cuvier, 1830
Inhabits passes and outer reef slopes in 6–40 m depth; feeds on plankton and algae; distinguished by dark colouration and black spot covering pectoral fin base; Great Barrier Reef, offshore reefs of W. Australia and throughout S.E. Asia; W. Pacific; to 11 cm.

10. BLUESPOT DAMSEL
Pomacentrus grammorhynchus Fowler, 1918
Inhabits lagoon and inshore coral reefs, frequently among branching corals in less than 12 m depth; distinguished by general brown colour (often very pale) with brilliant blue spot-on upper tail base; Great Barrier Reef, offshore reefs of W. Australia and throughout S.E. Asia; Indo-Malay Archipelago to Taiwan and Solomon Islands; to 12 cm.

11. BLACKSPOT DAMSEL
Pomacentrus stigma Fowler & Bean, 1928
Inhabits sheltered coastal reefs, usually on fringing reef dropoffs in 2–15 m depth; distinguished by general pale colouration and black blotch on anal fin; Indonesia and Philippines; to 13 cm.

12. BURROUGH'S DAMSEL
Pomacentrus burroughi Fowler, 1918
Inhabits coastal reefs and silty lagoons in 2–16 m depth; feeds mainly on algae; distinguished by one or two pale blotches at base of soft dorsal fin; Philippines to Solomon Islands, but absent from Australia; to 8.5 cm.

13. THREESPOT DAMSEL
Pomacentrus tripunctatus Cuvier, 1830
Inhabits shallow bays and silty coastal reefs to 3 m depth; feeds mainly on algae; distinguished by black spot on upper tail base, young has ocellus on dorsal fin; Great Barrier Reef and throughout S.E. Asia; Sri Lanka to Melanesia; to 10 cm.

14. BLACKBANDED DAMSEL
Amblypomacentrus breviceps (Schlegel and Muller, 1839)
Inhabits inshore or lagoon areas with sand or silt bottoms around sponge or rock, sometimes in seagrass; distinguished by 3 black bars or saddles on whitish background; Great Barrier Reef and throughout S.E. Asia; Indonesia and Philippines to Solomon Islands; to 6.5 cm.

CIRRHITIDAE

15. WHITESPOTTED HAWKFISH
Cirrhitus pinnulatus (Forster, 1801)
Inhabits coral reefs, found in the shallow surge zone; feeds on shrimps, crabs, sea urchins, brittle stars and fishes; distinguished by blotchy brown pattern and white spots; Great Barrier Reef, offshore reefs of W. Australia and throughout S.E. Asia; Indo-C. Pacific; to 28 cm.

16. DWARF HAWKFISH
Cirrhitichthys falco Randall, 1963
Inhabits coral reefs, frequently seen perching on coral heads; feeds on crabs and shrimps; distinguished by series of red-brown saddles that are tapered ventrally, and vertical rows of red-brown blotches; Great Barrier Reef and throughout S.E. Asia; Maldives to W. Pacific; to 7 cm.

17. FLAME HAWKFISH
Neocirrhites armatus Castelnau, 1873
Inhabits coral reefs, usually seen hiding among branches of live coral; distinguished by brilliant red colouration and blackened area on back; Great Barrier Reef, Sunda Islands and Philippines; W. Pacific to Samoa; to 9 cm.

18. LONGNOSE HAWKFISH
Oxycirrhites typus Bleeker, 1857
Inhabits coral reefs, usually seen on outer slopes below 30 m depth perching on black coral or gorgonians; distinguished by red cross-hatched pattern and long snout; Great Barrier Reef, offshore reefs of N.W. Australia and throughout S.E. Asia; Indo-E. Pacific; to 13 cm.

PLATE 68: HAWKFISHES AND EEL-BLENNIES

PENTACEROTIDAE

1. THREEBAR BOARFISH
Histiopterus typus Temminck & Schlegel, 1844
Inhabits deep reefs on the continental shelf; distinguished by protruding snout, elevated dorsal fin and dark bars; N.W. Australia, Indonesia and Philippines; mainly W. Pacific; to 35 cm.

CIRRHITIDAE

2. TWINSPOT HAWKFISH
Amblycirrhitus bimacula (Jenkins, 1903)
Inhabits coral reefs; distinguished by pale-edged dark spots on gill cover and below rear base of dorsal fin; N.W. Australia, Great Barrier Reef and throughout S.E. Asia; Indo-C. Pacific; to 8 cm.

3. BLOTCHED HAWKFISH
Cirrhitichthys aprinus (Cuvier, 1829)
Inhabits coral or rocky reefs; distinguished by irregular-shaped brown to red bars on side, brown spot at upper corner of gill cover and filament at middle of dorsal fin; N.W. Australia, Great Barrier Reef and throughout S.E. Asia; to 10 cm.

4. SPOTTED HAWKFISH
Cirrhitichthys oxycephalus (Bleeker, 1855)
Inhabits coral or rocky reefs; distinguished by red to brown spots or blotches and prolonged filament at middle of dorsal fin; N.W. Australia, Great Barrier Reef and throughout S.E. Asia; Indo-E. Pacific; to 9 cm.

5. LYRETAIL HAWKFISH
Cyprinocirrhites polyactis (Bleeker, 1874)
Inhabits outer reefs and passes where currents are strong, often on rubble bottoms; forms small aggregations that swim a short distance above the bottom; distinguished by lack of marks on body, strongly forked tail and filament at middle of dorsal fin; found throughout the Indo-W. Pacific; to 15 cm.

6. FRECKLED HAWKFISH
Paracirrhites forsteri (Schneider, 1801)
Inhabits coral reefs; distinguished by red to brown spots on head and dark upper half of body; N.W. Australia, Great Barrier Reef and throughout S.E. Asia; Indo-C. Pacific; to 20 cm.

7. RINGEYE HAWKFISH
Paracirrhites arcatus (Cuvier, 1829)
Inhabits coral reefs; distinguished by orange loop behind eye, 3 orange streaks on lower edge of gill cover and white streak on sides; N.W. Australia, Great Barrier Reef and throughout S.E. Asia; Indo-C. Pacific; to 13 cm.

8. ORNATE HAWKFISH
Paracirrhites hemistictus (Günther, 1874)
Inhabits offshore coral reefs; distinguished by dense spotting on upper half of body; offshore reefs of N.W. Australia, Great Barrier Reef and throughout S.E. Asia; Indo-C. Pacific; to 29 cm.

PERCOPHIDAE

9. OBTUSE DUCKBILL
Squamicreedia obtusa Rendahl, 1921
Inhabits sand bottoms; distinguished by slender body, dorsally positioned eyes and pattern of small spots; N. Australia only; to 8 cm.

CREEDIIDAE

10. TOMMYFISH
Limnichthys fasciatus Waite, 1904
Inhabits sand bottoms, frequently buried below surface with only eyes protruding; distinguished by tiny size, pointed snout, dark stripe along middle of side and saddle-like spots on back; found throughout the region; E. Indian Ocean and W. Pacific; to 4.5 cm.

CEPOLIDAE

11. YELLOWSPOTTED BANDFISH
Acanthocepola abbreviata (Valenciennes, 1835)
Inhabits sand or silt bottoms; distinguished by elongate, laterally compressed body with pointed tail; found throughout the region; E. Indian Ocean and W. Pacific; to 50 cm.

PSEUDOCHROMIDAE

12. OCELLATE EEL-BLENNY
Blennodesmus scapularis Günther, 1872
Inhabits shallow coastal reefs; similar to *Congrogadus spinifer* (13), but pale-edged dark spot above gill cover (not on it) and lacks distinct pale spots arranged in longitudinal rows; N.W. Australia and Queensland only; to 10 cm.

13. SPINY EEL-BLENNY
Congrogadus spinifer (Borodin, 1933)
Inhabits sand bottoms with weed and sponge; similar to *Blennodesmus scapularis* (12), but pale-edged dark spot on gill cover (not above it), pale stripe behind eye and distinct pale spots on side arranged in longitudinal rows; N. Australia only between Exmouth Gulf, W. Australia and Gulf of Carpentaria; to 13 cm.

14. CARPET EEL-BLENNY
Congrogadus subducens (Richardson, 1843)
Inhabits rock crevices in weedy areas near coral reefs; similar to *C. spinifer* (13), but much larger, bigger lips, less distinct spot on gill cover and pale spots on side more diffuse; found throughout the region; Andaman Sea and W. Pacific; to 45 cm.

PLESIOPIDAE

15. SPOTTED EEL-BLENNY
Notograptus guttatus Günther, 1867
Inhabits turbid inshore reefs; in rocky crevices; distinguished by elongate white body with longitudinal rows of small dark spots; N. Australia and S. New Guinea only; to 14 cm.

16. SHARK BAY EEL-BLENNY
Notograptus gregoryi Whitley, 1941
Inhabits sand-weed areas; distinguished by general dark colouration and several dark spots on head; a rare species known from only a few examples; known thus far only from Shark Bay, W. Australia; to 10 cm.

HAWKFISHES

Hawkfishes of the family Cirrhitidae are benthic inhabitants of coral reefs. Although found in all tropical seas, most of the 35 species are confined to the Indo-Pacific region. Hawkfishes have free-projecting rays on the lower part of the pectoral fins adapted for perching on coral branches, gorgonians, etc. They are predators of small fishes and crustaceans. Most are less than 15 cm in length.

Most of the remaining fishes on this plate are seldom seen due to their cryptic habits. The members of the family Creediidae are small fishes that bury themselves in the sand. The Yellowspotted Bandfish *Acanthocepola abbreviata* (11) of the family Cepolidae occurs over soft bottoms and shelters in burrows. Eel Blennies (12–16) were formerly classified in separate families (Congrogadidae and Notograptidae), but recent research indicates they belong in two different families (Pseudochromidae and Plesiopidae). They are usually found among weeds and rocks.

PLATE 69: MULLETS, THREADFINS AND BARRACUDAS

MUGILIDAE

1. GOLDSPOT MULLET ☆☆☆
Gracilimugil argenteus (Quoy & Gaimard, 1825)
Inhabits coastal waters including estuaries; a plain silvery species without distinguishing marks; has 35–38 scales in lateral line, lacks an enlarged pointed scale at upper pectoral fin base and has 10 soft (excluding 3 spines) anal fin-rays (versus 9 or 10 for other mullets on this page); also known as Jumping Mullet and Tiger Mullet; mainly confined to southern waters of Australia, but ranges north to Shark Bay, W. Australia; to 32 cm.

2. GREENBACK MULLET ☆☆☆
Planiliza subviridis (Valenciennes, 1836)
Inhabits coastal waters including estuaries; distinguished by greenish back, gelatinous membrane partially covering eye, 27–32 scales in lateral line and lacks an enlarged pointed scale at upper pectoral fin base, also tail narrowly dark-edged; found throughout the region; Indo-C. Pacific; to 30 cm.

3. DIAMONDSCALE MULLET ☆☆☆
Ellochelon vaigiensis (Quoy & Gaimard, 1825)
Inhabits coastal waters including estuaries; distinguished by square-shaped tail, scales on upper side with dark blotch giving appearance of stripes, and 24–27 scales in lateral line; juvenile has black pectoral fins; found throughout the region; Indo-C. Pacific; to 55 cm.

4. SAND MULLET ☆☆☆
Myxus elongatus Günther, 1861
Inhabits coastal waters, frequently off beaches or in estuaries; distinguished by pointed head, black spot at upper pectoral fin base and 43–46 scales in lateral line; also known as Tallegalane and Lano; mainly confined to subtropical and temperate seas of S. Australia; mainly W. Pacific; to 42 cm.

5. SEA MULLET ☆☆☆
Mugil cephalus Linneaus, 1758
Inhabits coastal waters, entering estuaries and fresh-water; distinguished by flattened head, gelatinous membrane covering eye, an enlarged, pointed scale at upper pectoral fin base, 38–42 scales in lateral line and diffuse stripes on side; found throughout the region; worldwide temperate and tropical seas; to 79 cm.

6. BLUETAIL MULLET ☆☆☆
Moolgarda buchanani (Bleeker, 1853)
Inhabits coastal waters including estuaries; distinguished by forked tail, gelatinous membrane around rim of eye, an enlarged pointed scale at upper pectoral fin base and 32–35 scales in lateral line; found throughout the region; Indo-W. Pacific; to 40 cm.

POLYNEMIDAE

7. STRIPED THREADFIN ☆☆☆
Polydactylus plebeius (Broussonet, 1782)
Inhabits coastal waters, frequently off beaches; distinguished by divided pectoral fin with lower part containing 5 free filamentous rays and narrow stripes on side; also known as Northern Threadfin; found throughout the region; Indo-C. Pacific; to 45 cm.

8. AUSTRALIAN THREADFIN ☆☆☆
Polydactylus multiradiatus (Günther, 1860)
Inhabits coastal waters over sand or mud bottoms; distinguished by divided pectoral fin with lower part containing 7 free filamentous rays and most of first dorsal fin blackish; found throughout the region; mainly W. Pacific; to 20 cm.

9. BLACKFIN THREADFIN ☆☆
Polydactylus nigripinnis Munro, 1964
Inhabits coastal waters over sand or mud bottoms; distinguished by divided pectoral fin with lower part containing 6 free filaments and upper part black; N. Australia and New Guinea only; to 20 cm.

10. BLUE THREADFIN ☆☆☆
Eleutheronema tetradactylum (Shaw, 1804)
Inhabits coastal waters over sand or mud bottoms, sometimes in estuaries; distinguished by divided pectoral fin with lower part containing 4 free filaments and lips absent except for small section at rear of lower jaw; also known as Cooktown Salmon and Rockhampton Kingfish; found throughout the region; Indo-W. Pacific; to 120 cm.

SPHYRAENIDAE

11. PICKHANDLE BARRACUDA ☆
Sphyraena jello Cuvier, 1829
Inhabits coastal waters and offshore reefs; similar to *S. barracuda* (**12**), but more slender, has smaller scales and caudal fin yellowish; found throughout the region; Indo-W. Pacific; to 150 cm.

12. GREAT BARRACUDA ☆
Sphyraena barracuda (Edwards, 1771)
Inhabits coastal waters and offshore reefs; distinguished by large-size, dark or dusky fins, diffuse dark bars on back, frequently with scattered dark blotches on side (not shown) and truncate tail, *S. qenie* (**13**) is similar, but more slender and has smaller scales (about 123–135 in lateral line versus 75–90); a curious fish that sometimes follows divers; has been known to attack humans in the Atlantic; found throughout the region; worldwide in tropical seas; to 180 cm.

13. BLACKFIN BARRACUDA ☆☆
Sphyraena qenie Klunzinger, 1870
Inhabits coastal waters; distinguished by chevron-shaped markings on side and dark tail; Onslow northwards; Indo-W. Pacific; to at least 90 cm.

14. STRIPED BARRACUDA ☆☆
Sphyraena obtusata Cuvier, 1829
Inhabits sand-weed areas, often in the vicinity of rocky or coral reefs, distinguished by pair of dusky yellowish stripes on side and yellow tail; found throughout the region; Indo-C. Pacific; to 55 cm.

MULLETS, THREADFINS AND BARRACUDAS

Mullets (**1–6**), Threadfins (**7–10**) and Barracudas (**11–14**) are placed together in the suborder Mugiloidei. They are primarily inhabitants of tropical and subtropical seas and estuaries, with a few species also penetrating the lower parts of freshwater streams. Mullets (Mugilidae; worldwide over 75 species) are mainly algal feeders that have very small teeth or may lack them entirely. The largest species is about 90 cm total length, but most are under about 40 cm. Barracudas (Sphyraenidae; worldwide over 25 species) are found near coastal reefs. They have large fang-like teeth and are known to occasionally attack humans. The largest species reaches about 2 m total length. Threadfins (Polynemidae; worldwide over 40 species) inhabit sand or mud bottoms.

PLATE 70: WRASSES

LABRIDAE

1. DIAMOND WRASSE ☆☆
Anampses caeruleopunctatus Rüppell, 1829
Inhabits coral reefs and rocky areas; females distinguished by blue spotting on head and body, male by greenish colour with blue streak on each scale and yellowish bar at level of pectoral fins; N.W. Australia, Great Barrier Reef and throughout S.E. Asia; Indo-C. Pacific; to 30 cm.

2. SCRIBBLED WRASSE ☆☆
Anampses geographicus Valenciennes, 1840
Inhabits coastal reefs, frequently in weedy areas; female distinguished by large spot at rear of dorsal and anal fins, male by blue lines on head and numerous blue spots or streaks on sides; found throughout the region; mainly W. Pacific; to 31 cm.

3. BLUE-AND-YELLOW WRASSE ☆☆
Anampses lennardi Scott, 1959
Inhabits coral reefs; female distinguished by blue and yellow stripes, male by yellowish patch above pectoral fin and blue streaks on tail; also known as Leonard's Wrasse; N.W. Australia to Gulf of Carpentaria only; to 28 cm.

4. SPECKLED WRASSE ☆☆
Anampses meleagrides Valenciennes, 1840
Inhabits coral reefs; female distinguished by white spots and yellow tail, male by pattern on tail which gives appearance of pointed tail lobes; N.W. Australia, Great Barrier Reef and throughout S.E. Asia; Indo-C. Pacific; to 22 cm.

5. CORAL PIGFISH ☆☆
Bodianus axillaris (Bennett, 1832)
Inhabits coral reefs; distinguished by large black spot on dorsal and anal fins, also at base of pectoral fin; N.W. Australia, Great Barrier Reef and throughout S.E. Asia; Indo-C. Pacific; to 20 cm.

6. SADDLEBACK PIGFISH ☆☆☆
Bodianus bilunulatus (Lacepède, 1801)
Inhabits coral reefs; distinguished by black saddle below rear of dorsal fin, juveniles with large black area at rear of body; W. Australia; scattered locations in Indo-C. Pacific; to 55 cm.

7. GOLDSPOT PIGFISH ☆☆☆
Bodianus perditio (Quoy and Gaimard, 1834)
Inhabits the vicinity of coral and rocky reefs, often over sand or rubble in deeper water; distinguished by yellow patch on middle of back followed by blackish area; N.W. Australia, Great Barrier Reef and throughout S.E. Asia; Indo-W. Pacific; to 53 cm and 3 kg.

8. WESTERN PIGFISH ☆☆☆☆
Bodianus vulpinus (Richardson, 1850)
Inhabits mainly rocky reefs; female (shown here) distinguished by narrow stripes and sometimes dark blotches on sides, male (Plate **71.18**) by black blotch at base of middle dorsal spines and reddish margin on upper and lower edges of tail; Ceduna, S. Australia northwards to Shark Bay, W. Australia; to 60 cm.

9. REDBREAST MAORI-WRASSE ☆☆☆
Cheilinus fasciatus (Bloch, 1791)
Inhabits coral reefs; distinguished by red area at front of body and prominent dark bars; N.W. Australia, Great Barrier Reef and throughout S.E. Asia; Indo-W. Pacific; to 38 cm.

10. FLORAL MAORI-WRASSE ☆☆☆
Cheilinus chlorourus (Bloch, 1791)
Inhabits inshore reefs, in both coral and weed areas; distinguished by mottled pattern with small pale spots on sides; N.W. Australia, Great Barrier Reef and throughout S.E. Asia; Indo-C. Pacific; to 45 cm.

11. RINGTAIL MAORI-WRASSE ☆☆
Oxycheilinus unifasciatus (Streets, 1877)
Inhabits coral reefs; distinguished by white bar at tail base, dark diagonal bands on lower edge of cheek, brownish mid-lateral stripe with white stripe above and below it and dark spot on each pelvic fin; N. Great Barrier Reef and offshore reefs of W. Australia; W. Pacific; to 20 cm.

12. TRIPLETAIL MAORI-WRASSE ☆☆☆
Cheilinus trilobatus Lacepède, 1801
Inhabits coral reefs; distinguished by numerous pale spots on head, elongated rear part of dorsal and anal fins and irregular outline of tail; N.W. Australia, Great Barrier Reef and throughout S.E. Asia; Indo-C. Pacific; to 45 cm.

INTRODUCING WRASSES

Wrasses (Plates 70–81) are the second largest family of reef fishes — only the goby family has more species. These rainbow-coloured fishes, members of the family Labridae, are one of the most conspicuous groups inhabiting tropical coral reefs. The family is also well represented in warmer temperate seas, for example along the southern coastline of Australia. Worldwide there are an estimated 500 species, including some which are still undescribed. The family is extremely diverse with respect to colours, shape, behaviour and ecological preferences. Most species live over sand, rubble, weed, or coral and rock substrata. Wrasses occur over a wide depth range, from shallow tidal pools, to depths of at least 100 m. They are diurnally active, feeding on a wide variety of benthic and pelagic invertebrates. At dusk some species bury themselves in the sand where they 'sleep' through the night. Razorwrasses (*Xyrichtys*) also dive under the sand when threatened. Female to male sex reversal is common in many species. Dramatic colour changes sometimes occur during growth, with juveniles, females and males exhibiting different patterns.

Most species are medium sized (about 20–40 cm), although the Humphead Maori-Wrasse or Giant Wrasse *Cheilinus undulatus* (Plate **71.11**) grows to a length of at least 230 cm and weight of 190 kg. In spite of its huge bulk it is a shy fish that is difficult to approach closely. The only thing it is likely to be confused with is the Bumphead Parrotfish, which reaches 130 cm. However, the parrotfish has a highly distinctive head profile, which is nearly square. The Giant Wrasse is usually seen singly in clear waters of outer reef slopes in 10–100 m depth. It feeds on a wide variety of molluscs, fishes, sea urchins, crustaceans and other invertebrates. The notorious coral-destroying Crown-of-thorns Seastar is also occasionally consumed. Large adults are popular display items in public aquaria.

PLATE 71: WRASSES

LABRIDAE

1. LYRETAIL PIGFISH ☆☆
Bodianus anthioides (Bennett, 1832)
Inhabits coral reefs, usually seen on outer slopes below 15–20 m depth; distinguished by obliquely demarcated bicolour pattern and lunate or deeply emarginate tail; offshore reefs of N.W. Australia, Great Barrier Reef and throughout S.E. Asia; Indo-C. Pacific; to 20 cm.

2. TWOSPOT PIGFISH
Bodianus bimaculatus Allen, 1973
Inhabits steep outer reef slopes at depths greater than 30 m; distinguished by small size, slender body, overall reddish-orange colour and black spot just behind head and at base of tail; Great Barrier Reef and throughout S.E. Asia; Indo-W. Pacific; to 10 cm.

3. ECLIPSE PIGFISH ☆☆
Bodianus mesothorax (Bloch & Schneider, 1801)
Inhabits coral reefs; similar to *B. axillaris* (Plate **70.5**), but lacks black spot on dorsal and anal fins, also juvenile has yellow instead of white spots; offshore reefs of N.W. Australia, Great Barrier Reef and throughout S.E. Asia; W. Pacific; to 20 cm.

4. DIANA'S PIGFISH ☆☆
Bodianus dictynna Gomon, 2006
Inhabits coral reefs; distinguished by purplish head and back, four small pale spots along back, black spot at base of tail and large red to black blotch on pelvic fins; juvenile with numerous white streaks and spots; offshore reefs of N.W. Australia, Great Barrier Reef and throughout S.E. Asia; Indo-C. Pacific; to 25 cm.

5. BLACKFIN PIGFISH ☆☆
Bodianus loxozonus (Snyder, 1908)
Inhabits coral reefs, usually seen on outer slopes; distinguished by broad diagonal black band across rear part of body; Great Barrier Reef and New Guinea; W. and C. Pacific; to 40 cm.

6. LITTLE MAORI-WRASSE
Oxycheilinus bimaculatus (Valenciennes, 1840)
Inhabits coral reefs, usually seen amongst rubble or weed; distinguished by small size compared to most other *Cheilinus* and dark stripe on middle of rear half of body; tail rhomboid with prolonged upper lobe in male, rounded in female; offshore reefs of N.W. Australia, Great Barrier Reef and throughout S.E. Asia; Indo-W. Pacific; to 15 cm.

7. VIOLETLINE MAORI-WRASSE ☆☆
Oxycheilinus diagramma (Lacepède, 1801)
Inhabits coral reefs; distinguished by dark diagonal lines across lower half of cheek and gill cover, sometimes with dark lateral stripe on side; also known as Cheeklined Maori-Wrasse; offshore reefs of N.W. Australia, Great Barrier Reef and throughout S.E. Asia; Indo-C. Pacific; to 30 cm.

8. SLENDER MAORI-WRASSE ☆
Oxycheilinus celebicus (Bleeker, 1853)
Inhabits coral reefs; distinguished by relatively slender shape, elongate pointed snout and diffuse blotches forming midlateral stripe; offshore reefs of N.W. Australia, Great Barrier Reef and throughout S.E. Asia; mainly W. Pacific; to 20 cm.

9. SAMURAI MAORI-WRASSE
Oxycheilinus samurai Fukui, Muto & Motomura, 2016
Inhabits coral reefs; distinguished by relatively small size, pointed snout, dark diagonal bands on lower edge of cheek, brownish mid-lateral stripe with white stripe above and below it and dark spot on each pelvic fin; N. Great Barrier Reef and throughout S.E. Asia; W. Pacific; to 20 cm.

10. RED MAORI-WRASSE ☆
Cheilinus oxycephalus Bleeker, 1853
Inhabits coral reefs, a shy species that stays close to shelter; distinguished by brown to red colouration with scattered pale spots, frequently with 3–4 dark spots in mid-lateral row on posterior fourth of body and on tail base; also known as Snooty Maori-Wrasse; Great Barrier Reef and throughout S.E. Asia; Indo-W. Pacific; to 17 cm.

11. HUMPHEAD MAORI-WRASSE ☆☆☆
Cheilinus undulatus Rüppell, 1835
Inhabits coral reefs, large adults usually seen on steep outer reef slopes in 10–100 m depth; distinguished by huge size and hump on forehead; juvenile has pair of dark diagonal stripes through eye; also known as Hump-headed Maori-Wrasse, Giant Maori-Wrasse and Napolean Wrasse; offshore reefs of N.W. Australia, Great Barrier Reef and throughout S.E. Asia; Indo-C. Pacific; the largest species in the family, to 229 cm and 190 kg.

12. ANCHOR TUSKFISH ☆☆☆
Choerodon anchorago (Bloch, 1791)
Inhabits coral reefs, frequently seen on silty inshore reefs; distinguished by pale diagonal bar at level of pectoral fin, black area on middle of upper side and large white saddle behind dorsal fin, also has white chin and belly; also known as Orange-dotted Tuskfish; Great Barrier Reef and throughout S.E. Asia; E. Indian Ocean and W. Pacific; to 38 cm.

13. PURPLE TUSKFISH ☆☆☆
Choerodon cephalotes (Castelnau, 1875)
Inhabits coral reefs, often in nearby seagrass beds; distinguished by pale spots on cheek, blue markings on head, white blotch above pectoral fin and wavy yellow bands on fins; also known as Grass Tuskfish; N. Australia; to 38 cm.

14. HARLEQUIN TUSKFISH ☆☆☆
Choerodon fasciatus (Günther, 1867)
Inhabits coral reefs; distinguished by brilliant red bars; Great Barrier Reef to New Caledonia and Ryukyu Islands to Taiwan; to 30 cm.

15. GRAPHIC TUSKFISH ☆☆☆
Choerodon graphicus (De Vis, 1885)
Inhabits sand-rubble bottoms with small coral heads in the vicinity of reefs; distinguished by green colour with dark bands through eye and irregular dark bars on side; *C. transversalis* is a synonym; Queensland and New Caledonia; to 46 cm.

16. VENUS TUSKFISH ☆☆☆
Choerodon venustus (De Vis, 1884)
Inhabits vicinity of reefs, often on sand-rubble or weed bottoms; distinguished by greenish to red background colour with numerous pale spots on side; Australia only, New South Wales and E. Queensland; to 65 cm.

17. BLACKBLOTCH TUSKFISH
Choerodon zosterophorus (Bleeker, 1868)
Inhabits sand-rubble bottoms in the vicinity of coral reefs; similar to *C. jordani* (Plate **76.6**), but black and white markings on side of body are different; Indo-Malay Archipelago, including Philippines; to 20 cm.

18. WESTERN PIGFISH ☆☆☆☆
Bodianus vulpinus (Richardson, 1850)
Inhabits mainly rocky reefs; male (shown here) distinguished by black blotch at base of middle dorsal spines and reddish margin on upper and lower edges of tail, female (Plate **70.8**) by narrow stripes and sometimes dark blotches on sides; Australia only from Ceduna, South Australia northwards to Shark Bay; to 60 cm.

PLATE 72: WRASSES

LABRIDAE

1. ORANGEBACK FAIRY-WRASSE
Cirrhilabrus aurantidorsalis Allen & Kuiter, 1999
Inhabits rubble bottoms and adjacent coral reef of lagoons and seaward slopes in 10–25 m depth; distinguished by broad orange zone on back; northern Sulawesi and nearby Togean Islands of Indonesia; to 10 cm.

2. PURPLE FAIRY-WRASSE
Cirrhilabrus beauperryi Allen, Drew & Barber, 2008
Inhabits rubble bottoms of lagoons and seaward slopes in 5–32 m depth; distinguished by broad pale zone on back and numerous blue markings on lower body and fins; northern New Guinea and Solomon Sea, including Solomon Islands; to 12 cm.

3. DUSKY FAIRY-WRASSE
Cirrhilabrus brunneus Allen, 2006
Inhabits rubble bottoms adjacent to seaward slopes in 30–60 m depth; distinguished by dark colouration and lunate marking on tail; central Indonesia and Philippines; to 7 cm.

4. CENDERAWASIH FAIRY-WRASSE
Cirrhilabrus cenderawasih Allen & Erdmann, 2006
Inhabits steep rubble slopes of coastal reefs in 20–60 m depth; distinguished by 4–5 irregular black blotches on back and yellow stripe or rectangular blotch on middle of side; Cenderawasih Bay, West Papua Province Indonesia; to 8.5 cm.

5. CONDE'S FAIRY-WRASSE
Cirrhilabrus condei Allen & Randall, 1996
Inhabits mixed coral and rubble bottoms of seaward slopes in 5–70 m depth; distinguished by bright red colour and black marking on dorsal fin; northern New Guinea to Solomon Islands; to 8 cm.

6. YELLOWFIN FAIRY-WRASSE
Cirrhilabrus flavidorsalis Randall & Carpenter, 1980
Inhabits mixed coral and rubble bottoms in 12–30 m depth; distinguished by red to pinkish bars on side and yellow dorsal fin; eastern Indonesia, Timor Leste, Malaysia, and Philippines; to 6.5 cm.

7. MONSOON FAIRY-WRASSE
Cirrhilabrus hygroxerus Allen & Hammer, 2016
Inhabits mixed coral and rubble slopes in 25–40 m depth; distinguished by short dorsal-fin 'pennant' mainly blackish upper body and bright red pelvic and anal fins; eastern Timor Sea off northern Australia; to 7 cm.

8. SUNSET FAIRY-WRASSE
Cirrhilabrus greeni Allen & Hammer, 2016
Inhabits mixed coral and rubble slopes in 18–40 m depth; distinguished by red upper body and yellow lower body with red 'scissor-tail' markings; eastern Timor Sea off northern Australia; to 6.5 cm.

9. HUMANN'S FAIRY-WRASSE
Cirrhilabrus humanni Allen & Erdmann, 2012
Inhabits rubble bottoms in 10–45 m depth; distinguished by short dorsal-fin 'pennant', yellow to brownish orange colour of body and red, fan-shaped pelvic fins; Timor Leste and eastern Lesser Sunda Islands of Indonesia; to 7 cm.

10. LUBBOCK'S FAIRY-WRASSE
Cirrhilabrus lubbocki Randall & Carpenter, 1980
Inhabits rubble bottoms of seaward reef slopes in 4–45 m depth; two distinct colour varieties — one mainly purple with yellowish back and dorsal fin and another pink or lavender with split level rows of purple spots on back and middle of posterior body; eastern Indonesia, Timor Leste, Malaysia, and Philippines; to 8 cm.

11. SAILFIN FAIRY-WRASSE
Cirrhilabrus marinda Allen, Erdmann & Dailami 2015
Inhabits mixed sand and rubble bottoms of seaward reefs in 25–40 m depth; similar to *C. condei* (5), but has more expansive black zone on dorsal fin and smaller maximum size; northern New Guinea to Vanuatu; to 5.5 cm.

12. MORRISON'S FAIRY-WRASSE
Cirrhilabrus morrisoni Allen, 1999
Inhabits rubble bottoms amongst *Halimeda* algae in 20–35 m depth; distinguished by short dorsal-fin 'pennant' and orange to blackish colour on upper body with black pelvic fins and broad black margin on dorsal and anal fins; Known only from Hibernia Reef, western Timor Sea; to 6 cm.

13. PYLE'S FAIRY-WRASSE
Cirrhilabrus pylei Allen & Randall, 1996
Inhabits rubble bottoms of seaward reefs in 45–80 m depth; distinguished by extremely elongate pelvic fins and yellowish colour with red dorsal fin; eastern Indonesia to Melanesia, including Papua New Guinea, Solomon Islands, and Vanuatu; to 13 cm.

14. REDMARGIN FAIRY-WRASSE
Cirrhilabrus rubrimarginatus Randall, 1992
Inhabits mixed coral and rubble areas in 25–52 m depth; distinguished by overall pinkish colour and bright red margin on dorsal and caudal fins; Indonesia (Bali eastward), Timor Leste, Philippines, and Papua New Guinea to Fiji and Tonga, and northward to Japan (Ryukyu Is.); to 15 cm.

15. REDFIN FAIRY-WRASSE
Cirrhilabrus rubripinnis Randall & Carpenter, 1980
Inhabits rubble bottoms in 15–40 m depth; distinguished by general red colour including dorsal, anal, and pelvic fins; Indonesia (N.E. Kalimantan and N. Sulawesi) and Philippines; to 9 cm.

16. RYUKYU FAIRY-WRASSE
Cirrhilabrus ryukyuensis Ishikawa, 1904
Inhabits mixed coral and rubble bottoms of lagoons and outer reefs in 2–25 m depth; distinguished by bluish area behind head and large triangular-shaped orange zone on anterior body; Eastern Indonesia, Malaysia, Brunei, Philippines, Taiwan, and Ryukyu Islands; to 11 cm.

17. SOLOR FAIRY-WRASSE
Cirrhilabrus solorensis Bleeker, 1853
Inhabits mixed coral and rubble bottoms of lagoons and outer reefs in 5–35 m depth; distinguished by green to bluish head, reddish-orange upper body, and red margin on dorsal fin; eastern Lesser Sunda Islands and Banda Sea of Indonesia; to 11 cm.

18. SQUIRE'S FAIRY-WRASSE
Cirrhilabrus squirei Walsh, 2014
Inhabits mixed coral and rubble bottoms of outer reefs in 28–65 m depth; distinguished by mainly red to yellow-orange colour and long, trailing caudal fin filaments; Great Barrier Reef of Australia and Coral Sea; to 7.5 cm.

19. TONO'S FAIRY-WRASSE
Cirrhilabrus tonozukai Allen & Kuiter, 1999
Inhabits mixed coral and rubble bottoms in 15–40 m depth; distinguished by thread-like dorsal fin filament and variable shades of red and yellow; eastern Indonesia (Sulawesi eastward) and Palau; to 7.5 cm.

20. WALINDI FAIRY-WRASSE
Cirrhilabrus walindi Allen & Randall, 1996
Inhabits steep rubble slopes of coastal reefs in 20–40 m depth; distinguished by pair of large black blotches on back; north-eastern Papua New Guinea, including New Britain and Bismarck Archipelago; to 8.5 cm.

PLATE 73: WRASSES

LABRIDAE

1. ALFIAN'S FLASHERWRASSE
Paracheilinus alfiani Allen, Erdmann & Yusmalinda, 2016
Inhabits mixed coral and rubble bottoms of coastal reefs in 15–30 m depth; distinguished by lack of filamentous dorsal rays, rounded tail, and very tall, reddish dorsal and anal fins; Known only from Lembata Island in the Lesser Sunda Group of Indonesia; to 6.5 cm.

2. ANGULAR FLASHERWRASSE
Paracheilinus angulatus Randall & Lubbock, 1981
Inhabits rubble and low coral patches of coastal reefs in 10–40 m depth distinguished by sharply angular, rear dorsal and anal fins, lunate tail, and general red colour; Brunei, Malaysia (Sabah), Indonesia (N.E. Kalimantan), and Philippines; to 7 cm.

3. CARPENTER'S FLASHERWRASSE
Paracheilinus carpenteri Randall & Lubbock, 1981
Inhabits rubble bottoms in 12–40 m depth; distinguished by 2–3 thread-like dorsal fin filaments, rounded tail, and yellow to orange body with mainly red anal fin; Brunei and Philippines; to 7 cm.

4. BLUE FLASHERWRASSE
Paracheilinus cyaneus Kuiter & Allen, 1999
Inhabits rubble bottoms of coral reefs in 6–35 m depth; distinguished by 5–8 thread-like dorsal fin filaments, deeply forked tail, and dark red nuptial colouration with shades of blue and green on head and back, and red anal fin; female mainly reddish with faint pale bars on back; Indonesia only from N.E. Kalimantan to West Papua; to 8 cm.

5. YELLOWFIN FLASHERWRASSE
Paracheilinus flavianalis Kuiter & Allen, 1999
Inhabits rubble bottoms in 6–35 m depth; distinguished by single thread-like dorsal fin filament, rounded tail, red to yellowish body with prominent yellow anal fin; Indonesia (Bali eastward) and Northwest Shelf of Australia (Scott & Hibernia reefs); to 7 cm.

6. LINESPOT FLASHERWRASSE
Paracheilinus lineopunctatus Randall & Lubbock, 1981
Inhabits rubble bottoms of coastal reefs in 18–40 m depth; distinguished by 6–9 thread-like dorsal fin filaments, rounded tail, relatively tall, red anal fin; Philippines, Taiwan, and southern Japan; to 7 cm.

7. NURSALIM FLASHERWRASSE
Paracheilinus nursalim Allen & Erdmann, 2008
Inhabits rubble bottoms of coral reefs in 5–50 m depth; distinguished by 6–8 thread-like dorsal fin filaments, deeply forked tail, and rectangular blackish areas below front of dorsal fin and on lower tail base; female mainly reddish with faint dark stripes on side; southern portion of West Papua Province of Indonesia; to 8 cm.

8. PAINE'S FLASHERWRASSE
Paracheilinus paineorum Allen, Erdmann & Yusmalinda, 2016
Inhabits rubble bottoms of reef slopes in 15–50 m depth; distinguished by 4–7 thread-like dorsal fin filaments, deeply forked tail, and orange-red colouration with yellow anterior dorsal fin and red dorsal-fin filaments; female reddish with faint dark stripes on side; central Indonesia from Java and Lesser Sunda Islands to N.E. Kalimantan and Sulawesi; to 9 cm.

9. RENNY'S FLASHERWRASSE
Paracheilinus rennyae Allen, Erdmann & Yusmalinda, 2013
Inhabits mixed coral and rubble bottoms of coastal reefs in 15–40 m depth; distinguished by lack of filamentous dorsal rays, relatively elongate body, rounded tail, and very tall, bright red dorsal and anal fins; Known only from Komodo Islands and west Flores Island of Indonesia; to 8 cm.

10. REDTAIL FLASHERWRASSE
Paracheilinus rubricaudalis Randall & Allen, 2003
Inhabits rubble bottoms in 15–46 m; distinguished by single thread-like dorsal fin filament and rounded, red tail; male nuptial colour is mainly yellow; eastern Papua New Guinea (Manus I. and Bismarck Archipelago), Vanuatu, northern Coral Sea, and Fiji; to 7 cm.

11. TOGEAN FLASHERWRASSE
Paracheilinus togeanensis Kuiter & Allen, 1999
Inhabits rubble bottoms of coastal reef systems in 16–40 m depth; distinguished by lack of filamentous dorsal rays, tall, rounded dorsal fin, and deeply forked tail; Known only from northern Sulawesi, Indonesia; to 7 cm.

12. WALTON'S FLASHERWRASSE
Paracheilinus waltoni Allen & Erdmann, 2006
Inhabits mixed coral and rubble bottoms in 18–45 m depth; distinguished by 3–4 thread-like dorsal fin filaments (white during nuptial display), lunate tail, and strong blue highlights on tail; Cenderawasih Bay on northern portion of West Papua Province of Indonesia; to 6 cm.

13. YELLOWTHREAD FLASHERWRASSE
Paracheilinus xanthocirrhitus Allen, Erdmann & Yusmalinda, 2016
Inhabits rubble bottoms of reef slopes in 15–25 m depth; distinguished by 4–7 thread-like dorsal fin filaments, deeply forked tail, and mainly yellow dorsal fin, including filaments; South China Sea at Anambas Islands of Indonesia and Brunei; to 7 cm.

FLASHER AND FAIRY-WRASSES

Flasherwrasses (*Paracheilinus*) and the closely related Fairy-Wrasses (*Cirrhilabrus*) are among the most colourful members of the family Labridae. They are common inhabitants of rubble bottoms of coral reefs, often frequenting outer reef slopes, usually at depths below about 15 m. The species are distinguished on the basis of adult male colouration shown here, which is greatly enhanced during spectacular courtship and spawning displays that occur daily, beginning 1–2 hours before sunset. Females of the various species are often difficult to distinguish and are generally reddish or pink, lacking dorsal fin appendages (or these are much reduced), and are generally much smaller in size (usually under about 4 cm). Only a few representative females are illustrated here.

PLATE 74: WRASSES

LABRIDAE

1. BLUESIDE FAIRY-WRASSE
Cirrhilabrus cyanopleura (Bleeker, 1851)
Inhabits coral reefs over rubble bottoms; distinguished by large, dark blue patch behind head; female (not shown) is light red; Andaman Sea to to W. Indonesia; to 15 cm.

2. LABOUTE'S FAIRY-WRASSE
Cirrhilabrus laboutei Randall & Lubbock, 1982
Inhabits coral reefs over rubble bottoms; distinguished by magenta stripes edged in yellow; Great Barrier Reef to New Caledonia and Loyalty Islands; to 12 cm.

3. EXQUISITE FAIRY-WRASSE
Cirrhilabrus exquisitus Smith, 1957
Inhabits outer reefs and passes, usually seen over rubble bottoms in less than 10 m depth; distinguished by brilliant red margin on fins, blue spots on tail and black spot on tail base, female mainly reddish with white patch on snout; Great Barrier Reef, offshore reefs of W. Australia and throughout S.E. Asia; Indo-C. Pacific; to 12 cm.

4. LAVENDER FAIRY-WRASSE
Cirrhilabrus lineatus Randall and Lubbock, 1982
Inhabits coral reefs over rubble bottoms; distinguished by bold blue stripes on head that break up into spots on body, blue stripe along upper back and lowermost part of body and red tail with blue cross-bands; Great Barrier Reef to New Caledonia and Loyalty Islands; to 12 cm.

5. FINESPOT FAIRY-WRASSE
Cirrhilabrus punctatus Randall & Kuiter, 1989
Inhabits coral reefs over rubble bottoms; distinguished by numerous pale dots on upper three-fourths of body and black bar across pectoral-fin base, female (not shown) mainly red; New South Wales northward to Great Barrier Reef and S.E. Papua New Guinea east to Fiji; to 13 cm.

6. SCOTT'S FAIRY-WRASSE
Cirrhilabrus scottorum Randall & Pyle, 1989
Inhabits coral reefs over rubble bottoms; distinguished by overall dark appearance with shades of red and red dorsal and anal fins with deep purple outer margin; Great Barrier Reef and across tropical South Pacific to Pitcairn Group; to 13 cm.

7. RANDALL'S FAIRY-WRASSE
Cirrhilabrus randalli Allen, 1995
Inhabits rubble bottoms of lagoons and outer reefs in 10–40 m depth; distinguished by broad orange stripe on middle of side; offshore reefs of W. Australia including Rowley Shoals and Scott, Seringapatam, Ashmore, Cartier and Hibernia Reefs; also Savu Sea, Indonesia; to 11 cm.

8. WHIPFIN FAIRY-WRASSE
Cirrhilabrus filamentosus (Klausewitz, 1976)
Inhabits rubble bottoms of sheltered reefs in 10–40 m depth; male has long filamentous extension on middle of dorsal fin, an abruptly white belly, long pelvic fins and fan-shaped tail; female mainly red; Indo-Malay Archipelago; to 7 cm.

9. FILAMENTOUS FLASHERWRASSE
Paracheilinus filamentosus Allen, 1974
Inhabits rubble areas in passages and on the outer reef slope, occasionally seen in lagoons; distinguished by reddish, striped body, filamentous dorsal rays and lunate caudal fin; male is brighter than female, has longer dorsal fin filaments and a more lunate tail; Papua New Guinea and Solomon Islands; to 9 cm.

10. McCOSKER'S FLASHERWRASSE
Paracheilinus mccoskeri Randall & Harmelin-Vivien, 1977
Inhabits rubble bottoms of outer slopes in 12–40 m depth; distinguished by single thread-like dorsal fin; similar to *P. flavianalis* (Plate **73.5**), but anal fin is mainly red rather than yellow; widely distributed in Indian Ocean from East Africa to Andaman Sea; to 7 cm.

11. PINKLINED WRASSE
Coris dorsomacula Fowler, 1908
Inhabits areas of mixed sand, weed and rubble near coral reefs; distinguished by narrow pale bars on side, ocellated 'ear-spot' and small ocellated spot at base of rear part of dorsal fin; Great Barrier Reef and throughout S.E. Asia; W. Pacific; to 20 cm.

12. VARIEGATED WRASSE
Coris batuensis (Bleeker, 1856-57)
Inhabits sand-rubble areas near coral reefs; distinguished by variegated pattern with short blackish bars on back; usually misidentified as *C. variegata* (a Red Sea species) or *C. schroederi*; Great Barrier Reef, offshore reefs of W. Australia and throughout S.E. Asia Indo-W. Pacific; to 17 cm.

13. PELVIC-SPOT WRASSE
Pseudocheilinops ataenia Schultz, 1960
Inhabits coral reefs, usually seen among rubble; a secretive fish that rarely exposes itself; distinguished by small size, 'stubby' body shape, reddish colour and dark spot on each pelvic fin; Indo-Malay Archipelago; to 5 cm.

14. CONNIE'S WRASSE
Conniella apterygia Allen, 1983
Inhabits rubble bottom with scattered coral outcrops on outer reefs in 25–50 m depth; distinguished by candy-striped pattern and lack of pelvic fins; offshore reefs of W. Australia including Rowley Shoals and Scott and Seringapatam Reefs; to 7 cm.

15. EIGHTLINE WRASSE
Pseudocheilinus octotaenia Jenkins, 1901
Inhabits rubble and live coral areas on seaward reefs to depths of 50 m; distinguished by overall reddish colour and eight dark stripes on side; Great Barrier Reef, offshore reefs of W. Australia and throughout S.E. Asia; Indo-C. Pacific; to 13.5 cm.

16. PINSTRIPE WRASSE
Pseudocheilinus evanidus Jordan & Evermann, 1903
Inhabits coral reef crevices, a very secretive fish; distinguished by bluish-white streak on cheek, general red colouration and thin white stripes on side; Great Barrier Reef and throughout S.E. Asia; Indo-C. Pacific; to 8 cm.

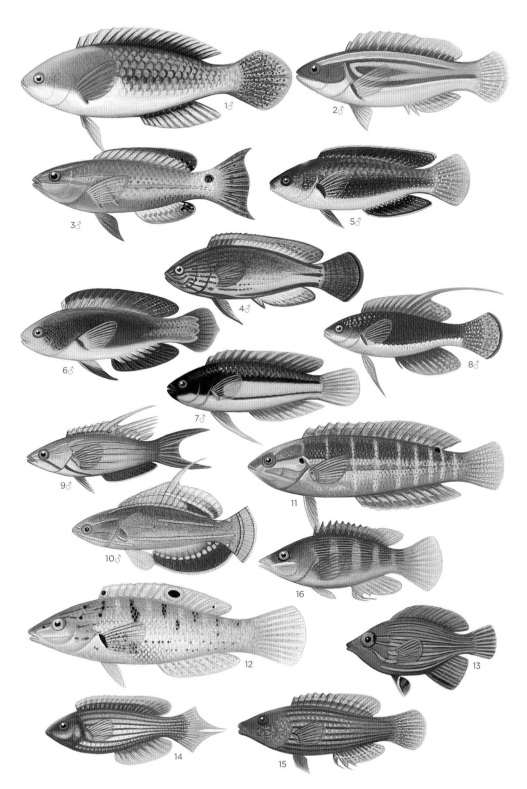

PLATE 75: WRASSES

LABRIDAE

1. BLUETAIL WRASSE

Anampses femininus Randall, 1972
Inhabits coral and rocky reefs; female recognised by brilliant orange colour with narrow blue stripes, becoming entirely blue on tail and rear part of body; male (not shown) similar to male of *A. caeruleopunctatus* (Plate **70.1**), but has broad blue stripes on head; also known as Feminine Wrasse; New South Wales and S. Great Barrier Reef across S. Pacific to Easter Island; to 24 cm.

2. BLACKTAIL WRASSE

Anampses melanurus Bleeker, 1857
Inhabits coral reefs; distinguished by white spotting and black tail with pale yellow bar across basal part; offshore reefs of N.W. Australia and throughout S.E. Asia; Indo-C. Pacific; to 12 cm.

3. BLACKBACK WRASSE

Anampses neoguinaicus Bleeker, 1878
Inhabits coral reefs; distinguished by blackish back and white colour on most of head and body, males and females are similar; Great Barrier Reef, offshore reefs of N.W. Australia and throughout S.E. Asia; W. Pacific; to 17 cm.

4. YELLOWBREAST WRASSE

Anampses twistii Bleeker, 1856
Inhabits coral reefs; distinguished by yellow region on breast and lower part of head, also by pattern of dark-edged pale spots and ocellus at rear of dorsal and anal fins; Great Barrier Reef, offshore reefs of N.W. Australia and throughout S.E. Asia; Indo-C. Pacific; to 18 cm.

5. YELLOWTAIL WRASSE

Diproctacanthus xanthurus (Bleeker, 1856)
Inhabits rich coral areas, usually seen in shallow, protected lagoons; feeds mainly on coral polyps, juveniles 'clean' other fishes; distinguished by black and white stripes and yellow tail; Great Barrier Reef, Kimberley coast of N.W. Australia and throughout S.E. Asia; Indo-Australian Archipelago; to 10 cm.

6. PASTEL SLENDER WRASSE

Hologymnosus doliatus (Lacepède, 1801)
Inhabits coral reefs; distinguished by elongate shape, pointed snout and series of thin bars on side; males are predominately bluish with a broad, blue-margined pale zone just behind pectoral fin base; Great Barrier Reef, offshore reefs of N.W. Australia and throughout S.E. Asia; Indo-W. Pacific; to 50 cm.

7. BREASTSPOT CLEANERFISH

Labroides pectoralis Randall & Springer, 1975
Inhabits coral reefs; 'cleans' parasites from other fishes; similar to *L. dimidiatus* (Plate **79.3**), but has large black spot at lower edge of pectoral fin base; Great Barrier Reef, offshore reefs of N.W. Australia and throughout S.E. Asia; mainly W. Pacific; to 8 cm.

8. TAILBLOTCH TUBELIP

Labropsis manabei Schmidt, 1931
Inhabits coral reefs, often seen on steep slopes in 10–30 m depth; male distinguished by yellow blotch on anterior body region and another on basal half of tail; female (not shown) is similar, but lacks yellow markings; Indo-Malay and Melanesian archipelagos; W. Pacific; to 13 cm.

9. ALLEN'S TUBELIP

Labropsis alleni Randall, 1981
Inhabits coral reefs, usually seen on outer reef slopes to 52 m depth; juveniles 'clean' other fishes, adults probably feed on coral polyps; distinguished by dark head, greenish body, white tail and prominent pale-edged black spot at base of pectoral fin; Philippines, Indonesia, Micronesia and Melanesia; to 10 cm.

10. YELLOWBACK TUBELIP

Labropsis xanthonota Randall, 1981
Inhabits coral reefs, most often seen on outer reef slopes in 10–50 m depth; feeds on coral polyps, juveniles 'clean' other fishes; female distinguished by yellow back and dorsal fin; male by dark caudal fin lobes and orange streak on rear edge of gill cover; Great Barrier Reef, offshore reefs of N.W. Australia and throughout S.E. Asia; Indo-W. Pacific; to 13 cm.

11. SOUTHERN TUBELIP

Labropsis australis Randall, 1981
Inhabits coral reefs, usually seen on outer slopes to 55 m depth; feeds on coral polyps; juveniles (black and white striped) 'clean' other fishes; female with grey head and three faint brown stripes, male as illustrated; Melanesia and Great Barrier Reef to Samoa; to 10 cm.

12. CHOAT'S WRASSE

Macropharyngodon choati Randall, 1978
Inhabits coral reefs between 1–30 m depth; distinguished by white background with irregular longitudinal red-orange bands and blotches; S. Great Barrier Reef; to 10 cm.

13. KUITER'S WRASSE

Macropharyngodon kuiteri Randall, 1978
Inhabits coral and rocky reefs in depth range of 5–55 m; distinguished by yellow-orange colour with prominent blue-rimmed black spot on upper part of gill cover; New South Wales, S. Great Barrier Reef and New Caledonia; to 10 cm.

14. LEOPARD WRASSE

Macropharyngodon meleagris (Valenciennes, 1839)
Inhabits coral reefs; female distinguished by leopard-like spotting and male (not shown) by dark-edged green spot on each scale of body, also has green spots and short bands on head; Great Barrier Reef, offshore reefs of N.W. Australia and throughout S.E. Asia; mainly W. and C. Pacific; to 15 cm.

TUBELIPS

Wrasses belonging to the genus *Labropsis* are closely associated with areas of rich coral development. They are called tubelips because of the rounded shape of their mouth and swollen lips. The latter feature is possibly an adaptation for feeding on live corals. Juveniles are often seen picking at the bodies of other reef fishes, presumably feeding on external parasites in the same manner as the Cleaner Wrasses (Plate **79.2–3**). Unlike the latter fishes, which are territorial, tubelips range over a larger area.

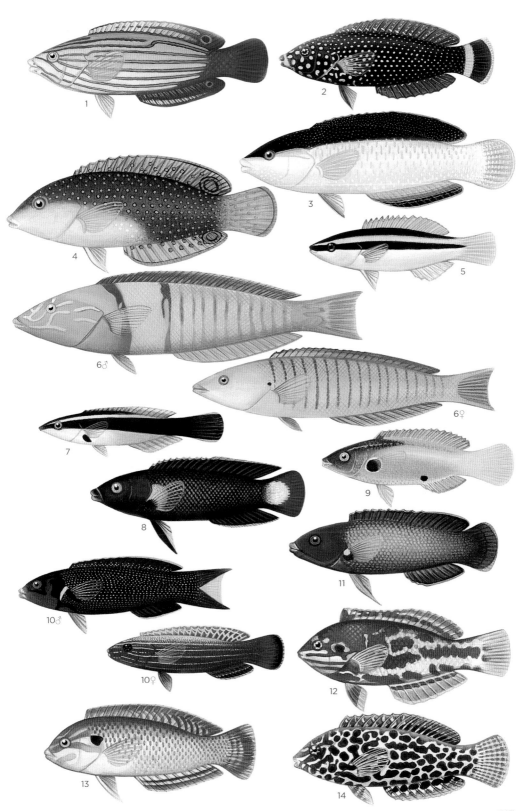

PLATE 76: WRASSES

LABRIDAE

1. SHARPNOSE WRASSE ☆☆
Cheilio inermis (Forsskål, 1775)
Inhabits weed beds; distinguished by elongate shape; males have blackish patch behind pectoral fins, females frequently display a narrow dark stripe along middle of sides; found throughout the region; Indo-C. Pacific; to 50 cm.

2. PEACOCK WRASSE
Cirrhilabrus temminckii Bleeker, 1853
Inhabits outer coral reefs, usually where there is loose rubble; male distinguished by red colour on upper half of head and body and very elongate pelvic fin filaments, females less vivid and lack pelvic filaments; W. Australia, Abrolhos to North West Cape and scattered locations in S.E. Asia; mainly W. Pacific; to 10 cm.

3. BLUE TUSKFISH ☆☆☆
Choerodon cyanodus (Richardson, 1843)
Inhabits coral reefs and flat bottoms, distinguished by white chin, white spot on middle of back, and scribble markings on tail; also known as Bluebone; N. Australia and Daru I., Papua New Guinea; to 60 cm and 7 kg.

4. PURPLE TUSKFISH ☆☆☆
Choerodon cephalotes (Castelnau, 1875)
Inhabits coral reefs, often in nearby seagrass beds; distinguished by pale spots on cheek, blue markings on head, white blotch above pectoral fin and wavy yellow bands on fins; also known as Grass Tuskfish; N. Australia; to 38 cm.

5. BALDCHIN GROUPER ☆☆☆
Choerodon rubescens (Günther, 1862)
Inhabits coral reefs and rock-weed areas; distinguished by abruptly pale chin and pale area at base of pectoral fins, the head profile becomes increasingly steep with growth, W. Australia only, between Geographe Bay and Coral Bay; to 65 cm and 6.3 kg.

6. DAGGER TUSKFISH
Choerodon jordani (Snyder, 1908)
Inhabits sandy areas adjacent to reefs; distinguished by blackish wedge on rear part of body and large white spot below end of dorsal fin; Great Barrier Reef, W. Australia, S. Japan, Vanuatu, and New Caledonia; mainly W. Pacific; to 13 cm.

7. REDSTRIPE TUSKFISH ☆☆
Choerodon vitta Ogilby, 1910
Inhabits flat sandy or weedy areas; distinguished by reddish stripe along middle of sides; N. Australia and Aru Islands, Indonesia; to 20 cm.

8. BLACKSPOT TUSKFISH ☆☆☆
Choerodon schoenleinii (Valenciennes, 1839)
Inhabits sand and weed areas adjacent to coral reefs; distinguished by overall bluish colour and black spot at base of middle of dorsal fin; found throughout the region; mainly W. Pacific; to 80 cm and 9 kg.

9. BLUESPOTTED TUSKFISH ☆☆
Choerodon cauteroma Gomon & Allen, 1987
Inhabits sand and weed areas adjacent to coral reefs; distinguished by yellow colouration and dark streak below middle of spiny dorsal fin; N.W. Australia only; to 36 cm.

10. WEDGETAIL TUSKFISH ☆☆
Choerodon sugillatum Gomon, 1987
Inhabits flat sandy or weedy areas; distinguished by blue band at pectoral fin base and blue streak above pectoral fin; N. Australia only; to 24 cm.

11. DARKSPOT TUSKFISH ☆☆
Choerodon monostigma Ogilby, 1910
Inhabits flat sandy or weedy areas; distinguished by prominent black spot at middle of dorsal fin and striped tail; N. Australia and W. Papua, Indonesia; to 25 cm.

12. EYEBROW TUSKFISH ☆☆
Choerodon zamboangae (Seale & Bean, 1907)
Inhabits flat sandy or weedy areas; distinguished by dark back and wedge-shaped reddish mark; N.W. Australia and throughout S.E. Asia; W. Pacific; to 25 cm.

13. CLOWN WRASSE
Coris gaimard (Quoy & Gaimard, 1824)
Inhabits sandy areas adjacent to coral reefs; distinguished by bright colour pattern and elongate spines at front of dorsal fin, juveniles bright red with white saddles; Great Barrier Reef, N.W. Australia and throughout S.E. Asia; mainly W.-C. Pacific; to 30 cm..

14. REDBLOTCHED WRASSE
Coris aygula Lacepède, 1801
Inhabits rubble-weed and sandy areas adjacent to reefs; male distinguished by hump on forehead and ragged tail margin, females by bicolour pattern with spots on the head and fins, juveniles with twin 'eye-spots'; found throughout the region; Indo-C. Pacific; to 100 cm.

15. PIXY WRASSE
Coris pictoides Randall & Kuiter, 1982
Inhabits rubble, sand or weedy areas adjacent to coral reefs; distinguished by black stripes on upper sides; Dampier Archipelago northwards; New South Wales, Great Barrier Reef, N.W. Australia and throughout S.E. Asia; W. Pacific and E. Indian Oceans; to 11 cm.

16. SPOT-TAIL WRASSE
Coris caudimacula (Quoy & Gaimard, 1834)
Inhabits sand or weedy areas adjacent to coral reefs; distinguished by dark band or blotches along upper side, broken bands or spots on tail and usually a prominent 'ear-spot' at rear edge of gill cover; N.W. Australia to E. Africa; Indian Ocean; to 20 cm.

LIVING RAINBOWS

The striking Clown Wrasse *Coris gaimard* (**13**) frequents sand and rubble patches intermingled with coral where it feeds on small invertebrates. Juveniles are brilliant red with four white saddles along the top of the head and back. This pattern gradually disappears with increased growth and is replaced by the adult colours shown here. Males and females of this species are very similar in appearance, but in many other wrasses the terminal male phase exhibits a gaudy colouration that is significantly different from that of the female. Like most wrasses, the Clown Wrasse begins its adult life as a female and can later change sex. In some species the initial adult stage contains both males and females, which tend to be relatively dull in colour. These initial-phase fish tend to spawn in aggregations. In contrast, the brightly coloured terminal-male phase usually engages in pair spawning with a single partner, which appears to be the reproductive pattern of the Clown Wrasse. At night this species buries itself in the sand.

PLATE 77: WRASSES

LABRIDAE

1. SLINGJAW WRASSE ☆☆
Epibulus insidiator (Pallas, 1770)
Inhabits coral reefs; distinguished by its highly protrusible jaw — two colour varieties are commonly encountered, one that is largely bright yellow, and a dark variety; Great Barrier Reef, N.W. Australia and throughout S.E. Asia; Indo-C. Pacific; to 35 cm.

2. BIRDNOSE WRASSE
Gomphosus varius Lacepède, 1801
Inhabits coral reefs; distinguished by elongate snout — females are generally lighter in colour than males; Great Barrier Reef, N.W. Australia and throughout S.E. Asia; Indo-C. Pacific; to 28 cm.

3. CHECKERBOARD WRASSE
Halichoeres hortulanus (Lacepède, 1801)
Inhabits coral reefs; female distinguished by blackish area below spiny dorsal fin and ocellus on middle of dorsal fin, male by yellow spot below front of dorsal fin and broad, pale bar behind head; Great Barrier Reef, N.W. Australia and throughout S.E. Asia; Indo-C. Pacific; to 26 cm.

4. FALSE-EYED WRASSE
Halichoeres biocellatus Schultz, 1960
Inhabits coral reefs; distinguished by series of red streaks and lines on head and sides; Great Barrier Reef, N.W. Australia and throughout S.E. Asia; mainly W. Pacific; to 15 cm.

5. DUSKY WRASSE
Halichoeres marginatus Rüppell, 1835
Inhabits coral reefs; distinguished by dark green-brown colour with darker stripes (most apparent anteriorly) and yellow margin on tail, young have striped pattern with an ocellus on the dorsal fin; Great Barrier Reef, N.W. Australia and throughout S.E. Asia; Indo-C. Pacific; to 18 cm.

6. THREESPOT WRASSE
Halichoeres trimaculatus (Quoy & Gaimard, 1834)
Inhabits sand and rubble flats adjacent to coral reefs; female distinguished by overall pale colour and spot on upper tail base, male is more ornate, but also has prominent spot on upper tail base; found throughout the region; Indo-C. Pacific; to 25 cm.

7. ORANGEFIN WRASSE
Halichoeres melanochir Fowler & Bean, 1928
Inhabits coral reefs; distinguished by overall purple-brown colour and yellow-orange pelvic fins, young specimens have 2 spots on the dorsal fin and a third spot on the upper tail base; N.W. Australia and throughout S.E. Asia; mainly W. Pacific, to 10 cm.

8. BUBBLEFIN WRASSE
Halichoeres nigrescens (Bloch & Schneider, 1801)
Inhabits rubble and weed areas near coral reefs; distinguished by 4–5 diffuse, broad, dark bars on upper two-thirds of side with yellow areas in between and dark spot at pectoral fin base; N.W. Australia and throughout S.E. Asia; Indo-Australian Archipelago; to 13 cm.

9. PEARLY WRASSE
Halichoeres margaritaceus (Valenciennes, 1839)
Inhabits rubble and weed areas near coral reefs; similar to *H. nebulosus* (**10**), but the bands running across cheek rise posteriorly (/) and usually has 13 pectoral fin-rays; Great Barrier Reef and throughout S.E. Asia; Indo-C. Pacific; to 12 cm.

10. CLOUD WRASSE
Halichoeres nebulosus (Valenciennes, 1839)
Inhabits rubble and weed near coral reefs; similar to *H. margaritaceus* (**9**), but the bands running across cheek descend posteriorly (\) and usually has 14 pectoral fin-rays; Great Barrier Reef, N.W. Australia and throughout S.E. Asia; Indo-W. Pacific; to 12 cm.

11. FIVEBAND WRASSE
Hemigymnus fasciatus (Bloch, 1792)
Inhabits coral reefs; distinguished by fleshy lips and broad dark bands on sides; Great Barrier Reef, N.W. Australia and throughout S.E. Asia; Indo-C. Pacific; to 80 cm.

12. THICKLIP WRASSE
Hemigymnus melapterus (Bloch, 1791)
Inhabits coral reefs; distinguished by large size and fleshy lips, smaller individuals (up to about 40–50 cm) have characteristic bicolour pattern, pale anteriorly and dark posteriorly; Great Barrier Reef, N.W. Australia and throughout S.E. Asia; Indo-C. Pacific; to 90 cm.

THE SLINGJAW

The colourful Slingjaw Wrasse *Epibulus insidiator* (**1**) is equipped with a unique feeding apparatus. It slowly and deliberately stalks its prey, mainly small fishes, crabs and prawns. When the victim is within range it shoots its distensible jaws forward with lightning speed, forming a peculiar tube-like structure that efficiently sucks in the meal. When not in use the jaws are neatly tucked away, giving the fish a normal wrasse profile.

Three distinct colour patterns are evident in this species. Females are either bright yellow or entirely dark brown. Terminal-phase males are brown with bright green scale edges, with a diffuse yellow bar on the sides just behind the pectoral fin. They also have a light grey head with dark lines radiating from the eye. The species ranges widely in the Indo-Pacific region, from the Red Sea and Africa eastward to the Hawaiian Islands and from Australia north to Japan.

WRASSE POWER

Wrasses are extremely abundant on coral reefs. As far as species total is concerned they are surpassed only by gobies. These colourful fishes, which range in size from 4 cm long dwarfs to over 2 m, have successfully invaded every reef habitat. The genus *Halichoeres*, of which several representatives are illustrated on the opposite plate, is the largest genus in the family, with approximately 50 species occurring in the Indo-Pacific region and several others in the tropical Atlantic. They are active fishes, constantly foraging for small crabs, shrimps, worms and other small, bottom-living invertebrates. They will quickly congregate to feed on the encrusting growth when a diver turns over a dead coral slab.

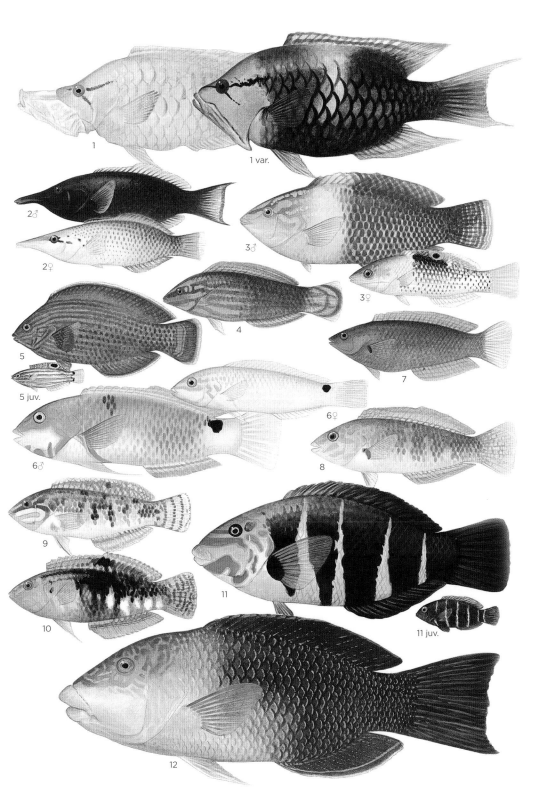

1

1 var.

2♂

2♀

3♂

3♀

4

5

5 juv.

6♂

6♀

7

8

9

10

11

11 juv.

12

PLATE 78: WRASSES

LABRIDAE

1. PASTEL-GREEN WRASSE
Halichoeres chloropterus (Bloch, 1791)
Inhabits protected lagoons and silty inshore reefs; female (shown here) distinguished by lime colour and small dark spots on side and frequently has dark smudge on middle of body, male with lavender-pink stripes on head and spots of same colour on side; also known as Green-spotted Wrasse; Great Barrier Reef and throughout S.E. Asia; W. Pacific; to 19 cm.

2. GOLDEN WRASSE
Halichoeres chrysus Randall, 1981
Inhabits vicinity of coral reefs, usually seen around small bommies in sand or rubble areas to 50 m depth; distinguished by bright yellow colour and black spot at front of dorsal fin; offshore reefs of W. Australia, Great Barrier Reef and throughout S.E. Asia; W. Pacific; to 19 cm.

3. REDHEAD WRASSE
Halichoeres rubricephalus Kuiter & Randall, 1995
Inhabits protected inner reefs between 15–35 m depth; distinguished by dark body and contrasting red colour of head; known thus far only from Maumere Bay on the Indonesian island of Flores; to 10 cm.

4. ORANGELINE WRASSE
Halichoeres hartzfeldii (Bleeker, 1852)
Inhabits open coral or sand-rubble bottoms, sometimes near isolated coral heads; female distinguished by broad yellow stripe on middle of side, male (shown here) by similar stripe, but with jagged edge and dark blotch on side beneath outer part of pectoral fin; Great Barrier Reef, Kimberley coast of N.W. Australia and throughout S.E. Asia; W. Pacific; to 20 cm.

5. RICHMOND'S WRASSE
Halichoeres richmondi Fowler & Bean, 1928
Inhabits coastal coral reefs, frequently in silty areas; distinguished by greenish body, dark head and blue stripes on side; Kimberley coast of N.W. Australia and throughout S.E. Asia; mainly W. Pacific; to 14 cm.

6. HOEVEN'S WRASSE
Halichoeres melanurus (Bleeker, 1851)
Inhabits shallow coral reefs; female distinguished by blue stripes and small ocellus on upper base of tail, male by red stripes and yellow pectoral fin base; *H. hoeveni* is a synonym; also known as Three-eyed Wrasse and Tailspot Wrasse; N.W. Australia, Great Barrier Reef and throughout S.E. Asia; mainly W. Pacific; to 10 cm.

7. GREYHEAD WRASSE
Halichoeres leucurus (Walbaum, 1792)
Inhabits silty inshore reefs; female similar to female of *H. richmondi* (5), but stripes less distinct, male distinguished by blue stripes on head, yellowish-brown spots on body and blue submarginal band on tail; Kimberley coast of N.W. Australia and throughout S.E. Asia; mainly W. Pacific; to 12 cm.

8. GREEN-TAIL WRASSE
Halichoeres podostigma (Bleeker, 1854)
Inhabits coastal coral reefs; distinguished by dark, pale-edged scales over most of body, pale head and tail base, and prominent black spot on pectoral fin base, juveniles have dark spot on pelvic fins; Indonesia and Philippines; to 18 cm.

9. EARMUFF WRASSE
Halichoeres melasmapomus Randall, 1981
Inhabits steep outer reef slopes in 20–55 m depth; distinguished by yellow bands on head and blue-edged ocellus behind eye; also known as Cheekspot Wrasse; Great Barrier Reef, offshore reefs of W. Australia, Christmas and Cocos-Keeling Is. and throughout S.E. Asia; E. Indian Ocean and W. and C. Pacific; to 14 cm.

10. CHEEK-RING WRASSE
Halichoeres miniatus (Valenciennes, 1839)
Inhabits shallow coral reefs; male distinguished by irregular dusky bars on lower side, dark blotch on middle of dorsal fin and pinkish bands on head; female (not shown) has series of close-set dark stripes on side; *H. nebulosus* (Plate **77.10**) and *H. margarataceus* (Plate **77.9**) are very similar species, particularly males, but the dominant pink markings on the cheek tends to form a diagonal band rather than a partial or fully formed ring; N. Queensland and throughout S.E. Asia; W. edge of Pacific; to 10 cm.

11. SEAWEED WRASSE
Halichoeres papilionaceus (Valenciennes, 1839)
Inhabits shallow coral reefs, frequently in weedy areas; distinguished by irregular bar pattern on side, pinkish bands on head and blackish outer edge of tail; Indo-Malay Archipelago; to 12 cm.

12. ARGUS WRASSE
Halichoeres argus (Bloch & Schneider, 1801)
Inhabits shallow coral reefs, frequently in sand-weed areas or seagrass beds; distinguished by strongly reticulated pattern composed of pale scale centres surrounded by thick dark margins; Indo-Malay and Melanesian archipelagos; to 11 cm.

13. ORNAMENTAL WRASSE
Halichoeres claudia Randall & Rocha, 2009
Inhabits coral reefs of lagoons and outer slopes; distinguished by irregular pink stripes on sides, a row of iridescent green spots on back and small black spot behind eye; females less than about 10 cm with ocellated black spot on middle of dorsal fin; Great Barrier Reef and offshore reefs of W. Australia; mainly island areas of W. and C. Pacific; to 15 cm.

14. TWOTONE WRASSE
Halichoeres prosopeion (Bleeker, 1853)
Inhabits coral reefs, frequently seen on outer slopes; distinguished by purplish head and anterior part of body, and yellowish colour posteriorly; juvenile has black and white stripes; Great Barrier Reef and throughout S.E. Asia; W. Pacific; to 13 cm.

15. ZIGZAG WRASSE
Halichoeres scapularis (Bennett, 1832)
Inhabits shallow reefs, usually in lagoons or bays on sand, rubble or seagrass bottoms; distinguished by general pale colouration with dark 'zipper-like' stripe on upper side, male is generally greenish with lavender bands on head and similar zigzag stripe (female shown here); Great Barrier Reef, offshore reefs of W. Australia and throughout S.E. Asia; Indo-W. Pacific; to 20 cm.

16. GREEN WRASSE
Halichoeres solorensis (Bleeker, 1853)
Inhabits coral reefs; distinguished by overall greenish-grey colour with pink stripes on yellow head and pale spots on scales of body; female purplish with yellow head; Indo-Malay Archipelago; to 18 cm.

PLATE 79: WRASSES

LABRIDAE

1. RINGED SLENDER WRASSE
Hologymnosus annulatus (Lacepède, 1801)
Inhabits coral reefs, often seen over sand or rubble areas; male distinguished by series of narrow dark bars on side, these also visible in female, which has a more slender body; juveniles black except golden yellow on back and top of head; Great Barrier Reef, N.W. Australia and throughout S.E. Asia; Indo-W. Pacific; to 40 cm.

2. BICOLOR CLEANERFISH
Labroides bicolor Fowler & Bean, 1928
Inhabits coral reefs, feeds on ectoparasites from other fishes; distinguished by light coloured tail region; Great Barrier Reef, N.W. Australia and throughout S.E. Asia; Indo-C. Pacific; to 14 cm.

3. COMMON CLEANERFISH
Labroides dimidiatus (Valenciennes, 1839)
Inhabits coral reefs, feeds on ectoparasites from other fishes; similar to *L. pectoralis* (Plate **75.7**), but lacks dark spot on pectoral fin base; found throughout the region; Indo-C. Pacific; to 12 cm.

4. ONELINE WRASSE
Labrichthys unilineatus (Guichenot, 1847)
Inhabits coral reefs, frequently seen amongst branching *Acropora* coral; distinguished by thin blue lines on side, male has pale bar behind head and juveniles have single pale stripe along middle side; Great Barrier Reef, N.W. Australia and throughout S.E. Asia; Indo-W. Pacific; to 17 cm.

5. SHOULDERSPOT WRASSE
Leptojulis cyanopleura (Bleeker, 1853)
Inhabits coral reefs or at least areas in the vicinity of reefs, sometimes on sand-rubble bottoms; occurs in aggregations with females greatly outnumbering males; female distinguished by whitish background and dark mid-lateral stripe, male is bluish grey with blue-edged orange stripes and blotches on head, body and fins; Great Barrier Reef and throughout S.E. Asia; Indo-W. Pacific; to 13 cm.

6. SIXLINE WRASSE
Pseudocheilinus hexataenia (Bleeker, 1857)
Inhabits coral reef crevices; distinguished by 6 red-orange stripes on side and small black spot on upper edge of tail base; Great Barrier Reef, N.W. Australia and throughout S.E. Asia; Indo-C. Pacific; to 8 cm.

7. COCKEREL WRASSE
Pteragogus enneacanthus (Bleeker, 1853)
Inhabits weedy patches on coral reefs; distinguished by free filamentous spines at front of dorsal fin and dark spot on gill cover; Great Barrier Reef, N.W. Australia and throughout S.E. Asia; mainly W. Pacific; to 20 cm.

8. ORNATE LEOPARD WRASSE
Macropharyngodon ornatus Randall, 1978
Inhabits coral reefs; female distinguished by pale spots in rows on side and reddish fins with light markings, males similar, but generally darker; N.W. Australia and throughout S.E. Asia; E. Indian Ocean and W. Pacific; to 11 cm.

9. BLACK LEOPARD WRASSE
Macropharyngodon negrosensis Herre, 1932
Inhabits coral reefs; female distinguished by blackish colour with blue-green scale margins, also dark streaks on upper and lower edges of tail; Great Barrier Reef, N.W. Australia and throughout S.E. Asia; mainly W. Pacific; to 12 cm.

10. REDSPOT WRASSE
Stethojulis bandanensis (Bleeker, 1851)
Inhabits coral and rocky reefs, often in weed or rubble areas; distinguished by red patch above pectoral fin base, male has curved blue stripe on cheek and female has pale spotting on back; found throughout the region; Indo-C. Pacific; to 15 cm.

11. SILVERSTREAK WRASSE
Stethojulis strigiventer (Bennett, 1833)
Inhabits weedy areas in the vicinity of coral and rocky reefs; female distinguished by narrow stripes on ventral half of body, male similar to *S. bandanensis* (**10**), but lacks blue stripe on the cheek; found throughout the region; Indo-W. Pacific; to 15 cm.

12. SOELA WRASSE
Suezichthys soelae Russell, 1985
Inhabits sandy areas in 50–80 m depth; distinguished by dark spots on tail; N.W. Australia only; to 10 cm.

13. PINKSPECKLED WRASSE
Xenojulis margaritaceus (Macleay, 1883)
Inhabits weedy areas in the vicinity of coral reefs; distinguished by dorsal fin shape (short in front and elevated posteriorly) and mottled pattern with pearly or pinkish spots on side; N.W. Australia and throughout S.E. Asia; mainly W. Pacific; to 15 cm.

FISH SERVICE STATIONS

The Cleaner Wrasses (**2–3** and Plate **75.7**) are small, colourful reef inhabitants which render an important service to other fishes. They remove parasites from the body, mouth cavity and gill chamber of numerous species spanning a considerable size range. Cleaning 'stations' occur at regular intervals on coral reefs. Research shows they are an integral component for maintaining good health within the local fish community. Each station is occupied by one or more cleaner wrasses. The demand for their services is readily apparent to even casual observers. Several fishes often queue while patiently waiting their turn to be inspected for parasites. Cleaner wrasses are not timid. They even enter the mouth of large voracious predators such as moray eels and groupers. The False Cleanerfish *Aspidontus taeniatus* (Plate **86.2**) is a member of the blenny family that is cleverly disguised as a cleaner wrasse. Not only is the colour pattern identical, but it also swims with an exaggerated undulating motion, exactly like the wrasse. Its uses this disguise to approach unsuspecting victims. But instead of removing their parasites the blenny dashes in and rips off a chunk of flesh, scales, or fin with its vampire-like fangs.

Like other wrasses, the Common Cleanerfish *Labroides dimidiatus* (**3**) exhibits sex change, but with an interesting twist. Each cleaner station is composed of a single dominant male and several females. Sex change in this species is dependent on behavioural interactions between the male and its harem of females. The normal aggressive behaviour of the male prevents its female companions from changing sex. However, if the male is experimentally removed, the dominant female assumes command within a few hours and after several days it can sexually function as a male.

PLATE 80: WRASSES

LABRIDAE

1. SURGE WRASSE ☆☆☆
Thalassoma purpureum (Forsskål, 1775)
Inhabits rocky reefs and inshore coral reefs, usually where there is wave action; male distinguished by ornate pattern highlighted by reddish-pink to purple stripes, female and juvenile greenish with double row of elongate red to brown blotches or stripes on middle and lower side; also known as Red-and-Green Wrasse; Great Barrier Reef, N.W. Australia and throughout S.E. Asia; Indo-C. Pacific; to 40 cm.

2. BLUEHEAD WRASSE
Thalassoma amblycephalum (Bleeker, 1856)
Inhabits coral and rocky reefs, usually several females seen with each male; male distinguished by bluish head with broad pale band just behind head, female has dark stripe or is overall brownish on upper half of body and white below; Great Barrier Reef, N.W. Australia and throughout S.E. Asia; Indo-W. Pacific; to 15 cm.

3. SEVENBAND WRASSE ☆☆
Thalassoma septemfasciatum Scott, 1959
Inhabits rocky and weedy reefs; male distinguished by uniform dark body and yellow pectoral fins, female by broad greenish bars on side and yellow colour on pectoral fin base; W. Australia only, between Rottnest Island and Coral Bay; to 31 cm.

4. MOON WRASSE ☆☆
Thalassoma lunare (Linnaeus, 1758)
Inhabits coral and rocky reefs; distinguished from *T. lutescens* (**5**) by magenta central portion of pectoral fin; juveniles (not shown) have a bluish belly and large black spot at base of tail; Great Barrier Reef, N.W. Australia and throughout S.E. Asia; Indo-W. Pacific; to 30 cm.

5. GREEN MOON WRASSE
Thalassoma lutescens (Lay & Bennett, 1839)
Inhabits coral and rocky reefs; male similar to *T. lunare* (**4**), but with blue-edged pectoral fin and lighter body colour, juvenile (not shown) with black midlateral stripe; Great Barrier Reef, N.W. Australia and throughout S.E. Asia; Indo-C. Pacific; to 30 cm.

6. SIXBAR WRASSE
Thalassoma hardwicke (Bennett, 1830)
Inhabits coral reefs; distinguished from *T. jansenii* (**7**) by narrower bars, some of which extend to belly region; Great Barrier Reef, N.W. Australia and throughout S.E. Asia; Indo-C. Pacific; to 18 cm.

7. JANSEN'S WRASSE
Thalassoma jansenii (Bleeker, 1856)
Inhabits coral reefs; similar to *T. hardwicke* (**6**), but has broader bars that do not extend onto belly; Great Barrier Reef, N.W. Australia and throughout S.E. Asia; Indo-W. Pacific; to 18 cm.

8. LONG GREEN WRASSE
Pseudojuloides elongatus Ayling & Russell, 1977
Inhabits weed beds; distinguished by elongate shape, male has orange blotch at pectoral base and blue spots on upper side, female uniform greenish; W. Australia (between Abrolhos Islands and Dampier Archipelago), New South Wales, New Zealand and Japan; to 15 cm.

9. BLUETOOTH TUSKFISH
Choerodon typus (Bleeker, 1857)
Inhabits flat sandy bottoms or rubble; distinguished by blue and yellow stripes in front of eye and yellowish fins; N. Australia (North West Shelf to Cape York) and throughout S.E. Asia to S. India; to 14 cm.

10. BLUE RAZORFISH
Iniistius pavo (Valenciennes, 1840)
Inhabits sand bottoms, uses keeled forehead to burrow into the sand when threatened; distinguished by broad brown bars and antenna-like first dorsal fin; Great Barrier Reef, N.W. Australia and throughout S.E. Asia; Indo-C. Pacific; to 35 cm.

11. LEAF WRASSE
Iniistius dea (Temminck & Schlegel, 1845)
Inhabits sand bottoms, burrows in sand when threatened; distinguished by antenna-like first dorsal fin, red or pinkish colour with vague bars and small black spot below front of dorsal fin, juveniles variable, black to pale in colour; North West Shelf; mainly W. Pacific; to 35 cm.

12. CARPET WRASSE
Novaculichthys taeniourus (Lacepède, 1801)
Inhabits rubble and weedy areas near coral reefs; distinguished by diagonal stripes on cheek, speckled fins and white bar across base of tail, juvenile has elongate spines at front of dorsal fin; Great Barrier Reef, N.W. Australia and throughout S.E. Asia; Indo-C. Pacific; to 25 cm.

OF RAZORS AND KNIVES

Razorfishes (**10** and Plate **81.14–15**) and knifefishes (Plate **81.13** and **16**) are peculiar wrasses that usually live on beds of clean white or black sand in 10–40 m depth. Their head and body is specially adapted for burrowing into the bottom — they are very compressed from side to side (i.e. thin) and the forehead forms a relatively sharpened keel (which is responsible for their common names). Reef-dwelling wrasses rely on the shelter afforded by the myriad of crevices and fissures. In their desert-like surroundings, which are absolutely devoid of hiding places, razorfishes and knifefishes have evolved an ingenious escape mechanism when threatened by predators or passing divers. They quickly vanish by plunging headlong into the sand. On several occasions when the author attempted to dig them out, it was obvious these fishes do not just simply bury themselves, but are adept at moving at a fairly rapid rate beneath the sandy surface. These fishes can sometimes be taken with a baited hook, but extreme care must be exercised when handling them. The powerful jaws are equipped with large tusk-like teeth that can inflict a nasty wound. Normally the teeth are used for feeding on sand-dwelling invertebrates such as shellfish, crabs and shrimps.

Like most other wrasses, razorfishes have different colour patterns according to sex and growth stage. Juveniles appear to mimic drifting debris, leaning over to one side and swimming with a peculiar swaying motion. The small young of the Blue Razorfish *Iniistius pavo* (**10**) and a few other species have a very elongate antenna on top of the head, which is actually part of the dorsal fin.

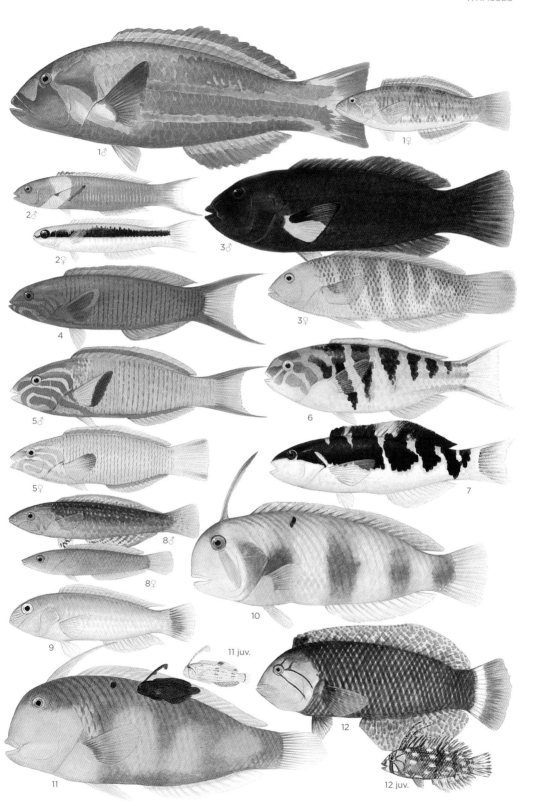

1♂

1♀

2♂

2♀

3♂

3♀

4

5♂

5♀

6

7

8♂

8♀

9

10

11 juv.

11

12

12 juv.

PLATE 81: WRASSES

LABRIDAE

1. JAPANESE WRASSE
Pseudocoris yamashiroi (Schmidt, 1931)
Inhabits coral reefs, usually seen in aggregations on outer slopes; females greatly outnumber males; feeds on zooplankton; male greyish on upper two-thirds and white below, further distinguished by dark-edged caudal fin lobes and prolonged spines at front of dorsal fin; female (not shown) is mainly pink to reddish; Great Barrier Reef, offshore reefs of N.W. Australia and throughout S.E. Asia; W. and C. Pacific; to 15 cm.

2. ZEBRA WRASSE
Pseudocoris heteroptera (Bleeker, 1857)
Inhabits coral reefs, frequently seen on outer slopes; distinguished by brilliant male colour pattern of black and yellow bars on rear half of body; Indo-Malay Archipelago; to 24 cm.

3. BROKENLINE WRASSE
Stethojulis interrupta (Bleeker, 1851)
Inhabits coral reefs in areas with scattered sand pockets; male distinguished by interrupted blue stripe on middle of sides; female (not shown) is brownish above and white below with black dots on lower half; Great Barrier Reef and throughout S.E. Asia; Indo-W. Pacific; to 13 cm.

4. CRYPTIC WRASSE
Pterogogus cryptus Randall, 1981
Inhabits reefs with abundant hard or soft corals between 4–70 m; a secretive fish that never exposes itself for more than a few seconds at a time; distinguished by white stripe on snout, continuing above eye to back of head and vertically elongate dark spot on gill cover; Great Barrier Reef, offshore reefs of W. Australia and throughout S.E. Asia; Indo-W. Pacific; to 7 cm.

5. RUST-BANDED WRASSE
Pseudocoris aurantiofasciata Fourmanoir, 1971
Inhabits coral reefs, most frequently on steep drop-offs, occurring in small aggregations; male distinguished by elongate first dorsal fin, relatively deep body with several dark bars on side and single pale bar on posterior half of body; Indo-Malay Archipelago; W. and C. Pacific to Tuamotus; to 24 cm.

6. PHILIPPINES WRASSE
Pseudocoris bleekeri (Hubrecht, 1876)
Inhabits coral reefs; male distinguished by black first dorsal spine, yellow blotch on middle of side and dark margins on tail; female is light brown with brown band on snout and dark blotches on end of gill cover and upper tail base; Indonesia and Philippines to Ryukyu Islands; to 15 cm.

7. CHISELTOOTH WRASSE
Pseudodax moluccanus (Valenciennes, 1840)
Inhabits coral reefs, usually seen on outer slopes; juvenile picks parasites from other fishes; distinguished by orange-red wash on nape and dorsal fin and pair of large spatulate teeth at front of jaws; juvenile resembles *Labroides* and has pair of blue stripes on side; Great Barrier Reef, offshore reefs of W. Australia and throughout S.E. Asia; Indo-C. Pacific; to 25 cm.

8. THREE-RIBBON WRASSE
Stethojulis trilineata (Bloch & Schneider, 1801)
Inhabits shallow reefs exposed to mild or moderate wave action; a very fast-swimming fish; male distinguished by three bright blue stripes running full length of body and shorter stripe from snout to pectoral region; female (not shown) is dark above and white below with numerous small white spots on upper half of body; Great Barrier Reef, offshore reefs of W. Australia and throughout S.E. Asia; E. Indian Ocean and W. Pacific; to 15 cm.

9. RED-RIBBON WRASSE
Thalassoma quinquevittatum (Lay & Bennett, 1839)
Inhabits shallow coral reefs from shallow surge areas down to 30 m depth; male distinguished by green and purplish bands on head, pink to purplish mid-lateral stripe and horizontal row of vertically elongate green spots on upper side; female relatively dull greenish with small black spot at front of dorsal fin; Great Barrier Reef, offshore reefs of N.W. Australia and throughout S.E. Asia; Indo-C. Pacific; to 17 cm.

10. LADDER WRASSE
Thalassoma trilobatum (Lacepède, 1801)
Inhabits shallow coral reefs, usually seen in areas exposed to surge; male distinguished by broad, red, mid-lateral stripe with double row of vertically elongate rectangular patches of green; female is very similar to that of *T. purpureum* (Plate **80.1**); Great Barrier Reef, offshore reefs of N.W. Australia and throughout S.E. Asia; Indo-C. Pacific; to 30 cm.

11. DOUBLELINE WRASSE
Wetmorella albofasciata Schultz & Marshall, 1954
Inhabits reef crevices and caves, rarely seen; distinguished by narrow white bars on body, ocellated spots on dorsal and anal fins and black spot on pelvic fins; Great Barrier Reef, offshore reefs of N.W. Australia and throughout S.E. Asia; Indo-C. Pacific; to 5.5 cm.

12. POSSUM WRASSE
Wetmorella nigropinnata (Seale, 1901)
Inhabits reef crevices and caves, rarely seen; distinguished by yellow bars behind eye and across tail base, also ocellated spot on dorsal and anal fins and black spot on pelvic fin; Great Barrier Reef, offshore reefs of N.W. Australia and throughout S.E. Asia; Indo-C. Pacific; to 8 cm.

13. KNIFE WRASSE
Cymolutes praetextatus (Quoy & Gaimard, 1834)
Inhabits clean sandy areas near coral reefs; dives under sand when disturbed; a slender, highly compressed pale-coloured fish without distinguishing marks; Great Barrier Reef, offshore reefs of N.W. Australia and throughout S.E. Asia; Indo-C. Pacific; to 12 cm.

14. WHITEBLOTCH RAZORFISH
Iniistius aneitensis (Günther, 1862)
Inhabits clean sandy areas near coral reefs; dives under sand when disturbed; distinguished by large white patch above belly; also known as Pale Razorfish; Great Barrier Reef and throughout S.E. Asia; Indo-W. Pacific; to 20 cm.

15. FIVEFINGER RAZORFISH
Iniistius pentadactylus (Linnaeus, 1758)
Inhabits clean sandy areas near coral reefs; dives under sand when disturbed; male distinguished by several black spots behind eye, female (not shown) has blackish spot on side near tip of pectoral fin; Great Barrier Reef and throughout S.E. Asia; Indo-W. Pacific; to 25 cm.

16. RAZOR WRASSE
Cymolutes torquatus (Valenciennes, 1840)
Inhabits clean sandy areas near coral reefs; dives under sand when disturbed; similar to *Wetmorella nigropinnata* (**12**), but has faint bars on side and dark diagonal bar above pectoral fin; Great Barrier Reef and throughout S.E. Asia; Indo-W. Pacific; to 12 cm.

17. SEAGRASS WRASSE
Novaculoides macrolepidotus (Bloch, 1791)
Inhabits seagrass beds, usually in small groups; distinguished by green colouration and dark stripe on middle of side; Queensland and S.E. Asia; Indo-W. Pacific; to 15 cm.

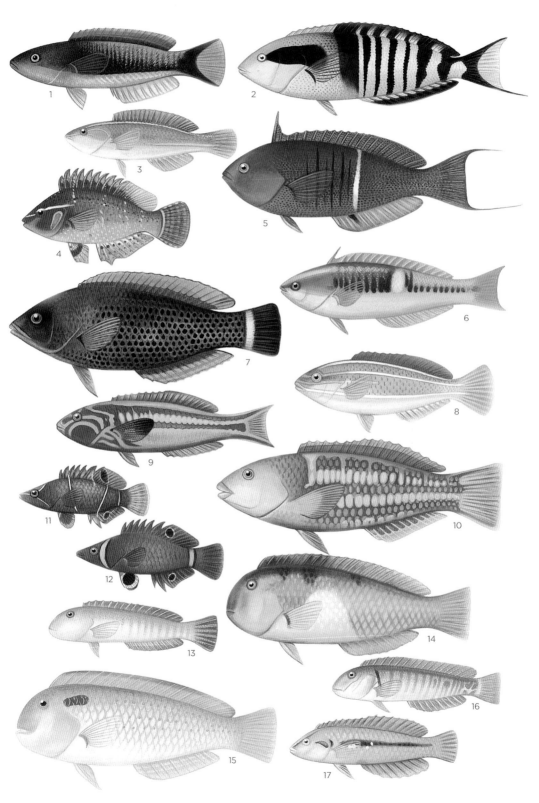

PLATE 82: PARROTFISHES

SCARIDAE

1. BUMPHEAD PARROTFISH ☆☆☆
Bolbometopon muricatum (Valenciennes, 1840)
Inhabits coral reefs; distinguished by large size and hump on forehead; the largest of all parrotfishes; Great Barrier Reef, N.W. Australia and throughout S.E. Asia; Indo-C. Pacific; to 130 cm.

2. BICOLOR PARROTFISH ☆☆☆
Cetoscarus ocellatus (Valenciennes, 1840)
Inhabits coral reefs, often in pairs; male distinguished by orange-red to pink scale margins, spots on head and front part of body and pale stripe from mouth to anal fin, females by dense black spotting on lower two-thirds of side, juvenile mainly white with broad orange bar on head; Great Barrier Reef, N.W. Australia and throughout S.E. Asia; E. Indo-C. Pacific; to 50 cm.

3. SPINYTOOTH PARROTFISH
Calotomus spinidens (Quoy & Gaimard, 1824)
Inhabits weed and seagrass beds; distinguished by marbled pattern of green and brown, differs from most other parrotfishes in having separate teeth (not fused to form beaklike structure); can change colour rapidly to blend with surroundings; Great Barrier Reef, N.W. Australia and throughout S.E. Asia; Indo-C. Pacific; to 19 cm.

4. MARBLED PARROTFISH
Leptoscarus vaigiensis (Quoy & Gaimard, 1824)
Inhabits weed and seagrass beds; similar to *Calotomus spinidens* (3), but has fused teeth, male has pale stripe along sides and small blue spots on head, female mottled and spotted with whitish and dark brown; Great Barrier Reef, N.W. Australia and throughout S.E. Asia; Indo-C. Pacific; to 38 cm.

5. LONGNOSE PARROTFISH ☆☆☆
Hipposcarus longiceps (Valenciennes, 1840)
Inhabits coral reefs, sometimes seen over sand or rubble bottoms, often forms schools; distinguished by pointed head, female has yellowish fins and is overall pale, male bluish on sides and on snout with blue margins on most fins; Great Barrier Reef, N.W. Australia and throughout S.E. Asia; Indo-C. Pacific; to 45 cm.

6. SIXBAND PARROTFISH ☆☆☆
Scarus frenatus Lacepède, 1802
Inhabits coral reefs, usually occurring in small groups; male distinguished by abruptly lighter colour on lower half of head and posterior part of body female by series of 6–7 dark stripes on side and reddish fins; Great Barrier Reef, N.W. Australia and throughout S.E. Asia; Indo-C. Pacific; to 40 cm.

7. BLUEBRIDLE PARROTFISH ☆☆☆
Scarus dimidiatus Bleeker, 1859
Inhabits coral reefs, usually alone or in small groups; male distinguished by dusky band from eye across gill cover with white band below, female by 3 saddle-like bars on back; Great Barrier Reef, N.W. Australia and throughout S.E. Asia; Indo-C. Pacific; to 34 cm.

8. BLUEBARRED PARROTFISH ☆☆☆
Scarus ghobban Forsskål, 1775
Inhabits coral reefs, seagrass and weed areas, and deeper offshore trawling grounds; male distinguished by broad blue scale margins, 3 dark streaks behind and below eye, and short blue stripe on chin, female by overall yellowish colour with diffuse blue bars and spots on side; found throughout the region; Indo-E:. Pacific; to 100 cm and 6.5 kg.

9. CHAMELEON PARROTFISH ☆☆
Scarus chameleon Choat & Randall, 1986
Inhabits coral reefs; male distinguished by dark stripe from snout, passing below eye across gill cover, another short stripe behind eye and vertical band above eye, also usually has large oval-shaped pale area occupying most of lower side, female generally dusky (may also have pale blotches) on upper half of side and abruptly pale below; Great Barrier Reef, N.W. Australia and throughout S.E. Asia; mainly W. Pacific; to 28 cm.

PARROTFISHES

Parrotfishes of the family Scaridae (Plates 82–84) are closely related to the wrasses (Plates 70–81), but rather than having individual teeth in the jaws, the dental plates are usually fused to form a distinctive beak-like structure. This structure is well adapted for scraping algal food from the surface of the reef. Parrotfishes also ingest large amounts of coral rock and sand along with the algae. This material is ground to a fine powder by special teeth at the back of the throat and is passed out with the faeces, contributing significantly to the bottom sediment.

Like the closely related wrasses, parrotfishes undergo female to male sex change and display different colour patterns according to growth stage or sex. Three decades ago, this discovery was considered a unique revelation, but detailed studies indicate that sex reversal is extremely common for a large portion of reef fishes belonging to many different families. In many species, the male and female colour patterns are so different they have long been regarded as different species. Diving scientists have been able to link most male–female pairings by observing courtship and spawning.

The estimated 100 species occurring worldwide are mainly inhabitants of coral reefs, although a few are found in weedy areas. They occur both individually or in large schools, grazing over the reef. At dusk parrotfishes retire to shelter in the form of crevices and ledges. Many of the species exude a strange cocoon-like mucus envelope which they remain inside during the night. This appears to be an adaptation which masks their scent, thus preventing predation by fishes such as moray eels that rely heavily on their sense of smell in locating prey. The largest parrotfishes are slightly over 1 m in length, but most species are under 50 cm.

PLATE 83: PARROTFISHES

SCARIDAE

1. STEEPHEAD PARROTFISH ☆☆☆
Chlorurus microrhinos (Bleeker, 1854)
Inhabits coral reefs and southern rocky reefs; distinguished by steep, blunt snout profile, becoming steeper with increased size, male and female similar but 2 colour phases are exhibited, a more common green one and a red one, large terminal male sometimes mainly purple with blue area ventrally, juvenile (not shown) is dark brown with 3 white stripes on side; Great Barrier Reef, N.W. Australia and throughout S.E. Asia; Indo-C. Pacific; to 50 cm.

2. VIOLETLINE PARROTFISH ☆☆☆
Scarus globiceps Valenciennes, 1840
Inhabits coral reefs; male distinguished by 'maze' pattern of spots and dashes on upper back and top of head, female difficult to separate from that of *S. rivulatus* (**9**), but often seen in company with male; Great Barrier Reef, N.W. Australia and throughout S.E. Asia; Indo-C. Pacific; to 30 cm.

3. DARKCAP PARROTFISH ☆☆
Scarus oviceps Valenciennes, 1840
Inhabits coral reefs; male distinguished by abruptly dark area on upper part of head and adjacent portion of back, female by similar darkened area followed by a pair of light and dark patches below dorsal fin; Great Barrier Reef, N.W. Australia and throughout S.E. Asia; mainly W. and C. Pacific; to 35 cm.

4. GREENCHEEK PARROTFISH ☆☆☆
Scarus prasiognathos Valenciennes, 1840
Inhabits coral reefs; male distinguished by blue-green colour on head below eyes and orange colour above, female by blackish or dark brown colour, numerous small white spots on side and reddish fins; N.W. Australia and throughout S.E. Asia; W. Pacific and E. Indian Ocean; to 70 cm.

5. PALENOSE PARROTFISH ☆☆☆
Scarus psittacus Forsskål, 1775
Inhabits coral reefs; male distinguished by 2–3 blue bands behind eye and lavender or bluish-grey colour on snout and forehead, female by overall dark colour, red pelvic fins and pale snout; Great Barrier Reef, N.W. Australia and throughout S.E. Asia; mainly W. and C. Pacific; to 30 cm.

6. BLACKVEIN PARROTFISH ☆☆☆
Scarus rubroviolaceus Bleeker, 1847
Inhabits coral reefs; male distinguished by blunt snout and bicolour pattern, female by red colour with irregular dark stripes; found throughout the region; Indo-E. Pacific; to 65 cm.

7. SCHLEGEL'S PARROTFISH ☆☆☆
Scarus schlegeli (Bleeker, 1861)
Inhabits coral reefs; male distinguished by 2 yellow patches below dorsal fin, the rear one forming a narrow bar between the dorsal and anal fin, female by overall dark colour and 4–5 narrow pale bars (often faint, sometimes absent) on side; found throughout the region; mainly W. and C. Pacific; to 35 cm.

8. GREENFIN PARROTFISH ☆☆☆
Chlorurus spilurus (Valenciennes, 1840)
Inhabits coral reefs; male distinguished by overall green colour with pale tail base and bluish cheeks, throat and breast, female by white tail with round black spot at base; Great Barrier Reef, N.W. Australia and throughout S.E. Asia; Indo-C. Pacific; *C. sordidus* (not shown) is a similar species found at Christmas and Cocos-Keeling Islands, ranging to Red Sea and W. Indian Ocean; to 45 cm.

9. SURF PARROTFISH ☆☆☆
Scarus rivulatus Valenciennes, 1840
Inhabits coral reefs; male distinguished by orange patch on cheek, wavy lines on snout and light yellow-green colour of pectoral fins, females are variable, but generally very pale; found throughout the region; mainly W. Pacific; to 45 cm.

PARROTFISH REPRODUCTION

Parrotfishes have a reproductive mode very similar to that of wrasses (Labridae). In both groups the male and female usually exhibit dramatically different colour patterns. The first mature phase in the life cycle is termed the initial phase and may include both female and male individuals. Females of most species in this phase can change to the male sex and alter their colouration to that of the more gaudy terminal phase. The initial phase is frequently drab brownish or grey compared to a terminal phase that is often dominated by green. Two styles of reproduction are found in many species: group spawning of initial-phase fish, in which males greatly outnumber females, and pair spawning of an initial-phase female and a terminal male. In both cases eggs and sperm are released at the apex of a rapid rush toward the surface. Terminal males tend to establish territories and maintain harems consisting of a number of females. Parrotfish eggs are spherical, ranging in diameter between 0.6–1.1 mm. They have a single yellow or orange oil droplet and are positively buoyant. The eggs hatch in about 25 hours at 26 degrees Celcius and the fry are slightly under 2.0 mm in length. The larvae begin feeding after about three days and are planktonic for an undetermined period, probably at least several weeks.

PLATE 84: PARROTFISHES

SCARIDAE

1. MINI-FIN PARROTFISH ☆☆☆
Scarus altipinnis (Steindachner, 1879)
Inhabits coral reefs; differs from other parrotfishes in having the middle part of the dorsal fin distinctly taller and forming short filament, female (not shown) also has elevated rays in the middle of the dorsal fin and is reddish-brown with 4–5 vertical series of small whitish spots on side; Great Barrier Reef and islands of the tropical W. and C. Pacific Ocean; to 60 cm.

2. BLEEKER'S PARROTFISH ☆☆☆
Chlorurus bleekeri (de Beaufort, 1940)
Inhabits coral reefs; male distinguished by large, squarish patch on cheek bordered by green; female is dark brown, usually with about four pale bars on side; Great Barrier Reef, offshore reefs of N.W. Australia and throughout S.E. Asia; W. Pacific; to 30 cm.

3. YELLOWFIN PARROTFISH ☆☆☆
Scarus flavipectoralis Schultz, 1958
Inhabits sheltered coral reefs; distinguished by yellowish pectoral fin, male has broad green band from snout to region above pectoral fin, also a lime-green patch often evident on middle of tail base, female (not shown) pale greyish to brown on back and head, sometimes yellowish ventrally with whitish stripes on belly; Great Barrier Reef, offshore reefs of N.W. Australia and throughout S.E. Asia; W. Pacific; to 30 cm.

4. WHITESPOT PARROTFISH ☆☆☆
Scarus forsteni (Bleeker, 1861)
Inhabits coral reefs; male distinguished by green 'moustache' that continues as green stripe below eye, bluish belly, darkened area on upper half of head and adjacent part of body and large diffuse pale patch on side; female has blue to yellowish streak or patch under pectoral fin and white spot on upper side; Great Barrier Reef, offshore reefs of N.W. Australia and throughout S.E. Asia; W. and C. Pacific; to 40 cm.

5. REEFCREST PARROTFISH ☆☆☆
Chlorurus frontalis (Valenciennes, 1840)
Inhabits coral reefs, usually seen in small schools in shallow water; differs from other parrotfishes in not having distinct male and female colour patterns — generally green with salmon-pink bar on each scale of body and irregular light salmon-pink to lavender bands in front of and above eye and on chin; Great Barrier Reef and scattered localities in SE Asia; W. and C. Pacific; to 50 cm.

6. HIGHFIN PARROTFISH ☆☆☆
Scarus longipinnis Randall & Choat, 1980
Inhabits coral reefs, usually between 20–55 m depth; distinguished by unusual shape of dorsal fin, which is more elevated than in other parrotfishes (similar to that of wrasses in genus *Cirrhilabrus*); female is light brownish-orange, often with dark brown bars, and has trio of blue-green stripes ventrally on the side and head markings similar to the male (shown here); Great Barrier Reef and Coral Sea across the S. Pacific to Pitcairn Island; to 40 cm.

7. SWARTHY PARROTFISH ☆☆☆
Scarus niger Forsskål, 1775
Inhabits coral reefs; distinguished by overall dark colouration (female reddish-brown) with pale mark just above upper corner of gill cover; Great Barrier Reef, offshore reefs of N.W. Australia and throughout S.E. Asia; Indo-W. Pacific; to 35 cm.

8. REDTAIL PARROTFISH ☆☆☆
Chlorurus japanensis (Bloch, 1789)
Inhabits coral reefs; male distinguished by broad orange band on dorsal and anal fins, large yellowish or tan area on posterior part of side and pale cheek, female (not shown) is overall dark brown with reddish tail; Great Barrier Reef, E. Indonesia, New Guinea and Philippines; W. Pacific; to 30 cm.

9. YELLOWHEAD PARROTFISH ☆☆☆
Scarus spinus (Kner, 1868)
Inhabits coral reefs, usually seen on outer slopes; male distinguished by greenish snout and broad yellowish area on head, female (not shown) is dark brown, often with 4–5 indistinct pale bars on side; Great Barrier Reef, offshore reefs of N.W. Australia and throughout S.E. Asia; W. and C. Pacific; to 30 cm.

10. GREENBLOTCH PARROTFISH ☆☆☆
Scarus quoyi Valenciennes, 1840
Inhabits coral reefs, usually in sheltered areas; distinguished by mainly orange dorsal fin and lime-green saddle on base of tail; throughout S.E. Asia; E. Indian Ocean and W. Pacific; to 30 cm.

11. TRICOLOUR PARROTFISH ☆☆☆
Scarus tricolor Bleeker, 1847
Inhabits coral reefs, usually seen on outer slopes; female distinguished by bright red fins and prominent reticulated pattern due to dark scale edges; male has blue or green stripes above and below eye, on chin and on margins of all fins except pelvics, also has exceptionally long pointed lobes on tail; Great Barrier Reef and throughout S.E. Asia; Indo-C. Pacific; to 45 cm.

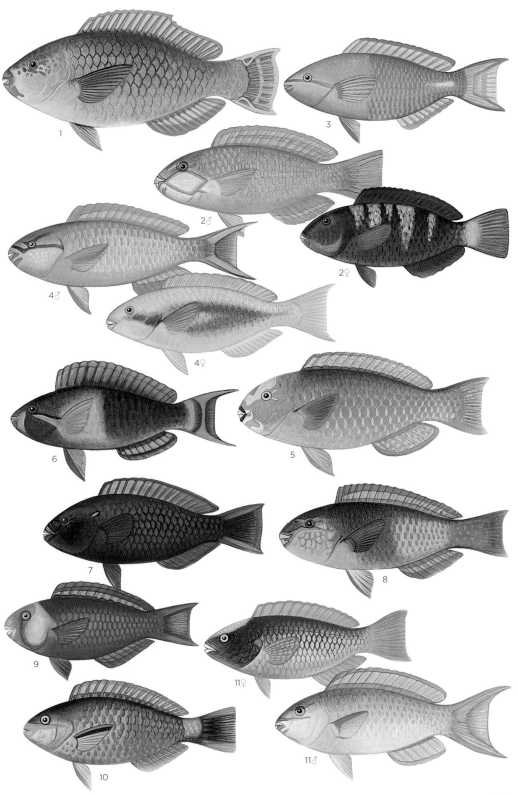

PLATE 85: GRUBFISHES, JAWFISHES AND STARGAZERS

PINGUIPEDIDAE

1. BLUENOSE GRUBFISH
Parapercis alboguttata (Günther, 1872)
Inhabits trawling grounds; distinguished by diffuse dark bars or blotches on side and bluish snout; N.W. Australia and S.E. Asia; N. Indian Ocean and W. Pacific; to 22 cm.

2. DOUBLESPOT GRUBFISH
Parapercis diplospilus Gomon, 1981
Inhabits trawling grounds; distinguished by diffuse dark spots or blotches on side and 2 spots on tail base; Exmouth Gulf northwards; Indo-Australian Archipelago; to 9 cm.

3. SPOTHEAD GRUBFISH
Parapercis clathrata Ogilby, 1910
Inhabits coral reefs; distinguished by row of enlarged spots along lower side, these usually connected by a thin stripe, also frequently with pale-edged black spot above gill cover; Great Barrier Reef, N.W. Australia and throughout S.E. Asia; Indo-C. Pacific; to 17 cm.

4. NARROW-BARRED GRUBFISH
Parapercis macrophthalma (Pietschmann, 1911)
Inhabits trawling grounds; distinguished by 5 narrow bars on side and dark spot on upper tail base; N.W. Australia and S.E. Asia; mainly W. Pacific; to 14 cm.

5. ROSY GRUBFISH
Parapercis gushikeni Yoshino, 1975
Inhabits trawling grounds; distinguished by narrow lines on upper side and spotted tail with pointed upper edge; N.W. Australia and S.E. Asia; mainly W. Pacific; to 30 cm.

6. BANDED GRUBFISH
Parapercis striolata Weber, 1913
Inhabits trawling grounds; distinguished by black spot at front of dorsal fin, wavy stripes on upper side and narrow bars on tail; N.W. Australia and S.E. Asia; mainly W. Pacific; to 20 cm.

7. DOUBLESTITCH GRUBFISH
Parapercis multiplacata Randall, 1984
Inhabits offshore coral reefs; distinguished by black spiny dorsal fin and series of red bars on side; Great Barrier Reef, N.W. Australia and Indonesia; mainly W. Pacific; to 10 cm.

8. PINKBANDED GRUBFISH
Parapercis nebulosa (Quoy & Gaimard, 1825)
Inhabits trawling grounds; similar to *P. multiplacata* (**7**), but cross bars wider and more diffuse, also lacks row of dark spots along lower side; Australia only, New South Wales northward to Great Barrier Reef and across far north to W. Australia; to 20 cm.

OPISTOGNATHIDAE

9. ABROLHOS JAWFISH
Opistognathus alleni Smith-Vaniz, 2004
Inhabits rubble and sand bottoms below 20 m depth; distinguished by small size and irregular, dark, longitudinal band on sides; Abrolhos to Montebello Islands, Western Australia; to 10 cm.

10. DARWIN JAWFISH
Opistognathus darwiniensis Macleay, 1878
Inhabits shallow reefs, usually in sandy or rubble areas; distinguished by yellowish colour of fins, dense spotting on head and sides and prominent banding on dorsal, anal and tail fins; N. Australia only, between Ningaloo Reef, W. Australia and Gulf of Carpentaria; to 50 cm.

11. BLOTCHED JAWFISH
Opistognathus latitabundus (Whitley, 1937)
Inhabits coastal waters, usually on rubble or soft bottoms; distinguished by large dark blotches on back and base of dorsal fin; also known as Spotted Pug; N. Australia only, between Broome, W. Australia and Gulf of Carpentaria; to 30 cm.

12. BLACK JAWFISH
Opistognathus inornatus Ramsay & Ogilby, 1887
Inhabits coastal waters, usually on rubble or soft bottoms; distinguished by overall dark colour without markings; N. Australia only, between Exmouth Gulf, W. Australia and Gulf of Carpentaria; to 55 cm.

13. LEOPARD JAWFISH
Opistognathus reticulatus (McKay, 1969)
Inhabits coastal waters, usually on rubble or soft bottoms; distinguished by large black spots; has bitten people wading in shallow water, but usually harmless; N. Australia only, between Exmouth Gulf, W. Australia and Gulf of Carpentaria; to 50 cm.

URANOSCOPIDAE

14. BANDED STARGAZER   VENOMOUS
Ichthyscopus fasciatus Haysom, 1957
Inhabits trawling grounds; distinguished by 5 dark bars on upper side; N. Australia only; to 25 cm.

15. DOUBLEBAND STARGAZER   VENOMOUS
Ichthyscopus insperatus Mees, 1960
Inhabits trawling grounds; distinguished by narrow double-bars on back and barred tail; N. Australia only; to 30 cm.

16. MARBLED STARGAZER   VENOMOUS
Uranoscopus bicinctus Temminck & Schlegel, 1843
Inhabits trawling grounds; distinguished by white patches on back and diffuse broad bar below each dorsal fin, has stout spine behind upper edge of gill cover; N.W. Australia and S.E. Asia; mainly W. Pacific; to 20 cm.

17. YELLOWTAIL STARGAZER   VENOMOUS
Uranoscopus cognatus Cantor, 1849
Inhabits trawling grounds; distinguished by overall brown colour except for black spot on first dorsal fin and lighter tail, has stout spine behind upper edge of gill cover; N.W. Australia and S.E. Asia; Indo-Australian Archipelago; to 22 cm.

18. KAI STARGAZER   VENOMOUS
Uranoscopus kaianus Günther, 1880
Inhabits trawling grounds; similar to *U. cognatus* (**17**), has variegated pattern on upper half of body; N.W. Australia and S.E. Asia; Indo-Australian Archipelago; to 22 cm.

19. WHITESPOTTED STARGAZER   VENOMOUS
Uranoscopus sp.
Inhabits trawling grounds; distinguished by small white spots on upper part of head and body, has stout spines behind upper edge of gill cover; possibly N. Australia only; to 15 cm.

PLATE 86: BLENNIES

BLENNIIDAE

1. LANCE BLENNY
Aspidontus dussumieri (Valenciennes, 1836)
Inhabits coral reefs and southern rocky reefs; similar to
A. taeniatus (**2**), but has yellow fins; Great Barrier Reef, W.
Australia and throughout S.E. Asia; Indo-C Pacific; to 14 cm.

2. FALSE CLEANERFISH
Aspidontus taeniatus Quoy & Gaimard, 1834
Inhabits coral reefs; nearly identical in colour to the
Common Cleanerfish *Labroides dimidiatus* (Plate **79.3**), but
has more pointed snout, longer dorsal fin base and enlarged
fangs at back of lower jaw; uses its 'disguise' to attack other
fishes, taking bites of skin and scales; Great Barrier Reef, W.
Australia and throughout S.E. Asia; Indo-C. Pacific; to 12 cm.

3. DUSKY BLENNY
Atrosalarias fuscus (Rüppell, 1838)
Inhabits coral reefs; distinguished by blackish to brown
body and relatively tall dorsal and anal fins with abruptly
pale tail; an entirely yellow colour phase is sometimes seen;
Great Barrier Reef, N.W. Australia and throughout
S.E. Asia; Indo-C. Pacific; to 10 cm.

4. MANYSPOT BLENNY
Laiphognathus multimaculatus Smith, 1955
Inhabits coral reefs, distinguished by numerous small red
spots and 1–2 rows of white spots just below base of dorsal
fin; found throughout the region; W. Australia and S.E. Asia;
W. Pacific and E. Indian Ocean; to 5.5 cm.

5. MIMIC BLENNY
Mimoblennius atrocinctus (Regan, 1909)
Inhabits coral reefs; distinguished by faint bars and row of
double-spots along midside, underside of head is dusky to
black; W. Australia and S.E. Asia; W. Pacific and E. Indian
Ocean; to 4 cm.

6. TALBOT'S BLENNY
Stanulus talboti Springer, 1968
Inhabits coral reefs; distinguished by small white spots on
cheek and lower part of head, larger white spots or blotches
on body and dark irregular blotches above pectoral fin;
Great Barrier Reef, N.W. Australia and throughout
S.E. Asia; Indo-W. Pacific; to 7 cm.

7. LEOPARD BLENNY
Exallias brevis (Kner, 1868)
Inhabits coral reefs, usually seen among branches of
Pocillopora and other corals; feeds on coral polyps;
distinguished by dense network of leopard-like spotting;
Great Barrier Reef, N.W. Australia and throughout
S.E. Asia; Indo-C Pacific; to 12 cm.

8. SHORTHEAD SABRETOOTH BLENNY
Petroscirtes breviceps (Valenciennes, 1836)
Inhabits weed-sand areas in the vicinity of reefs;
distinguished by mottled colour, usually with dark stripe or
broken band along middle of side; also known as Weed
Blenny; W. Australia and throughout S.E. Asia; Indo-W.
Pacific; to 15 cm.

9. CRESTED SABRETOOTH BLENNY
Petroscirtes mitratus Rüppell, 1830
Inhabits weed-sand areas in the vicinity of reefs;
distinguished by tall 'mast' at front of dorsal fin, juvenile
similar to *P. breviceps* (**8**), but slightly deeper-bodied;
Great Barrier Reef, W. Australia and throughout
S.E. Asia; Indo-W. Pacific; to 7 cm.

10. LINESPOT FANGBLENNY
Meiacanthus grammistes (Valenciennes, 1836)
Inhabits sand-weed areas and coral reefs; distinguished by
black stripes that become broken into spots on rear of body
and tail; Great Barrier Reef, N.W. Australia and throughout
S.E. Asia; mainly W. Pacific; to 10 cm.

11. GERMAIN'S BLENNY
Omobranchus germaini (Sauvage, 1883)
Inhabits shallow reefs, usually in crevices just below the level
of low tide; distinguished by 'ear-spot' and series of narrow
white to blue lines on side; Great Barrier Reef, N.W.
Australia and S.E. Asia; to 8 cm.

12. GOSSAMER BLENNY
Omobranchus ferox (Herre, 1927)
Inhabits mangrove bays or estuaries; distinguished by
semi-transparent body and white streak behind eye; N.W.
Australia and S.E. Asia; Indian Ocean and Indo-Australian
Archipelago; to 7 cm.

13. ROUNDHEAD BLENNY
Omobranchus lineolatus (Kner, 1868)
Inhabits mangrove bays and estuaries; distinguished by
'ear-spot', pronounced dark bars on head and fainter irregular
bars on side; found throughout the region; N. Australia and
S. New Guinea; to 9 cm.

14. MUZZLED BLENNY
Omobranchus punctatus (Valenciennes, 1836)
Inhabits inshore reefs and estuaries; distinguished by vertical
bars on head and broken thin stripes on side; Great Barrier
Reef, W. Australia and S.E. Asia; Indo-W. Pacific; to 9 cm.

15. PIANO FANGBLENNY
Plagiotremus tapeinosoma (Bleeker, 1857)
Inhabits coral and rocky reefs; distinguished by broad black
stripe which becomes broken (or has wavy margin) towards
rear of body, and broad dark margins on dorsal and anal fins;
this fish and *Xiphasia setifer* (**17**) have pair of enlarged fangs
and sometimes bite divers; Great Barrier Reef, N.W. Australia
and throughout S.E. Asia; Indo-C. Pacific; to 13 cm.

16. BLUESTRIPED FANGBLENNY
Plagiotremus rhinorhynchos (Bleeker, 1852)
Inhabits coral and rocky reefs, distinguished by narrower
blue stripes on each side of broad brownish to orange stripe
and has pale fins; Great Barrier Reef, N.W. Australia and
throughout S.E. Asia; Indo-C. Pacific; to 12 cm.

17. HAIRTAIL BLENNY
Xiphasia setifer Swainson, 1839
Inhabits sand-silt bottoms in the vicinity of coral reefs,
occupies a burrow; distinguished by extremely elongate,
tapering body; Great Barrier Reef, N.W. Australia and
throughout S.E. Asia; Indo-W. Pacific; to 56 cm.

FANGED FISHES

Blennies of the family Blenniidae (Plates 86–88)
are small, elongate, scaleless fishes that are common
on shallow reefs, mainly in tropical seas. Most of
the estimated 400 species occurring worldwide
are under 10–15 cm. They feed mainly on small
invertebrates, algae and bottom detritus. Several of
the species shown on this plate (**1–3, 8–10, 15–17**)
are commonly referred to as sabre-toothed blennies.
The name refers to the large teeth of the lower jaw
which appear to be used mainly for defence. Scale
and fin predation is a characteristic feeding habit
of *Aspidontus* (**1–2**) and *Plagiotremus* (**15–16**).

PLATE 87: BLENNIES

BLENNIIDAE

1. FILAMENTOUS BLENNY
Cirripectes filamentosus (Alleyne & Macleay, 1877)
Inhabits inshore reef crevices, frequently where there is wave action; distinguished by fringe of tentacles on neck, overall dusky colour and elevated fin-rays at front of dorsal fin; found throughout the region; Indo-W. Pacific; to 10 cm.

2. CHESTNUT BLENNY
Cirripectes castaneus (Valenciennes, 1836)
Inhabits inshore reef crevices exposed to surge; distinguished by fringe of tentacles on neck, pale spots on chin, and series of narrow dark bars on side (sometimes barely visible); found throughout the region; Indo-W. Pacific; to 13 cm.

3. BICOLOR COMBTOOTH-BLENNY
Ecsenius bicolor (Day, 1888)
Inhabits coral reef crevices; 2 colour varieties shown here are common: one is bright orange posteriorly and the other is overall dark brown; C. Indian Ocean to W. Pacific; to 8 cm.

4. LINED COMBTOOTH-BLENNY
Ecsenius lineatus Klausewitz, 1962
Inhabits coral reefs, distinguished by black stripe on upper side with brown area above and abruptly whitish on lower half; W. Australia, W. Indonesia and Philippines; Indo-W. Pacific; to 7 cm.

5. OCULAR COMBTOOTH-BLENNY
Ecsenius oculatus Springer, 1988
Inhabits coral reef crevices distinguished by series of pale-edged black spots connected by pale lines on side; W. Australia and Christmas Island (Indian Ocean); mainly W. Pacific; *E. paroculus* (not shown) is a similar species occurring in W. Indonesia and W. coast of Malay peninsula; to 6.5 cm.

6. PALESPOTTED COMBTOOTH-BLENNY
Ecsenius yaeyamensis (Aoyagi, 1954)
Inhabits coral reef crevices; distinguished by dark stripe behind eye, pale spots on side and pair of thin lines across base of pectoral fin; throughout S.E. Asia and N.W. Australia to Gulf of Carpentaria; mainly W. Pacific; *E. stictus* (not shown), a nearly identical species, occurs on the Great Barrier Reef; to 6.5 cm.

7. TWINSPOT ROCKSKIPPER
Entomacrodus thalassinus (Jordan & Seale, 1906)
Inhabits shallow coral reefs; distinguished by dark streak behind eye, row of large spots arranged in pairs along middle of side and spotted dorsal and tail fins; found throughout the region; Indo-W. Pacific; to 6.5 cm.

8. WAVYLINE ROCKSKIPPER
Entomacrodus decussatus (Bleeker, 1858)
Inhabits shallow reefs exposed to wave action; distinguished by wavy lines and irregular light and dark blotches on sides; Great Barrier Reef, N.W. Australia and throughout S.E. Asia; Indo-C. Pacific; to 18 cm.

9. BLACKSPOTTED ROCKSKIPPER
Entomacrodus striatus (Valenciennes, 1836)
Inhabits shallow reefs exposed to wave action; distinguished by clusters of dark spots on back superimposed on 4–5 broad diffuse dark bars; Great Barrier Reef, N.W. Australia and throughout S.E. Asia; Indo-C. Pacific; to 10 cm.

10. REDSPOTTED ROCKSKIPPER
Blenniella chrysospilos (Bleeker, 1857)
Inhabits shallow reefs and tide pools exposed to wave action; distinguished by small red spots on head and body and series of dark vertical streaks arranged in pairs on side; Great Barrier Reef, N.W. Australia and throughout S.E. Asia; Indo-C. Pacific; to 13 cm.

11. RIPPLED ROCKSKIPPER
Istiblennius edentulus (Forster & Schneider 1801)
Inhabits shallow reefs and tide pools exposed to wave action; male has skin flap on top of head, dark bars (usually in pairs) and pale streaks on side, female has lighter bars on sides, spots or lines on dorsal and anal fins, and often has numerous red to brown spots on rear part of body; Great Barrier Reef, N.W. Australia and throughout S.E. Asia; Indo-C. Pacific; to 13 cm.

12. PEACOCK ROCKSKIPPER
Istiblennius meleagris (Valenciennes, 1836)
Inhabits shallow reefs and tide pools exposed to wave action; male with low skin flap on top of head and rows of pale spots on side, female lacks skin flap and has faint forward-slanting bars and scattered pale spots on side; Australia only, occurs around entire coastline, except extreme south; to 15 cm.

13. LINED ROCKSKIPPER
Istiblennius lineatus (Valenciennes, 1836)
Inhabits shallow reefs and tide pools exposed to wave action; distinguished by skin flap on head and general pale colouration with narrow longitudinal lines on side; Great Barrier Reef, N.W. Australia and throughout S.E. Asia; C. Indian Ocean to C. Pacific; to 20 cm.

14. BLUESTREAKED ROCKSKIPPER
Blenniella periophthalmus (Valenciennes, 1836)
Inhabits shallow reef and tide pools exposed to wave action; distinguished by H-shaped bars on side and double row of silvery-blue streaks or spots on middle of side; found throughout the region; Indo-W. Pacific; *B. paula* (not shown), a nearly identical species, occurs on the Great Barrier Reef; to 14 cm.

15. BANDED BLENNY
Salarias fasciatus (Bloch, 1786)
Inhabits inshore coral reefs, often in weeds; distinguished by light and dark bars with overlay of narrow dark lines; Great Barrier Reef, N.W. Australia and throughout S.E. Asia; Indo-W. Pacific; to 13 cm.

16. STARRY BLENNY
Salarias ramosus Bath, 1992
Inhabits sand-weed areas on rocky outcrops; distinguished by frilly tentacles above eye and numerous small white spots; N.W. Australia, Indonesia and Philippines; Indo-Australian Archipelago; to 9 cm.

17. SPALDING'S BLENNY
Salarias sexfilum Günther, 1861
Inhabits coral reefs; distinguished by narrow dark bars on side and 'pepper-spotting' on upper side; N. Australia only, between Exmouth Gulf, Western Australia and Gulf of Carpentaria; to 9 cm.

TIDEPOOL BLENNIES

Most of the blennies shown on this plate, particularly **7–17**, are common inhabitants of shallow reef flats, the intertidal zone and splash pools along rocky shores. They are one of the most frequently observed groups of fishes encountered by beachcombers. A few of the species are commonly called rockskippers because, when disturbed, they use their body musculature and stout pelvic fins to skip over rocks from one pool to another.

PLATE 88: BLENNIES

BLENNIIDAE

1. EYELASH FANGBLENNY
Meiacanthus atrodorsalis (Günther, 1877)
Inhabits coral reefs, swims close to bottom with rapid darting motion interspersed with stationary hovering; nearly identical to *Plagiotremus laudandus* (5), but is not as slender and has diagonal dark band through eye; Great Barrier Reef, offshore reefs of W. Australia and E. Indonesia; mainly W. Pacific; to 11 cm.

2. SCHOOLING FANGBLENNY
Meiacanthus ditrema Smith-Vaniz, 1976
Inhabits coral reefs, behaviour as for *M. atrodorsalis* (1); distinguished by pair of black stripes on lower part of head that join into one stripe at pectoral fin base; Great Barrier Reef and Indonesia; W. Pacific; to 6.5 cm.

3. SMITH'S FANGBLENNY
Meiacanthus smithi Klausewitz, 1962
Inhabits coral reefs, behaviour as for *M. atrodorsalis* (1); distinguished by broad black stripe on dorsal fin and oblique dark band above eye; W. Indonesia and W. coast of Malay Peninsula; C. Indian Ocean to Java; Great Barrier Reef and Indonesia; W. Pacific; to 7 cm.

4. YELLOW FANGBLENNY
Meiacanthus luteus Smith-Vaniz, 1987
Inhabits coral reefs, behaviour as for *M. atrodorsalis* (1); distinguished by broad black stripe on middle of side and much narrower one at base of dorsal fin with bright yellow between; is mimicked by *Petroscirtes fallax* (not shown); N. Australia only; to 10 cm.

5. BICOLOR FANGBLENNY
Plagiotremus laudandus (Whitley, 1961)
Inhabits coral reefs; it mimics the nearly identical *M. atrodorsalis* (1), but is more slender and lacks diagonal dark band through eye; Great Barrier Reef, offshore reefs of W. Australia and E. Indonesia; mainly W. Pacific; to 7.5 cm.

6. REDSTREAKED BLENNY
Cirripectes stigmaticus Strasburg & Schultz, 1953
Inhabits coral reefs; distinguished by scarlet (male) to rust-coloured (female) spots and lines on side; Great Barrier Reef, offshore reefs of W. Australia, E. Indonesia and Melanesia; Indo-W. Pacific; to 12 cm.

7. KIMBERLEY BLENNY
Cirripectes alleni Williams, 1993
Inhabits coral reefs in turbid water; distinguished by frill of skin flaps on nape and whitish colour with broad dark stripe on middle of side; Kimberley region of N.W. Australia only, to 6.5 cm.

8. TRIPLESPOT BLENNY
Crossosalarias macrospilus Smith-Vaniz & Springer, 1971
Inhabits coral reefs, usually in less than 10 m depth; distinguished by mottled, pale-spotted pattern, low fleshy flap in front of dorsal fin and pair of dark spots on each side of throat; Great Barrier Reef and S.E. Asia; mainly W. Pacific; to 8 cm.

9. MIDAS COMBTOOTH-BLENNY
Ecsenius midas Starck, 1969
Inhabits coral reefs, usually on outer slopes; mimics *Pseudanthias squamipinnis* (Plate **27.4**); colour variable, usually orange-yellow or dark slate blue, also has small dark spot in front of anus; Great Barrier Reef and throughout S.E. Asia; Indo-W. Pacific; to 13 cm.

10. ALLEN'S COMBTOOTH-BLENNY
Ecsenius alleni Springer, 1988
Inhabits coral reefs; distinguished by black spot on pectoral fin base and combination of white blotches and black bars on side; offshore reefs of W. Australia only; to 4 cm.

11. AUSTRALIAN COMBTOOTH-BLENNY
Ecsenius australianus Springer, 1988
Inhabits coral reefs; distinguished by black stripe behind eye and double row of rectangular white spots on side; N. Great Barrier Reef only; to 4 cm.

12. BATH'S COMBTOOTH-BLENNY
Ecsenius bathi Springer, 1988
Inhabits coral reefs; has two distinct patterns: one with double stripes shown here and another that is similar to *E. australianus* (**11**); E. Indonesia only; to 4 cm.

13. AXELROD'S COMBTOOTH-BLENNY
Ecsenius axelrodi Springer, 1988
Inhabits coral reefs; distinguished by black 'ear-spot', white stripe on middle of sides crossed by 6–7 black bars; *E. tigris* (not shown) from the Coral Sea and *E. dilemma* (not shown) from the Philippines are similar, but lack 'ear-spot'; Sulawesi to Solomon Islands; to 4 cm.

14. SHIRLEY'S COMBTOOTH-BLENNY
Ecsenius shirleyae Springer & Allen, 2004
Inhabits coral reefs; distinguished by pearly stripe with black stripe immediately above, between eye and upper edge of gill cover, with brown colour above and light colour below stripes; Indonesia only, between Java and Timor; to 4 cm.

15. BLACKASS COMBTOOTH-BLENNY
Ecsenius lividanalis Chapman & Schultz, 1952
Inhabits coral reefs; entirely yellow to mainly slate grey with yellow fins, all varieties with black spot covering anus; N.W. Australia (Kimberley district to Darwin) and Bali, Indonesia to Solomon Islands; to 4 cm.

16. JAVA COMBTOOTH-BLENNY
Ecsenius melarchus McKinney & Springer, 1976
Inhabits coral reefs; distinguished by bluish colour on lower part of head, small black spot behind eye and black spot covering anus; 2 varieties seen: 'bicolour' form as shown and one which is uniformly brown on body; E. Indonesia and Philippines; to 4 cm.

17. NAMIYE'S COMBTOOTH-BLENNY
Ecsenius namiyei (Jordan & Evermann, 1902)
Inhabits coral reefs; head and body dark brown to blackish; tail either greyish-white or bright yellow; Philippines, E. Indonesia and offshore reefs of N.W. Australia; W. Pacific; to 9 cm.

18. WHITELINED COMBTOOTH-BLENNY
Ecsenius pictus McKinney & Springer, 1976
Inhabits coral reefs; distinguished by dark brown body with thin white lines and spots; E. Indonesia to Solomon Islands; to 4.5 cm.

19. SEGMENTED BLENNY
Salarias segmentatus Bath & Randall, 1991
Inhabits sheltered coral reefs, often in silty areas; distinguished by broken dark bars on side and large dark-rimmed pale spot below pectoral-fin base; E. Indonesia to Solomon Islands; to 7.5 cm.

20. PATZNER'S BLENNY
Salarias patzneri Bath, 1992
Inhabits coral reefs; distinguished by mottled pattern with numerous small white spots on head and body; Indonesia and Philippines; to 5.5 cm.

21. AMBON ROCKSKIPPER
Paralticus amboinensis (Bleeker, 1857)
Inhabits protected shores, sometimes among mangroves; distinguished by strongly mottled pattern and bushy flap above each eye; Sabah and E. Indonesia; to 13 cm.

PLATE 89: THREEFINS, DRAGONETS AND GOBIES

TRIPTERYGIIDAE

1. BLACKTHROAT THREEFIN
Helcogramma decurrens McCulloch & Waite, 1918
Inhabits inshore reefs; male distinguished by black on lower half of head and body, female is variably coloured, either red, green or brown; Australia only, southward of N.W. Cape, W. Australia, ranging to S. Australia; to 7 cm.

2. STRIPED THREEFIN
Helcogramma striatum Hansen, 1986
Inhabits coral reef crevices; distinguished by reddish colour with 3 narrow golden stripes on side; found throughout the region; E. Indian Ocean to C. Pacific; to 3.5 cm.

3. SCALYFIN THREEFIN
Norfolkia brachylepis (Schultz, 1960)
Inhabits inshore coral reefs; distinguished by presence of scales on cheek and gill cover, a low fleshy flap above eye and diagonal cross-bands on anal fin; N.W. Australia, Indonesia and Philippines; Indo-W. Pacific; to 6 cm.

CALLIONYMIDAE

4. LONGSPINE DRAGONET
Pseudocalliurichthys goodladi (Whitley, 1944)
Inhabits trawling grounds, generally on sand bottoms; distinguished by overall pale colouration with brown mottling on back and spotted tail, male has 2 filamentous spines at front of first dorsal fin and female (not shown) has one filament; W. Australia only; to 22 cm.

5. OCELLATE DRAGONET
Bathycallionymus moretonensis (Johnson, 1971)
Inhabits trawling grounds, generally on sand bottoms; similar to *Calliurichthys australis* (**6**) and *C. afilum* (**7**), but has shorter tail and stout spine on lower edge of cheek has 2 large teeth on its upper surface (versus many small teeth); N. Australia, New Caledonia and New Ireland; to 12 cm.

6. AUSTRALIAN STINKFISH
Calliurichthys australis (Fricke, 1983)
Inhabits trawling grounds, generally on sand bottoms; similar to *Bathycallionymus moretonensis* (**5**), but has 5–7 small teeth on upper surface of cheek spine (versus 2 large teeth); also resembles *C. afilum* (**7**), but has only outer tips of anal fin-rays blackish (versus outer half of entire fin); N.W. Australia only, but another subspecies *C. margaretae* (not shown) is widespread in N: Indian Ocean; to 18 cm.

7. LOWFIN STINKFISH
Calliurichthys afilum (Fricke, 2000)
Inhabits trawling grounds, generally on sand bottoms; similar to *Bathycallionymus moretonensis* (**5**) and *C. australis* (**6**), but has wider black margin on anal fin and tail often wider and more elongate; N. Australia, New Guinea and Philippines; mainly W. Pacific; to 30 cm.

8. LONGNOSE STINKFISH
Calliurichthys grossi (Ogilby, 1910)
Inhabits trawling grounds, generally on sand bottoms; similar to *Pseudocalliurichthys goodladi* (**4**), but has larger, differently shaped dorsal fin; N. Australia only; to 20 cm.

9. RED DRAGONET
Synchiropus altivelis (Temminck & Schlegel, 1845)
Inhabits trawling grounds in deep (70–600 m) water; distinguished by overall reddish or pink colour and relatively short first dorsal fin (sometimes with filament); N.W. Australia and Philippines to Japan; to 20 cm.

10. WHITESPOTTED DRAGONET
Orbonymus rameus (McCulloch, 1926)
Inhabits trawling grounds, generally on sand or rubble bottoms; distinguished by huge sail-like dorsal fin and blue-spotted anal fin; N. Australia and New Caledonia; to 15 cm.

11. MORRISON'S DRAGONET
Synchiropus morrisoni Schultz, 1960
Inhabits coral reefs and rocky areas usually below 25 m depth; male distinguished by tall, flat-topped first dorsal fin with dark vertical streaks and broad, dark submarginal band on anal fin, female by large dark blotch covering pectoral fin base and diagonal dark streaks on anal fin; Great Barrier Reef, N.W. Australia and Indonesia; mainly W. Pacific; to 6.5 cm.

12. SPOTTED DRAGONET
Synchiropus picturatus (Peters, 1877)
Inhabits coral reefs; distinguished by robust shape and ornate pattern of ocellated spots and blotches; another closely related species *S. occidentalis* (Plate **90.3**) occurs only in N.W. Australia; Indo-Malay Archipelago; to 5.5 cm.

13. NORTHERN DRAGONET
Diplogrammus xenicus (Jordan & Thompson, 1914)
Inhabits sand-rubble areas near reefs; male distinguished by relatively short filament on first dorsal fin, blue spots and lines on head, dusky anal fin and fan-like, dark-edged pelvic fins, female differs from male in size, shape and colour of first dorsal and pelvic fins, also the anal fin is clear instead of dusky; W. Australia and Okinawa to Japan; to 7 cm.

14. FINGERED DRAGONET
Dactylopus dactylopus (Valenciennes, 1837)
Inhabits sand-weed bottoms; distinguished by detached first ray on large fan-like pelvic fin; Great Barrier Reef, W. Australia and S.E. Asia; E. Indian Ocean and W. Pacific; to 30 cm.

GOBIIDAE

15. SLEEPY GOBY
Psammogobius biocellatus (Valenciennes, 1837)
Inhabits brackish estuaries and tidal creeks; distinguished by dark blotches or bars on lower lobe of tail, also anal and pelvic fins and lower part of head frequently dark; found throughout the region; mainly W. Pacific: to 10 cm.

16. MANGROVE FLATHEAD GOBY
Glossogobius circumspectus (Macleay, 1883)
Inhabits brackish estuaries and tidal creeks; similar to *Psammogobius biocellatus* (**15**), but has blunter snout, is generally lighter in colour and lacks darkened areas on pelvic, anal and tail fins (except narrow dark bands across tail); found throughout the region; Indo-Australian Archipelago; to 12 cm.

17. SHOULDERSPOT GOBY
Gnatholepis cauerensis (Bleeker, 1853)
Inhabits sand bottoms adjacent to oral reefs; distinguished by narrow dark stripes on side, thin bar below eye and small orange spot above pectoral fin base; found throughout the region; Indo-Australian Archipelago; to 7 cm.

TRIPLEFINS AND STINKFISHES

The Threefins of the family Tripterygiidae (**1–3**), as their name suggests, are characterised by three separate dorsal fins. They are mainly tiny fishes with well over 150 species occurring worldwide. Due to their small size and numerous species the identification is usually difficult. They are bottom dwellers found on the surface of rocks or corals.

Stinkfishes of the family Callionymidae (**4–14**) occur in tropical and temperate seas where they generally are found on sand or mud bottoms in the vicinity of reefs. Some species occur on the continental shelf and slope to depths of about 900 m. Nearly all of the estimated 135 species are small in size (usually under 20 cm total length) and most are inhabitants of the Indo-Pacific region.

PLATE 90: DRAGONETS AND GOBIES

CALLIONYMIDAE

1. MANDARINFISH
Synchiropus splendidus (Herre, 1927)
Inhabits shallow reefs; distinguished by green 'maze' pattern on orange or orange-brown background; Great Barrier Reef, offshore reefs of N.W. Australia and S.E. Asia; W. Pacific; to 6 cm.

2. MARBLE DRAGONET
Synchiropus ocellatus (Pallas, 1770)
Inhabits rubble bottoms; distinguished by blue markings on head and sail-like first dorsal fin; N. Great Barrier Reef, E. Indonesia and Philippines; W. and C. Pacific; to 7 cm.

3. WESTERN DRAGONET
Synchiropus occidentalis Fricke, 1983
Inhabits coral reef crevices and among live coral branches; distinguished by robust shape and ornate pattern of ocellated spots and blotches; known only from Dampier Archipelago and Monte Bello Is., W. Australia; to 5.5 cm.

4. MOYER'S DRAGONET
Synchiropus moyeri Zaiser & Fricke, 1985
Inhabits sand rubble bottoms among coral reefs at depths of about 5–30 m; distinguished by variegated pattern; male with tall, sail-like first dorsal fin with numerous oblique bands; Great Barrier Reef, Indonesia, Philippines, and Papua New Guinea, north to Japan; to 8.3 cm.

5. WEEDY DRAGONET
Anaora tentaculata Gray, 1835
Inhabits weedy areas; has excellent camouflage colour, distinguished by numerous small skin flaps on body; Borneo and Philippines to New Guinea; to 5.5 cm.

GOBIIDAE

6. BLACKCHEST SHRIMPGOBY
Amblyeleotris guttata (Fowler, 1938)
Inhabits sand rubble; shares burrow with alpheid shrimp; distinguished by orange spots on head and body and black pelvics and belly region; Great Barrier Reef and S.E. Asia; W. Pacific; to 8 cm.

7. STEINITZ'S SHRIMPGOBY
Amblyeleotris steinitzi (Klausewitz, 1974)
Inhabits sand-rubble fringe of coral reefs; shares burrow with alpheid shrimp; distinguished by whitish body and 5 dull brown bars; Great Barrier Reef, offshore reefs of N.W. Australia and S.E. Asia; Indo-W. Pacific; to 8 cm.

8. BROADBANDED SHRIMPGOBY
Amblyeleotris periophthalma (Bleeker, 1853)
Inhabits sand rubble; shares burrow with alpheid shrimp; distinguished by diffuse brown bars and horizontally elongate blotches on side; Great Barrier Reef and S.E. Asia; W. Pacific; to 8 cm.

9. SAILFIN SHRIMPGOBY
Amblyeleotris randalli Hoese & Steene, 1978
Inhabits ledges on outer reef slopes; shares burrow with alpheid shrimp; distinguished by thin, yellow-orange bars and large first dorsal fin; Great Barrier Reef, E. Indonesia, Phillipines, New Guinea and Solomon Islands; to 8 cm.

10. METALLIC SHRIMPGOBY
Amblyeleotris latifasciata Polunin & Lubbock, 1979
Inhabits sand rubble; shares burrow with alpheid shrimp; distinguished by broad brown bars, blue spotting on head and large, pale-rimmed dark spots on first dorsal fin; Indonesia; to 10 cm.

11. FLAGTAIL SHRIMPGOBY
Amblyeleotris yanoi Aonuma & Yoshino, 1996
Inhabits sand-rubble fringe of coral reefs; shares burrow with alpheid shrimp; distinguished by brightly marked tail fin; Indonesia to Malanesian Archipelago; W. Pacific; to 8 cm.

12. SADDLED SHRIMPGOBY
Cryptocentrus leucostictus (Günther, 1872)
Inhabits sand rubble; shares burrow with alpheid shrimp; distinguished by overall dark colour, white snout and saddles on back; Great Barrier Reef and S.E. Asia; W. Pacific; to 7 cm.

13. YELLOW SHRIMPGOBY
Cryptocentrus cinctus (Herre, 1936)
Inhabits sand-rubble fringe of coral reefs; shares burrow with alpheid shrimp; has two colour phases: one primarily yellow and another that is whitish with brown bars on side; Great Barrier Reef, offshore reefs of N.W. Australia and S.E. Asia; Indo-W. Pacific; to 8 cm.

14. TARGET SHRIMPGOBY
Cryptocentrus strigilliceps (Jordan & Seale, 1906)
Inhabits sand rubble; shares burrow with alpheid shrimp; distinguished by large black spots along middle of side; Great Barrier Reef, offshore reefs of N.W. Australia and throughout S.E. Asia; Indo-C. Pacific; to 7 cm.

15. TANGAROA SHRIMPGOBY
Ctenogobiops tangaroai Lubbock & Polunin, 1977
Inhabits sandy areas; pairs share burrow with alpheid shrimp; distinguished by very tall first dorsal fin; Great Barrier Reef, offshore reefs of N.W. Australia and throughout S.E. Asia; W. Pacific; to 5.5 cm.

16. GOLDSTREAKED SHRIMPGOBY
Ctenogobius aurocingulus (Herre, 1935)
Inhabits sand rubble; shares burrow with shrimp; distinguished by yellow-centred dark markings on head and vertical orange bands on lower side; Philippines, E. Indonesia and New Guinea; W. Pacific; to 6 cm.

17. CRAB-EYE GOBY
Signigobius biocellatus Hoese & Allen, 1977
Inhabits sandy fringe of coral reefs; Great Barrier Reef, offshore reefs of N.W. Australia and throughout S.E. Asia; Indo-Australian Archipelago; to 6.5 cm.

18. OLD GLORY GOBY
Koumansetta rainfordi Whitley, 1940
Inhabits caves and holes with sand-rubble bottom at base of coral reefs; similar to *K. hectori* (**19**), but is paler and lacks dark spot on first dorsal fin; Great Barrier Reef, New Guinea, offshore reefs of N.W. Australia, E. Indonesia and Philippines; mainly W. Pacific; to 6.5 cm.

19. HECTOR'S GOBY
Koumansetta hectori (Smith, 1957)
Inhabits coral reefs; similar to *K. rainfordi* (**18**), but body is darker and has pale-edged dark spot on first dorsal fin; Great Barrier Reef and throughout S.E. Asia; Indo-W. Pacific; to 5.5 cm.

GOBIES

Gobies (Plates 90–94) are by far the largest family of fishes in the region. There are no accurate estimates available, but in the area covered by this book there is probably in excess of 800 species. Worldwide it is the largest family of marine fishes with an estimated 250 genera and about 2,000 species — almost 1 out of every 10 fishes in the world, including both freshwater and saltwater species, belongs to this massive family. Although the family is large, many of its members are definitely not. Pygmy gobies belonging to the genus *Trimmatom* and *Pandaka* are full grown at about 1 cm, making them the smallest known vertebrate animals. It's difficult to define a typical goby, but they are usually small (less than 15 cm) bottom-resting fishes that depend on shelter in the form of rocks, coral, or sandy burrows. The majority live in the sea on reefs, but there are numerous freshwater species as well (particularly in the subfamily Eleotridinae). Most of the marine species have the pelvic fins completely or partially fused, forming a disk-like apparatus that is used as a 'tripod' when resting. Although gobies exhibit a wide range of feeding habits, most consume a variety of small invertebrates.

PLATE 91: GOBIES

GOBIIDAE

1. BLUESPOTTED MANGROVEGOBY
Amoya gracilis (Bleeker, 1875)
Inhabits mangrove estuaries; distinguished by overall pale colour with mid-lateral stripe composed of brown blotches and bright blue spots, also brown spots and blotches on back and fins; found throughout the region; Indo-Australian Archipelago; to 8 cm.

2. BURGUNDY SHRIMPGOBY
Amblyeleotris wheeleri (Polunin & Lubbock, 1977)
Inhabits sand bottoms near coral reefs, shares its burrow with an alpheid shrimp; distinguished by combination of wine-red bars and small bluish spots; Great Barrier Reef, N.W. Australia and throughout S.E. Asia; Indo-W. Pacific; to 6 cm.

3. STARRY GOBY
Asterropteryx semipunctata Rüppell, 1830
Inhabits rubble bottoms; distinguished by mottled green-brown colour with numerous small blue spots on head, body and fins, also has microscopic spines on edge of cheek; found throughout the region; Indo-C. Pacific; to 5 cm.

4. WHITEBARRED GOBY
Amblygobius phalaena (Valenciennes, 1837)
Inhabits sand-weed areas; distinguished by stripes that are interrupted by narrow dark bars on side, a large pale-edged dark spot on first dorsal fin and smaller dark spot on upper part of tail; also known as Whitespotted Goby; found throughout the region; Indo-W. Pacific; to 15 cm.

5. COCOS FRILLGOBY
Bathygobius cocosensis (Bleeker, 1854)
Inhabits shallow beach-rock reefs and tide pools; distinguished by diffuse dark saddles and row of elongated dark spots slightly below middle of side, also scales on top of head extend only to rear margin of cheek (preopercle); Great Barrier Reef, N.W. Australia and throughout S.E. Asia; Indo-W. Pacific; to 8 cm.

6. DUSKY FRILLGOBY
Bathygobius fuscus (Rüppell, 1830)
Inhabits shallow beach-rock reefs and tide pools distinguished by blunt snout, bulbous cheeks and often with large irregular-shaped blotches and small pale spots on head and side, scales on top of head extend almost to rear of eyes; found throughout the region; Indo-C. Pacific; to 12 cm.

7. WHISKERED GOBY
Callogobius sp.
Inhabits rubble areas and coral reef crevices; distinguished by rows of raised papillae (whiskers) on head, easily shed scales and blotchy colour pattern; possibly Australia only; to 6 cm.

8. TRIPLEBAND GOBY
Callogobius sclateri (Steindachner, 1879)
Inhabits coral reefs; distinguished by pair of dark bars, one below each dorsal fin, and rows of raised papillae (whiskers) on head; Great Barrier Reef, N.W. Australia and throughout S.E. Asia; Indo-C. Pacific; to 5 cm.

9. HALE'S DROMBUS
Drombus hale Whitley, 1935
Inhabits coastal waters, including estuaries; distinguished by abruptly pale back and small white spots on head and side; N. Australia; to 5 cm.

10. BLUE-SPECKLED PRAWN-GOBY
Cryptocentrus caeruleomaculatus (Herre, 1933)
Inhabits sand-rubble areas near coral reefs, shares its burrow with an alpheid shrimp; distinguished by broad green-brown bars with narrower pale areas between them, also blackish spot in middle of each dark bar; *C. caeruleomaculatus* is a synonym; N.W. Australia and throughout S.E. Asia; Indo-W. Pacific; to 5 cm.

11. PINKSPOT SHRIMPGOBY
Cryptocentrus leptocephalus Bleeker, 1876
Inhabits sandy areas near coral reefs, shares its burrow with an alpheid shrimp; distinguished by pink or red spots and stripes on head and dorsal fins, and oblique dark bars on body, also small white spots on head and side; *C. obliquus* and *C. singapurensis* are synonyms; N.W. Australia and throughout S.E. Asia; W. Pacific; to 10 cm.

12. GOLDSPECKLED SHRIMPGOBY
Ctenogobiops pomastictus Lubbock & Polunin, 1977
Inhabits sandy areas near coral reefs, shares its burrow with an alpheid shrimp; distinguished by brown spots on head and body and white blotch on lower edge of pectoral fins; Great Barrier Reef, N.W. Australia and throughout S.E. Asia; E. Indian Ocean and W. Pacific; to 6 cm.

13. QUEENSLAND EVIOTA
Eviota queenslandica Whitley, 1932
Inhabits coral reefs; distinguished by tiny size, semi-transparent appearance, red spots on head, black spot above gill cover, diffuse dark bars above anal fin and dark spot on middle of tail base; possibly N. Australia to Philippines; to 2 cm.

14. SHOULDERMARK EVIOTA
Eviota infulata (Smith, 1957)
Inhabits coral reefs; distinguished by tiny size, filamentous first and second dorsal spines (males) and black spot or blotch above pectoral fin base; Great Barrier Reef and W. Australia; Indo-C. Pacific; to 2 cm.

15. TWOSPOT SANDGOBY
Fusigobius duospilus Hoese & Reader, 1985
Inhabits sand bottoms adjacent to coral reefs; distinguished by semi-transparent appearance, 2 dark blotches on first dorsal fin, small brown spots on head and body and black spot at middle of tail base; Great Barrier Reef, N.W. Australia and throughout S.E. Asia; Indo-C. Pacific; to 6 cm.

GOBIES AND PARTNERS

Reef gobies offer some of the best examples of 'symbiosis'. Some live among the branches of particular corals, others are found on the surface of sponges, soft corals and tunicates, but the most fascinating examples involve associations with alpheid shrimps. The fish (often in pairs and usually in the genera *Amblyeleotris, Cryptocentrus, Ctenogobiops, Stonogobiops* and *Vanderhorstia*) stands sentry duty at the entrance of the burrow, its body or tail constantly maintaining contact with the long antennae of the shrimp. If the coast is clear of intruders, the fish signals its shrimp partner with a little wiggle. The shrimp then emerges with a load of sediment, carefully balanced on its large claw. It dumps the load a short distance from the entrance, then re-enters the burrow to repeat the process. Burrows are generally constructed in areas of very soft sand or silt and therefore require constant maintenance. Both fish and shrimp benefit greatly from their association and it is doubtful they could survive without it. The shrimp provides the fish with a home and also helps to unearth food. The fish performs a 'watchdog' role for the shrimp, allowing it to dig a burrow and forage (on algae, detritus and bacteria) without fear of predators.

PLATE 92: GOBIES

GOBIIDAE

1. MAORI CORALGOBY
Gobiodon histrio (Valenciennes, 1837)
Wedges amongst branching corals; distinguished by large rounded head and red-brown bars and stripes; found throughout the region; W. and C. Pacific; to 6 cm.

2. FIVELINE CORALGOBY
Gobiodon quinquestrigatus (Valenciennes, 1837)
Wedges amongst branching corals; similar shape to *G. histrio* (1), but overall dark with narrow blue lines on head; found throughout the region; Indo-C. Pacific; to 4 cm.

3. DECORATED SANDGOBY
Istigobius decoratus (Herre, 1927)
Inhabits sand bottoms in the vicinity of coral reefs; similar to *I. nigroocellatus* (4), but lacks black spot on rear part of first dorsal fin and less than 5 dark spots on top of head between eyes and first dorsal fin; Great Barrier Reef, W. Australia and S. E. Asia; Indo-W. Pacific; to 12 cm.

4. BLACKSPOTTED SANDGOBY
Istigobius nigroocellatus (Günther, 1873)
Inhabits sand or silt bottoms in turbid water near inshore reefs; similar to *I. decoratus* (3), but has black spot at rear of first dorsal fin and about 10–15 small black spots on top of head between eyes and first dorsal fin; Great Barrier Reef, W. Australia and Philippines; mainly W. Pacific; to 7 cm.

5. EYELINE SANDGOBY
Istigobius diadema (Steindachner, 1876)
Inhabits sand-rubble areas near inshore reefs; distinguished by reddish colour and narrow dark line connecting eyes over top of head; found throughout the region; Great Barrier Reef and N.W. Australia; E. Indian Ocean to N. Australia; to 11 cm.

6. ORNATE SANDGOBY
Istigobius ornatus (Rüppell, 1830)
Inhabits mangrove areas and shallow rubble reefs; distinguished by 3–4 free (filamentous) upper pectoral rays and enlarged canine tooth on each side of lower jaw, colour variable; found throughout the region; Indo-W. Pacific; to 10 cm.

7. GIRDLED REEFGOBY
Priolepis cincta (Regan, 1908)
Inhabits reef crevices; distinguished by series of dark-edged brown bars with narrower pale bars between; found throughout the region; Great Barrier Reef, N.W. Australia and throughout S. E. Asia; Indo-C. Pacific; to 6 cm.

8. HALFBARRED REEFGOBY
Priolepis semidoliata (Valenciennes, 1837)
Inhabits coral reef crevices and caves; distinguished by narrow blue bars on head and elongate filament on first dorsal fin; N.W. Australia, New Guinea, S. Indonesia and Philippines; Indo-W. Pacific; to 3 cm.

9. REDHEAD STYLOPHORA GOBY
Paragobiodon echinocephalus (Rüppell, 1830)
Inhabits coral reefs, found amongst branches of *Stylophora* coral; distinguished by red or pinkish head and black body, also has tiny bristles covering head; found throughout the region; Indo-W. Pacific; to 3.5 cm.

10. LANTANA PYGMYGOBY
Trimma lantana Winterbottom & Villa, 2003
Inhabits coral reef crevices and caves; distinguished by tiny size, irregular red and white blotches on head and body, and red spots on fins; N. Australia, Indonesia, Papua New Guinea and Solomon Islands; to 2.5 cm.

11. ORANGE-RED PYGMYGOBY
Trimma okinawae (Aoyagi, 1949)
Inhabits coral reef crevices and caves, distinguished by dense network of red-orange spots on body and fins; Great Barrier Reef, N.W. Australia and throughout S. E. Asia; E. Indian Ocean and W. Pacific; to 4 cm.

12. HOESE'S SILHOUETTE GOBY
Silhouettea hoesei Larson & Miller, 1986
Inhabits sand bottoms close to shore; distinguished by eyes on dorsal profile of head and overall pale colour with brown speckling; N.W. Australia only; to 3.5 cm.

13. BRAVO'S BEARDED GOBY
Gobiopsis bravoi (Herre, 1940)
Inhabits inshore reefs; distinguished by flattened head, rows of raised papillae on head, short skin tentacles around mouth and irregular dark bars and pale patches on body; N.W. Australia, Philippines, E. Indonesia and New Guinea; mainly W. Pacific; to 4 cm.

14. MURAL GLIDERGOBY
Valenciennea muralis (Valenciennes, 1837)
Inhabits sand-rubble areas near coral reefs; distinguished by broad white band and series of narrower brown stripes along side, and black spot at rear of first dorsal fin; found throughout the region; mainly W. Pacific; to 13 cm.

15. OCELLATE GLIDERGOBY
Valenciennea longipinnis (Lay & Bennett, 1839)
Inhabits sand-rubble areas near coral reefs; distinguished by blue-edged saddles or bars on side with dark spot at lower part of each bar; Great Barrier Reef, N.W. Australia and throughout S. E. Asia; mainly W. Pacific; to 15 cm.

16. ORANGESPOTTED GLIDERGOBY
Valenciennea puellaris (Tomiyama, 1956)
Inhabits sand-rubble areas near coral reefs; distinguished by orange longitudinal band from mouth to tail and orange spots on back; Great Barrier Reef, N.W. Australia and throughout S.E. Asia; Indo-W. Pacific; to 14 cm.

17. ORNATE SHRIMPGOBY
Vanderhorstia sp.
Inhabits sand bottoms; lives in burrow with alpheid shrimp; has long filament on first dorsal fin and blue-edged yellow spots on body; Great Barrier Reef and W. Australia; to 8 cm

18. WHITECAP SHRIMPGOBY
Lotilia klausewitzi Shibukawa, Suzuki & Senou, 2012
Inhabits sand-rubble fringe of coral reefs; shares burrow with shrimp, distinguished by black body with broad white band on top of head; Great Barrier Reef and throughout S.E. Asia; W. Pacific; to 4.5 cm.

19. HAIRFIN GOBY
Yongeichthys nebulosus (Forsskål, 1775)
Inhabits silt bottoms; large brown spots on side; found throughout region; Indo-W. Pacific; to 18 cm.

20. PYJAMA GOBY
Amblygobius nocturnus (Herre, 1945)
Inhabits sheltered inshore reefs; is pale greyish with orange to pinkish-red stripes on upper half of body and greyish spots along base of dorsal fin; W. Pacific; to 8 cm.

21. CROSSHATCH GOBY
Amblygobius decussatus (Bleeker, 1855)
Inhabits silty-sandy edge of sheltered reefs; pale-edged orange spot on tail base; Great Barrier Reef, offshore reefs of N.W. Australia and throughout S.E. Asia; W. Pacific; to 8 cm.

MICRODESMIDAE

22. BEAUTIFUL HOVER GOBY
Parioglossus formosus (Smith, 1931)
Inhabits mangrove areas, tidal creeks and inshore reefs, occurring in schools; distinguished by prominent black stripe along lower side and extending on to tail; found throughout the region; mainly W. Pacific; to 3.5 cm.

23. THREAD-TAIL DARTGOBY
Ptereleotris hanae (Jordan & Snyder, 1901)
Inhabits sand bottoms near coral reefs, distinguished by slender shape, pale blue colour and elongate filaments on first dorsal fin and tail; Great Barrier Reef, N.W. Australia and Philippines; W. and C. Pacific; to 10 cm.

PLATE 93: GOBIES, DARTFISHES, SAND-DIVERS AND CONVICT BLENNIES

GOBIIDAE

1. MUD-REEF GOBY
Exyrias belissimus (Smith, 1959)
Inhabits sandy or silty fringe of coral reefs; distinguished by elevated dorsal and anal fins, filamentous tips on first dorsal fin, about 10 diffuse brown bars on side and small white spots on head; *E. puntang* (not shown) is very similar, but has 10 or more predorsal scales (8–10 in *bellissimus*); Great Barrier Reef, offshore reefs of N.W. Australia and throughout S.E. Asia; Indo-W. Pacific; to 13 cm.

2. ALLEN'S GLIDERGOBY
Valenciennea alleni Hoese & Larson, 1994
Inhabits sand-rubble fringe of coral reefs; distinguished by general pale colour with white stripe on side of head and body, also a pair of dark-edged orange stripes on side of head; N.W. Australia and Great Barrier Reef; to 9 cm.

3. BLACKLINED GLIDERGOBY
Valenciennea helsdingenii (Bleeker, 1858)
Inhabits sand-rubble fringe of coral reefs; usually seen in pairs that share sandy burrow; distinguished by pair of dark stripes on head and body; Great Barrier Reef and S.E. Asia; Indo-W. Pacific; to 16 cm.

4. SIXSPOT GLIDERGOBY
Valenciennea sexguttata (Valenciennes, 1837)
Inhabits sand-rubble fringe of coral reefs; generally pale, but has black tip on first dorsal fin; Great Barrier Reef, offshore reefs of W. Australia and throughout S.E. Asia; Indo-W. Pacific; to 14 cm.

5. BLUEBAND GLIDERGOBY
Valenciennea strigata (Broussonet, 1782)
Inhabits sand-rubble fringe of coral reefs; often seen in pairs that share burrow; distinguished by yellow colour on head and blue stripe below eye; Great Barrier Reef, offshore reefs of W. Australia and throughout S.E. Asia; Indo-W. Pacific; to 18 cm.

6. LITTLE GLIDERGOBY
Valenciennea parva Hoese & Larson, 1994
Inhabits sand-rubble fringe of coral reefs; distinguished by pair of thin orange stripes on side with dark 'lattice' pattern on upper back; yellow colour on head and blue stripe below eye; Great Barrier Reef, offshore reefs of W. Australia, New Guinea and Philippines; Indo-W. Pacific; to 7 cm.

7. DECORATED GLIDERGOBY
Valenciennea decora Hoese & Larson, 1994
Inhabits sand-rubble fringe of coral reefs; distinguished by thin dark 'moustache' and orange 'lattice' pattern (sometimes faint, but orange bar just behind pectoral base usually evident); Great Barrier Reef; S.W. Pacific to Fiji; to 12 cm.

8. IMMACULATE GLIDERGOBY
Valenciennea immaculata (Ni, 1981)
Inhabits sand-rubble fringe of coral reefs; distinguished by pair of blue-edged orange stripes on head and body and pointed, dark-edged tail; W. Australia, Great Barrier Reef, Indonesia and Philippines; W. Pacific; to 10 cm.

MICRODESMIDAE

9. PURPLE FIREGOBY
Nemateleotris decora Randall & Allen, 1973
Inhabits outer reef slopes to 68 m depth; lives in sandy burrow; distinguished by short dorsal fin 'spike', violet snout and magenta hue on posterior part of body; Great Barrier Reef and throughout S.E. Asia; Indo-W. Pacific; to 8.5 cm.

10. RED FIREGOBY
Nemateleotris magnifica Fowler, 1938
Inhabits outer reef slopes to 60 m depth; pairs live in sandy burrow; distinguished by dorsal fin 'spike', yellow snout and reddish hue on posterior part of body and adjoining fins; Great Barrier Reef, offshore reefs of N.W. Australia and throughout S.E. Asia; Indo-W. Pacific; to 8 cm.

11. ZEBRA DARTGOBY
Ptereleotris zebra (Fowler, 1938)
Inhabits exposed coral reefs subject to surge; sometimes in schools that retreat to holes in bottom; distinguished by dark-edged light bars on side; Great Barrier Reef, offshore reefs of N.W. Australia and throughout S.E. Asia; Indo-C. Pacific; to 12 cm.

12. ARROW DARTGOBY
Ptereleotris evides (Jordan & Hubbs, 1925)
Inhabits sandy fringe of coral reefs; pairs often share burrows; distinguished by moderately elevated dorsal and anal fins; Great Barrier Reef, offshore reefs of N.W. Australia and throughout S.E. Asia; Indo-C. Pacific; to 14 cm.

13. GREENEYE DARTGOBY
Ptereleotris microlepis (Bleeker, 1856)
Inhabits sandy fringe of coral reefs; occurs in pairs or groups; distinguished by plain pale pattern with elongate dark bar across pectoral fin base; Great Barrier Reef, N.W. Australia and throughout S.E. Asia; Indo-C. Pacific; to 13 cm.

14. TAILSPOT DARTGOBY
Ptereleotris heteroptera (Bleeker, 1855)
Inhabits sandy fringe of coral reefs; occurs in pairs or groups; distinguished by plain pale pattern with dark blotch on middle of tail; Great Barrier Reef, offshore reefs of N.W. Australia and throughout S.E. Asia; Indo-C. Pacific; to 12 cm.

15. ONESPOT WORMFISH
Gunnelichthys monostigma Smith, 1958
Inhabits sand-rubble fringe of coral reefs; buries into sand when disturbed; distinguished by long slender body and small dark 'ear-spot'; Great Barrier Reef and throughout S.E. Asia; Indo-W. Pacific; to 11 cm.

16. CURIOUS WORMFISH
Gunnelichthys curiosus Dawson, 1968
Inhabits sand-rubble fringe of coral reefs; buries into sand when disturbed; distinguished by long slender body and broad orange stripe along middle of side; Coral Sea and Indonesia; Indo-C. Pacific; to 11 cm.

17. BLUEBARRED RIBBONGOBY
Oxymetopon cyanoctenosum Klausewitz & Condé, 1981
Inhabits silty bottoms; in pairs that live in burrow; distinguished by laterally compressed body and neon-blue bars and bands on head and body; Indonesia and Philippines; to 20 cm.

PHOLIDICHTHYIDAE

18. CONVICT BLENNY
Pholidichthys leucotaenia Bleeker, 1856
Inhabits coral reefs, often seen along drop-offs; swims in mid water close to reef, sometimes in large aggregations; similar to young of *Plotosus lineatus* (Plate **11.5**), but lacks 'whiskers' around mouth; Indonesia and Philippines to Solomon Islands; to 12 cm.

TRICHONOTIDAE

19. SPOTTED SAND-DIVER
Trichonotus setiger Bloch & Schneider, 1801
Inhabits sandy fringe of coral reefs; occurs in schools, which hover near the bottom; dives into sand when threatened; distinguished from *T. elegans* (**20**) by about 12 faint brown bars and longitudinal rows of small pale spots; Great Barrier Reef, S.E. Asia and W. Australia; Indo-W. Pacific; to 15 cm.

20. ELEGANT SAND-DIVER
Trichonotus elegans Shimada & Yoshino, 1984
Inhabits sandy fringe of coral reefs; behaviour same as *T. setiger* (**19**), but distinguished by black spot on first few dorsal fin-rays; male has extremely elongate rays at beginning of dorsal fin; Great Barrier Reef, offshore reefs of N.W. Australia and S.E. Asia; mainly W. Pacific; to 18 cm.

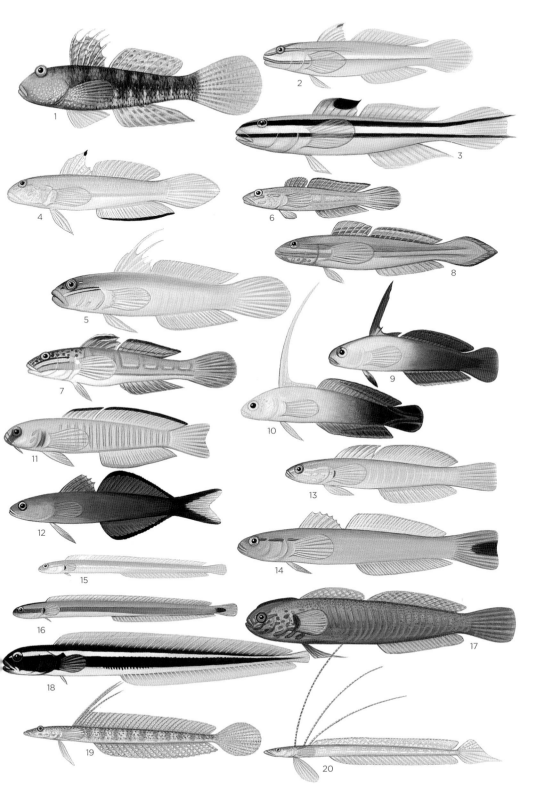

PLATE 94: GOBIES, GUDGEONS AND SPINEFEET

GOBIIDAE

1. PEPPERED MUDSKIPPER
Apocryptodon madurensis (Bleeker, 1849)
Inhabits brackish mangrove estuaries; distinguished by overall whitish colour, scattered dark spots on head and body, and dark-edged pointed tail; found throughout the region; Indo-W. Pacific; to 8 cm.

2. SILVERLINED MUDSKIPPER
Periophthalmus argentilineatus Valenciennes, 1837
Inhabits brackish mangrove estuaries, often seen resting on muddy banks; several similar species in region, but this is one of the most common; distinguished by protruding eyes and sail-like dorsal fin; found throughout the region; Indo-W. Pacific; to 27 cm.

3. BEARDED MUDSKIPPER
Scartelaos histiophorus (Valenciennes, 1837)
Inhabits brackish mangrove estuaries; distinguished by a row of short barbels (whiskers) along lower surface of head and antenna-like dorsal fin; found throughout the region; mainly W. Pacific; to 15 cm.

4. BLUESPOTTED MUDSKIPPER
Boleophthalmus caeruleomaculatus McCulloch & Waite, 1918
Inhabits brackish mangrove estuaries; distinguished by huge first dorsal fin with filamentous edge; N. Australia only, between Onslow, W. Australia and Gulf of Carpentaria; mainly W. Pacific; to 12 cm.

5. BLIND GOBY
Karsten totoyensis (Garman, 1903)
Inhabits soft mud, usually buried below surface; distinguished by reddish-pink colour and lack of eyes; found throughout the region; N. Australia, New Guinea and Indonesia; Indo-Australian Archipelago; to 5 cm.

ELEOTRIDAE

6. SMALLEYE GUDGEON
Prionobutis microps (Weber, 1907)
Inhabits brackish mangrove estuaries; distinguished by diagonal bands on head, striped fins and robust shape; N. Australia and New Guinea; to 23 cm.

7. OLIVE FLATHEAD GUDGEON
Butis amboinensis (Bleeker, 1853)
Inhabits brackish mangrove estuaries; distinguished by flattened, shovel-like snout; found throughout the region; Indo-Australian and Melanesian archipelagos; to 14 cm.

8. CHINESE GUDGEON
Bostrychus sinensis Lacepède, 1801
Inhabits coastal mudflats and estuaries; distinguished by pale-rimmed spot at upper tail base; found throughout the region; mainly W. Pacific and Andaman Sea; to 12 cm.

ZANCLIDAE

9. MOORISH IDOL
Zanclus cornutus Linnaeus, 1758
Inhabits coral reefs; distinguished by elongate snout, dorsal fin filament and conspicuous pattern; found throughout the region; Indo-C. Pacific; to 24 cm.

SIGANIDAE

10. SPOTTED RABBITFISH   VENOMOUS ☆☆☆
Siganus punctatus (Schneider & Forster, 1801)
Inhabits coral and rocky reefs; distinguished by numerous spots on head, body and fins; found throughout the region; Great Barrier Reef, W. Australia and throughout S.E. Asia; mainly W. Pacific; to 40 cm.

11. BLACK RABBITFISH   VENOMOUS ☆☆☆
Siganus nebulosus (Quoy & Gaimard, 1825)
Inhabits rock and weed areas, sometimes found in estuaries, occurs in schools; similar to *S. canaliculatus* (**13**), but body colour more uniform (generally lacks spotting) and edge of gill cover darkly outlined; found throughout the region; mainly W. Pacific; to 41 cm.

12. GOLDLINED SPINEFOOT   VENOMOUS ☆☆
Siganus lineatus (Valenciennes, 1835)
Inhabits coral reefs and mangrove estuaries; distinguished by yellow-orange lines and large spot below rear part of dorsal fin; N. Australia, New Guinea and Philippines, mainly W. Pacific; to 30 cm.

13. WHITESPOTTED RABBITFISH   VENOMOUS ☆☆☆
Siganus canaliculatus (Park, 1797)
Inhabits sand-weed areas; similar to *S. nebulosus* (**11**), but has more prominent spots on body and fins, frequently with dark blotch behind upper edge of gill cover; N.W. Australia and throughout S.E. Asia; Indo-W. Pacific; to 20 cm.

14. THREESPOT RABBITFISH   VENOMOUS ☆☆☆
Siganus trispilos Woodland & Allen, 1977
Inhabits coral reefs, often found amongst branching *Acropora* corals; distinguished by 3 black blotches on upper side; N.W. Australia only; to 23 cm.

15. BLUELINED RABBITFISH   VENOMOUS ☆☆
Siganus doliatus (Guérin-Méneville, 1829–38)
Inhabits coral reefs; distinguished by pair of diagonal dark bars on head and front of body; found throughout the region; *S. virgatus* (not shown) is a similar species from Malay Peninsula, W. Indonesia and Philippines; N. Australia, E. Indonesia and New Guinea; mainly W. Pacific; to 30 cm.

RABBITFISHES

Rabbitfishes (named because of their snout shape) of the family Siganidae (Plates 94–95) are plant feeders, sometimes forming large schools as they roam over the reef. They are also sometimes called 'spinefeet' in reference to the unusual arrangement of two pelvic fin spines separated by three soft rays. Another peculiarity is the high (7) number of anal fin spines. All dorsal, anal and pelvic fin spines are grooved and contain venom glands. If handled carelessly they are capable of inflicting very painful wounds.

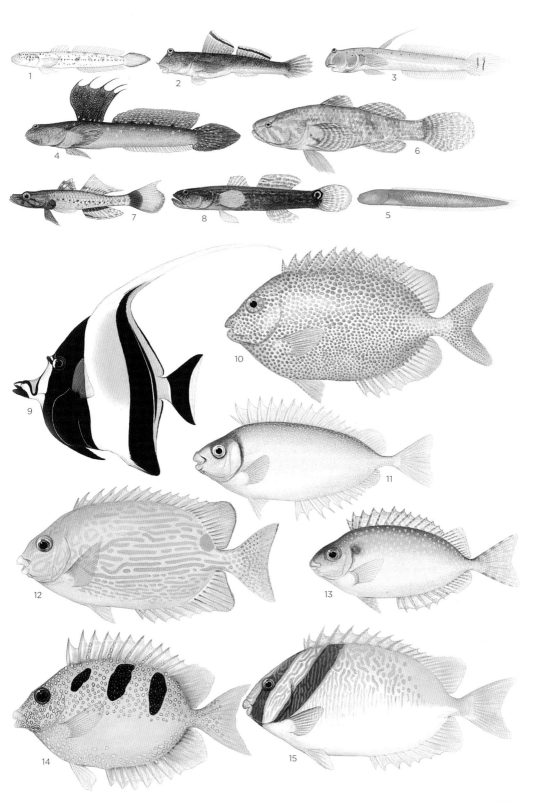

PLATE 95: SURGEONFISHES AND SPINEFEET

ACANTHURIDAE

1. ORANGE-TIP BRISTLETOOTH ☆☆
Ctenochaetus tominiensis Randall, 1955
Inhabits coral reefs; distinguished by pale tail and yellow outer portion of dorsal and anal fins; Indonesia, Philippines, New Guinea and Solomon Islands; to 22 cm.

2. YELLOWEYE BRISTLETOOTH ☆☆
Ctenochaetus cyanocheilus Randall & Clements, 2001
Inhabits coral reefs; distinguished by yellow ring around eye and small pale spots covering head, juvenile entirely bright yellow; Great Barrier Reef, offshore reefs of W. Australia and scattered localities throughout S.E. Asia; E. Indo-C. Pacific; to 20 cm.

3. RINGTAIL UNICORNFISH ☆☆
Naso annulatus (Quoy & Gaimard, 1825)
Inhabits steep outer reef slopes, adults usually below 20 m depth; distinguished long slender forehead 'spike' and 'webbed' markings on tail, juvenile has white ring around tail base; Great Barrier Reef, offshore reefs of W. Australia and throughout S.E. Asia; Indo-C. Pacific; to 100 cm.

4. HUMPBACK UNICORNFISH ☆☆
Naso brachycentron (Valenciennes, 1835)
Inhabits coral reefs; distinguished by angular profile of back; adult male has long tapering 'spike' in front of eye, female (shown here) with only a bump; Great Barrier Reef, offshore reefs of W. Australia and throughout S.E. Asia; Indo-W. Pacific; to 60 cm.

5. SLEEK UNICORNFISH ☆☆
Naso hexacanthus (Bleeker, 1855)
Inhabits steep outer reef slopes, usually seen in schools; brown to bluish-grey, but can quickly change to pale blue, has black markings on cheek; Great Barrier Reef, offshore reefs of W. Australia and throughout S.E. Asia; Indo-C. Pacific; to 75 cm.

6. SLENDER UNICORNFISH ☆☆
Naso lopezi Herre, 1927
Inhabits coral reefs, usually seen on edge of drop-offs below 20–30 m depth; distinguished by elongate shape and bluish-grey colouration with numerous dark grey spots; Great Barrier Reef and throughout S.E. Asia; Indo-C. Pacific; to 50 cm.

7. ONESPINE UNICORNFISH ☆☆
Naso thynnoides (Cuvier 1829)
Inhabits coral reefs, usually along the edge of lagoon and outer slopes to depth of 30 m; distinguished by elongate shape and numerous fine bars on side of body; throughout S.E. Asia; Indo-W. Pacific; to 30 cm.

8. BIGNOSE UNICORNFISH ☆☆
Naso vlamingii (Valenciennes, 1835)
Inhabits steep outer reef slopes; feeds on zooplankton; distinguished by vertical blue lines on side of body, blue band through eye and prolonged filament on upper and lower corner of tail; Great Barrier Reef, offshore reefs of W. Australia and throughout S.E. Asia; Indo-C. Pacific; to 55 cm.

9. HORSEFACE UNICORNFISH ☆☆
Naso fageni Morrow, 1954
Inhabits coral reefs, often in schools; distinguished by lack of forehead spike (although large males may develop protruding snout) and pearl-white ring around tail base (rapidly disappears after death); found throughout the region; N.W. Australia, Indonesia and Philippines; Indo-W. Pacific; to 80 cm.

SIGANIDAE

10. SCRIBBLED RABBITFISH VENOMOUS ☆☆
Siganus spinus (Linnaeus, 1758)
Inhabits coral reefs, usually seen in aggregations on shallow outer reefs; distinguished by 'maze' colour pattern; Great Barrier Reef and throughout S.E. Asia; Andaman Sea to C. Pacific; to 20 cm.

11. JAVA RABBITFISH VENOMOUS ☆☆
Siganus javus (Linnaeus 1766)
Inhabits silty coastal reefs and brackish areas; distinguished by white spots and lines on side and large black spot on tail; Queensland and throughout S.E. Asia; Indo-W. Pacific; to 53 cm.

12. MAZE RABBITFISH VENOMOUS ☆☆
Siganus vermiculatus (Valenciennes, 1835)
Inhabits shallow coastal reefs and brackish areas, usually seen in small aggregations; distinguished by vermiculated colour pattern; Great Barrier Reef and throughout S.E. Asia; E. Indian Ocean and W. Pacific; to 45 cm.

13. CORAL RABBITFISH VENOMOUS ☆☆
Siganus corallinus (Valenciennes, 1835)
Inhabits coral reefs, usually seen in pairs; distinguished by dense covering of blue spots on yellow background colour; also known as Coral Spinefoot; Great Barrier Reef, offshore reefs of W. Australia and throughout S.E. Asia; Indo-W. Pacific; to 28 cm.

14. MASKED RABBITFISH VENOMOUS
Siganus puellus (Schlegel, 1852)
Inhabits coral reefs, usually seen in pairs; distinguished by diagonal dark bar through eye and narrow blue lines on side; Great Barrier Reef, offshore reefs of W. Australia and throughout S.E. Asia; mainly W. Pacific; to 38 cm.

15. FORKTAIL RABBITFISH VENOMOUS ☆☆☆
Siganus argenteus (Quoy & Gaimard, 1825)
Inhabits coral reefs, frequently seen in aggregations; distinguished by numerous yellow spots on side, yellow 'wash' on top of head and deeply forked tail; also known as Silver Spinefoot; Great Barrier Reef, offshore reefs of W. Australia and throughout S.E. Asia; Indo-W. Pacific; to 37 cm.

16. ORANGESPOTTED SPINEFOOT VENOMOUS ☆☆
Siganus guttatus (Bloch, 1787)
Inhabits coastal reefs and lagoons, frequently among mangroves and in brackish water; distinguished by spotted pattern and large golden spot below posterior part of dorsal fin; *S. lineatus* (Queensland and S.E. Asia) is very similar, but has horizontal lines on the body instead of spots; throughout S.E. Asia; E. Indian Ocean and W. Pacific; to 42 cm.

17. FOXFACE VENOMOUS ☆☆
Siganus vulpinus (Schlegel & Müller, 1845)
Inhabits coral reefs, adults seen in pairs; distinguished by elongate snout, diagonal dark bar through eye, black breast and bright yellow body; Great Barrier Reef, Kimberley coast and offshore reefs of W. Australia and throughout S.E. Asia; W. Pacific; to 30 cm.

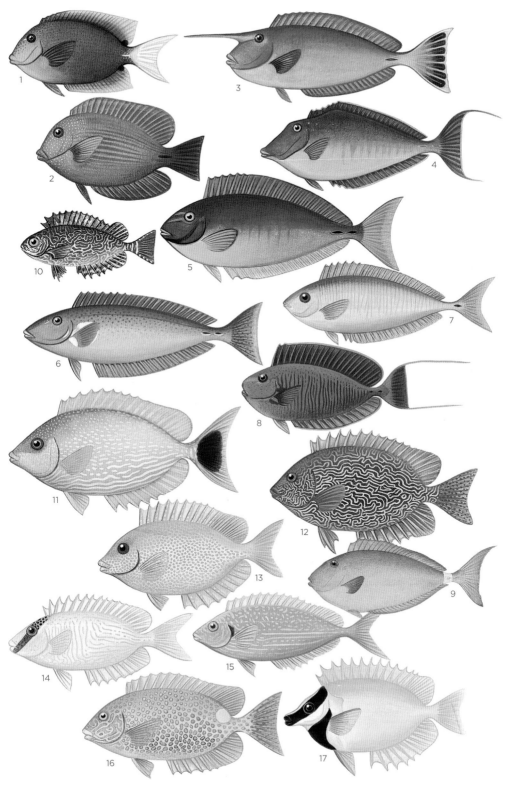

PLATE 96: SURGEONFISHES

ACANTHURIDAE

1. PALE SURGEONFISH ☆☆
Acanthurus mata (Cuvier, 1829)
Inhabits coral reef areas; distinguished by narrow stripes on side and yellow bands in front of eye; sharp spine on each side of tail base; formerly known as *A. bleekeri;* Great Barrier Reef, N.W. Australia and throughout S.E. Asia; Indo-C. Pacific; to 50 cm.

2. VELVET SURGEONFISH ☆☆
Acanthurus nigricans (Linnaeus, 1758)
Inhabits coral reefs; distinguished by white patch below eye; sharp spine on each side of tail base; formerly known as *A. glaucoparieus;* Great Barrier Reef, N.W. Australia and throughout S.E. Asia; mainly tropical Pacific Ocean to Central America and the Galapagos; to 21 cm.

3. PENCIL SURGEONFISH ☆☆
Acanthurus dussumieri Valenciennes, 1835
Inhabits coral reefs; distinguished by yellowish fins and black outline around spine on base of tail; also known as Dussumier's Surgeonfish; Great Barrier Reef, N.W. Australia and throughout S.E. Asia; Indo-W. Pacific; to 54 cm.

4. BLUELINED SURGEONFISH **VENOMOUS** ☆☆
Acanthurus lineatus (Linnaeus, 1758)
Inhabits shallow coral reefs usually where there is some wave action; distinguished by blue stripes on side, and sharp spine on each side of tail base; Great Barrier Reef, N.W. Australia and throughout S.E. Asia; Indo-C. Pacific; to 38 cm.

5. INSHORE SURGEONFISH ☆☆
Acanthurus grammoptilus Richardson, 1843
Inhabits coral and rocky reefs, often in silty inshore areas; distinguished by uniform dark colour and pale bar at base of tail; sharp spine on each side of tail base; N. Australia and Aru Islands, Indonesia; to 30 cm.

6. ORANGEBLOTCH SURGEONFISH ☆☆
Acanthurus olivaceus Forster, 1801
Inhabits sand and rubble areas adjacent to coral reefs; distinguished by elliptical orange band behind eye, juveniles entirely yellow; sharp spine on each side of tail base; Great Barrier Reef, N.W. Australia and throughout S.E. Asia; Indo-C. Pacific; to 32 cm.

7. DUSKY SURGEONFISH ☆☆
Acanthurus nigrofuscus (Forsskål, 1775)
Inhabits coral and rocky reefs; distinguished by black spot at rear base of dorsal and anal fins; sharp spine on each side of tail base; found throughout the region; Great Barrier Reef, N.W. Australia and throughout S.E. Asia; Indo-C. Pacific; to 20 cm.

8. CONVICT SURGEONFISH ☆☆
Acanthurus triostegus (Linnaeus, 1758)
Inhabits coral and rocky reefs; distinguished by bold black bars on side, and sharp spine on each side of tail base; Great Barrier Reef, N.W. Australia and throughout S.E. Asia; Indo-E. Pacific; to 25 cm.

9. LINED BRISTLETOOTH ☆☆
Ctenochaetus striatus (Quoy & Gaimard, 1825)
Inhabits coral reefs; distinguished by overall dark colour and flexible, bristle-like teeth (versus fixed teeth), and sharp spine on each side of tail base; Great Barrier Reef, N.W. Australia and throughout S.E. Asia; Indo-C. Pacific; to 18 cm.

10. CLOWN UNICORNFISH ☆☆
Naso lituratus (Forster, 1801)
Inhabits coral reefs; distinguished by dark stripe on snout and yellow patches at tail base; pair of sharp spines on each side of tail base; Great Barrier Reef, N.W. Australia and throughout S.E. Asia; E. Indo-C. Pacific; to 15 cm.

11. SPOTTED UNICORNFISH ☆☆
Naso brevirostris (Cuvier, 1829)
Inhabits coral reefs; distinguished by long spike on snout and short white tail, and a pair of sharp spines on each side of tail base; Great Barrier Reef, N.W. Australia and throughout S.E. Asia; Indo-C. Pacific; to 50 cm.

12. HUMPNOSE UNICORNFISH
Naso tonganus (Valenciennes, 1835)
Inhabits coral reefs; distinguished by bulbous snout and plain greyish colour, and pair of sharp spines on each side of tail base; Great Barrier Reef, N.W. Australia and throughout S.E. Asia; found throughout the region; Indo-W. Pacific; to 60 cm.

13. BLUESPINE UNICORNFISH ☆☆
Naso unicornis (Forsskål, 1775)
Inhabits coral reefs; distinguished by relatively short forehead spike, blue spots around pair of spines on each side of tail base and elongate tail filaments; Great Barrier Reef, N.W. Australia and throughout S.E. Asia; Indo-C. Pacific; to 70 cm.

14. SAILFIN TANG ☆☆
Zebrasoma veliferum Bloch, 1795
Inhabits coral reefs; distinguished by sail-like fins and bars on side; sharp spine on each side of tail base; Great Barrier Reef, N.W. Australia and throughout S.E. Asia; E. Indo-C. Pacific; *Z. desjardinii* (not shown) is a similar species occurring in the Indian Ocean; to 40 cm.

15. BROWN TANG ☆☆
Zebrasoma scopas (Cuvier, 1829)
Inhabits coral reefs; distinguished by overall dark colour, protruding snout and white spine on each side of tail base; Great Barrier Reef, N.W. Australia and throughout S.E. Asia; Indo-C. Pacific; to 20 cm.

THE MEAN SURGEON

Most surgeonfishes have a peaceful disposition, travelling in schools, as they graze on algae from the reef's surface. However, the beautiful and pugnacious Bluelined Surgeonfish *Acanthurus lineatus* (**4**) is an exception. It is strongly territorial, aggressively chasing away intruders that enter its domain. The territory of each adult occupies about 6–8 square metres of bottom. Attacks are mainly directed against algal-feeding fishes, particularly fellow Bluelined surgeons and other members of the family, as well as parrotfishes and triggerfishes. This behaviour ensures an adequate supply of seaweed-covered turf, which is its sole food source. The fish often occurs in colonies, with adjacent territories in close proximity. Adults occupy the central area and juveniles are scattered around the periphery. Like other surgeonfishes, this species possesses a collapsible, scalpel-like spine on each side of the tail base. However, the spines of the Bluelined Surgeonfish differ by being venomous and are capable of inflicting painful wounds if handled carelessly.

1

2

3

4

5

6 juv.

6

7

8

9

10

11

12

13

14

14 juv.

15

PLATE 97: SURGEONFISHES

ACANTHURIDAE

1. POWDERBLUE SURGEONFISH ☆☆
Acanthurus leucosternon Bennett, 1833
Inhabits coral reefs, usually on upper seaward slope or on nearby reef flats; distinguished by overall blue colour, white area on chin and yellow dorsal fin; S.W. Indonesia; widely distributed in Indian Ocean; to 23 cm.

2. MIMIC SURGEONFISH ☆☆
Acanthurus pyroferus Kittlitz, 1834
Inhabits coral reefs; distinguished by dark brown area on lower and rear part of head and yellow edge on tail; juvenile mimics the pygmy angelfish *Centropyge vroliki* (Plate **60.5**); also known as Orange-gilled Surgeonfish; Great Barrier Reef, offshore reefs of W. Australia and throughout S.E. Asia; W. and C. Pacific; to 25 cm.

3. BLUE TANG ☆☆
Paracanthurus hepatus (Linnaeus, 1766)
Inhabits coral reefs, young hide amongst branching corals; feeds on zooplankton; distinguished by deep blue colouration and black marking on side; also known as Palette Surgeonfish; Great Barrier Reef and throughout S.E. Asia; Indo-W. Pacific; to 31 cm.

4. WHITESPOTTED SURGEONFISH ☆☆
Acanthurus guttatus Forster, 1801
Inhabits coral reefs, usually found in surge zone, often in schools; distinguished by pair of white bars, small white spots on side and yellow pelvic fins; Great Barrier Reef and scattered localities in other parts of S.E. Asia; Indo-C. Pacific; to 26 cm.

5. DARK SURGEONFISH ☆☆
Acanthurus blochii Valenciennes, 1835
Inhabits coral reefs; distinguished by yellow patch behind eye, white bar at base of tail and narrow blue and orange stripes on dorsal and anal fin; Great Barrier Reef, offshore reefs of W. Australia and throughout S.E. Asia; Indo-C. Pacific; to 42 cm.

6. WHITEFIN SURGEONFISH ☆☆
Acanthurus albipectoralis Allen & Ayling, 1987
Inhabits coral reefs on steep outer slopes between 5–20 m depth; swims well above the bottom while feeding on zooplankton; outer half of pectorals white; Great Barrier Reef and Coral Sea eastward to Tonga; to 33 cm.

7. NIGHT SURGEONFISH ☆☆
Acanthurus thompsoni (Fowler, 1923)
Inhabits steep outer reef slopes; feeds on zooplankton; distinguished by dark brown colouration with white tail; also known as Thompson's Surgeonfish; Great Barrier Reef, offshore reefs of W. Australia and throughout S.E. Asia; Indo-C. Pacific; to 27 cm.

8. SPOTTED-FACE SURGEONFISH ☆☆
Acanthurus maculiceps (Ahl, 1923)
Inhabits coral reefs; distinguished by blue bar behind upper rear corner of gill cover, pale spots on head and pale bar across tail base; throughout S.E. Asia; E. Indian Ocean and W. and C. Pacific; to 35 cm.

9. EYELINE SURGEONFISH ☆☆
Acanthurus nigricauda Duncker & Mohr, 1929
Inhabits coral reefs; distinguished by horizontal black band behind eye, white bar at tail base (sometimes absent) and black streak on middle of tail base; Great Barrier Reef, offshore reefs of W. Australia and throughout S.E. Asia; Indo-C. Pacific; to 40 cm.

10. EYESPOT SURGEONFISH ☆☆
Acanthurus bariene Lesson, 1831
Inhabits coral reefs, usually seen on outer slope below 30 m depth; distinguished by round marking behind eye, yellow bar behind gill cover and yellow dorsal fin; Great Barrier Reef and throughout S.E. Asia; C. Indian Ocean to W. Pacific; to 50 cm.

11. PALELIPPED SURGEONFISH
Acanthurus leucocheilus Herre, 1927
Inhabits coral reefs in the vicinity of drop-offs between 5–35 m depth; distinguished by whitish lips, white bar on chin and pale ring around tail base; throughout S.E. Asia; Indo-W. Pacific; to about 40 cm.

12. PINSTRIPE SURGEONFISH ☆☆
Acanthurus nubilus (Fowler and Bean, 1929)
Inhabits coral reefs in the vicinity of drop-offs in 5–40 m depth; distinguished by pattern of fine blue horizontal lines on side and spot on head; overall colouration changeable from relatively pale to very dark, nearly blackish; shape is relatively rounded; throughout S.E. Asia; Indo-C. Pacific; to 26 cm.

13. YELLOWMASK SURGEONFISH ☆☆
Acanthurus xanthopterus Valenciennes, 1835
Inhabits sandy areas near coral reefs; distinguished by yellow pectoral fins and yellow area in front and behind eye; also known as Ring-tailed Surgeonfish; Great Barrier Reef, offshore reefs of W. Australia and throughout S.E. Asia; Indo-E. Pacific; to 56 cm.

14. HORSESHOE SURGEONFISH ☆☆
Acanthurus fowleri de Beaufort, 1951
Inhabits coral reefs, usually seen on seaward slopes and adjacent to drop-offs in 10–50 m depth; distinguished by horseshoe-shaped marking behind head; also known as Fowler's Surgeonfish; E. Indonesia and Philippines to New Britain; to 27 cm.

15. RINGTAIL SURGEONFISH ☆☆
Acanthurus auranticavus Randall, 1956
Inhabits coral reefs, usually seen in small schools at shallow depths in lagoons and on outer reefs; distinguished by elliptical mark behind head and orange border around caudal spine; Great Barrier Reef and throughout S.E. Asia; Maldive Islands to Indonesia and Philippines; to 35 cm.

16. TWOSPOT BRISTLETOOTH ☆☆
Ctenochaetus binotatus Randall, 1955
Inhabits coral reefs; distinguished by blue iris, narrow, pale lines on side and small black spot at rear base of dorsal and anal fin; juvenile has yellowish tail; Great Barrier Reef, offshore reefs of W. Australia and throughout S.E. Asia; Indo-C. Pacific; to 22 cm.

SURGEONFISHES

The estimated 85 species of surgeonfishes in the family Acanthuridae are widely distributed in tropical and sub-tropical seas. Their common name is derived from the scalpel-like spines on each side of the tail base, a handy defensive weapon. Surgeons are solitary in habit or form schools. The largest genus, *Acanthurus,* contains mainly algal feeders that graze widely over their home reefs. However, most members of the genus *Naso* and a few *Acanthurus* feed high above the bottom on zooplankton.

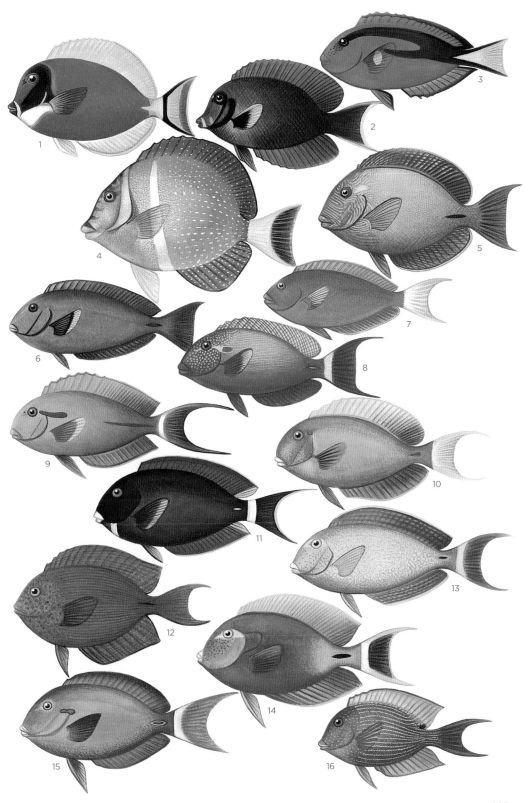

PLATE 98: BILLFISHES AND TUNAS

ISTIOPHORIDAE

1. BLACK MARLIN ☆☆☆
Istiompax indica (Cuvier, 1832)
Inhabits oceanic waters, generally well offshore; distinguished by lack of cross-bars and the rigid pectoral fin which cannot be folded against side of body; found throughout the region; Indo-C. Pacific; to 500 cm. All-tackle world record 707.6 kg, Australian record 600.1 kg.

2. INDO-PACIFIC BLUE MARLIN ☆☆☆
Makaira nigricans Lacepède, 1802
Inhabits oceanic waters, generally well offshore; distinguished from *Istiompax indica* (1) by narrow bars on sides and non-rigid pectoral fin and from *Kajikia audax* (4) by its lower dorsal fin; found throughout the region; Indo-E. Pacific; to 500 cm. All-tackle world record 624.1 kg, Australian record 452.2 kg.

3. SHORTBILL SPEARFISH ☆☆
Tetrapturus angustirostris Tanaka, 1915
Inhabits oceanic waters, generally well offshore; distinguished by very short bill and slender shape; found throughout the region; Indo-E. Pacific; to 200 cm. All-tackle world and Australian record 50.0 kg.

4. STRIPED MARLIN ☆☆☆
Kajikia audax (Philippi, 1887)
Inhabits oceanic waters, generally well offshore; similar to *Makaira nigricans* (2), but has taller dorsal fin; found throughout the region; Indo-E. Pacific; to 420 cm. All-tackle world record 224.1 kg, Australia record 174.8 kg.

5. SAILFISH ☆☆
Istiophorus platypterus (Shaw, 1792)
Inhabits oceanic waters, generally well offshore; distinguished by sail-like dorsal fin; found throughout the region; Indo-E. Pacific; to 360 cm. All-tackle world record 100.2 kg, Australian record 77.95 kg.

XIPHIIDAE

6. SWORDFISH ☆☆☆
Xiphias gladius Linnaeus, 1758
Inhabits oceanic waters, generally well offshore; distinguished by the long flattened sword; found throughout the region; worldwide in temperate and tropical seas; to 450 cm. All-tackle world record 536.15 kg, Australian record 267.4 kg.

SCOMBRIDAE

7. ALBACORE ☆☆☆
Thunnus alalunga (Bonnaterre, 1788)
Inhabits oceanic waters, generally well offshore; occurs in schools; distinguished by the very long pectoral fins, these are shorter in juveniles and sub-adults which resemble *T. albacares* (8) and *T. obesus* (9), but differ from them by having a white rear border on the tail; found throughout the region; worldwide in temperate and tropical seas; to 150 cm. All-tackle world record 39.97 kg, Australian record 26.0 kg.

8. YELLOWFIN TUNA ☆☆☆
Thunnus albacares (Bonnaterre, 1788)
Inhabits oceanic waters, generally well offshore; occurs in schools; distinguished by yellow dorsal and anal fins that become elongated with increased age; found throughout the region; worldwide tropical and temperate seas, to 210 cm. All-tackle world record 193.68 kg, Australian record 124.0 kg.

9. BIGEYE TUNA ☆☆
Thunnus obesus (Lowe, 1839)
Inhabits oceanic waters, generally well offshore; occurs in schools; similar to *T. albacares* (8), but has much larger eye and lacks elongate dorsal and anal rays; found throughout the region; worldwide in tropical and temperate seas; to 240 cm. All-tackle world angling record 197.3 kg, Australian record 120.0 kg.

10. SOUTHERN BLUEFIN TUNA ☆☆
Thunnus maccoyii (Castelnau, 1872)
Inhabits oceanic waters, generally well offshore; occurs in schools; distinguished by short pectoral fins and robust body shape; S. Queensland, W. Australia and S. Indonesia; Southern Hemisphere in mainly temperate seas, but ranges to tropics in Australia and S. Indonesia; to 240 cm. All-tackle world and Australian record 167.0 kg.

11. LONGTAIL TUNA ☆☆
Thunnus tonggol (Bleeker, 1851)
Inhabits oceanic waters, generally well offshore; occurs in schools; distinguished by short pectoral fins and slender body shape; found throughout the region; mainly W. Pacific and N. Indian Ocean; to 150 cm. All-tackle world and Australian record 35.9 kg.

12. SKIPJACK TUNA ☆☆
Katsuwonus pelamis (Linnaeus, 1758)
Inhabits oceanic waters, generally well offshore; occurs in schools; distinguished by dark stripes on sides; found throughout the region; worldwide in tropical and temperate seas. All-tackle world record 20.54 kg, Australian record 12.0 kg.

KINGS OF THE SEA

Marlins are swift predatory inhabitants of the high seas, well known among anglers for their fighting ability. The Indo-Pacific Blue Marlin is the largest species, reported to reach unofficial weights in excess of 906 kg (2,000 lb). Numerous Black Marlin *Istiompax indica* (1) weighing in excess of 500 kg have been caught in waters off Cairns, Queensland. These fishes range widely in tropical and temperate seas of the Indo-Pacific region. There is still much to be learned about their biology, but tagging programs by sport anglers have been helpful in establishing their extensive migration routes. At certain times of the year they migrate to spawning grounds on the edge of continental shelves or off oceanic islands. One of the best known Black Marlin grounds in our region is the outer Great Barrier Reef off Cairns, Queensland, where dense concentrations appear between August and November.

Fully grown marlin probably have few enemies, but they are occasionally attacked and killed by large pelagic sharks and killer whales while struggling after being hooked. Humans are definitely their biggest threat, although sport anglers often tag and release their catches. Commercial fishing operations take a heavy toll, utilising longlines. Large quantities of marlin flesh are marketed in Japan, Taiwan and other Asian countries.

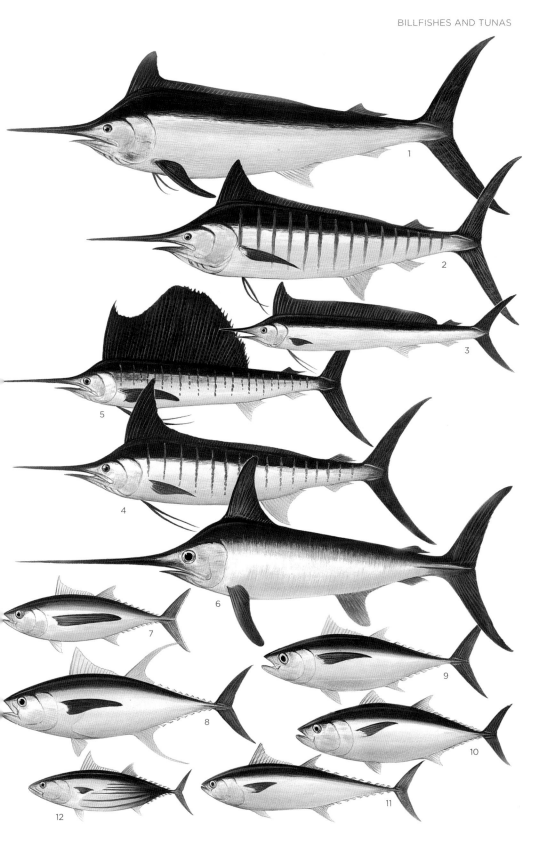

PLATE 99: MACKERELS AND TUNAS

SCOMBRIDAE

1. WAHOO ☆☆☆
Acanthocybium solandri (Cuvier, 1832)
Inhabits oceanic waters, generally well offshore; occurs solitarily or in loose aggregations; distinguished from mackerels by its more elongate shape, more numerous spines in the first dorsal fin and by its banded pattern — except also in *Scomberomorus commerson* (**2**); found throughout the region; all tropical seas; to 210 cm. All-tackle world record 83.46 kg, Australian record 47.0 kg.

2. SPANISH MACKEREL ☆☆☆☆
Scomberomorus commerson (Lacepède, 1800)
Inhabits coastal seas, frequently near reefs; similar to *Acanthocybium solandri* (**1**), but has fewer dorsal spines (15–18 versus 23–27) and shorter first dorsal fin; found throughout the region; Indo-W. Pacific; to 235 cm. All-tackle world record 44.9 kg, Australian record 38.75 kg.

3. GREY MACKEREL ☆☆☆
Scomberomorus semifasciatus (Macleay, 1883)
Inhabits coastal seas in the vicinity of reefs; distinguished by dark bars extending part way down sides and black area at front of dorsal fin; N. Australia and S. New Guinea only; to 120 cm and 8.5 kg. All-tackle world and Australian record 9.3 kg.

4. SPOTTED MACKEREL ☆☆☆
Scomberomorus munroi Collette & Russo, 1980
Inhabits coastal seas; distinguished by broad band of small spots along middle of sides; tropical and subtropical Australia and S. New Guinea only; to 104 cm and 10 kg. All-tackle world and Australian record 9.25 kg.

5. SCHOOL MACKEREL ☆☆☆
Scomberomorus queenslandicus Munro, 1943
Inhabits inshore coastal waters; distinguished by large dark spots on sides and black area at front of dorsal fin; N. Australia and S. New Guinea only; to 100 cm and 12 kg. All-tackle world and Australian record 3.8 kg.

6. ORIENTAL BONITO ☆☆
Sarda orientalis (Temminck & Schlegel, 1844)
Inhabits coastal seas, sometimes in large schools; distinguished by narrow stripes on upper half of body; found throughout the region; Indo-E. Pacific; to 102 cm and 3.5 kg. All-tackle world record 9.67 kg, Australian record 9.4 kg.

7. MACKEREL TUNA ☆☆
Euthynnus affinis (Cantor, 1849)
Inhabits oceanic waters, sometimes well offshore; colour pattern is similar to *Auxis thazard* (**10**), but distinguished by the lack of space between the dorsal fins; found throughout the region; Indo-C. Pacific; to 100 cm. All-tackle world record 15.05 kg, Australian record 11.8 kg.

8. LEAPING BONITO ☆☆
Cybiosarda elegans (Whitley, 1935)
Inhabits coastal waters, sometimes entering estuaries; distinguished by spots on back and stripes on lower side, also has tall, dark-coloured first dorsal fin; Australia (except south coast) and S. New Guinea; to 54 cm. All-tackle world and Australian record 0.96 kg.

9. BULLET TUNA ☆☆
Auxis rochei (Risso, 1810)
Inhabits coastal and oceanic waters, forming large schools; distinguished by widely separated dorsal fins, elongate patch of short bars or blotches on back at rear half of body, and by its slender shape; found throughout the region; worldwide tropical and subtropical seas; to 50 cm. All-tackle world record 1.84 kg.

10. FRIGATE MACKEREL ☆☆
Auxis thazard (Lacepède, 1800)
Inhabits coastal and oceanic waters, forming large schools; similar to *Euthynnus affinis* (**7**), but has wide gap between dorsal fins and more slender shape; found throughout the region; worldwide tropical and subtropical seas; to 58 cm. All-tackle world record 1.6 kg, Australian record 1.46 kg.

11. MOUTH MACKEREL ☆☆☆
Rastrelliger kanagurta (Cuvier, 1816)
Inhabits coastal waters, near reefs; forms large schools; distinguished by widely separate dorsal fins; narrow lines or rows of spots on upper part of body and black spot near lower margin of pectoral fin; found throughout the region; Indo-W. Pacific; to 35 cm. All-tackle world record 0.86 kg.

12. DOGTOOTH TUNA
Gymnosarda unicolor (Rüppell, 1836)
Inhabits offshore waters, usually in the vicinity of coral reefs; distinguished by large conical teeth, relatively large eye and undulating lateral line; found throughout the region; Indo-C. Pacific, to 150 cm. All-tackle world record 107.5 kg, Australian record 81.0 kg.

13. SHARK MACKEREL ☆☆
Grammatorcynus bicarinatus (Quoy & Gaimard, 1825)
Inhabits offshore waters, usually in the vicinity of coral reefs; has double lateral line, similar to *G. bilineatus* (**14**), but eye smaller and frequently has dark spots along belly; Australia only (except south coast); to 130 cm. All-tackle world and Australian record 12.3 kg.

14. SCAD MACKEREL ☆☆
Grammatorcynus bilineatus (Rüppell, 1836)
Inhabits offshore waters, usually in the vicinity of coral reefs; has double lateral line, similar to *G. bicarinatus* (**13**), but eye larger and lacks spotting along belly; found throughout the region; Indo-W. Pacific; to 70 cm. All-tackle world and Australian record 3.0 kg.

TONNES OF TUNA

The fishes featured on Plates 98–99 occur worldwide, primarily in tropical and temperate seas. They occur both inshore and far out to sea. Tunas, mackerels and bonitos (family Scombridae; 53 species worldwide) are well known for their fine eating qualities. Over the past 10 years world catches have generally fluctuated between about 5–6 million tonnes annually. These fishes are also highly prized by recreational anglers and throughout much of the world they support important subsistence fisheries. All species are powerful swimmers and some undertake extensive annual migrations. The largest species is about 300 cm, but most grow to between 100–200 cm total length.

Billfishes exhibit similar habits and are close relatives of tunas, being distinguished by their elongate, spear-like snout. The group is comprised of the swordfish (Xiphidae; l species worldwide) and the marlins and sailfishes (Istiophoridae; 10 species worldwide). They are favourite angling fishes and some may reach the massive size of over 450 cm total length and 700 kg in weight. Although the billfishes and larger tunas are distributed widely throughout the N. Australian-S.E. Asian region, their occurrence is dependent on deep, clear blue, oceanic seas.

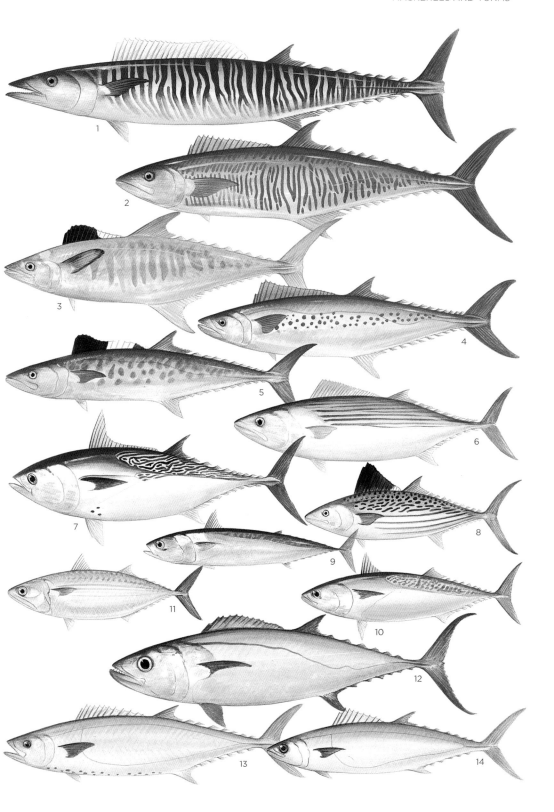

PLATE 100: FLOUNDERS AND SOLES

PSETTODIDAE

1. AUSTRALIAN HALIBUT ☆☆☆
Psettodes erumei (Bloch & Schneider, 1801)
Inhabits sand or mud bottoms; distinguished by large mouth and large, sharp teeth; found throughout the region; Indo-W. Pacific; to 64 cm.

PARALICHTHYIDAE

2. LARGETOOTH FLOUNDER ☆☆☆
Pseudorhombus arsius (Hamilton, 1822)
Inhabits sand or mud bottoms, sometimes in estuaries; distinguished by several enlarged teeth at front of mouth, large brown blotch behind pectoral fin, smaller blotch about halfway between first spot and tail base, and scattered dark-edged pale spots; found throughout the region; Indo-W. Pacific; to 31 cm.

3. BIGTOOTH TWINSPOT FLOUNDER ☆☆
Pseudorhombus diplospilus Norman, 1926
Inhabits sand bottoms; distinguished by 4 pairs of 'eye-spots'; other similar species (not shown) include *P. argus* (same 'eye-spot' pattern except 1 or 2 additional sets of spots on middle of body near tail base), *P. dupliocellatus* (same 'eye-spot' pattern as *P. diplospilus* but lacks enlarged canine teeth [versus strong canines]), *P. quinquocellatus* (similar pattern to *P. argus* but only a single eye-spot instead of double-spots in each marking) and *P. spinosus* (3 well-separated single spots on back); N. Australia and Indo-Malay Archipelago; to 25 cm.

4. DEEP FLOUNDER
Pseudorhombus elevatus Ogilby, 1912
Inhabits sand or mud bottoms; similar to *P. arsius* (2), but lacks enlarged teeth, is deeper-bodied (rounder) and generally has more pale spots; N. Australia and Indo-Malay Archipelago; N. Indian Ocean and Indo-Australian Archipelago; to 15 cm.

5. SMALLTOOTH FLOUNDER ☆☆☆
Pseudorhombus jenynsii (Bleeker, 1855)
Inhabits sand or mud bottoms; distinguished by 6 pale-edged spots as shown in illustration; Australia only; to 34 cm.

BOTHIDAE

6. BLOTCHED FLOUNDER
Asterorhombus intermedius (Bleeker, 1865)
Inhabits sand bottoms; distinguished by dense scattering of dark speckles and blotches on fins and body; also known as Intermediate Flounder; N.W. Australia and Indonesia; Indian Ocean and Indo-Australian Archipelago; to 13 cm.

7. SPOT-TAIL WIDE-EYE FLOUNDER
Engyprosopon grandisquama (Temminck & Schlegel, 1846)
Inhabits sand bottoms; distinguished by well-separated eyes and pair of black spots on margin of tail; also known as Mottled Wide-eyed Flounder; found throughout the region; Indo-W. Pacific; to 13 cm.

8. THREESPOT FLOUNDER
Grammatobothus polyophthalmus (Bleeker, 1865)
Inhabits sand bottoms; distinguished by mottled pattern and 3 pale-edged dark spots; N. Australia and Indo-Malay Archipelago; N.E. Indian Ocean and Indo-Australian Archipelago; to 14 cm.

9. LEOPARD FLOUNDER ☆☆
Bothus pantherinus (Rüppell, 1830)
Inhabits sand bottoms near coral reefs; distinguished by mottled appearance with numerous brown and white spots and large brown patch in middle of rear part of body, males have filamentous pectoral rays reaching tail base; also known as Panther Flounder; found throughout the region; Indo-W. Pacific; to 24 cm.

SOLEIDAE

10. THICKRAY SOLE
Aesopia cornuta Kaup, 1858
Inhabits sand or mud bottoms; similar to *Zebrias craticula* (14) and *Z. cancellatus* (15), but has darker stripes, *Soleichthys heterorhinos* (not shown) also similar but has irregular-shaped broken bars and white black-tipped tail; N. Australia only; to 18 cm.

11. TUFTED SOLE
Dexillus muelleri (Steindachner, 1879)
Inhabits sand bottoms; distinguished by light brown colour with patches of dark skin filaments; N. Australia and S. New Guinea only; to 20 cm.

12. DARKSPOTTED SOLE
Liachirus melanospilus (Bleeker, 1854)
Inhabits sand bottoms; distinguished by numerous small dark spots and pair of large dark blotches superimposed on mottled pattern; found throughout the region; mainly W. Pacific; to 15 cm.

13. PEACOCK SOLE
Pardachirus pavoninus (Lacepède, 1802)
Inhabits sand bottoms; distinguished by numerous black spots with broad, pale margins; experiments have shown that the mucus of this fish has shark-repellent qualities; found throughout the region; Indo-C. Pacific; to 25 cm.

14. WICKER-WORK SOLE
Zebrias craticula (McCulloch, 1916)
Inhabits sand bottoms; similar to *Aesopia cornuta* (10) and *Z. cancellatus* (15), but dark bars more numerous and narrower; N. Australia only; to 15 cm.

15. HARROWED SOLE
Zebrias cancellatus (McCulloch, 1916)
Inhabits sand bottoms; bars lighter and body more elongate than *Aesopia cornuta* (10); bars wider and less numerous than *Z. craticula* (14); N. Australia only; to 27 cm.

16. SPOTTED SOLE
Phyllichthys punctatus McCulloch, 1916
Inhabits sand bottoms; distinguished by dense covering of diffuse white blotches; N. Australia only; to 24 cm.

SAMARIDAE

17. COCKATOO FLOUNDER
Samaris cristatus Gray, 1831
Inhabits sand bottoms; distinguished by filamentous dorsal fin-rays on top of head; also known as Cockatoo Righteye Flounder; N. Australia and Indo-Malay Archipelago; N. Indian Ocean and W. Pacific; to 17 cm.

PLEURONECTIDAE

18. FRECKLED RIGHTEYE FLOUNDER
Psammodiscus ocellatus Günther, 1862
Inhabits sand bottoms; distinguished by dense mottled or speckled pattern, also 3 or 4 pale-edged dark spots usually present; found throughout the region; Indo-Australian Archipelago; to 15 cm.

CYNOGLOSSIDAE

19. LEMON TONGUE SOLE ☆☆☆
Paraplagusia bilineata (Bloch, 1787)
Inhabits sand bottoms; distinguished by elongate shape and fringe of branched tentacles on lips; other elongate soles (not shown) from this region without fringe of tentacles belong to the genus *Cynoglossus;* found throughout the region; Indo-W. Pacific; to 40 cm.

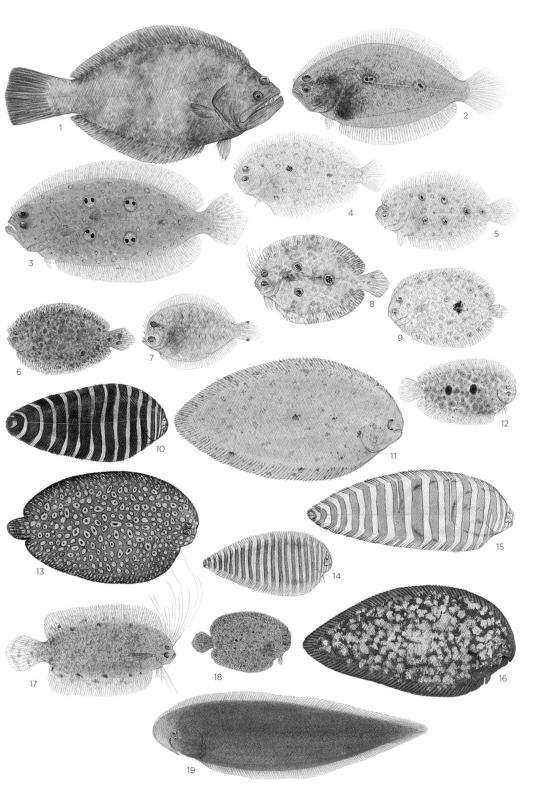

PLATE 101: DUCKBILLS, DRIFTFISHES AND TRIPODFISHES

PERCOPHIDAE

1. PHILIPPINE DUCKBILL
Bembrops philippinus Fowler, 1939
Inhabits offshore trawling grounds; distinguished by 2 spines on gill cover, a loose flap of skin on rear part of upper jaw and small black spots on back; N.W. Australia only; to 20 cm.

2. SHARPNOSE DUCKBILL
Bembrops filiferus Gilbert, 1905
Inhabits offshore trawling grounds; similar to *B. philippinus* (**1**), but lacks distinct spotting and tail has dark margin with dark spot on upper part of base; found throughout the region; mainly W. Pacific; to 20 cm.

3. BLOTCHED DUCKBILL
Chironema chlorotaenia McKay, 1971
Inhabits offshore trawling grounds; distinguished by 2 spines on gill cover, no flap of skin at rear of upper jaw, elongate orange spots and diffuse brown blotches on sides; N.W. Australia only; to 21 cm.

ARIOMMATIDAE

4. INDIAN DRIFTFISH
Ariomma indicum (Day, 1871)
Inhabits oceanic waters usually well offshore; distinguished by ovate silvery body and rounded snout with small mouth; similar to *Psenopsis humerosa* (**5**), but has 2 dorsal fins; found throughout the region; Indo-W. Pacific; to 25 cm.

CENTROLOPHIDAE

5. BLACKSPOT BUTTERFISH
Psenopsis humerosa Munro, 1958
Inhabits oceanic waters usually well offshore; similar to *Ariomma indicum* (**4**), but has only one dorsal fin; N.W. Australia only; to 20 cm.

NOMEIDAE

6. COASTAL CUBEHEAD
Cubiceps whiteleggii (Waite, 1894)
Inhabits oceanic waters usually well offshore; distinguished by elongate shape, 2 dorsal fins and overall darkish colour; N. Australia only; to 13 cm.

TRIODONTIDAE

7. THREETOOTH PUFFER   POISONOUS
Triodon macropterus Lesson, 1831
Inhabits coastal waters and offshore trawling grounds; distinguished by large skin flap on belly and black spot on middle of side; found throughout the region; Indo-W. Pacific; to 60 cm.

TRIACANTHIDAE

8. SHORTNOSE TRIPODFISH
Triacanthus biaculeatus (Bloch, 1786)
Inhabits trawling grounds; similar to *T. nieuhofii* (**9**), but spiny dorsal fin entirely black (versus only front half of fin black); found throughout the region; Indo-W. Pacific; to 25 cm.

9. SILVER TRIPODFISH
Triacanthus nieuhofii Bleeker, 1852
Inhabits trawling grounds; similar to *T. biaculeatus* (**8**), but rear half of spiny dorsal fin pale (versus black); N.W. Australia and Indo-Malay Archipelago; to 28 cm.

10. BLACKTIP TRIPODFISH
Trixiphichthys weberi (Chaudhuri, 1910)
Inhabits trawling grounds; distinguished by black tip on spiny dorsal fin and diffuse dark blotches on side similar to *Pseudotriacanthus strigilifer* (**11**), but has longer, narrower snout; N.W. Australia, Indo-Malay Archipelago and Philippines; Andaman Sea and Indo-Australian Archipelago; to 20 cm.

11. BLOTCHED TRIPODFISH
Pseudotriacanthus strigilifer (Cantor, 1849)
Inhabits trawling grounds; similar to *Trixiphichthys weberi* (**10**), but has more pronounced pattern of blotches on side and shorter snout; N.W. Australia and throughout S.E. Asia; Indian Ocean and Indo-Australian Archipelago; to 24 cm.

TRIACANTHODIDAE

12. LONGSNOUT SPIKEFISH
Halimochirurgus centriscoides Alcock, 1899
Inhabits trawling grounds; similar to *Macrorhamphosodes platycheilus* (**14**), but snout is directed upwards and lacks enlarged mouth opening at tip; N.W. Australia and Indo-Malay Archipelago; Andaman Sea and Indo-Australian Archipelago; to 15 cm.

13. SHORTSNOUT SPIKEFISH
Triacanthodes ethiops Alcock, 1894
Inhabits trawling grounds; similar in general shape to species **8–11**, but has 6 spines (versus 5) in first dorsal fin and much shorter and thicker tail base, usually has 3 diverging stripes on side; N.W. Australia and throughout S.E. Asia; Indo-W. Pacific; to 9 cm.

14. LARGEGILL TRUMPETSNOUT
Macrorhamphosodes platycheilus Fowler, 1934
Inhabits trawling grounds; similar to *Halimochirurgus centriscoides* (**12**), but has snout directed straightforward and enlarged mouth opening at tip; N.W. Australia, Indonesia and Philippines; Andaman Sea and Indo-Australian Archipelago; to 13 cm.

FLATFISHES

Flatfishes (Plate 100) are amazing bottom-dwelling creatures with highly compressed bodies and both eyes oddly situated on the same side of the head. The larvae actually begin life looking very much like normal, symmetrical fish larvae, but profound changes occur during their first few weeks. One of the eyes slowly migrates across the top of the head and at the same time the mouth and other body parts become asymmetrically distorted. The end result is a creature that looks more like a camouflaged pancake than a fish. Camouflage is the operative word as flatfishes possess chameleon-like powers enabling them to quickly match their surroundings. In stark contrast, the underside of these fishes is usually devoid of pigment. Their spectacular colour changes are useful for hiding from larger predators or for deceiving its own prey, usually small fishes and small invertebrates. The flatfish group includes 7 families with about 540 species worldwide. Most are marine fishes, inhabiting continental shelves and slopes, but fresh and brackish waters are also inhabited.

TRASH FISHES

Most of the species featured on this plate, particularly the duckbills, tripodfishes and spikefishes, are classed as 'trash' by commercial fishermen. These species, along with many other small bottom fishes are often captured in large numbers while trawling. Because of their small size or poor edibility they are dumped overboard after sorting out the marketable species. Unfortunately most of the trash catch dies during this process, resulting in tremendous waste of this resource. However, in some parts of the world the trash catch is effectively harvested for use as fishmeal and fertiliser.

PLATE 102: TRIGGERFISHES

BALISTIDAE

1. ORANGESTRIPE TRIGGERFISH
Balistapus undulatus (Park, 1797)
Inhabits coral reefs; distinguished by red diagonal stripes; Great Barrier Reef, N.W. Australia and throughout S.E. Asia; Indo-C. Pacific; to 35 cm.

2. STARRY TRIGGERFISH
Abalistes stellatus (Anonymous, 1798)
Inhabits coral and rocky reefs; distinguished by relatively elongate shape, blue to orange spotting on body and frequently with 3 white patches on back at base of dorsal fin; large adults have elongate filaments on tail; found throughout the region; Indo-W. Pacific; to 60 cm and 2.4 kg.

3. TITAN TRIGGERFISH
Balistoides viridescens (Bloch & Schneider, 1801)
Inhabits coral and rocky reefs; nest-guarding females may attack divers, inflicting painful bites; distinguished by relatively large size, dark area with pale 'bridle' around upper part of mouth, yellowish cheeks, diffuse dark bar through eye and dark fin margins; Great Barrier Reef, N.W. Australia and throughout S.E. Asia; Indo-C. Pacific; to 60 cm and 2.3 kg.

4. BLACK TRIGGERFISH
Melichthys niger (Bloch, 1786)
Inhabits coral reefs; distinguished by black colour of body and fins; *Melichthys vidua* (**12**) is a similar species, but has pale dorsal, anal and tail fins; Great Barrier Reef, N.W. Australia and throughout S.E. Asia; Indo-E. Pacific; to 35 cm.

5. HAWAIIAN TRIGGERFISH
Rhinecanthus aculeatus (Linnaeus, 1758)
Inhabits coral reefs; distinguished by white diagonal bars above anal fin base; Great Barrier Reef, N.W. Australia and throughout S.E. Asia; Indo-C. Pacific; to 30 cm.

6. WEDGETAILED TRIGGERFISH
Rhinecanthus rectangulus (Bloch & Schneider, 1801)
Inhabits coral reefs on limestone platforms exposed to wave action; distinguished by black wedge-shaped mark at tail base; Great Barrier Reef, N.W. Australia and throughout S.E. Asia; Indo-C. Pacific; to 24 cm.

7. YELLOWSPOTTED TRIGGERFISH
Pseudobalistes fuscus (Bloch & Schneider, 1801)
Inhabits coral reefs; distinguished by dense network of yellow-orange spots on body and pointed lobes of tail; Great Barrier Reef, N.W. Australia and throughout S.E. Asia; Indo-C. Pacific; to 50 cm.

8. EYE-STRIPE TRIGGERFISH
Sufflamen chrysopterum (Bloch & Schneider, 1801)
Inhabits coral reefs; distinguished by dark colour of body, pale line below eye and white-edged tail; Great Barrier Reef, N.W. Australia and throughout S.E. Asia; Indo-C. Pacific; to 30 cm.

9. PALLID TRIGGERFISH
Sufflamen bursa (Bloch & Schneider, 1801)
Inhabits coral reefs, often in rubble areas; distinguished by general grey colouration with narrow brown to orange bar through eye and another from dorsal fin to pectoral base; Great Barrier Reef, N.W. Australia and throughout S.E. Asia; Indo-C. Pacific; to 30 cm.

10. BRIDLED TRIGGERFISH
Sufflamen fraenatum (Latreille, 1804)
Inhabits coral reefs and hard, flat-bottom areas with occasional outcrops; distinguished by brown colour and bridle-like marking behind mouth; Great Barrier Reef, N.W. Australia and throughout S.E. Asia; Indo-C. Pacific; to 30 cm.

11. LINED TRIGGERFISH
Xanthichthys lineopunctatus (Hollard, 1854)
Inhabits offshore reefs, often seen well above the bottom; distinguished by narrow lines on head and body, and orange outline on tail; N.W. Australia and possibly S. Indonesia; Indo-W. Pacific; to 30 cm.

12. PINKTAIL TRIGGERFISH
Melichthys vidua (Richardson, 1845)
Inhabits coral reefs; similar to *M. niger* (**4**), but distinguished by pale dorsal, anal and tail fins; found throughout the region; Indo-C. Pacific; to 38 cm.

TRIGGERFISHES

Triggerfishes (family Balistidae) are characterised by a rugby-ball shape, leathery skin and small mouth with powerful crushing jaws. Their common name is derived from the peculiar mechanism by which the first dorsal spine can be locked into an erect position by the second dorsal spine — if pressure is exerted on the trigger-like second spine, the first spine can be 'unlocked' and depressed. This device is used to good advantage at night when the fish wedges into a coral crevice and 'locks' itself in. Most of the 40 triggerfish species inhabit the tropical Indo-Pacific region, but a few are found in other warm seas. They are usually solitary in habit, although the Whitespotted Trigger *Canthidermis maculata* (Plate **103.4**) forms large schools. Swimming is slow and deliberate, usually accomplished by gentle undulations of the second dorsal and anal fins, but when threatened they retreat quickly to a hole in the reef by using their tail. In many species the same hole is always used and also serves as a nocturnal resting place. Some triggers, for example *Rhinecanthus aculeatus* (**5**) and *R. rectangulus* (**6**), are capable of producing grunt-like sounds when disturbed. Although the mouth is relatively small, triggers possess powerful jaws and strong teeth. These are used for crushing a variety of hard-shelled prey, including crabs, molluscs and echinoderms. Sponges, gorgonians, hydroids, corals and algae are also consumed by several species. A few triggers including the Redtooth *Odonus niger* (Plate **103.3**), Whitespotted *Canthidermis maculata* (Plate **103.4**) and the species of *Xanthichthys* (**11** and Plate **103.5**) feed heavily on zooplankton. Triggerfishes lay eggs on the bottom, which are aggressively guarded by the female. Divers should exercise caution when swimming through a nest area. It is best to give the Titan Trigger *Balistoides viridescens* (**3**) a wide berth on these occasions as it is particularly belligerent and can inflict nasty bites.

The Clown Trigger *B. conspicillum* (Plate **103.2**) is easily the most spectacular member of the family. It has long been a favourite of marine aquarists. Several decades ago, when it first appeared in pet shops, the price tag was over US$300 per fish. Nowadays it is more common, but still fetches at least $50.

PLATE 103: TRIGGERFISHES AND LEATHERJACKETS

BALISTIDAE

1. YELLOWMARGIN TRIGGERFISH
Pseudobalistes flavimarginatus (Rüppell, 1829)
Inhabits coral reefs; distinguished by raised spines on scales of tail base, yellow margins on fin and cross-hatch pattern on side; Great Barrier Reef, offshore reefs of W. Australia and throughout S.E. Asia; Indo-C. Pacific; to 60 cm.

2. CLOWN TRIGGERFISH
Balistoides conspicillum (Bloch & Schneider, 1801)
Inhabits coral reefs, usually seen on outer slopes; distinguished by yellow lips and large white spots on lower half of head and body; Great Barrier Reef, offshore reefs of W. Australia and throughout S.E. Asia; Indo-C. Pacific; to 50 cm.

3. REDTOOTH TRIGGERFISH
Odonus niger (Rüppell, 1836)
Inhabits coral reefs, sometimes seen in groups on outer reefs; feeds on zooplankton; distinguished by dark blue to purplish-blue colour, lunate tail (with prolonged lobes in adult), blue fin margins and red teeth; Great Barrier Reef, offshore reefs of W. Australia and throughout S.E. Asia; Indo-C. Pacific; to 35 cm.

4. WHITESPOTTED TRIGGERFISH
Canthidermis maculata (Bloch, 1786)
Inhabits steep outer reef slopes, sometimes seen far out to sea around logs or other floating debris; distinguished by relatively elongate body, triangular dorsal and anal fins, rounded caudal fin with upper and lower lobes slightly elongate, colour changeable from grey to blackish, often with small white spots covering head and body; islands adjacent to deep water throughout S.E. Asia; tropical circumglobal; to 35 cm.

5. GILDED TRIGGERFISH
Xanthichthys auromarginatus (Bennett, 1832)
Inhabits steep outer reef slopes in 15–70 m depth; feeds on zooplankton; male distinguished by blue patch on cheek and yellow fin margins; female (not shown) is bluish-grey with pale scale centres; Great Barrier Reef and throughout S.E. Asia; Indo-C. Pacific; to 22 cm.

6. BLACKPATCH TRIGGERFISH
Rhinecanthus verrucosus (Linnaeus, 1758)
Inhabits sheltered coral reefs, including silty inshore areas; distinguished by large black patch on lower side and narrow dark bar through eye to pectoral fin base; Great Barrier Reef and throughout S.E. Asia; Indo-W. Pacific; to 23 cm.

7. HALFMOON TRIGGERFISH
Rhinecanthus lunula Randall & Steene, 1983
Inhabits coral reefs, usually seen in depths below 10 m; distinguished by black first dorsal fin, black spot at pectoral fin base, another in front of anal fin and black ring around tail base; Great Barrier Reef and islands of the South Pacific eastward to Pitcairn Group; to 28 cm.

MONACANTHIDAE

8. LARGESCALE LEATHERJACKET
Cantheschenia grandisquamis Hutchins, 1977
Inhabits coral and rocky reefs; distinguished by orange tail with broad blue margins and dark blotch in front of anal fin; S. Great Barrier Reef and New South Wales; to 26 cm.

9. BROOM FILEFISH
Amanses scopas (Cuvier, 1829)
Inhabits coral reefs; distinguished by overall dark brown colouration with several incomplete blackish bars on middle of side; males with patch of numerous long spines and females with toothbrush-like patch of bristles in front of tail base; Great Barrier Reef and throughout S.E. Asia; Indo-W. Pacific; to 20 cm.

10. BARRED LEATHERJACKET
Cantherhines dumerilii (Hollard, 1854)
Inhabits coral reefs; distinguished by yellowish iris and tail, also by two pairs of forward-curved spines on tail base; Great Barrier Reef, offshore reefs of W. Australia and throughout S.E. Asia; Indo-E. Pacific; to 35 cm.

11. SPOTTED FILEFISH
Pseudomonacanthus macrurus (Bleeker, 1857)
Inhabits shallow weedy areas and trawling grounds; a nondescript species which can change its colours to match the surroundings; found throughout S.E. Asia; to 24 cm.

12. RHINOCEROS LEATHERJACKET
Pseudalutarius nasicornis (Temminck & Schlegel, 1850)
Inhabits trawling grounds to 75 m depth, also found in shallow weedy areas; distinguished by pair of dark stripes on back and unusual placement (in front of eye) of dorsal spine; Queensland and throughout S.E. Asia; W. Pacific; to 18 cm.

13. ORANGETAIL LEATHERJACKET
Pervagor aspricaudus (Hollard, 1854)
Inhabits coral reefs; distinguished by orange tail and numerous fine dark spots on head and body; similar to *P. janthinosoma* (Plate **104.12**), but lacks prominent black blotch above gill opening; Great Barrier Reef; anti-equatorial distribution, mainly around oceanic islands from Mauritius to New Caledonia and Taiwan to Hawaii; to 12 cm.

14. BLACKHEAD LEATHERJACKET
Pervagor melanocephalus (Bleeker, 1853)
Inhabits coral reefs; distinguished by bright orange body and brown head; also known as Dark-headed Leatherjacket; Great Barrier Reef and throughout S.E. Asia; W. Pacific; to 10 cm.

15. BLACKLINED LEATHERJACKET
Pervagor nigrolineatus (Herre, 1927)
Inhabits sheltered coral reefs; distinguished by pale stripe extending from cheek to middle of body and by prolonged rays at front of second dorsal fin; offshore reefs of W. Australia and throughout S.E. Asia; W. Pacific; to 7 cm.

16. BRISTLE-TAIL LEATHERJACKET
Acreichthys tomentosus (Linnaeus, 1758)
Inhabits weed-rubble bottoms on shallow reefs; distinguished by chameleon-like colour pattern and numerous skin-flap appendages on body; found throughout S.E. Asia; W. edge of Pacific, excluding Australia; to 12 cm.

17. RADIAL LEATHERJACKET
Acreichthys radiatus (Popta, 1900)
Inhabits coral reefs, frequently seen among soft corals; distinguished by narrow white bars (may be faint) on side and filamentous appendages on dorsal spine; Great Barrier Reef and throughout S.E. Asia; W. Pacific; to 7 cm.

18. BLACKSADDLE FILEFISH
Paraluteres prionurus (Bleeker, 1851)
Inhabits coral reefs; a mimic of *Canthigaster valentini* (Plate **106.13**), a poisonous puffer; distinguished from the nearly identical puffer by the presence of the spinous first dorsal fin and the longer-based dorsal and anal fins (these have 22–28 rays, versus 9 rays in the puffer); Great Barrier Reef and throughout S.E. Asia; Indo-W. Pacific; to 10 cm.

PLATE 104: LEATHERJACKETS

MONACANTHIDAE

1. UNICORN LEATHERJACKET ☆☆☆
Aluterus monoceros (Linnaeus, 1758)
Inhabits coral reefs and flat-bottom trawling grounds; distinguished by large ovate shape and slender dorsal spine, similar to *A. scriptus* (**2**), but has rounder head, shorter tail and lacks ornate pattern; found throughout the region; worldwide tropical and subtropical seas; to 76 cm.

2. SCRAWLED LEATHERJACKET ☆☆☆
Aluterus scriptus (Osbeck, 1765)
Inhabits coral reefs; distinguished by relatively elongate shape, slender dorsal spine, spotted pattern and elongate tail; found throughout the region; worldwide tropical and subtropical seas; to 100 cm.

3. HONEYCOMB LEATHERJACKET ☆☆☆
Cantherhines pardalis (Rüppell, 1837)
Inhabits coral reefs; distinguished by network of dark spots on sides; Great Barrier Reef, N.W. Australia and throughout S.E. Asia; Indo-C. Pacific; to 20 cm.

4. SPECTACLED LEATHERJACKET ☆☆☆
Cantherhines fronticinctus (Günther, 1867)
Inhabits coral reefs; distinguished by white bar on tail base, sometimes with irregular dark blotches on sides; N.W. Australia, S. New Guinea, Indonesia and Philippines; Indo-W. Pacific, to 23 cm.

5. BEARDED LEATHERJACKET
Anacanthus barbatus Gray, 1830
Inhabits sand-weed bottoms; distinguished by unusually elongate shape and barbel on chin; found throughout the region; E. Indian Ocean and Indo-Australian Archipelago; to 35 cm.

6. BLUESPOTTED LEATHERJACKET ☆☆☆
Eubalichthys caeruleoguttatus Hutchins, 1977
Inhabits trawling grounds; male has distinctive pattern of stripes on head and body, and elevated dorsal and anal fin lobes, female distinguished by blue to whitish spots on side; W. Australia only; to 38 cm.

7. FANBELLY LEATHERJACKET ☆☆☆
Monacanthus chinensis (Osbeck, 1765)
Inhabits reef and weed bottoms, also trawling grounds; distinguished by triangular back profile, huge skin flap on belly and filamentous extension on tail; found throughout the region; mainly W. Pacific; to 38 cm.

8. TASSELLED LEATHERJACKET ☆☆☆
Chaetodermis penicilligerus (Cuvier, 1816)
Inhabits sea grass and trawling grounds; distinguished by round shape and tentacles on head and body; found throughout the region; mainly W. Pacific; to 31 cm.

9. HARLEQUIN FILEFISH
Oxymonacanthus longirostris (Bloch & Schneider, 1801)
Inhabits coral reefs, usually associated with branching or plate corals; distinguished by tubular snout and orange spots; Great Barrier Reef, N.W. Australia and throughout S.E. Asia; Indo-W. Pacific; to 9 cm

10. THREADFIN LEATHERJACKET ☆☆☆
Paramonacanthus filicauda (Günther, 1880)
Inhabits trawling grounds; distinguished by relatively deep body, dark blotch below front of dorsal fin and filament on upper lobe of tail; tropical and subtropical Australia only; to 22 cm.

11. PIGFACE LEATHERJACKET ☆☆☆
Paramonacanthus choirocephalus (Bleeker, 1852)
Inhabits trawling grounds; distinguished by slightly diagonal dark stripes on side with intense blotch in middle stripe just behind pectoral fin; female shown here, male is much more slender; N. Australia and Indo-Malay Archipelago; N.E. Indian Ocean and Indo-Australian Archipelago; to 14 cm.

12. GILLBLOTCH LEATHERJACKET
Pervagor janthinosoma (Bleeker, 1854)
Inhabits coral reefs; distinguished by brownish body and fan-shaped red tail; Great Barrier Reef, W. Australia and throughout S.E. Asia; Indo-W. Pacific; to 14 cm.

13. MODEST LEATHERJACKET
Thamnaconus modestoides (Barnard, 1927)
Inhabits trawling grounds; distinguished by relatively elongate shape and nondescript pattern; N.W. Australia and Indonesia; Indian Ocean and W. Pacific; to 30 cm.

14. BROWN-BLOTCHED LEATHERJACKET ☆☆☆
Stephanolepis sp.
Inhabits trawling grounds; an undescribed species distinguished by a relatively deep body and dense pattern of dark blotches; W. Australia only; to 34 cm.

15. POT-BELLIED LEATHERJACKET ☆☆☆
Pseudomonacanthus peroni (Hollard, 1854)
Inhabits trawling grounds; distinguished by moderately large skin flap on belly and small spots on body and tail; N. Australia only; to 40 cm.

16. PAXMAN'S LEATHERJACKET
Colurodontis paxmani Hutchins, 1977
Inhabits sea grass; distinguished by movable pelvic spine and flattened teeth at front of jaws; W. Australia only, between Shark Bay and Dampier Archipelago; to 15 cm.

LEATHERJACKETS

Leatherjackets (family Monacanthidae) are closely related to triggerfishes (Plates 102–103) and share many of their anatomical peculiarities. However they are generally more laterally compressed and usually have 2 dorsal spines instead of 3. Members of both groups are able to swim slowly by undulating movements of the soft dorsal and anal fins. Rapid bursts are achieved mainly by vigorous tail movement. Australia has more leatherjackets than any other region, with nearly 60 of the estimated total of 85 species being represented. However, the majority are confined to temperate and subtropical seas. The flesh of many species is good eating and in places such as Australia and Japan they are important commercial fishes. Food items are similar to those of triggerfishes, mainly consisting of benthic invertebrates.

PLATE 105: BOXFISHES AND PUFFERFISHES

OSTRACIIDAE

1. LONGHORN COWFISH POISONOUS
Lactoria cornuta (Linnaeus, 1758)
Inhabits weed-sand areas near rock or coral reefs; distinguished from *L. diaphana* (**2**) by longer horns and flatter belly that is not semi-transparent; found throughout the region; Indo-C. Pacific; to 46 cm.

2. ROUNDBELLY COWFISH POISONOUS
Lactoria diaphana (Bloch & Schneider, 1801)
Inhabits coastal waters, the young sometimes in estuaries; distinguished from *L. cornuta* (**1**) by shorter horns; 'thorn' on back and semi-transparent, rounded belly; found throughout the region; Indo-W. Pacific; to 25 cm.

3. YELLOW BOXFISH POISONOUS
Ostracion cubicus Linnaeus, 1758
Inhabits coral and rocky reefs; distinguished by yellow to brown colour with small black spots arranged in clusters on side, juvenile bright yellow with black spots; found throughout the region; Indo-W. Pacific; to 45 cm.

4. BLACK BOXFISH POISONOUS
Ostracion meleagris Shaw, 1796
Inhabits coral reefs; male distinguished by blue sides with yellow-orange spots, female by black colour and numerous white spots, found throughout the region; Great Barrier Reef, N.W. Australia and throughout S.E. Asia; Indo-C. Pacific; to 16 cm.

5. HORN-NOSE BOXFISH POISONOUS
Ostracion rhinorhynchos (Bleeker, 1852)
Inhabits reefs and flat-bottom areas; distinguished by bump on snout; found throughout the region; mainly Indo-Australian Archipelago; to 35 cm.

6. SHORTNOSE BOXFISH POISONOUS
Ostracion nasus Bloch, 1785
Inhabits reefs and flat-bottom areas; distinguished by lack of horns, a ridged back and dull spots on side; found throughout the region; Indo-W. Pacific; to 30 cm.

7. HUMPBACK TURRETFISH POISONOUS
Tetrosomus gibbosus (Linnaeus, 1758)
Inhabits coastal waters, sometimes trawled; distinguished by prominent peak on back; found throughout the region; Indo-W. Pacific; to 30 cm.

8. TURRETFISH POISONOUS
Tetrosomus concatenatus (Bloch, 1785)
Inhabits coastal waters; distinguished by ridge on back with 2 stout spines and blue lines on body; young have peak on back similar to *T. gibbosus* (**7**), but with 2 spines at apex; *Trioris reipublicae* is a synonym; found throughout the region; Indo-W. Pacific; to 22 cm.

TETRAODONTIDAE

9. FINESPINE PUFFERFISH POISONOUS
Tylerius spinosissimus (Regan, 1908)
Inhabits trawling grounds; distinguished by short bristles covering body; N.W. Australia and S. Indonesia; Indo-W. Pacific; to 12 cm.

10. FEROCIOUS PUFFER POISONOUS
Feroxodon multistriatus (Richardson, 1854)
Inhabits trawling grounds and offshore reefs; distinguished by curved bars on top half of head and body with spots below; N.W. Australia; mainly S.W. Pacific; to 15 cm.

11. NARROWLINED PUFFER POISONOUS
Arothron manilensis Marion de Procé, 1822
Inhabits relatively turbid inshore waters over silty sand or mud bottoms, sometimes amongst weeds; distinguished by numerous thin stripes on side; found throughout the region; mainly W. Pacific; to 31 cm.

12. RETICULATE TOADFISH POISONOUS
Arothron reticularis (Bloch & Schneider, 1801)
Inhabits shallow coastal waters, usually over sand or mud bottoms; similar to *A. hispidus* (**13**), but with dark lines on snout and cheek; N.W. Australia and S.E. Asia; W. Pacific and E. Indian Ocean; to 30 cm.

13. STARS-AND-STRIPES PUFFER POISONOUS
Arothron hispidus (Linnaeus, 1758)
Inhabits shallow waters near rock or coral reefs; similar to *A. reticularis* (**12**), but without lines on snout and cheek; Queensland, N.W. Australia and throughout S.E. Asia; Indo-C. Pacific; to 51 cm.

14. YELLOWEYE PUFFER POISONOUS
Arothron immaculatus (Bloch & Schneider, 1801)
Inhabits sand or mud bottoms, often amongst weed; distinguished by lack of markings and dark rim around tail; Indo-Malay Archipelago; mainly Indian Ocean; to 30 cm.

15. STARRY PUFFER POISONOUS
Arothron stellatus (Bloch & Schneider, 1801)
Inhabits sand and mud bottoms, often amongst weeds; distinguished by large size and dense spotting on head and body, juvenile with curved black bars on belly; Great Barrier Reef, N.W. Australia and throughout S.E. Asia; Indo-C. Pacific; to 90 cm.

16. BLACKSPOTTED PUFFER POISONOUS
Arothron nigropunctatus (Bloch & Schneider, 1801)
Inhabits clear waters of offshore coral reefs; distinguished by scattered black spots and dark lips, background colour ranges from grey to yellow; also known as Dog-faced Puffer; found throughout the region; Indo-C. Pacific; to 30 cm.

BOXFISHES AND BLOWIES

Boxfishes of the family Ostraciidae (Plates 105–106) are strange creatures found mainly on tropical and subtropical reefs. Their bodies are encased in a bony carapace and the fins are relatively small. They are slow swimmers, but capable of short, rapid bursts. When feeding, boxfishes sometimes squirt a jet of water into the sand to uncover small plants and invertebrates that are then sucked into the mouth. Some species produce a toxic mucus that can kill other fishes, or even themselves when confined in a small aquarium.

The puffers or blowies (family Tetraodontidae) and the related porcupinefishes (family Diodontidae) can inflate their bodies by swallowing water (or air if out of water). Presumably this adaptation serves as a deterrent to potential predators. The estimated 190 species of puffers occur worldwide in tropical and warm temperate seas and estuaries. The flesh, especially the viscera, contains a potent toxin that has caused many human fatalities. However, they are considered a great delicacy in Japan, where they are prepared by specially trained and licensed chefs. The largest species grow to about 1 m TL, but most are considerably smaller.

PLATE 106: BOXFISHES, PUFFERFISHES AND PORCUPINEFISHES

OSTRACIIDAE

1. THORNBACK COWFISH   **POISONOUS**
Lactoria fornasini (Bianconi, 1846)
Inhabits weed bottoms near coral reefs; distinguished by spine in front of each eye, 'thorn' on back and blue dots and dashes covering head and body; Great Barrier Reef and throughout S.E. Asia; Indo-C. Pacific; to 15 cm.

2. STRIPED BOXFISH   **POISONOUS**
Ostracion solorensis Bleeker, 1853
Inhabits coral reefs; female distinguished by reticulum of gold lines on side, male by bluish head and anterior body region and by dark-edged pale stripes and pale spots on side; also known as Solar Boxfish; Great Barrier Reef, offshore reefs of N.W. Australia and throughout S.E. Asia; Indo-Australian Archipelago; to 11 cm.

TETRAODONTIDAE

3. BLUESPOTTED PUFFER   **POISONOUS**
Arothron caeruleopunctatus Matsuura, 1994
Inhabits coral reefs, distinguished by bluish-white spots on body and dark rings around eye; Indonesia, New Guinea and Coral Sea; Indo-W. Pacific; to 50 cm.

4. SCRIBBLED PUFFER   **POISONOUS**
Arothron mappa (Lesson, 1831)
Inhabits coral reefs; distinguished by spoke-like black lines radiating from eye, black blotch around gill opening and pectoral fin base, and highly irregular reticulum of black lines with pale spots; Great Barrier Reef and throughout S.E. Asia; Indo-W. Pacific; to 60 cm.

5. AMBON TOBY   **POISONOUS**
Canthigaster amboinensis (Bleeker, 1864)
Inhabits coral reefs in areas exposed to surge; distinguished by ocellated dark spot below dorsal fin and white to blue-white spots and lines on head and body, also prominent spotting on tail; Great Barrier Reef and throughout S.E. Asia; Indo-C. Pacific; to 11 cm.

6. BLACKSPOT TOBY   **POISONOUS**
Canthigaster bennetti (Bleeker, 1854)
Inhabits vicinity of coral reefs, usually seen on rubble or sand bottoms or in sea grass and algal beds; distinguished by brown upper half and white lower half, also has large, pale-edged dark spot at base of dorsal fin; Great Barrier Reef, offshore reefs of N.W. Australia and throughout S.E. Asia; Indo-C. Pacific; to 10 cm.

7. LANTERN TOBY   **POISONOUS**
Canthigaster epilampra (Jenkins, 1903)
Inhabits outer reef slopes, usually below 20 m depth; distinguished by yellow area around eye with blue 'spokes', blue spotting on side and brown back with ocellus-like mark below dorsal fin; Great Barrier Reef, New Guinea and Solomon Islands; E. Indian Ocean (Christmas Island) and W. and C. Pacific; to 11 cm.

8. TYLER'S TOBY   **POISONOUS**
Canthigaster tyleri Allen & Randall, 1977
Inhabits outer reef slopes, usually below 20 m depth; distinguished by white ground colour and numerous brown spots on head and body; Christmas Island (Indian Ocean) and Indonesia (Moluccas); mainly Indian Ocean; to 7.5 cm.

9. LEOPARD TOBY   **POISONOUS**
Canthigaster leoparda Lubbock & Allen, 1979
Inhabits outer reef slopes, usually below 25 m depth; distinguished by leopard-like brown spotting on side; Philippines and Indonesia (Molucca Islands); E. Indian Ocean (Christmas Island) and W. Pacific; to 7 cm.

10. SHY TOBY   **POISONOUS**
Canthigaster ocellicincta Allen & Randall, 1977
Inhabits coral reefs, very secretive and seldom seen; distinguished by pair of dark bars with narrow white bar between them on middle of side and ocellated spot below dorsal fin; Great Barrier Reef, Indonesia, Philippines and Melanesian Archipelago; to 6.5 cm.

11. NETTED TOBY   **POISONOUS**
Canthigaster papua (Bleeker, 1848)
Inhabits coral reefs; distinguished by ocellated dark spot below dorsal fin, and white to blue-white spots and lines on head and body, also prominent spotting on tail; fish from Oceania are slightly different in colour, having smaller, more numerous spots; W. Pacific; to 11 cm.

12. COMPRESSED TOBY   **POISONOUS**
Canthigaster compressa (Marion de Procé, 1822)
Inhabits coral reefs, frequently seen in silty bays or harbours, often around wharf pilings; distinguished by wavy lines on sides and ocellated spot below dorsal fin, also spots on tail are frequently joined to form vertical bands; Indo-Malay Archipelago; to 10 cm.

13. BLACKSADDLE TOBY   **POISONOUS**
Canthigaster valentini (Bleeker, 1853)
Inhabits coral reefs; mimicked by the leatherjacket *Paraluteres prionurus* (Plate **103.18**); distinguished by dark saddle-like markings; Great Barrier Reef, offshore reefs of N.W. Australia and throughout S.E. Asia; Indo-C. Pacific; to 11 cm.

DIODONTIDAE

14. SPOTTED PORCUPINEFISH   **POISONOUS**
Diodon hystrix Linnaeus, 1758
Inhabits coral reefs; distinguished by pepper-like spotting on head and body and absence of dark saddles or bars; Great Barrier Reef, N.W. Australia and throughout S.E. Asia; worldwide in tropical seas; to 71 cm.

POISONOUS FISHES

Under no circumstance should any fish be eaten that is indicated **POISONOUS** in the text accompanying Plates 105–107. These fishes produce toxins and may cause serious illness or death. If caught while fishing it is advisable to release them immediately.

PLATE 107: PUFFERS AND PORCUPINEFISHES

TETRAODONTIDAE   POISONOUS

1. CROWNED TOBY

Canthigaster axiologus Whitley, 1931

Inhabits flat-bottom areas with coral, sponge and rocky outcrops; distinguished by 3 dark saddles on upper half of body; Great Barrier Reef, N.W. Australia and Philippines; W. and C. Pacific; to 13 cm.

2. SPOTTED TOBY   POISONOUS

Canthigaster janthinoptera (Bleeker, 1855)

Inhabits caves and crevices of coral reefs; distinguished by dense network of white lines and spots on head and body; Great Barrier Reef, N.W. Australia and throughout S.E. Asia; Indo-C. Pacific; to 8.5 cm.

3. OCCELATE TOBY   POISONOUS

Canthigaster rivulata (Temminck & Schlegel, 1850)

Inhabits offshore reefs and trawling grounds; distinguished by wavy lines on back and brown stripe on side that curves around front of pectoral fin base; N.W. Australia and S. China Sea; Indo-W. Pacific; to 20 cm.

4. MILKSPOT TOADFISH   POISONOUS

Chelonodontops patoca (Hamilton, 1822)

Inhabits bays and brackish mangrove estuaries; distinguished by network of large, dark-centred white spots on head and body; found throughout the region; Indo-W. Pacific; to 20 cm.

5. ROUGH GOLDEN TOADFISH   POISONOUS

Lagocephalus lunaris (Bloch & Schneider, 1801)

Inhabits coastal waters; similar to *L. inermis* (**6**) and *L. spadiceus* (**7**), but has bristles on dorsal surface between snout and dorsal fin; found throughout the region; Indo-W. Pacific; to 30 cm.

6. SMOOTH GOLDEN TOADFISH   POISONOUS

Lagocephalus inermis (Temminck & Schlegel, 1850)

Inhabits coastal waters; similar to *L. lunaris* (**5**) and *L. spadiceus* (**7**), but lacks bristles on dorsal surface (and elsewhere); N.W. Australia and S. Indonesia; Indo-W. Pacific; to 20 cm.

7. BROWNBACK TOADFISH   POISONOUS

Lagocephalus spadiceus (Richardson, 1845)

Inhabits coastal waters; similar to *L. lunaris* (**5**) and *L. inermis* (**6**), but has patch of bristles on dorsal surface from snout to about halfway to dorsal fin; found throughout the region; Indo-W. Pacific; to 30 cm.

8. SILVER TOADFISH   POISONOUS

Lagocephalus sceleratus (Gmelin, 1789)

Inhabits coastal waters, usually in schools; an aggressive species that can inflict painful bites, in a feeding frenzy it is very dangerous, attacking everything in sight; distinguished by spots and faint blotches on back and silvery stripe on sides, is also more elongate than *L. lunaris* (**5**), *L. inermis* (**6**) and *L. spadiceus* (**7**); found throughout the region; Indo-W. Pacific; to 85 cm.

9. DARWIN TOADFISH   POISONOUS

Marilyna darwinii (Castelnau, 1873)

Inhabits mud-bottom areas, frequently in mangrove estuaries or the lower reaches of freshwater streams; N. Australia and S. New Guinea; to 17 cm.

10. HICKS' TOADFISH   POISONOUS

Torquigener hicksi Hardy, 1983

Inhabits coastal waters; similar to *T. parcuspinus* (**11**) and *T. pallimaculatus* (**12**), but bristles sparsely distributed on head and body; N. Australia only; to 13 cm.

11. YELLOWEYE TOADFISH   POISONOUS

Torquigener parcuspinus Hardy, 1983

Inhabits coastal waters; similar to *T. hicksi* (**10**), but covered with well developed bristles, lacks distinctive spotting of *T. pallimaculatus* (**12**), which has shorter bristles, also distinguished by small yellow areas above each eye; N. Australia only; to 10 cm.

12. RUSTY-SPOTTED TOADFISH   POISONOUS

Torquigener pallimaculatus Hardy, 1983

Inhabits coastal waters; distinguished by pattern of spots and bristle development that is intermediate to *T. hicksi* (**10**) and *T. parcuspinus* (**11**), also by orange-brown spots on lower side; N. Australia only; to 15 cm.

DIODONTIDAE

13. FRECKLED PORCUPINEFISH   POISONOUS

Diodon holocanthus Linnaeus, 1758

Inhabits vicinity of coral reefs; distinguished by long movable spines on head and body, and combination of scattered small dark spots and larger dark blotches (often much darker than shown); *D. hystrix* (Plate **106.14**) is similar but lacks the larger dark patches and the small spots are more numerous; Great Barrier Reef, N.W. Australia and throughout S.E. Asia; worldwide in tropical seas; to 35 cm.

14. BLACKBLOTCHED PORCUPINEFISH POISONOUS

Diodon liturosus Shaw, 1804

Inhabits vicinity of coral reefs; distinguished by long movable spines on head and body, and large dark patches on side and dorsal surface, a solid broad bar across the top of the head just behind eyes is also distinctive; Great Barrier Reef, N.W. Australia and throughout S.E. Asia; mainly W. and C. Pacific; to 40 cm.

15. SPOTBASE BURRFISH   POISONOUS

Cyclichthys spilostylus (Leis & Randall, 1982)

Inhabits coastal waters in the vicinity of reefs; distinguished by short non-movable spines on head and body and small black spots at the base of most spines; N.W. Australia, Indonesia and Philippines; N. Indian Ocean to S. China Sea; to 35 cm.

16. SPOTFIN PORCUPINEFISH   POISONOUS

Chilomycterus reticulatus (Linnaeus, 1758)

Inhabits coastal waters in the vicinity of reefs; distinguished by short, non-movable spines on head and body, faint dark bars on side and spotted tail; *C. affinis* is a synonym; found throughout the region, but rare; worldwide in tropical seas; to 55 cm.

17. LONGSPINE PORCUPINEFISH   POISONOUS

Tragulichthys jaculiferus (Cuvier, 1818)

Inhabits coastal waters; distinguished by long, non-movable spines, 3–4 dark patches on back and a few dark spots on side; N. Australia and Arafura Sea, to 30 cm.

18. SHORTSPINE PORCUPINEFISH   POISONOUS

Cyclichthys orbicularis (Bloch, 1785)

Inhabits coastal waters; distinguished by short, non-movable spines on head and body and relatively large black spots on back and side; Indo-W. Pacific; Great Barrier Reef, N.W. Australia and throughout S.E. Asia; to 30 cm.

INDEX

PLATE NO. PLATE NO. PLATE NO.

"Books to Span the East and West"

Tuttle Publishing was founded in 1832 in the small New England town of Rutland, Vermont [USA]. Our core values remain as strong today as they were then—to publish best-in-class books which bring people together one page at a time. In 1948, we established a publishing outpost in Japan—and Tuttle is now a leader in publishing English-language books about the arts, languages and cultures of Asia. The world has become a much smaller place today and Asia's economic and cultural influence has grown. Yet the need for meaningful dialogue and information about this diverse region has never been greater. Over the past seven decades, Tuttle has published thousands of books on subjects ranging from martial arts and paper crafts to language learning and literature—and our talented authors, illustrators, designers and photographers have won many prestigious awards. We welcome you to explore the wealth of information available on Asia at **www.tuttlepublishing.com**.

Published in 2020 by Tuttle Publishing, an imprint of Periplus Editions (HK) Ltd.

www.tuttlepublishing.com

ISBN 978-0-8048-5279-1

Front cover: Lukiyanova Natalia frenta | Shutterstock; Back cover (from left, top to bottom): Andover Lionfish (*Pterois andover*) (G. Allen); Colourful shoals of fairy basslets (*Pseudanthias dispar*) (R. Steene); Plate 56: Butterflyfishes (p. 175); Plate 80: Wrasses (p. 223); (bottom, right) Potato Rockcod (*Epinephelus tukula*) (G. Allen) Frontispiece: A harem of Carpenter's Flasherwrasses (*Paracheilinus carpenteri*) (G. Allen)

Copyright © Western Australian Museum, 2018. All rights reserved. Apart from fair dealing for the purposes of research or private study, or criticism or review, this publication may not be reproduced, stored, or transmitted, in any form, or by any means, without the prior permission in writing of the publishers. All copyright inquiries should be addressed to the publisher.

Distributed by

North America, Latin America & Europe
Tuttle Publishing
364 Innovation Drive
North Clarendon, VT 05759-9436 U.S.A.
Tel: 1 (802) 773-8930; Fax: 1 (802) 773-6993
info@tuttlepublishing.com
www.tuttlepublishing.com

Asia Pacific
Berkeley Books Pte. Ltd
3 Kallang Sector #04-01, Singapore 349278
Tel (65) 67412178; Fax: (65) 67412179
inquiries@periplus.com.sg;
www.tuttlepublishing.com

Indonesia
PT Java Books Indonesia
Kawasan Industri Pulogadung,
JI. Rawa Gelam IV No. 9, Jakarta 13930
Tel: (62) 21 4682-1088; Fax: (62) 21 461-0206
crm@periplus.co.id
www.periplus.com

Printed in China   2412CM
27 26 25 24   6 5 4 3

TUTTLE PUBLISHING® is a registered trademark of Tuttle Publishing, a division of Periplus Editions (HK) Ltd.